Under Three Flags

Andris J. Kursietis

Under Three Flags

The German Navy under the Kaiser,
the Republic and the Third Reich

(1914 - 1945)

Aspekt Publishers

Under Three Flags
© Andris J. Kursietis
© 2016 Uitgeverij ASPEKT / Aspekt Publishers
Amersfoortsestraat 27, 3769 AD Soesterberg, The Netherlands
info@uitgeverijaspekt.nl – http://www.uitgeverijaspekt.nl

Cover: Mark Heuveling
Inside: Thomas Wunderink

ISBN: 9789461539410
NUR: 680

All rights reserved. No reproduction copy or transmission of this publication may be made without written permission.

I wish to thank my wife Rosemarie, who has supported and encouraged me during the many months that it took to finish this project. Although this is not the first time that she has kept the home fires burning while I delve into a writing project, her understanding of my absences (whether in front of a computer, or at a library or bookstore) has made the completion of this task so much easier. I am sure that other authors and their spouses know what I am talking about! I also wish to express my deep gratitude to military historians Hans H. Hildebrand and Ernest Henriot, whose masterful work "Deutschlands Admirale 1849 - 1945" (published by Biblio Verlag, Osnabrück, 1988 - 1996) formed the backbone for my research into this book.

ALSO BY ANDRIS J. KURSIETIS:

The Royal Hungarian Armed Forces 1919-1945 (1994)
The Fallen Generals (1995, 2015)
La Regia Marina 1919-1945 (1995)
The Hungarian Army and its Leadership in World War II (1996)
The Armed Forces of Latvia 1918 - 1940 (1998)
The Wehrmacht at War (1999)
The Luftwaffe 1935 - 1945 (2000)
A Lifetime for Hungary (2014)
The Imperial Japanese Navy (2015)

LIST OF CONTENTS:

Introduction	9
Chapter 1: Order of battle, 1914 - 1918	18
Chapter 2: Ships of the Reichsmarine, 1914 - 1918	24
Chapter 3: Order of battle, 1919 - 1933	38
Chapter 4: Ships of the Reichsmarine, 1919 - 1933	41
Chapter 5: Order of battle, 1933 - 1945	45
Chapter 6: Ships of the Kriegsmarine, 1933 - 1945	52
Chapter 7: Admirals of the German Navy, 1914 - 1945	66
Appendix: Alphabetical index of ships, 1914 - 1945	289
List of sources	295

INTRODUCTION

World War I

Imperial Germany entered World War I with one of the strongest navies in the world. The number of battleships alone at the disposal of the Naval High Command in 1914 (forty-six, including coastal battleships) is a testament to the power that had been built up over the years following the unification of Germany in 1871. However, the fact that this might still did not enable Germany to win the war is a testament partly to the lack of understanding of the High Command of how to use its naval power, and partly due to the co-existence of a powerful British fleet that resulted in a virtual stalemate in the war on the high seas. It is remarkable that such a large force did not make a significant impact on the course of the war, and yet it is indicative of the German Admiralty's inaction that following the Battle of Jutland in 1916 (where the German Navy lost 11 ships to the British 14 vessels lost), no further major encounters occurred on the high seas for the remainder of the war.

In 1914, at the outbreak of the war, the German Naval forces were made up of eight Squadrons (I - VI, Cruiser, Training). Split between these units were a total of 39 battleships (three more were added during the course of the war), 7 coastal battleships (used as coastal defense ships and barracks), 21 heavy cruisers (surprisingly, only one more, the *"Hindenburg"*, was launched during the war) and 39 light cruisers (with ten additional vessels completed and launched between 1915 - 1918).

The oldest of the vessels was the light cruiser *"Schwalbe"*, launched in 1887, however the vessel was used as a floating barracks rather than an active-duty warship at sea. The table below breaks down the years of launching of the battleships, coastal battleships, heavy cruisers and light cruisers. Not included in the listing are those vessels which were launched but not completed, and which therefore did not see service.

It is somewhat startling to realize that 35 out of the total 39 available battleships were no more than 15 years old at the outbreak of the war, and 20 out of the 21 heavy cruisers were less than 17 years old in 1914. Moreover, the building program for light cruisers did not really get under way until 1900, with a total of 33 out of 39 light cruisers available to the German Navy at the outbreak of hostilities being built between 1900 - 1914. This means that in fact 89% of the warships at the disposal of the Naval High Command in 1914 were less than 17 years old - the mark of a truly modern navy!

It is also interesting to note that of the ships launched and completed during the war years (essentially 1915 - 1918), the vast majority (10 out of 14, or over 71%) were light cruisers, perhaps indicating an increased awareness of the need for speed and mobility in the fleet. Nevertheless, in 1914 a stunning 37% of the fleet was made up of battleships, and if the coastal battleships and heavy cruisers are thrown into the mix, the percentage increases to 63%, showing a marked preponderance for power over mobility.

During the war years, the German Navy lost 2 battleships (the "*Pommern*" was sunk by torpedoes, while the "*Rheinland*" was beached in 1918), 7 heavy cruisers (of which 5 were lost within the first six months of the war) and 20 light cruisers, including several vessels that were damaged enough to be withdrawn from service.

Table 1: Major warships available to the German Navy 1914 - 1918

Launch Year	Coastal Battleships	Heavy Battleships	Cruisers	Light Cruisers	TOTAL
1887			1		1
1888					0
1889		1			1
1890		1			1
1891	1	1			2
1892	1	2		1	4
1893		1	1		2
1894		1			1
1895			1		1
1896	1				1
1897	1			5	6
1898			1	1	2
1899	2		2		4
1900	2		4	1	7

Year					Total
1901	4			1	5
1902	1		3	1	5
1903	3		3	1	7
1904	2		1	1	4
1905	2		3		5
1906	2		2	2	6
1907			2		2
1908	4		2	1	7
1909	3		3	1	7
1910	1			1	2
1911	3		4	1	8
1912	2		2	1	5
1913	3		1	2	6
1914	1		3		4
PRE-WAR TOTAL	**39**	**7**	**39**	**21**	**106**
1915	2		4	1	7
1916			5		5
1917			1		1
1918	1				1
TOTAL	**42**	**7**	**49**	**22**	**120**

The High Command of the Imperial German Navy during the war was dominated by such personalities as the Chief of the Imperial Naval Office, Großadmiral Alfred von Tirpitz (who could arguably be called the father of the modern German navy), Großadmiral Henning von Holtzendorf, Chief of the Admiralty Staff for a major portion of the war, Admiral Hugo von Pohl, who was successively Chief of the Admiralty Staff and Commander-in-Chief of the High Seas Fleet and Admiral Reinhard Scheer, who also held both these commands, although in reverse order. It was Scheer who commanded the fleet at the Battle of Jutland on May 31/June 1, 1916. Although he neither won nor lost the battle, and even though his forces inflicted greater casualties on the British fleet than his own forces suffered, this battle signaled the end of any aggressive attempts by the German fleet to break the Allied blockade of Germany, and the British fleet maintained supremacy in the North Atlantic for the remainder of the war. Both von Tirpitz and von Pohl retired in 1916, and von Holtzendorf (who had retired already in 1910 but had been recalled) and

Scheer were retired at the end of 1918. Their years of seniority and experience of the highest levels of command were not to be used in the post-war navy, as the "old guard" gave way to a younger generation of naval officers.

The German Republic

Following Germany's defeat in 1918, the Treaty of Versailles, imposed by the victorious Allies, severely restricted the permissible strength of the German Navy. The terms limited the German Navy to six battleships, six light cruisers and twelve torpedo boats, with no submarines allowed. The manpower strength was not to exceed 15,000 officers and men, clearly a significant cut from the sizeable headcount that the German Navy wielded during World War I.

Under the terms of the November 1918 Armistice, signaling the end of World War I, the High Seas Fleet was interned at Scapa Flow (in the Orkney Islands, off the coast of Scotland). On June 21, 1919, one week prior to the signing of the Treaty of Versailles, the commander of the interned fleet, Konteradmiral Ludwig von Reuter, ordered the scuttling of the vessels to prevent their use by the Allies. A total of 21 major warships (11 battleships, 5 heavy cruisers and 5 light cruisers) were scuttled, and an attempt to scuttle a further 3 light cruisers failed. Of these vessels, only the battleship "Baden" was salvaged by the Allies, only to be sunk in 1921 while being used for target practice. Several other vessels were subsequently raised and scrapped.

Of the ships that remained intact, 7 battleships and 11 light cruisers were claimed by the Allies as prizes with France taking 6 vessels, Great Britain claiming 4 vessels, Japan claiming 3 vessels, the USA and Italy each taking 2 vessels, and Russia taking one battleship.

This left Germany with a theoretical choice of 9 battleships to use on active service. However, the "*Schlesien*" and "*Schleswig-Holstein*" had already been designated as barracks ships before the end of World War I, and the "*Zähringen*" was re-designated an exercise ship in 1916. Whilst several of the other battleships had been similarly re-designated by 1918, nevertheless the following vessels were initially called to fleet duties during the period of the German Republic: "*Braunschweig*", "*Elsaß*", "*Hannover*", "*Hessen*", "*Lothringen*", and "*Preussen*". The "*Preussen*" was decommissioned in 1929, while the remaining ships met the same fate in 1931 and 1935. In the meantime, the "*Schlesien*" and "*Schleswig-Holstein*" were re-armed in 1928 - 1929, and a new battleship, the "*Deutschland*" was launched in 1931. Further details of the ships available to and used by the German Navy during the period of the Republic (1919 - 1933) are shown in Chapter 4.

The Navy of the German Republic saw a multitude of changes in its High Command, on the one hand somewhat surprising given the fact that this was during peace time, yet understandable in view of the political turmoil going on in the country during this period. Six Commanders-in-Chief oversaw the Navy between 1919 - 1933, with four of them being appointed during 1919 - 1920 alone. It was not until Admiral Paul Behncke took charge in August 1920 that a period of stability began in the High Command. He served for 4 years, followed by Admiral Hans Zenker for a further 4 years, and in 1928 Admiral Erich Raeder was appointed Commander-in-Chief, a position he was to hold until 1943. During this same period (1919 - 1933), there were ten Chiefs of Naval General Staff and six Commanders of the High Seas Fleet. These senior naval officers were faced with the unenviable task of supervising a bare-bones navy, within the strict limitations of the terms of the Treaty of Versailles. The focus during this period was on training, with an eye to the future when the limitations would be lifted.

The Third Reich & World War II
With the ascent to power of Adolf Hitler in 1933, Germany's adherence to the terms of all former treaties ended. Under Hitler, the German Navy began a major restructuring and rebuilding project, whose ultimate aim (at least in Hitler's mind) was to dominate the high seas and support the expansionist aims of the Third Reich.

Although the Navy retained a few of the old battleships ("*Hessen*", "*Schlesien*", "*Schleswig-Holstein*" and "*Zähringen*"), these were used as auxiliary or training vessels, and a series of new battleships and pocket battleships was launched, starting with the "*Admiral Scheer*" in 1933 and culminating with the launch of the renowned "*Bismarck*" and "*Tirpitz*" in 1939. None of these new battleships survived the war, being either sunk of scuttled. Plans were also laid for the construction of several aircraft carriers, but just as in World War I, none came to fruition. The strategic planners of the Kriegsmarine did not see the value of such vessels, focusing their attention instead on the mass production of U-Boats.

Three heavy cruisers were launched in 1937 and 1938: "*Admiral Hipper*", *Blücher*", and "*Prinz Eugen*". Of these, only the latter survived the war, ending up being destroyed in a US Navy atomic bomb test at Bikini Atoll in 1946. Only one light cruiser was launched during the Third Reich era, the *"Nürnberg"* in 1934. The remaining light cruisers used during World War II were of 1925 - 1929 vintage, and none of these survived the end of the war. Essentially replacing the role of the light cruisers were the destroyers, and starting in 1935 through 1943, a total of 40 new such vessels were launched. Of these, 25 destroyers, or 62.5% were lost during the war years.

As stated previously, the main focus of the Germany Navy in the years leading up to the outbreak of World War II, and indeed during the war years themselves, was the submarine force. On January 1, 1936, Captain Karl Dönitz became Flag Officer, U-Boats, and it is indeed telling that this same officer was to rise rapidly through the ranks to not only become, in 1943, Commander-in-Chief of the Navy (being promoted and appointed over the heads of many more senior Admirals), but also the last Head of State of the Third Reich, being appointed as such by Adolf Hitler in his last will and testament just prior to his suicide in his Berlin bunker on April 30, 1945.

A total of 1,364 U-Boats (including 202 midget submarines) were constructed and launched during the period 1935 - 1945, but the casualty rate amongst them was enormous. 821 submarines were lost at sea or otherwise destroyed, and it is estimated that around 70% of submariners (officers and crew together) did not survive their tour of service.

The war years saw a relative stability in the High Command of the Kriegsmarine. Essentially, there were two Commanders-in-Chief, Großadmiral Erich Raeder (1928 - 1943) and the aforementioned Großadmiral Karl Dönitz (1943 - 1945), although Generaladmiral Hans-Georg von Friedeburg and Generaladmiral Walter Warzecha oversaw the death throes of the Navy in the final week of the war and its immediate aftermath. Generaladmiral Otto Schniewind and Admirals Kurt Fricke and Wilhelm Meisel occupied the post of Chief of Naval General Staff between 1938 - 1945, while five officers served in the role of Commander-in-Chief of the High Seas Fleet. Of these, the unluckiest was Admiral Günther Lütjens, who had been in charge of the fleet for a little over a year when he went down with his flagship, the battleship *"Bismarck"*, on May 27, 1941. While in the North Atlantic, and having engaged in a naval battle with a British force that culminated in the sinking of the British battleship *"Hood"*, Admiral Lütjens' flagship was targeted by Royal Air Force torpedo bombers. A torpedo hit damaged the *"Bismarck's"* rudder, jamming it into such a position that the vessel could not steer for home port at any great speed. The ship was eventually attacked by the British battleships "*King George V*" and "*Rodney*", and Admiral Lütjens, who had been gravely wounded when the bridge of the "*Bismarck*" was hit by a shell, went down with the ship when the Germans themselves applied the coup de grace to the smashed hulk, scuttling the vessel to prevent it from falling into enemy hands.

Notwithstanding the High Seas Fleet, regional command over the Navy was administered by the Marineoberkommando or Marinegruppenkommando (Naval Groups). There were six such entities, covering the East/Baltic, North, North Sea, Norway, South, and West. At the next level down were senior area commanders, for example, Admiral Commanding, Adriatic, or Admiral Commanding, France. In addition, each vessel type had a Flag Officer who was responsible for the setting up and training of the various types of vessel, e.g. Flag Officer, Battleships, or Flag Officer, U-Boats.

When World War II finally came to an end in Europe, on May 8, 1945, the Kriegsmarine was a mere shadow of the force that had been built with the intention of supporting Hitler's "Thousand Year Reich". The majority of its ships and submarines had been destroyed, in one form or another, and the Kriegsmarine had lost countless officers and men during the conflict. Nevertheless, it is interesting to note that a handful of the Admirals (Konteradmiral Werner Ehrhardt, Konteradmiral Rolf Johannesson, Konteradmiral Hans Karl Meyer, Vizeadmiral Bernhard Rogge, Vizeadmiral Friedrich Ruge and Konteradmiral Gerhard Wagner) that survived the war went on to form the backbone of the post-war German Navy as part of the Bundeswehr (Federal Armed Forces).

General
Chapters 1 - 6 of this book present the order of battle of the German Navy and brief details of its ships during the period 1914 - 1945. In order for the reader to be better able to distinguish between the three separate and distinct political eras (Imperial Germany, under the Kaiser; the German Republic; the Third Reich, under Adolf Hitler), the order of battle and ships available during each era are listed in separate Chapters (1914 - 1918, 1919 - 1933, 1933 - 1945). However, for ease of reference, the biographical details of all the Admirals of the German Navy during the period 1914 - 1945 (Chapter 7) are presented in one alphabetical listing.

Table 2: Naval Officer (Flag Officer) Ranks

GERMAN	ENGLISH TRANSLATION
Großadmiral	Grand Admiral
Generaladmiral	General Admiral
Admiral	Admiral
Admiral (Ingeneur)	Engineer Admiral
Admiraloberstabsarzt	Admiral (Medical Service)
Admiraloberstabsintendant	Admiral (Administration)
Admiraloberstabsrichter	Admiral (Legal Service)
Vizeadmiral	Vice-Admiral
Vizeadmiral (Ingeneur)	Engineer Vice-Admiral
Marineoberbaudirektor	Engineer Vice-Admiral
Admiralstabsarzt	Vice-Admiral (Medical Service)
Marinegeneraloberstabsarzt	Vice-Admiral (Medical Service)
Admiralstabsintendant	Vice-Admiral (Administration)
Generalstabsintendant der Marine	Vice-Admiral (Administration)
Admiralstabsrichter	Vice-Admiral (Legal Service)
Reichskriegsgerichtsrat	Vice-Admiral (Legal Service)
Ministerialdirektor	Vice-Admiral
Konteradmiral	Rear-Admiral
Konteradmiral (Ingeneur)	Engineer Rear-Admiral
Hafenbaudirektor	Engineer Rear-Admiral
Wirkliche Geheime Oberbaurat	Engineer Rear-Admiral
Admiralarzt	Rear-Admiral (Medical Service)
Marinegeneralstabsarzt	Rear-Admiral (Medical Service)
Marineobergeneralarzt	Rear-Admiral (Medical Service)
Admiralintendant	Rear-Admiral (Administration)
Admiralrichter	Rear-Admiral (Legal Service)
Reichskriegsanwalt	Rear-Admiral (Legal Service)
Ministerialdirigent	Rear-Admiral
Wirkliche Geheime Admiralsrat	Rear-Admiral
Wirkliche Geheime Rat	Rear-Admiral
Feldbischof	Field Bishop (Naval Chief Chaplain)
Marinedekan	Rear-Admiral (Chaplains Service)
Marinepropst	Rear-Admiral (Chaplains Service)

| Generalmajor der Marinefestungspionere | Major-General of Naval Fortress Pioneers |
| Kommodore | Commodore |

Table 3: Naval Officer (Non-Flag Officer) Ranks

GERMAN	ENGLISH TRANSLATION
Kapitän zur See	Captain
Fregattenkapitän	Commander
Korvettenkapitän	Lieutenant-Commander
Kapitänleutnant	1st Lieutenant
Oberleutnant zur See	Sub-Lieutenant
Leutnant zu See	2nd Lieutenant
Fähnrich zur See	Ensign

CHAPTER 1:

ORDER OF BATTLE OF THE REICHSMARINE, 1914-1918

Note: The highest Command functions of the German Navy in World War I were split between the Chief/State Secretary of the Imperial Naval Office (Reichsmarineamt), the Chief of the Admiralty Staff (Admiralstab) and the Chief of the Naval Cabinet (Marinekabinett). In addition to these offices, the position of Inspector-General of the Navy accommodated the special status of the Kaiser's brother, Prince Heinrich of Prussia. In August 1918, the position of Chief of the Naval War Staff (Chef der Seekriegsleitung) was created; this office effectively carried out the functions of Commander-in-Chief of the Navy.

Inspector-General of the Navy
1 Oct 1909 - 10 Aug 1919: Großadmiral Heinrich Prinz von **PREUSSEN**

Chief (State Secretary) of the Imperial Naval Office
15 Jun 1897 - 15 Mar 1916: Großadmiral Alfred von **TIRPITZ**
15 Mar 1916 - 22 Sep 1918: Admiral Eduard von **CAPELLE**
22 Sep 1918 - 28 Dec 1918: Vizeadmiral Ernst Ritter von **MANN**, Edler von Tiechler
28 Dec 1918 - 16 Feb 1919: Vizeadmiral Maximilian **ROGGE**

Chief of the Naval Cabinet
8 Jul 1906 - 28 Nov 1918: Admiral Georg Alexander von **MÜLLER**

Chief of the Naval War Staff
28 Aug 1918 - 14 Nov 1918: Admiral Reinhard **SCHEER**

Chief of the Admiralty Staff
1 Apr 1913 - 1 Feb 1915: Admiral Hugo von **POHL**
8 Feb 1915 - 4 Sep 1915: Admiral Gustav **BACHMANN**
5 Sep 1915 - 10 Aug 1918: Großadmiral Henning von **HOLTZENDORF**
11 Aug 1918 - 14 Nov 1918: Admiral Reinhard **SCHEER**

14 Nov 1918 - 9 Dec 1918:
9 Dec 1918 - 2 Jan 1919: Konteradmiral Friedrich von **BÜLOW**

Deputy Chief of the Admiralty Staff
1 Jan 1914 - 2 Aug 1914:
2 Aug 1914 - 4 Sep 1915: Vizeadmiral Paul **BEHNCKE**
4 Sep 1915 - 16 Sep 1916: Admiral Reinhard **KOCH**
16 Sep 1916 - 6 Oct 1916: Vizeadmiral Albert **HOPMAN**
6 Oct 1916 - 15 Aug 1918: Admiral Reinhard **KOCH**
16 Aug 1918 - 2 Jan 1919: Konteradmiral Friedrich von **BÜLOW**

Chief of Naval Operations
7 Oct 1916 - 9 Dec 1916: Vizeadmiral Albert **HOPMAN**
26 Dec 1916 - 29 Jun 1917: Vizeadmiral Hermann **NORDMANN**
30 Jun 1917 - 4 Aug 1918: Konteradmiral Walter Freiherr
 von **KEYSERLINGK**

C-in-C, High Seas Fleet (Flottenchef)
30 Jan 1913 - 2 Feb 1915: Admiral Friedrich von **INGENOHL**
2 Feb 1915 - 23 Jan 1916: Admiral Hugo von **POHL**
23 Jan 1916 - 6 Aug 1918: Admiral Reinhard **SCHEER**
6 Aug 1918 - 12 Aug 1918:
12 Aug 1918 - 29 Nov 1918: Admiral Franz Ritter von **HIPPER**
29 Nov 1918 - 5 Jan 1919: Vizeadmiral Hugo **MEURER**

Commander, Baltic Naval Station
7 May 1912 - 22 Jul 1914: Admiral Carl von **COERPER**
23 Jul 1914 - 6 Feb 1915: Admiral Gustav **BACHMANN**
6 Feb 1915 - 16 Feb 1915: Admiral Reinhard **KOCH**
16 Feb 1915 - 13 Aug 1915: Admiral Friedrich von **INGENOHL**
14 Aug 1915 - 3 Sep 1915: Admiral Reinhard **KOCH**
5 Sep 1915 - 12 Aug 1916: Admiral Gustav **BACHMANN**
12 Aug 1916 - 30 Aug 1916: Admiral Hubert von **REBEUR-PASCHWITZ**
30 Aug 1916 - 27 Oct 1918: Admiral Gustav **BACHMANN**
28 Oct 1918 - 8 Nov 1918: Admiral Wilhelm **SOUCHON**
8 Nov 1918 - 10 Mar 1919: Konteradmiral Hans **KÜSEL**

Commander, North Sea Naval Station
13 Apr 1913 - 15 Jul 1914: Admiral August von **HEERINGEN**
16 Jul 1914 - 29 Dec 1918: Admiral Günther von **KROSIGK**

Commander, I. Squadron

27 Jan 1913 - 14 Feb 1915:	Admiral Wilhelm von **LANS**
16 Feb 1915 - 19 Jun 1915:	Vizeadmiral Richard **ECKERMANN**
20 Jun 1915 - 25 Aug 1915:	Vizeadmiral Friedrich **GÄDEKE**
27 Aug 1915 - 1 Jul 1916:	Admiral Ehrhard **SCHMIDT**
1 Jul 1916 - 10 Jul 1916:	Konteradmiral Walter **ENGELHARDT**
10 Jul 1916 - 3 Feb 1917:	Admiral Ehrhard **SCHMIDT**
3 Feb 1917 - 21 Feb 1917:	Konteradmiral Walter **ENGELHARDT**
21 Feb 1917 - 6 Sep 1917:	Admiral Ehrhard **SCHMIDT**
6 Sep 1917 - 2 Nov 1917:	Konteradmiral Gottfried Freiherr von **DALWIGK zu Lichtenfels**
2 Nov 1917 - 18 Jan 1918:	Admiral Ehrhard **SCHMIDT**
22 Jan 1918 - 3 Aug 1918:	Vizeadmiral Friedrich **BOEDICKER**
3 Aug 1918 - 8 Sep 1918:	Konteradmiral Johannes **HARTOG**
8 Sep 1918 - 23 Sep 1918:	Vizeadmiral Friedrich **BOEDICKER**
23 Sep 1918 - 2 Oct 1918:	Konteradmiral Johannes **HARTOG**
2 Oct 1918 - 27 Nov 1918:	Vizeadmiral Friedrich **BOEDICKER**

Deputy Commander, I. Squadron

1 Oct 1913 - 29 Jun 1915:	Vizeadmiral Friedrich **GÄDEKE**
29 Jun 1915 - 19 Feb 1916:	Vizeadmiral Richard **ENGEL**
20 Feb 1916 - 29 Feb 1916:	Konteradmiral Richard **LANGE**
1 Mar 1916 - 17 Jul 1916:	Konteradmiral Walter **ENGELHARDT**
17 Jul 1916 - 7 Sep 1916:	Konteradmiral Richard **LANGE**
7 Sep 1916 - 1 Feb 1917:	Konteradmiral Walter **ENGELHARDT**
1 Feb 1917 - 2 Feb 1917:	Konteradmiral Richard **LANGE**
2 Feb 1917 - 27 May 1917:	Konteradmiral Walter **ENGELHARDT**
28 May 1917 - 4 Dec 1917:	Konteradmiral Gottfried Freiherr von **DALWIGK zu Lichtenfels**
4 Dec 1917 - 27 Jan 1918:	
27 Jan 1918 - 12 Aug 1918:	Konteradmiral Johannes **HARTOG**
12 Aug 1918 - 23 Aug 1918:	Kapitän zur See Wilhelm von **KROSIGK**
23 Aug 1918 - 11 Sep 1918:	Konteradmiral Johannes **HARTOG**
11 Sep 1918 - 22 Sep 1918:	Kapitän zur See Wilhelm von **KROSIGK**
22 Sep 1918 - 30 Nov 1918:	Konteradmiral Johannes **HARTOG**

Commander, II. Squadron

9 Dec 1913 - 26 Dec 1914:	Admiral Reinhard **SCHEER**
27 Dec 1914 - 10 Aug 1915:	Vizeadmiral Felix **FUNKE**
10 Aug 1915 - 30 Nov 1916:	Vizeadmiral Franz **MAUVE**

19 Nov 1916 - 15 Aug 1917:   Admiral Hubert von **REBEUR-PASCHWITZ**
15 Aug 1917 - 30 Nov 1918:

Deputy Commander, II. Squadron
1 Oct 1913 - 3 Jun 1915:   Vizeadmiral Franz **MAUVE**
3 Jun 1915 - 19 Aug 1915:   Konteradmiral Hans **UTHEMANN**
20 Aug 1915 - 30 Nov 1916:   Konteradmiral Gottfried Freiherr
　　　　　　　　　　　　　　von **DALWIGK zu Lichtenfels**
30 Nov 1916 - 30 Nov 1918:

Commander, III. Squadron
1 Nov 1913 - 28 Feb 1914:   Vizeadmiral Christian **SCHÜTZ**
1 Mar 1914 - 26 Dec 1914:   Vizeadmiral Felix **FUNKE**
27 Dec 1914 - 12 Jan 1916:   Admiral Reinhard **SCHEER**
12 Jan 1916 - 12 Jun 1916:   Vizeadmiral Paul **BEHNCKE**
12 Jun 1916 - 20 Aug 1916:   Vizeadmiral Hermann **NORDMANN**
20 Aug 1916 - 15 Apr 1918:   Vizeadmiral Paul **BEHNCKE**
15 Apr 1918 - 9 May 1918:   Vizeadmiral Hugo **KRAFT**
9 May 1918 - 11 Aug 1918:   Vizeadmiral Paul **BEHNCKE**
12 Aug 1918 - 4 Nov 1918:   Vizeadmiral Hugo **KRAFT**

Deputy Commander, III. Squadron
1 Jan 1914 - 2 Aug 1914:
2 Aug 1914 - 11 Aug 1915:   Vizeadmiral Carl **SCHAUMANN**
12 Aug 1915 - 22 Dec 1915:   Vizeadmiral Hermann **NORDMANN**
22 Dec 1915 - 12 Jan 1916:   Konteradmiral Karl **SEIFERLING**
12 Jan 1916 - 15 Jan 1916:   Vizeadmiral Paul **BEHNCKE**
15 Jan 1916 - 31 Jan 1916:   Konteradmiral Karl **SEIFERLING**
31 Jan 1916 - 8 Dec 1916:   Vizeadmiral Hermann **NORDMANN**
12 Dec 1916 - 31 Oct 1917:   Konteradmiral Karl **SEIFERLING**
31 Oct 1917 - 15 Nov 1917:
15 Nov 1917 - 18 Aug 1918:   Konteradmiral Ernst **GOETTE**
19 Aug 1918 - 30 Nov 1918:   Konteradmiral Constanz **FELDT**

Commander, IV. Squadron
31 Jul 1914 - 26 Aug 1915:   Admiral Ehrhard **SCHMIDT**
26 Aug 1915 - 8 Dec 1915:   Admiral Friedrich **SCHULTZ**
8 Dec 1915 - 1 Dec 1916:
1 Dec 1916 - 18 Feb 1917:   Vizeadmiral Franz **MAUVE**
18 Feb 1917 - 14 Mar 1917:   Konteradmiral Gottfried Freiherr

	von **DALWIGK zu Lichtenfels**
14 Mar 1917 - 12 Aug 1917:	Vizeadmiral Franz **MAUVE**
13 Aug 1917 - 4 Sep 1917:	Konteradmiral Hugo **MEURER**
4 Sep 1917 - 19 Jan 1918:	Admiral Wilhelm **SOUCHON**
19 Jan 1918 - 13 Feb 1918:	Vizeadmiral Hugo **KRAFT**
13 Feb 1918 - 4 Jun 1918:	Admiral Wilhelm **SOUCHON**
4 Jun 1918 - 22 Jul 1918:	Vizeadmiral Hugo **KRAFT**
22 Jul 1918 - 30 Jul 1918:	Admiral Wilhelm **SOUCHON**
30 Jul 1918 - 4 Oct 1918:	Konteradmiral Hugo **MEURER**
4 Oct 1918 - 10 Oct 1918:	Konteradmiral Ernst **GOETTE**
10 Oct 1918 - 12 Nov 1918:	Konteradmiral Hugo **MEURER**
13 Nov 1918 - 16 Dec 1918:	Konteradmiral Ernst **GOETTE**

Deputy Commander, IV. Squadron

2 Aug 1914 - 24 Aug 1915:	Vizeadmiral Hermann **ALBERTS**
26 Aug 1915 - 10 Nov 1915:	Konteradmiral Walter **ENGELHARDT**
10 Nov 1915 - 1 Dec 1916:	
1 Dec 1916 - 18 Feb 1917:	Konteradmiral Gottfried Freiherr von **DALWIGK zu Lichtenfels**
18 Feb 1917 - 14 Mar 1917:	Konteradmiral Walter Freiherr von **KEYSERLINGK**
14 Mar 1917 - 28 Apr 1917:	Konteradmiral Gottfried Freiherr von **DALWIGK zu Lichtenfels**
28 Apr 1917 - 2 May 1917:	Konteradmiral Walter Freiherr von **KEYSERLINGK**
3 May 1917 - 19 May 1917:	Konteradmiral Hugo **LANGEMAK**
19 May 1917 - 27 May 1917:	Konteradmiral Gottfried Freiherr von **DALWIGK zu Lichtenfels**
28 May 1917 - 12 Aug 1917:	Konteradmiral Hugo **MEURER**
12 Aug 1917 - 7 Sep 1917:	Kapitän zur See Kurt **GRAßHOFF**
7 Sep 1917 - 5 Nov 1917:	Konteradmiral Hugo **MEURER**
5 Nov 1917 - 27 Nov 1917:	Konteradmiral Eduard **VARRENTRAPP**
27 Nov 1917 - 12 Aug 1918:	Konteradmiral Hugo **MEURER**
12 Aug 1918 - 19 Aug 1918:	
19 Aug 1918 - 16 Dec 1918:	Konteradmiral Ernst **GOETTE**

Commander, V. Squadron

5 Aug 1914 - 23 Jan 1915:	Admiral Max von **GRAPOW**
24 Jan 1915 - 15 Jan 1916:	Vizeadmiral Alfred **BEGAS**

Deputy Commander, V. Squadron
7 Aug 1914 - 23 Jan 1915:   Vizeadmiral Alfred **BEGAS**

Commander, VI. Squadron
12 Aug 1914 - 31 Aug 1914:   Vizeadmiral Richard **ECKERMANN**
3 Sep 1914 - 25 Jan 1915:   Vizeadmiral Herwarth **SCHMIDT von Schwind**
25 Jan 1915 - 17 Mar 1915:   Vizeadmiral Georg von **AMMON**
17 Mar 1915 - 31 Aug 1915:   Vizeadmiral Herwarth **SCHMIDT von Schwind**

Deputy Commander, VI. Squadron
12 Aug 1914 - 20 Aug 1914:   Konteradmiral Ehler **BEHRING**

Commander, Cruiser Squadron
15 Nov 1913 - 8 Dec 1914:   Vizeadmiral Maximilian Graf von **SPEE**

Commander, Training Squadron
30 Mar 1914 - 29 Apr 1914:   Vizeadmiral Richard **ECKERMANN**

CHAPTER 2:

SHIPS OF THE REICHSMARINE 1914-1918

Battleships

Baden
Launched in 1915. Interned at Scapa Flow in 1918 and scuttled, June 21, 1919. Salvaged by the Royal Navy and sunk as target on August 16, 1921.

Bayern
Launched in 1915. Interned at Scapa Flow in 1918 and scuttled, June 21, 1919. Raised in 1934 and broken up the following year.

Beowulf (Coastal Battleship)
Launched in 1890. Served as a coastal defense ship in 1915 and target ship in 1916. Decommissioned in 1919 and scrapped in 1921.

Brandenburg
Launched in 1891. Redesignated a coastal defense ship in 1915. Decommissioned in 1919 and scrapped one year later.

Braunschweig
Launched in 1902. Redesignated an exercise ship in 1916 and a barracks ship in 1917. Decommissioned in 1931 and scrapped the following year.

Deutschland
Launched in 1904. Redesignated a barracks ship in 1917. Decommissioned in 1920 and scrapped.

Elsaß
Launched in 1903. Redesignated an exercise ship in 1916. Decommissioned in 1931, sold and scrapped in 1936.

Friedrich der Grosse
Launched in 1911. Flagship of the High Seas Fleet (Admiral Scheer), 1916. Interned at Scapa Flow in 1918 and scuttled, June 21, 1919. Broken up in 1936-1937.

Frithjof (Coastal Battleship)
Launched in 1891. Served as a coastal defense ship and barracks ship from 1915. Decommissioned in 1919, sold and reconstructed as a freighter. Broken up in 1930.

Grosser Kurfürst
Launched in 1913. Interned at Scapa Flow in 1918 and scuttled, June 21, 1919. Raised and scrapped in 1938.

Hagen (Coastal Battleship)
Launched in 1893. Served as floating barracks, 1916-1918. Decommissioned in 1919 and broken up.

Hannover
Launched in 1905. Decommissioned in 1935 and broken up in 1944.

Heimdall (Coastal Battleship)
Launched in 1892. Served as coastal defense ship in 1915 and floating barracks in 1916. Decommissioned in 1919 and scrapped in 1921.

Helgoland
Launched in 1909. Decommissioned in 1919 and taken by the British as a prize. Broken up in 1921.

Hessen
Launched in 1903. Redesignated a tender in 1917. Decommissioned in 1935. Refitted as a target ship and recommissioned in 1937. Taken by the USSR in 1946 as a prize.

Hildebrand (Coastal Battleship)
Launched in 1892. Flagship of VI. Squadron (Vizeadmiral Eckermann), 1914. Served as a coastal defense ship in 1915 and barracks ship in 1916. Decommissioned in 1919 and sold to Holland. Broken up in 1933.

Imperator (ex Volga)
Launched in 1914 in Russia as "*Imperator Alexander III*". Commissioned under German flag in 1918, but trials halted at the time of the Armistice. Transferred to White Russian control in 1919 and interned a year later. Scrapped in 1936.

Kaiser
Launched in 1911. Flagship of V. Squadron (Admiral von Grapow), 1914. Interned at Scapa Flow in 1918 and scuttled, June 21, 1919. Raised in 1929 and scrapped the following year.

Kaiser Friedrich III
Launched in 1896. Redesignated a prison barracks ship in 1916. Decommissioned in 1919 and broken up in 1920.

Kaiser Karl Barbarossa
Launched in 1900. Redesignated as a prison barracks ship in 1916. Decommissioned in 1919 and scrapped.

Kaiser Karl der Grosse
Launched in 1899. Redesignated a prison barracks ship in 1916. Decommissioned in 1919 and scrapped in 1920.

Kaiser Wilhelm II
Launched iin 1897. Served as the Fleet commander's office ship at Wilhelmshaven, 1915-1918. Decommissioned in 1921 and scrapped in 1922.

Kaiser Wilhelm der Grosse
Launched in 1899. Redesignated as a harbor ship in 1916. Decommissioned in 1919 and broken up the following year.

Kaiserin
Launched in 1911. Interned at Scapa Flow in 1918 and scuttled, June 21, 1919. Raised and scrapped in 1936.

König
Launched in 1913. Interned at Scapa Flow in 1918 and scuttled, June 21, 1919.

König Albert
Launched in 1912. Interned at Scapa Flow in 1918 and scuttled, June 21, 1919. Raised in 1935 and scrapped the following year.

Kronprinz (Since 1918, *Kronprinz Wilhelm*)
Launched in 1914. Interned at Scapa Flow in 1918 and scuttled, June 21, 1919.

Lothringen
Launched in 1904. Redesignated as an exercise ship in 1917. Decommissioned in 1931 and scrapped.

Markgraf
Launched in 1913. Interned at Scapa Flow in 1918 and scuttled, June 21, 1919.

Mecklenburg
Launched in 1901. Redesignated as a prison barracks ship in 1916, and as a submarine crew barracks ship in 1918. Decommissioned in 1920 and broken up in 1921.

Nassau
Launched in 1908. Decommissioned and transferred to Japan as scrap in 1920.

Odin (Coastal Battleship)
Launched in 1894. Served as a coastal defense ship in 1915 and redesignated as a tender in 1916. Decommissioned in 1919 and refitted as a freighter. Scrapped in 1935.

Oldenburg
Launched in 1910. Decommissioned in 1919 and taken by the Japanese as a prize. Sold in 1920 and scrapped a year later.

Ostfriesland
Launched in 1909. Flagship of I. Squadron (Admiral von Lans), 1914. Decommissioned in 1919 and taken by the USA as a prize. Sunk in bombing practice in 1921.

Pommern
Launched in 1905. Sunk on June 1, 1916 by torpedoes.

Posen
Launched in 1908. Decommissioned in 1919 and taken by the British as a prize. Scrapped in 1922.

Preussen
Launched in 1903. Flagship of II. Squadron (Admiral Scheer), 1914. Redesignated as a tender in 1919. Decommissioned in 1929, sold and scrapped in 1931.

Prinzregent Luitpold
Launched in 1912. Flagship of III. Squadron (Vizeadmiral Funke), 1914. Interned at Scapa Flow in 1918 and scuttled, June 21, 1919. Raised in 1931 and scrapped in 1933.

Rheinland
Launched in 1908. Beached on April 11, 1918. Refloated but not repaired. Decommissioned in 1920 and scrapped the following year.

Sachsen
Launched in 1916 but never completed. Decommissioned in 1919 and broken up in 1922.

Schlesien
Launched in 1906. Redesignated as an exercise ship and barracks ship in 1917. Scuttled near Swinemünde on May 4, 1945 after suffering damage from mines, bombs and torpedoes.

Schleswig-Holstein
Launched in 1906. Redesignated as a tender in 1917 and a barracks ship in 1918. Converted to a training ship in 1936. Bombed and sunk in Gotenhafen harbor on December 18, 1944. Hulk scuttled on March 21, 1945.

Schwaben
Launched in 1901. Redesignated as an exercise ship in 1916. Decommissioned and scrapped in 1921.

Siegfried (Coastal Battleship)
Launched in 1889. Served as a coastal defense ship and floating barracks, 1915 1918. Decommissioned in 1919 and scrapped the following year.

Thüringen
Launched in 1909. Decommissioned in 1919 and taken by France as a prize. Scrapped in 1922-1923.

Westfalen
Launched in 1908. Taken by the British as a prize in 1920 and scrapped in 1924.

Wettin
Launched in 1901. Redesignated as an exercise ship in 1916. Decommissioned in 1920 and broken up in 1922.

Wittelsbach
Launched in 1900. Flagship of IV. Squadron (Admiral Schmidt), 1914. Redesignated as an exercise ship in 1916. Decommissioned and scrapped in 1921.

Wörth
Launched in 1892. Redesignated as a coastal defense ship in 1915. Decommissioned and broken up in 1919.

Württemberg
Launched in 1917 but never completed. Decommissioned in 1919 and broken up in 1921.

Zähringen
Launched in 1901. Redesignated as an exercise ship in 1916. Decommissioned in 1920.

Aircraft Carriers
I
Launched in 1915 as Italian passenger ship "*Ausonia*". Intended for refitting as an aircraft carrier in 1918, but not completed. Scrapped in 1920.

Heavy Cruisers
Blücher
Launched in 1908. Sunk by British gunfire and torpedoes in the North Sea, on January 24, 1915.

Derfflinger
Launched in 1913. Interned at Scapa Flow in 1918 and scuttled, June 21, 1919. Raised in 1939 and scrapped in 1948.

Freya
Launched in 1897. Redesignated as a coastal defense ship in 1914, then as a training ship in 1915. Decommissioned in 1920 and scrapped the following year.

Friedrich Carl
Launched in 1902. Flagship of Deputy Commander, Baltic Fleet (Konteradmiral Behring), 1914. Sunk by mines in the Baltic Sea, on November 17, 1914.

Fürst Bismarck
Launched in 1897. Used as as coastal defense ship and training ship 1914-1918. Decommissioned in 1919 and broken up.

Gneisenau
Launched in 1906. Sunk by gunfire off the Falkland Islands, on December 8, 1914.

Goeben
Launched in 1911. Flagship of Cruiser Squadron (Admiral Souchon), 1914. In Turkish service throughout the war (renamed "*Jawus Sultan Selim*", then transferred to Turkey in 1918. Scrapped in 1976.

Graf Spee
Launched in 1917 but never completed. Broken up, 1921-1922.

Hansa
Launched in 1898. Served as a coastal defense ship and floating barracks, 1914-1918. Decommissioned in 1919 and scrapped in 1920.

Hertha
Launched in 1897. Served as a coastal defense ship and barracks ship from 1914. Decommissioned in 1919 and scrapped the following year.

Hindenburg
Launched in 1915. Interned at Scapa Flow in 1918 and scuttled, June 21, 1919. Raised in 1930 and broken up, 1931-1932.

Kaiserin Augusta
Launched in 1892. Served as gunnery training ship, 1914-1918. Decommissioned in 1919 and scrapped the following year.

Lützow
Launched in 1913. Torpedoed and scuttled in the North Sea, on June 1, 1916.

Mackensen
Launched in 1917 not never completed. Broken up in 1922.

Moltke
Launched in 1910. Interned at Scapa Flow in 1918 and scuttled, June 21, 1919. Raised in 1927 and scrapped in 1929.

Prinz Adalbert
Launched in 1901. Sunk by torpedoes in the Baltic Sea, on October 23, 1915.

Prinz Heinrich
Launched in 1900. Served as an office ship from 1916. Decommissioned in 1920 and broken up.

Roon
Launched in 1903. Flagship of IV. Reconnaissance Group (Admiral von Rebeur - Paschwitz), 1914. Served as a floating barracks, 1916-1918. Decommissioned in 1920 and scrapped the following year.

Scharnhorst
Launched in 1906. Flagship of the Cruiser Squadron (Vizeadmiral von Spee), 1914. Sunk by gunfire off the Falkland Islands, on December 8, 1914.

Seydlitz
Launched in 1912. Flagship of I. Reconnaissance Group (Admiral von Hipper), 1914. Interned at Scapa Flow in 1918 and scuttled, June 21, 1919. Raised in 1928 and scrapped in 1930.

Victoria Louise
Launched in 1897. Served as a coastal defense ship, minelayer and floating barracks, 1914-1918. Decommissioned in 1919, sold and refitted as a freighter. Broken up in 1923.

Vineta
Launched in 1897. Served as a coastal defense ship and floating barracks, 1914 1918. Decommissioned in 1919 and scrapped the following year.

Von der Tann
Launched in 1909. Interned at Scapa Flow in 1918 and scuttled, June 21, 1919. Raised in 1930 and scrapped in 1934.

Yorck
Launched in 1904. Sunk accidentally by German mines on November 4, 1914.

Light Cruisers

Amazone
Launched in 1900. Decommissioned in 1931 and used as an auxiliary ship. Broken up in 1954.

Arcona
Launched in 1902. Decommissioned in 1930 and refitted as a floating anti-aircraft artillery battery in 1940. Scuttled on May 3, 1945. Broken up, 1948-1950.

Ariadne
Launched in 1900. Flagship of III. Reconnaissance Group, 1914. Sunk by gunfire in the North Sea, on August 28, 1914.

Augsburg
Launched in 1909. Taken as a prize by Japan in 1920. Broken up in 1922.

Berlin
Launched in 1903. Served as coastal defense ship, 1917-1918. Scuttled on May 31, 1947.

Bremen
Launched in 1903. Sunk by torpedoes in the Baltic Sea, on December 17, 1915.

Bremse (Cruiser Minelayer)
Launched in 1916. Interned at Scapa Flow in 1918 and scuttled, June 21, 1919. Raised in 1929 and broken up, 1932-1933.

Breslau
Launched in 1911. Sunk by mines in the Aegean Sea, on January 20, 1918.
Brummer (Cruiser Minelayer)

Launched in 1915. Interned at Scapa Flow in 1918 and scuttled, June 21, 1919.

Cöln
Launched in 1909. Flagship of II. Reconnaissance Group (Konteradmiral Maaß), 1914. Sunk by gunfire in the North Sea, on August 28, 1914.

Cöln (II)
Launched in 1916. Interned at Scapa Flow in 1918 and scuttled, June 21, 1919.

Danzig
Launched in 1905. Decommissioned in 1919 and taken by the British as a prize, 1920. Scrapped in 1921-1923.

Dresden
Launched in 1907. Damaged by gunfire and scuttled in the South Atlantic, on March 14, 1915.

Dresden (II)
Launched in 1917. Interned at Scapa Flow in 1918 and scuttled, June 21, 1919.

Elbing
Launched in 1914. Sunk in the North Sea, in a collision with the battleship "*Posen*" on June 1, 1916.

Emden
Launched in 1908. Damaged by gunfire and beached in the Cocos Islands, on November 9, 1914.

Emden (II)
Launched in 1916. Interned at Scapa Flow in 1918. Unsuccessful attempt made to scuttle the ship on June 21, 1919. Taken by France as a prize and scrapped in 1926.

Frankfurt
Launched in 1915. Interned at Scapa Flow in 1918. Unsuccessful attempt made to scuttle the ship on June 21, 1919. Beached and salvaged, then sunk in U.S. bomb test in 1921.
Frauenlob

Launched in 1902. Sunk by gunfire and torpedoes in the North Sea, on May 31, 1916.

Frauenlob (II)
Launched in 1918 but never completed. Broken up in 1921.

Gazelle
Launched in 1898. Badly damaged by a mine in 1916 and taken out of service. Decommissioned and scrapped in 1920.

Gefion
Launched in 1893. Served as floating barracks, 1916-1918. Decommissioned in 1919 and scrapped in 1923.

Graudenz
Launched in 1913. Decommissioned in 1920 and taken by Italy as a prize. Broken up in 1937.

Hamburg
Launched in 1903. Decommissioned in 1931. Used as floating barracks for submarine crews, 1936-1944. Sunk by bombs at Hamburg in 1944. Raised and broken up, 1949-1956.

Hela
Launched in 1895. Sunk by torpedoes in the North Sea, on September 13, 1914.

Karlsruhe
Launched in 1912. Sunk in the West Indies by an explosion, on November 4, 1914.

Karlsruhe (II)
Launched in 1916. Interred at Scapa Flow in 1918 and scuttled, June 21, 1919.

Kolberg
Launched in 1908. Decommissioned in 1919 and taken by France as a prize. Scrapped in 1929.

Königsberg
Launched in 1905. Scuttled in the Rufiji delta (East Africa) on July 11, 1915.

Königsberg (II)
Launched in 1915. Decommissioned in 1920 and taken by France as a prize. Broken up in 1936.

Leipzig
Launched in 1905. Sunk by gunfire off the Falkland Islands, on December 8, 1914.

Leipzig (II)
Launched in 1918 but never completed. Decommissioned in 1919 and scrapped in 1921.

Magdeburg
Launched in 1911. Beached and blown up in the Baltic Sea, on August 26, 1914.

Magdeburg (II)
Launched in 1917 but never completed. Decommissioned in 1919, sold and broken up in 1922.

Mainz
Launched in 1909. Sunk by gunfire and torpedoes in the North Sea, on August 28, 1914.

Medusa
Launched in 1900. Decommissioned in 1929 and refitted as a floating anti-aircraft artillery battery in 1940. Scuttled on May 3, 1945. Broken up, 1948 - 1950.

München
Launched in 1904. Damaged by torpedoes and decommissioned in 1915. Taken by the British as a prize and broken up in 1920.

Niobe
Launched in 1899. Decommissioned in 1925 and taken over by the Yugoslav Navy, then the Italian Navy in 1941 (renamed "*Cattaro*"). Returned to Germany in 1943. Ran aground and torpedoed on December 22, 1943, and abandoned. Raised in 1947 and scrapped in 1949.

Nürnberg
Launched in 1906. Sunk off the Falkland Islands by gunfire, on December 8, 1914.

Nürnberg (II)
Launched in 1916. Interred at Scapa Flow in 1918. An attempt to scuttle the ship on June 21, 1919 failed. Salvaged and sunk in gunnery tests in 1922.

Nymphe
Launched in 1899. Decommissioned in 1931 and scrapped the following year.

Pillau
Launched in 1914. Decommissioned in 1919 and taken by Italy as a prize (renamed "*Bari*"). Sunk by U.S. aircraft at Livorno on June 28, 1943.

Regensburg
Launched in 1914. Decommissioned in 1920 and taken by France as a prize (renamed "*Strasbourg*"). Scuttled at Lorient in 1944.

Rostock
Launched in 1912. Damaged by gunfire and torpedoes, scuttled in the North Sea, on June 1, 1916.

Rostock (II)
Launched in 1918 but never completed. Broken up in 1921.

Schwalbe
Launched in 1887. Served as floating barracks, 1914-1918. Decommissioned in 1919 and scrapped in 1922.

Stettin
Launched in 1907. Decommissioned in 1919, then sold and scrapped, 1921-1923.

Stralsund
Launched in 1911. Decommissioned in 1920 and taken by France as a prize. Scrapped in 1933.

Straßburg
Launched in 1911. Decommissioned in 1920 and taken by Italy as a prize (re-

named "*Taranto*"). Scuttled in La Spezia harbor on September 9, 1943. Raised but sunk by bombs on October 23, 1943. Raised again and sunk by bombs for the final time on September 23, 1944.

Stuttgart
Launched in 1906. Decommissioned in 1919 and broken up the following year.

Thetis
Launched in 1900. Decommissioned in 1929 and scrapped the following year.

Undine
Launched in 1902. Sunk by torpedoes in the Baltic Sea, on November 7, 1915.

Wiesbaden
Launched in 1915. Sunk by gunfire in the North Sea, on June 1, 1916.

Wiesbaden (II)
Launched in 1917, but never completed. Decommissioned in 1919 and scrapped the following year.

CHAPTER 3:

ORDER OF BATTLE OF THE REICHSMARINE, 1919-1933

Commander-in-Chief
(1919: Leiter des Reichsmarineamtes)
(1919-1920: Chef der Admiralität)
(1920-1935: Chef der Marineleitung)

17 Feb 1919 - 26 Mar 1919:	Vizeadmiral Maximilian **ROGGE**
26 Mar 1919 - 22 Mar 1920:	Admiral Adolf von **TROTHA**
22 Mar 1920 - 5 Aug 1920:	Vizeadmiral William **MICHAELIS**
5 Aug 1920 - 18 Aug 1920:	Vizeadmiral Heinrich **LÖHLEIN**
18 Aug 1920 - 31 Aug 1920:	Vizeadmiral William **MICHAELIS**
31 Aug 1920 - 18 Sep 1924:	Admiral Paul **BEHNCKE**
18 Sep 1924 - 24 Sep 1928:	Admiral Hans **ZENKER**
24 Sep 1928 - 30 Jan 1943:	Großadmiral Erich **RAEDER**

Chief of Naval General Staff
(1919: Chef des Admiralstabs)
(1919 - 1937: Chef des Marinekommandoamtes)

9 Dec 1918 - 3 Jan 1919:	Konteradmiral Friedrich von **BÜLOW**
3 Jan 1919 - 1 Aug 1919:	Admiral Hans **ZENKER**
1 Aug 1919 - 1 Oct 1919:	
1 Oct 1919 - 22 May 1920:	Vizeadmiral William **MICHAELIS**
22 May 1920 - 1 Jul 1920:	Admiral Iwan **OLDEKOP**
2 Jul 1920 - 10 Apr 1922:	Vizeadmiral Theodor **PÜLLEN**
11 Apr 1922 - 21 Sep 1924:	Admiral Conrad **MOMMSEN**
22 Sep 1924 - 30 Sep 1928:	Vizeadmiral Adolf **PFEIFFER**
1 Oct 1928 - 28 Sep 1930:	Vizeadmiral Friedrich **BRUTZER**
29 Sep 1930 - 27 Sep 1931:	Admiral Walter **GLADISCH**
28 Sep 1931 - 28 Sep 1934:	Admiral Dr. Otto **GROOS**

Chief of Naval Operations
(1919-1936: Chef der Flottenabteilung)

17 May 1920 - 26 Sep 1922:	Admiral Iwan **OLDEKOP**
27 Sep 1922 - 24 Jun 1923:	Admiral Walter **GLADISCH**
24 Jun 1923 - 30 Sep 1925:	Konteradmiral Arno **SPINDLER**
1 Oct 1925 - 10 Mar 1927:	Vizeadmiral Wilfried von **LOEWENFELD**
13 Mar 1927 - 22 Sep 1929:	Vizeadmiral Kurt **AßMANN**
28 Sep 1929 - 27 Sep 1932:	Generaladmiral Hermann **BOEHM**
27 Sep 1932 - 28 Sep 1934:	Admiral Günther **GUSE**

C-in-C, High Seas Fleet (Flottenchef)

29 Nov 1918 - 5 Jan 1919:	Vizeadmiral Hugo **MEURER**
6 Jan 1919 - 30 Jun 1919:	Konteradmiral Victor **HARDER**
30 Jun 1919 - 15 Oct 1923:	POSITION ABOLISHED
15 Oct 1923 - 17 Sep 1924:	Admiral Hans **ZENKER**
26 Sep 1924 - 29 Sep 1927:	Admiral Conrad **MOMMSEN**
29 Sep 1927 - 30 Sep 1931:	Admiral Iwan **OLDEKOP**
30 Sep 1931 - 22 Sep 1933:	Admiral Walter **GLADISCH**

Admiral Commanding, Baltic

12 Mar 1919 - 8 Jan 1920:	Vizeadmiral Hugo **MEURER**
8 Jan 1920 - 18 Mar 1920:	Konteradmiral Magnus von **LEVETZOW**
18 Mar 1920 - 23 Mar 1920:	Konteradmiral Ernst **EWERS**
23 Mar 1920 - 3 Jun 1920:	
3 Jun 1920 - 11 Jul 1921:	Admiral Ernst Freiherr von **GAGERN**
11 Jul 1921 - 14 Jul 1921:	Vizeadmiral Hugo **DOMINIK**
14 Jul 1921 - 10 Jan 1925:	Admiral Ernst Freiherr von **GAGERN**
10 Jan 1925 - 28 Oct 1925:	Großadmiral Erich **RAEDER**
28 Oct 1925 - 10 Nov 1925:	Vizeadmiral Martin **HOSEMANN**
10 Nov 1925 - 1 Oct 1928:	Großadmiral Erich **RAEDER**
1 Oct 1928 - 10 Oct 1930:	Admiral Gottfried **HANSEN**
10 Oct 1930 - 23 Oct 1930:	Vizeadmiral Ernst **JUNKERMAN**
23 Oct 1930 - 30 Sep 1932:	Admiral Gottfried **HANSEN**
1 Oct 1932 - 1 Nov 1938:	Generaladmiral Conrad **ALBRECHT**

Admiral Commanding, North Sea

2 Jan 1919 - 16 Mar 1920:	Vizeadmiral Andreas **MICHELSEN**
16 Mar 1920 - 24 May 1920:	
24 May 1920 - 30 Sep 1923:	Admiral Hans **ZENKER**
30 Sep 1923 - 5 Oct 1928:	Admiral Hermann **BAUER**
5 Oct 1928 - 28 Sep 1932:	Admiral Werner **TILLESSEN**
28 Sep 1932 - 3 Aug 1933:	Admiral Richard **FOERSTER**

Flag Officer, Battleships
1 Jan 1930 - 27 Feb 1930:   Vizeadmiral Walther **FRANZ**
27 Feb 1930 - 27 Sep 1932: Admiral Richard **FOERSTER**
1 Oct 1932 - 28 Sep 1934:   Admiral Max **BASTIAN**

Flag Officer, Reconnaissance Forces
1 Jan 1930 - 28 Sep 1930:   Admiral Walter **GLADISCH**
28 Sep 1930 - 1 Oct 1932:   Generaladmiral Conrad **ALBRECHT**
1 Oct 1932 - 24 Sep 1934:   Vizeadmiral Hans **KOLBE**

CHAPTER 4:

SHIPS OF THE REICHSMARINE 1919-1933

Battleships

Braunschweig
Launched in 1902. Fleet duties, 1921-1926. Decommissioned in 1931 and scrapped.

Deutschland
Launched in 1931. Renamed "*Lützow*" in 1939. Sunk by bombs in Swinemünde on April 16, 1945. Raised by the USSR and scrapped in 1948-1949.

Elsaß
Launched in 1903. Fleet duties, 1924-1930. Decommissioned in 1931 and scrapped in 1936.

Hannover
Launched in 1905. Fleet duties, 1921-1931. Decommissioned in 1935 and broken up, 1944-1946.

Hessen
Launched in 1903. Fleet duties, 1925-1934. Decommissioned in 1935 and refitted as a target ship. Recommissioned in 1937. Taken by the USSR as a prize in 1946.

Lothringen
Launched in 1904. Fleet duties, 1922-1936. Decommissioned in 1931 and scrapped.

Preussen
Launched in 1903. Fleet duties, 1919-1929. Decommissioned in 1929, sold and scrapped in 1931.

Schlesien
Launched in 1906. Rearmed in 1926-1928. Scuttled near Swinemünde on May 4, 1945 after suffering mine, bomb and torpedo damage.

Schleswig-Holstein
Launched in 1906. Rearmed in 1926-1928. Coverted to a training ship in 1936. Sunk by bombs in Gotenhafen harbor on December 18, 1944 and the hulk scuttled on March 21, 1945. Raised in 1945-1946 by the USSR and used for training purposes.

Zähringen
Launched in 1901. Decommissioned in 1920. Refitted as a target ship in 1927 1928. Bombed in Gotenhafen harbor and scuttled on March 21, 1945. Broken up in 1949-1950.

Cruisers

Amazone
Launched in 1900. Decommissioned in 1931 and used as an auxiliary ship. Broken up in 1954.

Arcona
Launched in 1902. Decommissioned in 1930 and refitted as a floating anti-aircraft artillery battery in 1940. Scuttled on May 3, 1945. Broken up, 1948 - 1950.

Berlin
Launched in 1903. Served as coastal defense ship, 1917-1918. Scuttled on May 31, 1947.

Emden (III)
Launched in 1925. Served as a training cruiser, then saw active service from 1939. Scuttled in Heikendorfer Bay on May 3, 1945 after sustaining bomb damage. Broken up in 1949.

Graudenz
Launched in 1913. Fleet service, 1919-1920. Decommissioned in 1920 and taken by Italy as a prize. Broken up in 1937.

Hamburg
Launched in 1903. Decommissioned in 1931. Used as floating barracks for submarine crews, 1936-1944. Sunk by bombs at Hamburg in 1944. Raised and broken up, 1949-1956.

Karlsruhe (III)
Launched in 1927. Served as a training cruiser, then fleet duties from 1936. Damaged by torpedoes at Kristiansand (Norway) and scuttled on April 9, 1940.

Köln
Launched in 1928. Served as a training cruiser, then saw active service from 1939. Sunk by bombs at Wilhelmshaven on March 30, 1945 and the hulk blown up on May 2, 1945.

Königsberg (III)
Launched in 1927. Fleet duties 1929-1936. Served as gunnery training ship after 1936. Active service, 1939-1940. Bombed and destroyed off Bergen (Norway) on April 10, 1940. Raised in 1942 and broken up.

Leipzig (III)
Launched in 1929. Fleet duties, 1931-1939. Severely damaged by a torpedo in 1939 and removed from service the following year. Refitted and reentered service as a training cruiser. Scuttled by the British on   December 16, 1946.

Medusa
Launched in 1900. Decommissioned in 1929 and refitted as a floating anti-aircraft artillery battery in 1940. Scuttled on May 3, 1945. Broken up, 1948 - 1950.

Niobe
Launched in 1899. Decommissioned in 1925 and taken over by the Yugoslav Navy, then the Italian Navy in 1941 (renamed "*Cattaro*"). Returned to Germany in 1943. Ran aground and torpedoed on December 22, 1943, and abandoned. Raised in 1947 and scrapped in 1949.

Nymphe
Launched in 1899. Decommissioned in 1931 and scrapped the following year.

Pillau
Launched in 1914. Fleet duties, 1919. Decommissioned in 1919 and taken by Italy as a prize (renamed "*Bari*"). Sunk by U.S. aircraft at Livorno on June 28, 1943.

Prinz Eitel Friedrich
Launched in 1920 (under the name "*Noske*"), but never completed. Broken up in 1921.

Regensburg
Launched in 1914. Fleet duties, 1919-1920. Decommissioned in 1920 and taken by France as a prize (renamed "*Strasbourg*"). Scuttled at Lorient in 1944.

Straßburg
Launched in 1911. Fleet duties, 1919-1920. Decommissioned in 1920 and taken by Italy as a prize (renamed "*Taranto*"). Scuttled in La Spezia harbor on September 9, 1943. Raised but sunk by bombs on October 23, 1943. Raised again and sunk by bombs for the final time on September 23, 1944.

Thetis
Launched in 1900. Decommissioned in 1929 and scrapped the following year.

CHAPTER 5:

ORDER OF BATTLE OF THE KRIEGSMARINE, 1933-1945

Commander-in-Chief
(1920-1935: Chef der Marineleitung)
(1935-1945: Oberbefehlshaber der Kriegsmarine)

24 Sep 1928 - 30 Jan 1943:   Großadmiral Erich **RAEDER**
30 Jan 1943 - 1 May 1945:   Großadmiral Karl **DÖNITZ**
1 May 1945 - 23 May 1945:   Generaladmiral Hans-Georg
                             von **FRIEDEBURG**
23 May 1945 - 26 May 1945:   Admiral Otto **BACKENKÖHLER**
26 May 1945 - 22 Jul 1945:   Generaladmiral Walter **WARZECHA**

Chief of Naval General Staff
(1919-1937: Chef des Marinekommandoamtes)
(1937-1945: Chef des Stabes der Seekriegsleitung)

28 Sep 1931 - 28 Sep 1934:   Admiral Dr. Otto **GROOS**
29 Sep 1934 - 31 Oct 1938:   Admiral Günther **GUSE**
31 Oct 1938 - 13 Jun 1941:   Generaladmiral Otto **SCHNIEWIND**
13 Jun 1941 - 20 Feb 1943:   Admiral Kurt **FRICKE**
20 Feb 1943 - 22 Jul 1945:   Admiral Wilhelm **MEISEL**

Chief of Naval Operations
(1919-1936: Chef der Flottenabteilung)
(1936-1945: Chef der Operationsabteilung)

29 Sep 1934 - 22 Sep 1936:   Admiral Otto **CILIAX**
22 Sep 1936 - 1 Oct 1937:   Generaladmiral Wilhelm **MARSCHALL**
1 Oct 1937 - 12 Jun 1941:   Admiral Kurt **FRICKE**
12 Jun 1941 - 29 Jun 1944:   Konteradmiral Gerhard **WAGNER**
29 Jun 1944 - 22 Jul 1945:   Konteradmiral Hans Karl **MEYER**

C-in-C, High Seas Fleet (Flottenchef)

30 Sep 1931 - 22 Sep 1933:	Admiral Walter **GLADISCH**
22 Sep 1933 - 21 Dec 1936:	Admiral Richard **FOERSTER**
21 Dec 1936 - 1 Nov 1938:	Generaladmiral Rolf **CARLS**
1 Nov 1938 - 20 Oct 1939:	Generaladmiral Hermann **BOEHM**
20 Oct 1939 - 11 Mar 1940:	Generaladmiral Wilhelm **MARSCHALL**
11 Mar 1940 - 23 Apr 1940:	Admiral Günther **LÜTJENS**
23 Apr 1940 - 18 Jun 1940:	Generaladmiral Wilhelm **MARSCHALL**
18 Jun 1940 - 27 May 1941:	Admiral Günther **LÜTJENS**
27 May 1941 - 12 Jun 1941:	Vizeadmiral Leopold **SIEMENS** (Acting)
12 Jun 1941 - 31 Jul 1944:	Generaladmiral Otto **SCHNIEWIND**
31 Jul 1944 - 23 May 1945:	Vizeadmiral Wilhelm **MEENDSEN-BOHLKEN**

Baltic Fleet

21 Sep 1941 - 21 Oct 1941:	Admiral Otto **CILIAX**

Naval Group North

21 Sep 1940 - 2 Mar 1943:	Generadmiral Rolf **CARLS**
2 Mar 1943 - 30 Jul 1944:	Generaladmiral Otto **SCHNIEWIND**

Naval Group North Sea

22 Jun 1943 - 10 Jul 1945:	Admiral Erich **FÖRSTE**

Naval Group Norway

4 Mar 1943 - 25 Apr 1945:	Admiral Otto **CILIAX**
25 Apr 1945 - 26 Aug 1945:	Admiral Theodor **KRANCKE**

Naval Group East/Baltic

1 Nov 1938 - 30 Oct 1939:	Generaladmiral Konrad **ALBRECHT**
31 Oct 1939 - 20 Sep 1940:	Generaladmiral Rolf **CARLS**
22 Jun 1943 - 1 Mar 1944:	Admiral Hubert **SCHMUNDT**
1 Mar 1944 - 23 Jul 1945:	Generaladmiral Oskar **KUMMETZ**

Naval Group South

30 Jun 1941 - Dec 1941:	Admiral Karlgeorg **SCHUSTER**
Dec 1941 - Mar 1942:	Generaladmiral Wilhelm **MARSCHALL**
Mar 1942 - 21 Mar 1943:	Admiral Karlgeorg **SCHUSTER**
21 Mar 1943 - 11 Dec 1944:	Admiral Kurt **FRICKE**
11 Dec 1944 - 1 Jan 1945:	POSITION NOT FILLED
1 Jan 1945 - 2 May 1945:	Vizeadmiral Werner **LÖWISCH**

Naval Group West
23 Aug 1939 - 21 Sep 1942:   Generaladmiral Alfred **SAALWÄCHTER**
21 Sep 1942 - 19 Apr 1943:   Generaladmiral Wilhelm **MARSCHALL**
20 Apr 1943 - 18 Apr 1945:   Admiral Theodor **KRANCKE**
19 Apr 1945 - 8 May 1945:   Generaladmiral Wilhelm **MARSCHALL**

Admiral Commanding, Adriatic
10 Sep 1943 - 4 Jul 1944:   Vizeadmiral Joachim **LIETZMANN**
4 Jul 1944 - 16 Jul 1944:   Vizeadmiral Werner **LÖWISCH**
16 Jul 1944 - 7 Dec 1944:   Vizeadmiral Joachim **LIETZMANN**

Admiral Commanding, Aegean
1 Jul 1941 - 26 Sep 1941:   Vizeadmiral Hans-Hubertus von **STOSCH**
26 Sep 1941 - 23 Feb 1943:   Vizeadmiral Erich **FÖRSTE**
23 Feb 1943 - 28 Nov 1944:   Vizeadmiral Werner **LANGE**

Admiral Commanding, Atlantic Coast
1 Mar 1943 - 9 May 1945:   Vizeadmiral Ernst **SCHIRLITZ**

Admiral Commanding, Baltic
1 Oct 1932 - 1 Nov 1938:   Generaladmiral Conrad **ALBRECHT**
1 Nov 1938 - 3 Jan 1939:   Generaladmiral Rolf **CARLS**
3 Jan 1939 - 15 Jan 1939:   Vizeadmiral Friedrich **GÖTTING**
15 Jan 1939 - 15 May 1939:   Generaladmiral Rolf **CARLS**
15 May 1939 - 27 May 1939:   Admiral Günther **GUSE**
27 May 1939 - 16 Feb 1940:   Generaladmiral Rolf **CARLS**
16 Feb 1940 - 10 Apr 1942:   Admiral Günther **GUSE**
10 Apr 1942 - 2 May 1942:   Generaladmiral Wilhelm **MARSCHALL**
2 May 1942 - 8 Mar 1943:   Admiral Günther **GUSE**
9 Mar 1943 - 21 Jun 1943:   Admiral Hubert **SCHMUNDT**
22 Jun 1943:   REDESIGNATED MARINEOBERKOMMANDO OSTSEE

Admiral Commanding, East Baltic
17 Jun 1944 - 18 Apr 1945:   Admiral Theodor **BURCHARDI**
28 Apr 1945 - 12 May 1945:   Vizeadmiral August **THIELE**

Admiral Commanding, West Baltic
29 Nov 1944 - 30 Mar 1945:   Vizeadmiral Werner **LANGE**
30 Mar 1945 - 22 Jul 1945:   Konteradmiral Günther **SCHUBERT**

Admiral Commanding, Belgium & the Netherlands
20 May 1940 - 18 Jun 1940:	Vizeadmiral Lothar von ARNAULD de la Perière
18 Jun 1940 - 1 Jul 1942:	Konteradmiral Helmuth **KIENAST**
1 Jul 1942 - 4 Mar 1943:	Vizeadmiral Kurt Caesar **HOFFMANN**
4 Mar 1943 - 31 Dec 1944:	Vizeadmiral Gustav **KLEIKAMP**
31 Dec 1944 - 9 Jun 1945:	Vizeadmiral Rudolf **STANGE**

Admiral Commanding, Black Sea
1 Jul 1941 - 2 May 1942:	Admiral FriedrichWilhelm **FLEISCHER**
2 May 1942 - 15 May 1942:	Konteradmiral Wolff-Ehrenreich von **ARNSWALDT**
15 May 1942 - 15 Sep 1942:	Admiral Hans-Dietrich **WURMBACH**
15 Sep 1942 - 10 Nov 1942:	Vizeadmiral Hellmuth **HEYE**
10 Nov 1942 - 28 Feb 1943:	Vizeadmiral Robert **WITTHOEFT-EMDEN**
28 Feb 1943 - 19 Nov 1943:	Vizeadmiral Gustav **KIESERITZKY**
19 Nov 1943 - 22 Nov 1943:	Kapitän zur See Heinz-Dietrich von **CONRADY**
22 Nov 1943 - 9 Nov 1944:	Vizeadmiral Hellmuth **BRINKMANN**

Admiral Commanding, Channel Coast
26 Jul 1940 - 19 Feb 1941:	Admiral FriedrichWilhelm **FLEISCHER**
19 Feb 1941 - 10 May 1943:	Admiral Hermann von **FISCHEL**
10 May 1943 - 8 Sep 1944:	Vizeadmiral Friedrich **RIEVE**

Admiral Commanding, Denmark
1 Jun 1940 - 18 Mar 1943:	Admiral Raul **MEWIS**
18 Mar 1943 - 8 May 1945:	Admiral Hans-Dietrich **WURMBACH**

Admiral Commanding, East Asia
21 Mar 1940 - 8 May 1945:	Admiral Paul **WENNEKER**

Admiral Commanding, France
22 Jun 1941 - 1 Mar 1941:	Admiral Karlgeorg **SCHUSTER**
1 Mar 1941 - 12 Aug 1942:	Generaladmiral Otto **SCHULTZE**
12 Aug 1942 - 30 Nov 1942:	Generaladmiral Wilhelm **MARSCHALL**

Admiral Commanding, French South Coast
26 Jun 1943 - 31 Aug 1943:	Konteradmiral Adalbert **ZUCKSCHWERDT**
2 Sep 1943 - 11 Aug 1944:	Vizeadmiral Paul **WEVER**
13 Aug 1944 - 6 Sep 1944:	Vizeadmiral Ernst **SCHEURLEN**

Admiral Commanding, Heligoland Bight
7 Sep 1944 - 11 Feb 1945: Vizeadmiral Ernst **SCHEURLEN**
11 Feb 1945 - 14 Mar 1945: Konteradmiral Rolf **JOHANNESSON**
14 Mar 1945 - 8 May 1945: Vizeadmiral Gustav **KLEIKAMP**

Admiral Commanding, North Sea
28 Sep 1932 - 3 Aug 1933: Admiral Richard **FOERSTER**
3 Aug 1933 - 16 Sep 1933: Admiral Otto **FEIGE**
16 Sep 1933 - 21 Sep 1933: Admiral Richard **FOERSTER**
2 Oct 1933 - 4 Oct 1937: Generaladmiral Otto **SCHULTZE**
4 Oct 1937 - 28 Oct 1938: Generaladmiral Hermann **BOEHM**
28 Oct 1938 - 23 Aug 1939: Generaladmiral Alfred **SAALWÄCHTER**
23 Aug 1939 - 28 Nov 1939: Generaladmiral Otto **SCHULTZE**
28 Nov 1939 - 28 Feb 1943: Admiral Hermann **DENSCH**
28 Feb 1943 - 21 Jun 1943: Admiral Erich **FÖRSTE**
22 Jun 1943: REDESIGNATED MARINEOBERKOMMANDO NORTH SEA

Admiral Commanding, Northern Waters
15 Oct 1941 - 27 Aug 1942: Admiral Hubert **SCHMUNDT**
27 Aug 1942 - Sep 1942: Vizeadmiral August **THIELE**
Sep 1942 - 14 Mar 1944: Konteradmiral Otto **KLÜBER**
15 Mar 1944 - 4 Jun 1944: Konteradmiral Rudolf **PETERS**

Admiral Commanding, Norway
10 Apr 1940 - 31 Jan 1943: Generaladmiral Hermann **BOEHM**
1 Feb 1943: REDESIGNATED MARINEOBERKOMMANDO NORWAY

Admiral Commanding, Norwegian North Coast
27 Apr 1940 - 19 Jun 1941: Vizeadmiral August **THIELE**
21 Jun 1941 - 30 Apr 1942: Vizeadmiral Leopold **SIEMENS**
30 Apr 1942 - 7 Jun 1942: Vizeadmiral Walter **KRASTEL**
7 Jun 1942 - 6 Nov 1944: Vizeadmiral Leopold **SIEMENS**
8 Nov 1944 - 17 Aug 1945: Vizeadmiral Erich **SCHULTE-MÖNTING**

Admiral Commanding, Norwegian Polar Coast
31 Aug 1940 - 3 Aug 1941: Vizeadmiral Otto **SCHENK**
3 Aug 1941 - 27 Oct 1941: Vizeadmiral Walter **KRASTEL**

27 Oct 1941 - 13 Aug 1942:   Vizeadmiral Otto **SCHENK**
18 Sep 1942 - 8 Jan 1945:   Vizeadmiral Heinz **NORDMANN**
8 Jan 1945 - 21 Jul 1945:   Vizeadmiral Bruno **MACHENS**

Admiral Commanding, Norwegian South Coast
9 Apr 1940 - 30 Aug 1940:   Vizeadmiral Otto **SCHENK**

Admiral Commanding, Norwegian West Coast
9 Apr 1940 - 19 Jul 1945:   Admiral Otto von **SCHRADER**

Admiral Commanding, Polar Coast
8 Jan 1945 - 21 Jul 1945:   Vizeadmiral Bruno **MACHENS**

Admiral Commanding, West
22 Jun 1940 - 1 Mar 1941:   Admiral Karlgeorg **SCHUSTER**

Flag Officer, Battleships
1 Oct 1932 - 28 Sep 1934:   Admiral Max **BASTIAN**
28 Sep 1934 - 23 Nov 1936:   Generaladmiral Rolf **CARLS**
25 Nov 1936 - 8 Feb 1938:   Admiral Hermann von **FISCHEL**
8 Feb 1938 - 20 Oct 1939:   Generaladmiral Wilhelm **MARSCHALL**
20 Oct 1939 - 16 Jun 1941:   POSITION ABOLISHED
16 Jun 1941 - 2 Jun 1942:   Admiral Otto **CILIAX**
2 Jun 1942 - 19 Feb 1943:   REDESIGNATED FLAG OFFICER, CRUISERS
19 Feb 1943:   REDESIGNATED COMMANDER, BATTLE GROUP
19 Feb 1943 - 9 Nov 1943:   Generaladmiral Oskar **KUMMETZ**
9 Nov 1943 - 26 Dec 1943:   Konteradmiral Erich **BEY**
26 Dec 1943 - 16 Jan 1944:   Konteradmiral Rolf **JOHANNESSON**
16 Jan 1944 - 30 Apr 1944:   Konteradmiral Hans Karl **MEYER**

Flag Officer, Cruisers
3 Jun 1942 - 18 Feb 1943:   Generaladmiral Oskar **KUMMETZ**
1 Aug 1940 - 14 Oct 1941:   Admiral Hubert **SCHMUNDT**

Flag Officer, Destroyers
26 Oct 1939 - 10 Apr 1940:   Kommodore Friedrich **BONTE**
10 Apr 1940 - 10 May 1940:   Kapitän zur See Alfred **SCHEMMEL**
10 May 1940 - 26 Dec 1943:   Konteradmiral Erich **BEY**

26 Dec 1943 - 26 Jan 1944:   Konteradmiral Max-Eckart **WOLFF**
26 Jan 1944 - 29 May 1945:   Vizeadmiral Leo **KREISCH**

Flag Officer, Submarines
1 Jan 1936 - 30 Jan 1943:   Großadmiral Karl **DÖNITZ**
30 Jan 1943 - 30 Apr 1945:   Generaladmiral Hans-Georg von **FRIEDEBURG**
30 Apr 1945 - 31 May 1945:   Konteradmiral Eberhard **GODT**

Flag Officer, Torpedo Boats
25 Sep 1933 - 4 Oct 1934:   Admiral Kurt **FRICKE**
4 Oct 1934 - 28 Sep 1937:   Generaladmiral Oskar **KUMMETZ**
8 Oct 1937 - 20 Oct 1939:   Admiral Günther **LÜTJENS**
20 Oct 1939 - 26 Oct 1939:
26 Oct 1939 - 29 Nov 1939:   Kommodore Friedrich **BONTE**
29 Nov 1939 - 19 Apr 1942:   Konteradmiral Hans von **BÜTOW**
19 Apr 1942 - 22 Jul 1945:   Kommodore Rudolf **PETERSEN**

Flag Officer, Minesweepers
2 Oct 1933 - 1 Jun 1937:   Konteradmiral Kurt **RAMIEN**
1 Jun 1937 - 31 Aug 1939:   Vizeadmiral Friedrich **RUGE**

Flag Officer, Reconnaissance Forces
1 Oct 1932 - 24 Sep 1934:   Vizeadmiral Hans **KOLBE**
24 Sep 1934 - 27 Sep 1937:   Generaladmiral Hermann **BOEHM**
2 Oct 1937 - 20 Oct 1939:   Admiral Hermann **DENSCH**
20 Oct 1939 - 17 Jun 1940:   Admiral Günther **LÜTJENS**

Flag Officer, Naval Security Forces
15 Jan 1945 - 22 Jun 1945:   Konteradmiral Ernst **LUCHT**

Flag Officer, Midget Weapons
20 Apr 1944 - 10 Sep 1945:   Vizeadmiral Helmuth **HEYE**

CHAPTER 6:

SHIPS OF THE KRIEGSMARINE 1933-1945

Battleships

Bismarck
Launched in 1939. Flagship of the High Seas Fleet (Admiral Lütjens). Damaged by airborne torpedoes and gunfire in the North Atlantic. Scuttled by depth charges on May 27, 1941.

Deutschland
Laid down in 1937 but never completed.

Gneisenau
Launched in 1936. Heavily damaged in air raids in February 1942 and taken out of service in July of the same year. Scuttled in Gotenhafen harbor on March 27, 1945. Raised in 1951 and broken up.

Hessen
Launched in 1903. Reconstructed in 1936-1937 and used as an auxiliary vessel. Taken by the USSR as a prize in 1946.

Hindenburg
Laid down in 1938 but never completed.

Scharnhorst
Launched in 1936. Sunk in the North Sea by British ships on December 26, 1943.

Schlesien
Launched in 1906. Rearmed in 1926-1928 and converted in 1935-1936 as a training ship. Used as a floating battery to bombard the Polish fortress of Hela in 1939. Scuttled near Swinemünde on May 4, 1945 after suffering mine, bomb and torpedo damage.

SchleswigHolstein
Launched in 1906. Rearmed in 1926-1928 and converted in 1935-1936 as a training ship. Used as a floating battery to bombard the Polish fortress of Hela in 1939. Sunk by bombs in Gotenhafen harbor on December 18, 1944 and the hulk scuttled on March 21, 1945. Raised in 1945-1946 by the USSR and used for training purposes.

Tirpitz
Launched in 1939. Sunk by Allied bombers near Tromsö, Norway, on November 12, 1944. Hulk broken up in 1948-1957.

Zähringen
Launched in 1901. Reconstructed in 1927-1928 and used as a target ship. Bombed in Gotenhafen harbor and scuttled on March 21, 1945. Broken up in 1949-1950.

Pocket Battleships
Admiral Graf Spee
Launched in 1934. Badly damaged by British warships while leaving Montevideo (Uruguay) harbor. Scuttled in the River Plate estuary on December 17, 1939. Broken up in 1942-1943.

Admiral Scheer
Launched in 1933. Capsized in Kiel harbor following a bombing raid on April 9, 1945.

Deutschland/Lützow
Launched in 1931. Renamed "*Lützow*" in November 1939. Badly damaged in an air raid on Swinemünde, on April 16, 1945 and grounded. Raised by the USSR and broken up in 1948-1949.

Lützow
Launched in 1939 but never completed. Sold to the USSR in February 1940. Sunk by German artillery on September 17, 1941. Later raised and repaired and used as floating artillery battery. Broken up in 1960.

Aircraft Carriers
Graf Zeppelin
Launched in 1938 but never completed. Scuttled in Stettin, on March 24, 1945. Salvaged by the USSR but damaged by mine and broken up in 1948-1949.

Peter Strasser
Launched in 1940 but never completed. Broken up that same year.

Seydlitz
Launched in 1939 as a heavy cruiser. Intended for conversion in 1942 as aircraft carrier ("*Weser*"), but never completed. Scuttled at Königsberg on January 29, 1945. Broken up in 1958.

Plans existed for the construction of other aircraft carriers and auxiliary aircraft carriers, but none were completed.

Heavy Cruisers
Admiral Hipper
Launched in 1937. Badly damaged in air raid in April 1945, and scuttled by depth charges on May 3, 1945. Refloated and broken up in 1948-1952.

Blücher
Launched in 1937. Torpedoed and sunk by shore batteries in Oslo Fjord, on April 9, 1940.

Prinz Eugen
Launched in 1938. Used in atomic bomb tests by the US Navy in June 1946. Sank due to leaks on December 22, 1946.

Light Cruisers
Emden (III)
Launched in 1925. Damaged in air raid on Kiel in April 1945. Scuttled at Heinkendorfer Bay on May 3, 1945, and broken up in 1949.

Karlsruhe (III)
Launched in 1927. Heavily damaged by torpedoes and scuttled off the south coast of Norway on April 9, 1940.

Köln
Launched in 1928. Sunk in air raid in Wilhelmshaven on March 30, 1945. Broken up in 1946.

Königsberg (III)
Launched in 1927. Bombed and sunk by aircraft at Bergen (Norway) on April 10, 1940. Raised in 1942 and broken up.

Leipzig (III)
Launched in 1929. Severely damaged by a torpedo in 1939 and removed from service the following year. Refitted and reentered service as a training cruiser. Scuttled by the British on December 16, 1946.

Nürnberg
Launched in 1934. Taken by the USSR as a prize in January 1946. Decommissioned and broken up in 1961.

Two further "M" Class light cruisers were laid down in 1938 and 1939, provisionally designated "M" and "N". They were not completed and were broken up in 1939.

Auxiliary Cruisers
Atlantis
Launched in 1937 and converted to an auxiliary cruiser in 1939. Sunk by British warships in the South Atlantic on 22 November, 1941.

Coronel
Launched as the freighter *Togo* in 1938 and commissioned as an auxiliary cruiser in December 1942. In February 1943 tried to break out into the Atlantic but failed, and never saw action as a raider. After the war taken as a prize by the British, transferred to the US Navy in 1946, then to the Norwegian Navy the following year. In 1954 reverted to private ownership, and ended up aground off the coast of Mexico on 21 November, 1984.

Hansa
Launched in 1939 and acquired in 1940 when Germany occupied Denmark. Converted to an auxiliary cruiser in 1943, but did not see action and was then used as a training ship as of 1944. At the end of the war, taken over by the British and used under various names until being scrapped in 1971.

Komet
Launched in 1937 and converted to an auxiliary cruiser during 1939/1940. Sunk with all hands by a British torpedo boat off Cap de la Haye on October 14, 1942.

Kormoran
Launched in 1938, converted to an auxiliary cruiser in 1940. Badly damaged in battle off the west coast of Australia and scuttled on November 19, 1941.

Michel
Launched in 1939 and converted into an auxiliary cruiser the following year. Sunk by an American submarine off the Japanese coast, on October 17, 1943.

Orion
Launched in 1930 as a freighter, and converted into an auxiliary cruiser in 1939. Decommissioned and taken out of service in August 1941. In March 1945 once again designated as an auxiliary cruiser. Bombed by Soviet aircraft on May 4, 1945, beached and abandoned. Raised and scrapped in 1952.

Pinguin
Launched in 1936 and converted in 1940. Sunk by a British heavy cruiser in the Indian Ocean, on May 8, 1941.

Stier
Launched in 1936, converted into an auxiliary cruiser in 1941. Badly damaged in battle in the South Atlantic and scuttled on September 27, 1942.

Thor
Launched in 1938 and converted during 1939/1940. Sunk by a series of accidental explosions in Yokohama harbor (Japan) on November 30, 1942.

Widder
Launched in 1929 as a freighter and converted into an auxiliary cruiser in 1939. Decommissioned in November 1940 and a reassigned as a repair ship. Ran onto rocks and was destroyed on October 4, 1955. Broken up the following year.

Destroyers
Anton Schmitt (Z 22)
Launched in 1938. Sunk by torpedoes at Narvik (Norway) on April 10, 1940.

Bernd von Arnim (Z 11)
Launched in 1936. Scuttled at Narvik (Norway) on April 13, 1940.

Bruno Heinemann (Z 8)
Launched in 1936. Sunk by a mine on January 25, 1942 north of Dunkirk.

Diether von Roeder (Z 17)
Launched in 1937. Scuttled off Narvik (Norway) on April 13, 1940.

Erich Giese (Z 12)
Launched in 1936. Sunk in battle at Narvik (Norway) on April 13, 1940.

Erich Koellner (Z 13)
Launched in 1937. Sprung a leak and beached at Narvik (Norway). Smashed by ships' gunfire on April 13, 1940.

Erich Steinbrinck (Z 15)
Launched in 1936. Taken as a prize by the British in 1945 and transferred to the USSR the following year. Broken up in 1961.

Friedrich Eckoldt (Z 16)
Launched in 1937. Sunk by gunfire in the Barents Sea, on December 31, 1942.

Friedrich Ihn (Z 14)
Launched in 1935. Taken by the USSR as a prize in 1946. Broken up in 1961.

Georg Thiele (Z 2)
Launched in 1935. Badly damaged and beached at Narvik (Norway) on April 13, 1940. Wreck broken up in 1963.

Hans Lody (Z 10)
Launched in 1936. Taken by the British as a prize in 1946. Broken up in 1949.

Hans Lüdemann (Z 18)
Launched in 1937. Badly damaged, abandoned and sunk by a torpedo at Narvik (Norway) on April 13, 1940.

Hermann Künne (Z 19)
Launched in 1937. Badly damaged and beached at Narvik (Norway) on April 13, 1940. Broken up in 1941.

Hermann Schoemann (Z 7)
Launched in 1936. Scuttled on May 2, 1942 in the North Sea, after engine failure in battle.

Karl Galster (Z 20)
Launched in 1938. Taken by the USSR as a prize in 1946. Broken up in 1961.

Leberecht Maaß (Z 1)
Launched in 1935. Damaged in battle off the Polish coast on September 3, 1939. Sank on February 22, 1940 off the Dutch north coast.

Max Schultz (Z 3)
Launched in 1935. Damaged in battle off the Polish fortress of Hela in September 1939. Sunk on February 22, 1940 off the Dutch north coast.

Paul Jacobi (Z 5)
Launched in 1936. Taken by the British as a prize in 1945, and transferred to France the following year. Decommissioned in 1954 and broken up.

Richard Beitzen (Z 4)
Launched in 1935. Taken by the British as a prize in 1945. Broken up in 1947.

Theodor Riedel (Z 6)
Launched in 1936. Taken by the British as a prize in 1945, and transferred to France the following year. Decommissioned in 1957 and broken up.

Wilhelm Heidkamp (Z 21)
Launched in 1938. Sunk by a torpedo at Narvik (Norway) on April 10, 1940.

Wolfgang Zenker (Z 9)
Launched in 1936. Scuttled off Narvik (Norway) on April 13, 1940.

Z 23
Launched in 1939. Damaged in bombing raid and scuttled at La Pallice (France) on August 21, 1944. Raised in 1945 but not repaired. Broken up in 1951.

Z 24
Launched in 1940. Sunk in a bombing raid at Le Verdon (France) on August 25, 1944. Broken up in 1946.

Z 25
Launched in 1940. Taken by the British as a prize in 1946 and then transferred to France. Decommissioned in 1958 and broken up.

Z 26
Launched in 1940. Sunk in a naval battle with British warships in the North Sea, on March 29, 1942.

Z 27

Launched in 1940. Sunk in a naval battle with British cruisers in the Bay of Biscay, on December 28, 1943.

Z 28

Launched in 1940. Sunk in a bombing raid off the north coast of Germany, on March 6, 1945. Later broken up.

Z 29

Launched in 1940. Taken by the USA as a prize in 1945 and cannibalized for parts. Hulk scuttled in the Skagerrak on December 16, 1946.

Z 30

Launched in 1940. Taken by the British as a prize in 1945 and destroyed during underwater explosives experiments.

Z 31

Launched in 1941. Taken by the British as a prize in 1945 and transferred to France the following year. Decommissioned in 1958 and broken up.

Z 32

Launched in 1941. Sunk in a naval battle with British destroyers off the coast of France, on June 9, 1944.

Z 33

Launched in 1941. Taken by the USSR as a prize in 1946. Broken up in 1964.

Z 34

Launched in 1942. Taken by the USA as a prize in 1945. Scuttled in the Skagerrak on March 26, 1946.

Z 35

Launched in 1942. Sunk in an explosion resulting from mine damage in the Baltic Sea, on December 12, 1944.

Z 36

Launched in 1943. Sunk in an explosion resulting from mine damage in the Baltic Sea, on December 12, 1944.

Z 37
Launched in 1941. Damaged in 1942 in a collision with *Z 32* off the north coast of Spain and taken out of service. Scuttled in Bordeaux docks on August 24, 1944. Broken up in 1949.

Z 38
Launched in 1941. Taken by the British as a prize in 1945 and used in experiments. Broken up in 1949.

Z 39
Launched in 1941. Taken by the USA as a prize in 1945 and transferred to France in 1947. Cannibalized for parts in 1951 and decommissioned in 1954. Used as a pontoon bridge in 1958 and broken up in 1964.

Z 40-42
Planned but never built.

Z 43
Launched in 1943. Badly damaged by mines and bombs, and scuttled in Geltinger Bay on May 3, 1945. Broken up in 1953.

Z 44
Launched in 1944. Sunk in an air raid prior to completion, on July 29, 1944. Broken up in 1948-1949.

Z 45
Launched in 1944 but never completed. Broken up in 1946.

Z 46 47
Construction begun in 1943 but never completed. Broken up after 1945.

The German Navy took over several French, Dutch, and Greek destroyers following the fall of those countries. Only the following were commissioned into the Kriegsmarine.

ZH 1
Launched in 1940 as the Dutch vessel "*Gerard Callenburgh*". Scuttled in May 1940 and raised by the Germans later that year. Completed in 1942. Scuttled following naval battle with British destroyers off the coast of France, on June 9, 1944.

ZG 3 (Hermes)

Launched in 1938 as the Greek vessel "*Vasileus Georgios*". Sunk by German aircraft in April 1941. Raised, repaired and commissioned into the Kriegsmarine in March 1942. Badly damaged in bomb attack in the Mediterranean and scuttled at La Goulette (Tunisia) on May 7, 1943.

Großadmiral Karl **DÖNITZ**

Großadmiral **GEORGE V,** King of Great Britain & Ireland

Großadmiral Kaiser **WILHELM II**

Großadmiral Henning von **HOLTZENDORF**

Großadmiral Kaiser **KARL** of Austria

Großadmiral Hans von **KOESTER**

Großadmiral Heinrich Prinz von **PREUSSEN**

Großadmiral Erich **RAEDER**

Großadmiral Alfred von **TIRPITZ**

Generaladmiral Conrad **ALBRECHT**

Generaladmiral Hermann **BOEHM**

Generaladmiral Rolf **CARLS**

Generaladmiral Hans-Georg von **FRIEDEBURG**

Generaladmiral Oskar **KUMMETZ**

Generaladmiral Wilhelm **MARSCHALL**

Generaladmiral Alfred **SAALWÄCHTER**

Generaladmiral Otto **SCHNIEWIND**

Generaladmiral Otto **SCHULTZE**

Generaladmiral Walter **WARZECHA**

Generaladmiral Karl **WITZELL**

Admiral Paul **BEHNCKE**

Admiral Eduard von **CAPELLE**

Admiral Otto **CILIAX**

Admiral Kurt **FRICKE**

Admiral Walter **GLADISCH**

Admiral Günther **GUSE**

Admiral Franz von **HIPPER**

Admiral Friedrich von **INGENOHL**

Admiral Theodor **KRANCKE**

Admiral Günther **LÜTJENS**

Admiral Wilhelm **MEISEL**

Admiral Conrad **MOMMSEN**

Admiral Hugo von **POHL**

Admiral Reinhard **SCHEER**

Admiral Adolf von **TROTHA**

Admiral Hans **ZENKER**

CHAPTER 7:

ADMIRALS OF THE GERMAN NAVY 1914-1945

Note: The focus of this section is on the careers of the officers at Admiral level. Accordingly, the biographical details given for each officer pertain to the latter part of their careers, in general, after they reached the rank of Kapitän zur See. In certain cases, career information covering the period prior to reaching this rank is given, when it can be considered pertinent or interesting to the particular officer's career. Foreign officers who held an honorary rank in the German Navy are also included in the following listing.

Admiral Luigi Amedeo, Principe di Savoia-Aosta, Duca degli **ABRUZZI** (29 Jan 1873 - 18 Mar 1933)
Admiral à la Suite (Honorary title)
Awards: *Order of the Black Eagle*

Konteradmiral Richard **ACKERMANN** (17 Nov 1869 - 27 Sep 1930)
4 Apr 1914 - 15 Jan 1918:	Commandant, Heavy Cruiser "*Goeben*"
15 Jan 1918 - 17 Mar 1918:	On leave
17 Mar 1918 - 19 Mar 1919:	Commander, 1. Shipyard Division
20 Mar 1919 - 7 Nov 1919:	Attached to the Commander, Baltic Naval Station
(7 Nov 1919:	Promoted to brevet Konteradmiral)
7 Nov 1919:	Retired

Konteradmiral (Ingeneur) Max **ADAM** (28 Dec 1894 - 22 Oct 1978)
27 Oct 1938 - 6 May 1940:	Engineer, Flag Officer of Reconnaissance Forces
7 May 1940 - 23 Jun 1942:	Engineer, Naval Group West
24 Jun 1942 - 30 Sep 1943:	Chief of Fuel Economics Section, Naval Quartermaster's Office
(1 Feb 1943:	Promoted to Konteradmiral Ingeneur)
1 Oct 1943 - 22 Jul 1945:	Chief of Supplies, Naval Quartermaster's Office

Konteradmiral Wilhelm **ADELUNG** (17 Dec 1867 - 3 Aug 1938)
1 Apr 1913 - 16 Nov 1914:	Commandant, Heavy Cruiser "*Vineta*"
17 Nov 1914 - 9 Jan 1915:	Attached to Technical Research Commission

9 Feb 1915 - 3 Mar 1915:	Commandant, Auxiliary Cruiser "*Vineta*"
4 Mar 1915 - 31 Mar 1915:	Member, Technical Research Commission
20 Apr 1915 - 7 Feb 1917:	Commandant, Training Ship "*Württemberg*"
8 Feb 1917 - 14 Jan 1918:	Commandant, Heavy Cruiser "*Roon*", President, Technical Research Commission
16 Jan 1918 - 23 Jan 1918:	Acting Commandant, Battleship "*Friedrich der Große*"
25 Jan 1918 - 8 Nov 1918:	Commandant, Battleship "*Kaiserin*"
25 Feb 1918 - 20 May 1918:	Acting Deputy Commander, IV. Squadron
13 Aug 1918 - 18 Aug 1918:	Acting Deputy Commander, IV. Squadron
9 Nov 1918 - 7 Nov 1919:	Attached to the Commander, Baltic Naval Station
(7 Nov 1919:	Promoted to brevet Konteradmiral)
7 Nov 1919:	Retired

Konteradmiral Georg **AHLERT** (24 Dec 1867 - 17 Jun 1963)

12 Nov 1911 - 9 Aug 1914:	Director of Pension Bureau, Naval Office
10 Aug 1914 - 17 Dec 1916:	Director of Central Office, Wilhelmshaven Shipyards
(25 Nov 1916:	Promoted to brevet Konteradmiral)
17 Dec 1916:	Retired
1 Feb 1917 - 31 Mar 1918:	Recalled; Deputy Director of Shipyard Department, Naval Office
(17 Sep 1917:	Confirmed as Konteradmiral from brevet rank)
31 Mar 1918:	Retired

Admiralarzt (Konteradmiral) Dr. Eberhard **AHRENS** (13 Jan 1892 - 29 Jun 1945)

23 Sep 1935 - 22 Oct 1938:	Medical Officer attached to the Deputy Commander, Baltic
24 Oct 1938 - 3 Sep 1939:	Medical Officer, Inspectorate of Naval Training
4 Sep 1939 - 30 May 1940:	Chief Medical Officer, KielHassee Naval Hospital
31 May 1940 - 13 Feb 1941:	Chief Medical Officer, Admiral France
14 Feb 1941 - 19 Aug 1942:	Chief Medical Officer, Kiel-Wik Naval Hospital
(1 Sep 1941:	Promoted to Admiralarzt)
20 Aug 1942 - 30 Sep 1943:	Chief Medical Officer, Naval Group South
1 Nov 1943 - 2 Nov 1944:	Chief Medical Officer, Malente Naval Hospital
3 Nov 1944 - 31 Dec 1944:	Attached to the Commanding Admiral, Baltic Naval Group
31 Dec 1944:	Retired

Wirkliche Geheime Admiralsrat (Konteradmiral) Dr. Bernhard **ALBATH**
(4 Feb 1857 - 20 Feb 1937)
1 Jun 1906 - 24 Mar 1919:	Chief of Construction Administration Office, Naval Office
(3 Mar 1917:	Appointed Wirkliche Geheime Admiralsrat)
24 Mar 1919:	Retired

Vizeadmiral Hermann **ALBERTS** (8 Mar 1865 - 13 Dec 1946)
(15 Nov 1913:	Promoted to Konteradmiral)
2 Aug 1914 - 24 Aug 1915:	Deputy Commander, IV. Squadron
25 Aug 1915 - 20 Oct 1915:	Acting Inspector, II. Naval Inspectorate
21 Oct 1915 - 14 Dec 1916:	Chief of Staff, Baltic Naval Station
(25 Nov 1916:	Promoted to brevet Vizeadmiral)
18 Dec 1916 - 23 May 1918:	Director of Nautical Department, Naval Office
23 May 1918:	Retired

Generaladmiral Conrad **ALBRECHT** (7 Oct 1880 - 18 Aug 1969)
28 Mar 1923 - 11 Sep 1925:	Commandant, Kiel Arsenal
12 Sep 1925 - 30 Sep 1928:	Chief of Staff, Baltic Naval Station
1 Oct 1928 - 30 Nov 1928:	Attached to the Commander-in-Chief of the Navy
1 Dec 1928 - 28 Sep 1930:	Chief of Officer Personnel Section, Naval High Command
(1 Apr 1930:	Promoted to Konteradmiral)
29 Sep 1930 - 30 Sep 1932:	Flag Officer, Reconnaissance Forces
(1 Oct 1932:	Promoted to Vizeadmiral)
1 Oct 1932 - 31 Oct 1938:	Commander, Baltic Naval Station
(1 Dec 1935:	Promoted to Admiral)
1 Nov 1938 - 31 Dec 1939:	C-in-C, Naval Group East
(1 Apr 1939:	Promoted to Generaladmiral)
31 Dec 1939:	Retired
1 Jan 1940:	Placed on reserve list; no appointment conferred

Admiral **ALFONSO XIII**, King of Spain (17 May 1886 - 28 Feb 1941)
Admiral à la Suite (Honorary title)
Awards: *Order of the Black Eagle*

Vizeadmiral Georg von **AMMON** (17 May 1869 - 2 Feb 1937)
2 Aug 1914 - 26 Nov 1914:	Chief of Supply, High Seas Fleet

25 Jan 1915 - 17 Mar 1915:	Acting Commander, VI. Squadron
18 Mar 1915 - 3 Sep 1915:	Attached to the Commander, Baltic Naval Station
4 Sep 1915 - 18 Dec 1916:	Chief of Kiel Fortifications
(18 Sep 1915:	Promoted to Konteradmiral)
1 Jan 1917 - 10 Nov 1917:	Commander, I. Naval Brigade, Flanders Marine Corps
11 Nov 1917 - 2 Sep 1918:	Commander, II. Naval Brigade, Flanders Marine Corps
3 Sep 1918 - 28 Oct 1918:	Attached to the Commander, Baltic Naval Station
(18 Sep 1918:	Promoted to brevet Vizeadmiral)
28 Oct 1918:	Retired

Vizeadmiral Heinrich **ANCKER** (7 Oct 1886 - 15 May 1960)

1 Jan 1933 - 26 Sep 1934:	Commandant of Wilhelmshaven
27 Sep 1934 - 24 Sep 1936:	Commandant, Battleship "*Schlesien*"
26 Sep 1936 - 29 Nov 1937:	Commandant, Kiel Naval Arsenal
(1 Oct 1936:	Promoted to Konteradmiral)
30 Nov 1937 - 31 Aug 1942:	Inspector, Defense Economics Inspectorate X
(1 Nov 1939:	Promoted to brevet Vizeadmiral)
(1 Nov 1940:	Confirmed as Vizeadmiral from brevet rank)
Jun 1941 - Jan 1942:	Acting Inspector, Defense Economics Inspectorate North
31 Aug 1942:	Retired
1 Sep 1942:	Recalled to reserve status
31 May 1943:	Retired

Vizeadmiral Lothar von **ARNAULD de la Perière**
(18 Mar 1886 - 24 Feb 1941)

24 Sep 1928 - 10 Oct 1930:	Commandant, Cruiser "*Emden*"
11 Oct 1930 - 26 Sep 1931:	Chairman of Ships Testing Committee
30 Sep 1931:	Retired
1932 - 1938:	Instructor, Turkish Naval Academy
(25 Jan 1937:	Promoted to brevet Konteradmiral)
(19 Aug 1939:	Promoted to brevet Vizeadmiral)
10 Sep 1939 - 14 Mar 1940:	Recalled from retirement; Naval Commissioner for Danzig & Polish Corridor Coast
20 May 1940 - 18 Jun 1940:	Naval Commander, BelgiumNetherlands
(1 Jun 1940:	Confirmed as Konteradmiral from brevet rank)

22 Jun 1940 - 3 Dec 1940:	Naval Commander, Brittany
4 Dec 1940 - 19 Feb 1941:	Naval Commander, West France
(1 Feb 1941:	Confirmed as Vizeadmiral from brevet rank)
20 Feb 1941 - 24 Feb 1941:	AdmiralDesignate, South

Awards: *Pour le Mérite*

Konteradmiral Wolff-Ehrenreich von **ARNSWALDT** (23 Mar 1898 - 4 Jan 1972)

9 Mar 1938 - 22 Jul 1940:	Staff Officer, Baltic Naval Station
23 Jul 1940 - 12 Feb 1941:	Commander of Sea Defenses, Flanders
13 Feb 1941 - 4 Apr 1941:	Chief of Staff to Naval Commander "B"
5 Apr 1941 - 30 Jun 1941:	Chief of Staff, Naval Mission to Romania
1 Jul 1941 - 7 Jun 1943:	Chief of Staff, Admiral Commanding, Black Sea
20 Jun 1943 - 28 Jul 1944:	Chief of Staff, Naval Artillery Inspectorate
29 Jul 1944 - 9 May 1945:	Commander of Sea Defenses, Latvia
(1 Jan 1945:	Promoted to Konteradmiral)

Vizeadmiral Theodor **ARPS** (11 Feb 1884 - 28 Apr 1947)

1 Oct 1933 - 30 Sep 1934:	Recalled from retirement; Chief of Foreign Navies Office, Naval High Command
1 Oct 1934 - 31 Dec 1939:	Chief of Naval Intelligence
(1 Jan 1940:	Promoted to Konteradmiral)
1 Jan 1940 - 8 May 1945:	Judge, Supreme Military Tribunal
(1 Apr 1942:	Promoted to Vizeadmiral)

Konteradmiral Karl **ASCHER** (5 Aug 1851 - 6 Feb 1940)

(11 Oct 1906:	Promoted to brevet Konteradmiral)
18 Jun 1917 - 27 Jul 1919:	Recalled from retirement; Commissioner, Berlin Prize Court
27 Jul 1919:	Retired

Vizeadmiral Kurt **AßMANN** (13 Jul 1883 - 26 Jul 1962)

7 Nov 1918 - 27 Sep 1923:	Department Head, Naval High Command
28 Sep 1923 - 15 Jul 1925:	First Officer, Battleship "*Hannover*"
16 Jul 1925 - 12 Mar 1927:	Department Head, Naval High Command
13 Mar 1927 - 22 Sep 1929:	Chief of Fleet Office, Naval High Command (Chief of Naval Operations)
23 Sep 1929 - 23 Sep 1932:	Commandant, Battleship "*Schlesien*"
24 Sep 1932 - 31 Dec 1932:	Attached to the Commander-in-Chief of the Navy

(1 Oct 1932:				Promoted to Konteradmiral)
31 Dec 1932:				Retired
1 Apr 1933 - 21 Jan 1936:		Reactivated; Chief of Naval Archives
22 Jan 1936 - 28 Jun 1943:		Chief of Technical Section,
					Naval High Command
(25 Jan 1937:				Promoted to brevet Vizeadmiral)
(1 Jan 1941:				Confirmed as Vizeadmiral from brevet rank)
30 Jun 1943:				Retired

Admiral Gustav **BACHMANN** (13 Jul 1860 - 31 Aug 1943)
(27 Mar 1909:				Promoted to Konteradmiral)
(5 Sep 1911:				Promoted to Vizeadmiral)
2 Aug 1914 - 6 Feb 1915:		Commander, Baltic Naval Station
8 Feb 1915 - 4 Sep 1915:		Chief of Naval General Staff
(22 Mar 1915:				Promoted to Admiral)
5 Sep 1915 - 27 Oct 1918:		Commander, Baltic Naval Station
13 Dec 1918:				Retired

Admiral Johannes **BACHMANN** (22 Mar 1890 - 2 Apr 1945)
29 Sep 1933 - 20 Sep 1935:		Chief of Königsberg Naval Office
21 Sep 1935 - 25 Aug 1936:		Commandant, Cruiser "*Emden*"
26 Aug 1936 - 20 Aug 1940:		Chief of Staff, North Sea Naval Station
(1 Apr 1939:				Promoted to Konteradmiral)
21 Aug 1940 - 13 Feb 1941:		Coastal Commander, East Friesland
14 Feb 1941 - 22 Jun 1942:		Coastal Commander, Heligoland Bight
(1 Apr 1941:				Promoted to Vizeadmiral)
8 Aug 1942 - 31 Jan 1943:		Naval Commander, West France
(1 Sep 1942:				Promoted to Admiral)
1 Feb 1943 - 6 Mar 1943:		Admiral Commanding, Atlantic Coast
7 Mar 1943 - 31 May 1943:		Attached to the Commander-in-Chief of the
					Navy
31 May 1943:				Retired
1 Jun 1943:				Recalled to reserve status; no
					appointment conferred
Awards: *German Cross in Silver*

Konteradmiral Otto **BACK** (31 Oct 1864 - 20 Jun 1943)
21 Feb 1914 - 30 Jun 1919:		Naval Commissioner, Kaiser Wilhelm Canal
(17 Mar 1914:				Promoted to brevet Konteradmiral)
(22 Mar 1916:				Confirmed as Konteradmiral from brevet rank)

30 Jun 1919 - 15 Jul 1919: Placed on inactive status
(15 Jul 1919: Promoted to brevet Vizeadmiral)
15 Jul 1919: Retired

Admiral Otto **BACKENKÖHLER** (1 Feb 1892 - 5 Feb 1967)
1 Oct 1935 - 15 Oct 1937: Commandant, Cruiser "*Köln*"
16 Oct 1937 - 30 Oct 1938: Chief of Staff, High Seas Fleet
31 Oct 1938 - 23 Oct 1939: Chief of Staff, Baltic Naval Station
24 Oct 1939 - 31 Jul 1940: Chief of Staff, High Seas Fleet
(1 Jan 1940: Promoted to Konteradmiral)
8 Aug 1940 - 8 Mar 1943: Chief of Torpedo Office, Naval Weapons Directorate, Naval High Command
(1 Apr 1942: Promoted to Vizeadmiral)
9 Mar 1943 - 30 Apr 1944: Chief of Naval Weapons Directorate, Naval High Command
(1 Apr 1943: Promoted to Admiral)
1 May 1944 - 15 Jul 1945: Chief of Naval Armaments, Naval High Command
23 May 1945 - 26 May 1945: Acting Commander-in-Chief of the Kriegsmarine

Awards: *German Cross in Silver; Knight's Cross of the War Merit Cross with Swords*

Vizeadmiral Martin **BALTZER** (10 Nov 1898 - 3 Apr 1971)
8 Apr 1937 - 24 Oct 1938: Commandant, Destroyer "*Max Schultz*"
25 Oct 1938 - 24 May 1942: Adjutant, Baltic Naval Station
25 May 1942 - 12 Dec 1942: Commandant, Light Cruiser "*Köln*"
6 Jan 1943 - 14 Jul 1945: Chief of Naval Personnel
(1 Mar 1943: Promoted to Konteradmiral)
(1 Apr 1945: Promoted to Vizeadmiral)

Konteradmiral Rudolf **BARTELS** (2 Jun 1871 - 25 Jun 1946)
12 Aug 1914 - 22 Sep 1915: Commandant, Coastal Defense Ship "*Heimdall*"
23 Sep 1915 - 14 Jul 1916: Commandant, Battleship "*Hessen*"
15 Jul 1916 - 31 Jul 1916: Commandant, Battleship "*Deutschland*"
1 Aug 1916: Placed on reserve list
1 Jan 1917 - 29 Mar 1919: Commander, 1. Torpedo Division
30 Mar 1919 - 27 May 1919: Attached to the Commander, Baltic Naval Station
27 May 1919: Retired
(30 Aug 1919: Promoted to brevet Konteradmiral)

Vizeadmiral Karl **BARTENBACH** (29 Nov 1881 - 24 Oct 1949)

1 Nov 1934 - 23 Sep 1935:	Recalled from retirement; Chief of Antisubmarine Section, Naval General Office, Naval High Command
24 Sep 1935 - 17 Oct 1935:	Chief of UBoat Section, Naval General Office, Naval High Command
18 Oct 1935 - 16 Feb 1938:	Chief of Statistical Section, Naval General Office, Naval High Command
(28 Feb 1938:	Promoted to brevet Konteradmiral)
28 Feb 1938:	Retired
15 Feb 1939:	Recalled to reserve status; no appointment conferred
(19 Aug 1939:	Promoted to brevet Vizeadmiral)
31 May 1943:	Retired

Awards: *Pour le Mérite*

Konteradmiral Joachim Adolph von **BASSEWITZ** (28 Apr 1859 - 22 Jul 1918)

(27 Jan 1908:	Promoted to brevet Konteradmiral)
1 Jul 1905 - 17 Dec 1916:	Reichskommissar of Lübeck, Rostock, Flensburg, Hamburg, Stettin and Stralsund Naval Offices
31 Aug 1914 - 17 Dec 1916:	Judge, Kiel Prize Court
18 Dec 1916 - 30 Jun 1918:	Director of War Office, Allenstein
30 Jun 1918:	Retired

Admiral Max **BASTIAN** (28 Aug 1883 - 11 Mar 1958)

1 Oct 1928 - 23 Sep 1929:	Commandant, Battleship "*Schlesien*"
24 Sep 1929 - 26 Sep 1932:	Chief of Naval Budget Office, Ministry of Defense
1 Oct 1932 - 28 Sep 1934:	Commodore & Flag Officer, Battleships
(1 Sep 1933:	Promoted to Konteradmiral)
2 Oct 1934 - 26 Sep 1935:	Deputy Commander, Baltic Naval Station
27 Sep 1935 - 3 Apr 1938:	Chief of General Naval Office, Naval High Command
(1 Dec 1935:	Promoted to Vizeadmiral)
(1 Apr 1938:	Promoted to Admiral)
4 Apr 1938 - 30 Sep 1938:	Attached to Armed Forces High Command (OKW)
1 Oct 1938 - 11 Sep 1939:	President, Armed Forces Welfare Court
12 Sep 1939 - 31 Oct 1944:	President, Supreme Military Tribunal

1 Nov 1944 - 30 Nov 1944:	Attached to the Commander-in-Chief of the Navy
30 Nov 1944:	Retired

Awards: *Knight's Cross of the War Merit Cross with Swords*

Konteradmiral Ernst **BATSCH** (27 Jan 1879 - 21 Dec 1948)

Jan 1919 - 15 Jan 1923:	Member, Navy Peace Commission
16 Feb 1923 - 21 Sep 1926:	President, Navy Peace Commission
22 Sep 1926 - 31 Mar 1928:	Member, League of Nations Naval Group, Ministry of Defense
(1 Oct 1926:	Promoted to brevet Konteradmiral)
31 Mar 1928:	Retired

Admiral Hermann **BAUER** (22 Jul 1875 - 11 Feb 1958)

21 Dec 1918 - 31 Mar 1919:	Commander, 2. Torpedo Division
12 May 1919 - 2 Oct 1919:	Armaments Director, Wilhelmshaven Shipyards
3 Oct 1919 - 18 May 1923:	Director of Wilhelmshaven Shipyards
(1 Apr 1922:	Promoted to Konteradmiral)
6 Jun 1923 - 30 Sep 1923:	Chief of General Naval Office, Naval High Command
1 Oct 1923 - 4 Oct 1928:	Commander, North Sea Naval Station
(1 Feb 1925:	Promoted to Vizeadmiral)
4 Oct 1928 - 30 Nov 1928:	Attached to the Commander-in-Chief of the Navy
(30 Nov 1928:	Promoted to brevet Admiral)
30 Nov 1928:	Retired
25 Jul 1939:	Placed on reserve list; no appointment conferred

Konteradmiral Otto **BECHTEL** (26 Aug 1868 - 14 Apr 1939)

12 Nov 1911 - 20 Jan 1915:	Inspector, III. Coastal District
21 Jan 1915 - May 1915:	Commandant, Kiel Coast
May 1915 - 19 Nov 1918:	Commander of East-Kiel Coastal Works
20 Nov 1918 - 8 May 1919:	Inspector, Coastal Inspectorate III
9 May 1919 - 8 Jun 1919:	Attached to the Commander, Baltic Naval Station
8 Jun 1919:	Retired
(18 Nov 1919:	Promoted to brevet Konteradmiral)

Admiralrichter (Konteradmiral) Paul **BECKER** (23 May 1881 - 11 Sep 1963)
15 Oct 1936 15 May 1944:	Chief Judge, Baltic Naval Station/ Baltic Naval Group
(17 Apr 1940:	Promoted to Konteradmiral rank)
(1 Oct 1942:	Rank changed to Marinechefrichter)
(1 May 1944:	Rank changed to Admiralrichter)
16 May 1944 31 Aug 1944:	Attached to the Commanding Admiral, Baltic Naval Group
31 Aug 1944:	Retired
1 Dec 1944 30 May 1945:	Recalled; President, Armed Forces Military 4th Criminal Court

Vizeadmiral Alfred **BEGAS** (20 Jan 1866 - 7 Apr 1938)
7 Aug 1914 - 23 Jan 1915:	Deputy Commander, V. Squadron
24 Jan 1915 - 15 Jan 1916:	Acting Commander, V. Squadron
(23 Feb 1915:	Promoted to Konteradmiral)
16 Jan 1916 - 16 Feb 1918:	Naval Commander, Liepaja & Courland
(14 Oct 1917:	Promoted to brevet Vizeadmiral)
17 Feb 1918 - 17 Mar 1918:	Attached to the Commander, Baltic Naval Station
17 Mar 1918:	Retired

Konteradmiral Karl **BEHM** (18 Mar 1864 - 13 Jun 1919)
1 Nov 1911 - 31 Mar 1919:	Director of Hamburg Naval Observatory
(18 Nov 1912:	Promoted to Konteradmiral)
31 Mar 1919:	Retired

Marinegeneralstabsarzt (Konteradmiral) Dr. Hans **BEHMER** (19 Nov 1865 - 20 Mar 1926)
14 Oct 1913 - 10 Apr 1916:	Garrison Medical Officer, Kiel
11 Apr 1918 - 30 Nov 1918:	Acting Chief Medical Officer, 4. Army
1 Dec 1918 - 25 Jul 1919:	Reserve status; no appointment conferred
(25 Jul 1919:	Promoted to brevet Marinegeneralstabsarzt)
25 Jul 1919:	Retired

Konteradmiral Friedrich **BEHNCKE** (29 Jun 1869 - 28 Apr 1957)
7 Aug 1914 - 28 Mar 1915:	Commandant, Battleship *"Friedrich der Große"*
29 Mar 1915 - 7 Apr 1915:	Commandant, Battleship *"Kaiser Friedrich III"*
8 Apr 1915 - 24 Sep 1916:	Commandant. Battleship *"Schlesien"*
29 Sep 1916 - 24 Aug 1917:	Commandant, Battleship *"Markgraf"*
25 Aug 1917 - 15 Sep 1918:	Chief of Military Section, Naval Office

16 Sep 1918 - 16 Oct 1918:	Attached to Kiel Naval Shipyards
17 Oct 1918 - 30 Jun 1920:	Director of Kiel Shipyards
(4 Feb 1920:	Promoted to brevet Konteradmiral)
30 Jun 1920:	Retired

Admiral Paul **BEHNCKE** (13 Aug 1866 - 4 Jan 1937)

(14 Jul 1914:	Promoted to Konteradmiral)
2 Aug 1914 - 4 Sep 1915:	Deputy Chief of Naval General Staff
5 Sep 1915 - 30 Nov 1915:	Attached to the High Seas Fleet
1 Dec 1915 - 11 Jan 1916:	Attached to the Chief of Naval General Staff
12 Jan 1916 - 15 Jan 1916:	Deputy Commander, III. Squadron
12 Jan 1916 -11 Aug 1918:	Commander, III. Squadron
(25 Nov 1916:	Promoted to Vizeadmiral)
28 Aug 1918 - 27 Sep 1918:	State Secretary, Naval Office
28 Sep 1918 - 12 Feb 1919:	Attached to the High Seas Fleet
13 Feb 1919 - 5 Nov 1919:	German Representative in Military Control Commission, Aaland Islands
5 Nov 1919 - 31 Aug 1920:	Placed on inactive status
31 Aug 1920 - 25 Sep 1924:	Commander-in-Chief of the Navy
(20 Dec 1920:	Promoted to Admiral)
30 Sep 1924:	Retired

Awards: *Pour le Mérite*

Konteradmiral Ehler **BEHRING** (7 Nov 1865 - 7 Jul 1918)

30 Sep 1912 - 22 Jun 1914:	Commandant, Battleship *"Wittelsbach"*
(22 Jun 1914:	Promoted to brevet Konteradmiral)
22 Jun 1914 - 2 Aug 1914:	Placed on Reserve List
2 Aug 1914 - 5 Aug 1914:	Acting Inspector, II. Naval Inspectorate
12 Aug 1914 - 20 Aug 1914:	Deputy Commander, VI. Squadron
23 Aug 1914 - 20 Apr 1915:	Detached Admiral, Eastern Baltic
21 Apr 1915 - 30 May 1915:	Attached to the Commander, Baltic Naval Station
30 May 1915 - 29 May 1918:	Placed on Reserve List
29 May 1918 - 7 Jul 1918:	Commander, I. Marine Brigade, Flanders Marine Corps
7 Jul 1918:	Retired

Admiraloberstabsintendant (Admiral) Hanns **BENDA**
(19 Aug 1877 - 27 Feb 1951)

15 Sep 1920 31 May 1935:	Attached to the staff, Commander-in-Chief of the Navy

(1 Jan 1935:	Promoted to Ministerialdirigent [Konteradmiral])
1 Jun 1935 31 Oct 1939:	Chief of General Section, Naval High Command
(1 Nov 1939:	Promoted to Ministerialdirektor [Vizeadmiral])
1 Nov 1939 28 Feb 1945:	Chief of Naval Administration Office, Naval High Command
(19 Aug 1942:	Promoted to Ministerialdirektor with Admiral rank)
(1 May 1944:	Rank changed to Admiraloberstabsintendant)
1 Mar 1945 30 Apr 1945:	Placed on inactive status
30 Apr 1945:	Retired

Awards: *German Cross in Silver*

Konteradmiral Waldemar **BENDER** (28 Dec 1885 - 6 Dec 1950)

28 Sep 1932 - 27 Sep 1935:	Chief of Nautical Office, Naval High Command
(30 Sep 1935:	Promoted to brevet Konteradmiral)
30 Sep 1935:	Retired
1 Mar 1941 - 4 May 1942:	Recalled; Chief of Staff, Drontheim Shipyards
5 May 1942 - 14 Mar 1943:	Director, Horten Shipyards
(1 Jul 1942:	Confirmed as Konteradmiral from brevet rank)
9 Jun 1943 - 10 Jan 1945:	Commandant of Kaiser-Wilhelm Canal
11 Jan 1945 - 31 Jan 1945:	Attached to the Admiral Commanding, Baltic Naval Group
31 Jan 1945:	Retired

Konteradmiral Hans **BENE** (17 Aug 1972 - 10 Jun 1943)

12 Aug 1914 - 14 Jan 1916:	Commandant, Coastal Defense Ship *"Siegfried"*
17 Sep 1914 - 22 Dec 1914:	Commander, Jade & Weser Harbor Flotilla
2 Sep 1915 - 26 Nov 1916:	Commander, Jade & Weser Harbor Flotilla
30 Nov 1916 - 29 Nov 1918:	Naval Staff Officer attached to Army von Mackensen
30 Nov 1918 - 28 Aug 1919:	Reserve status; no appointment conferred
28 Aug 1919:	Retired
(4 Feb 1920:	Promoted to brevet Konteradmiral)

Konteradmiral (Ingeneur) Walter **BERENDT** (16 Apr 1878 - 16 Aug 1978)

8 Jun 1922 - 23 Sep 1924:	Chief Engineer, Battleship *"Braunschweig"*

24 Sep 1924 - 30 Sep 1925:	Attached to the Commander, North Sea Naval Station
1 Oct 1925 - 25 Sep 1927:	Chief Engineer, North Sea Naval Station
26 Sep 1927 - 31 Oct 1929:	Chief Engineer, High Seas Fleet
(31 Oct 1929:	Promoted to brevet Konteradmiral Ingeneur)
31 Oct 1929:	Retired
1 May 1933 - 31 Mar 1939:	Recalled from retirement; Chief of Psychological Testing Office, North Sea Naval Station
31 Mar 1939:	Retired
1 Apr 1939:	Recalled to reserve status; no appointment conferred

Vizeadmiral (Ingeneur) Paul **BERNDT** (21 Mar 1879 - 10 Sep 1941)

9 Sep 1923 - 30 Sep 1924:	Engineer-Inspector, Naval Training Inspectorate
1 Oct 1924 - 30 Sep 1925:	Chief Engineer, Baltic Naval Station
1 Oct 1925 - 25 Sep 1927:	Fleet Engineer
26 Sep 1927 - 28 Sep 1933:	Engineer Officer attached to Naval High Command
(1 Jan 1928:	Promoted to Konteradmiral Ingeneur)
(30 Sep 1933:	Promoted to brevet Vizeadmiral Ingeneur)
30 Sep 1933:	Retired

Konteradmiral Ferdinand **BERTRAM** (26 Apr 1868 - 13 Oct 1941)

1 Nov 1912 - 1 Aug 1914:	Commandant, Heavy Cruiser "*Prinz Adalbert*"
6 Aug 1914 - 26 Nov 1914:	Commandant, Heavy Cruiser "*Kaiserin Augusta*"
28 Nov 1914 - 2 Apr 1915:	Commandant, Heavy Cruiser "*Fürst Bismarck*"
4 Apr 1915 - 2 Jul 1915:	Commandant, Battleship "*Wörth*"
26 Aug 1915 - 18 Nov 1915:	Commandant, Battleship "*Zähringen*"
20 Nov 1915 - 18 Jan 1917:	Director of Liepaja Naval Works
(25 Nov 1916:	Promoted to brevet Konteradmiral)
19 Jan 1917 - 10 Mar 1917:	Attached to the Commander, Baltic Naval Station
10 Mar 1917:	Retired

Konteradmiral Wilhelm **BERTRAM** (4 Nov 1865 - 3 Jun 1959)

(13 Oct 1913:	Promoted to brevet Konteradmiral)

Sep 1914 - Jan 1918: Recalled from retirement; Commandant, Celle POW Camp
Jan 1918: Retired

Konteradmiral (Ingeneur) Wilhelm **BETCHE** (24 Oct 1879 - 12 May 1941)
8 Oct 1928 - 29 Sep 1932: Station Engineer, Baltic Naval Station
(30 Sep 1932: Promoted to brevet Konteradmiral Ingeneur)
30 Sep 1932: Retired
1 Sep 1939 - 12 May 1941: Recalled from retirement; Chief of Construction Training, Hamburg Naval Office
(1 Feb 1941: Confirmed as Konteradmiral Ingeneur from brevet rank)

Vizeadmiral (Ingeneur) Werner **BETTENHÄUSER** (3 May 1886 - 11 Sep 1959)
30 Sep 1931 - 26 Nov 1939: Commander, Kiel Naval School
(1 Oct 1936: Promoted to Konteradmiral Ingeneur)
27 Nov 1939 - 31 Dec 1939: Attached to the Commander, Baltic Naval Station
(31 Dec 1939: Promoted to brevet Vizeadmiral Ingeneur)
1 Jan 1940 - 14 Jul 1941: Recalled to the Führer Reserve
15 Jul 1941 - 14 Feb 1943: Director of Naval Equipment & Repair Works, Libau
(1 Feb 1943: Confirmed as Vizeadmiral Ingeneur from brevet rank)
15 Feb 1943 - 31 Aug 1943: Chief of Shipyards Staff, Baltic
1 Sep 1943 - 23 Mar 1945: Liaison Officer to Schichau Shipyard, Elbing & Danzig

Konteradmiral Erich **BEY** (23 Mar 1898 - 26 Dec 1943)
26 Oct 1938 - 3 Apr 1939: Commandant, Destroyer *"Friedrich Ihn"*
4 Sep 1939 - 10 May 1940: Commander, 4. Destroyer Flotilla
10 May 1940 - 26 Dec 1943: Flag Officer, Destroyers
(10 Apr 1942: Promoted to Kommodore)
(1 Mar 1943: Promoted to Konteradmiral)
14 May 1940 - 14 Nov 1940: Commander, 6. Destroyer Flotilla
9 Nov 1943 - 26 Dec 1943: Acting Commander, Battle Group Norway
Awards: *Knight's Cross*

Marinegeneralstabsarzt (Konteradmiral) Prof. Dr. August **BIER**
(24 Nov 1861 - 12 Mar 1949)

1907 - 1932: Director of Berlin Surgical University Clinic
(29 Feb 1928: Promoted to brevet Marinegeneralstabsarzt)

Konteradmiral Ernst **BINDSEIL** (20 Jul 1880 - 5 Mar 1947)
30 Nov 1918 - 1 Apr 1923: Department Head, Fleet Office, Naval High Command
2 Apr 1923 - 30 Sep 1923: Attached to the Commander-in-Chief of the Navy
1 Oct 1923 - 30 Nov 1924: Commandant, Cruiser "*Thetis*"
1 Dec 1924 - 9 Jan 1925: Commandant, Cruiser "*Nymphe*"
10 Jan 1925 - 9 Feb 1928: Chief of Staff, Naval General Office, Naval High Command
10 Feb 1928 - 29 Feb 1928: Attached to the Commander-in-Chief of the Navy
(29 Feb 1928: Promoted to brevet Konteradmiral)
29 Feb 1928: Retired
22 Mar 1939: Placed on reserve status; no appointment conferred
31 May 1943: Retired

Konteradmiral Wilhelm **BLECKWENN**
(Transferred from Army as Generalmajor) (21 Oct 1906 - 10 May 1989)
15 Nov 1944 - 20 Feb 1945: Commander, 708. Volksgrenadier Division
(30 Jan 1945: Promoted to Generalmajor)
28 Feb 1945 8 May 1945: Commander, 1. Marine Infantry Division
(1 Mar 1945: Rank changed to Konteradmiral)
Awards: *Oakleaves to the Knight's Cross; Knight's Cross; German Cross in Gold; Iron Cross (1st & 2nd Class)*

Konteradmiral Bernhard **BOBSIEN** (30 Nov 1878 - 5 Dec 1934)
19 Jun 1920 - 6 Sep 1920: Recalled from retirement; Commander of Mines Group, North Sea Standing Naval Force Division
7 Sep 1920 - 22 Sep 1922: Commandant, Cruiser "*Hamburg*"
19 Oct 1922 - 28 Sep 1926: Commander of Cuxhaven Defenses
(30 Sep 1926: Promoted to brevet Konteradmiral)
30 Sep 1926: Retired

Konteradmiral Karl von **BODECKER** (29 Jan 1875 - 20 Oct 1957)
9 Jul 1920 - 31 Mar 1921: Inspector, Coastal Inspectorate V

9 Feb 1921 - 31 Mar 1921:	Harbor Captain, Wilhelmshaven
1 Apr 1921- 15 Aug 1921:	Deputy Chief of Personnel, North Sea Naval Station
16 Aug 1921 - 20 Feb 1922:	Chief of Personnel, North Sea Naval Station
21 Feb 1922 - 27 Sep 1923:	Chief of Bremen Naval Office
28 Sep 1923 - 31 Oct 1923:	Attached to the Commander, North Sea Naval Station
(31 Oct 1923:	Promoted to brevet Konteradmiral)
31 Oct 1923:	Retired
15 Jul 1941 - 30 Nov 1941:	Recalled from retirement; Chief of Construction Supervision, Nikolayev, Kherson & Oschakov Shipyards
1 Dec 1941 - 28 Feb 1943:	Chief of Shipyards Staff, Baltic
(1 Jul 1942:	Confirmed as Konteradmiral from brevet rank)
28 Feb 1943:	Retired

Vizeadmiral Friedrich **BOEDICKER** (13 Mar 1866 - 20 Sep 1944)

15 Jul 1914 - 27 Aug 1915:	Director of General Naval Department, Naval Office
(22 Mar 1915:	Promoted to Konteradmiral)
28 Aug 1915 - 10 Sep 1916:	Commander, II. Reconnaissance Group
27 Mar 1916 - 12 May 1916:	Acting Commander of Reconnaissance Forces
2 Sep 1916 - 14 Oct 1916:	Acting Commander of Reconnaissance Forces
15 Oct 1916 - 20 Jan 1918:	Deputy Commander of Reconnaissance Forces
24 Apr 1917 - 6 May 1917:	Acting Commander of Reconnaissance Forces
5 Sep 1917 - 5 Oct 1917:	Acting Commander of Reconnaissance Forces
22 Jan 1918 - 27 Nov 1918:	Commander, I. Squadron
(27 Jan 1918:	Promoted to Vizeadmiral)
16 Aug 1918 - 9 Sep 1918:	Commander of Special Forces, Operation "Schlußstein"
28 Nov 1918 - 17 Mar 1919:	Attached to the Commander, North Sea Naval Station
17 Mar 1919:	Retired

Generaladmiral Hermann **BOEHM** (18 Jan 1884 - 11 Apr 1972)

28 Sep 1929 - 29 Sep 1932:	Chief of Naval Operations, Naval High Command
30 Sep 1932 - 2 Oct 1933:	Chief of Staff, High Seas Fleet
3 Oct 1933 - 24 Sep 1934:	Commandant, Battleship "*Hessen*"
25 Sep 1934 - 27 Sep 1937:	Flag Officer, Reconnaissance Forces

(1 Oct 1934:	Promoted to Konteradmiral)
(1 Apr 1937:	Promoted to Vizeadmiral)
Aug 1936 - Aug 1937:	Intermittently, Commander of Naval Forces, Spain
4 Oct 1937 - 27 Oct 1938:	Commander, North Sea Naval Station
(1 Apr 1938:	Promoted to Admiral)
1 Nov 1938 - 20 Oct 1939:	CinC, High Seas Fleet
21 Oct 1939 - 9 Apr 1940:	Attached to the Commander-in-Chief of the Navy
10 Apr 1940 - 31 Jan 1943:	Admiral Commanding, Norway
(1 Apr 1941:	Promoted to Generaladmiral)
1 Feb 1943 - 3 Mar 1943:	CinC, Naval Group Norway
4 Mar 1943 - 31 May 1943:	Attached to the Commander-in-Chief of the Navy
31 May 1943:	Retired
1 Jun 1943:	Placed on reserve status
1 Mar 1944 - 31 Mar 1945:	Reactivated; attached to Naval Training Inspectorate
31 Mar 1945:	Retired

Awards: *German Cross in Gold*

Konteradmiral Paul **BOETHKE** (24 Sep 1872 - 7 Sep 1964)

8 Nov 1914 - 9 Mar 1920:	Prisoner of war in China
9 Mar 1920:	Retired
(10 Sep 1920:	Promoted to brevet Konteradmiral)

Konteradmiral Kurt **BÖHMER** (31 Dec 1892 - 1 Oct 1944)

21 Jul 1937 - 21 Jan 1940:	First Officer, Pocket Battleship *"Admiral Scheer"*
22 Jan 1940 - 31 May 1940:	Commander of Special Units, North Sea
1 Jun 1940 - 15 Oct 1940:	Chief of Staff, Commander of Naval Security Forces, North Sea
16 Oct 1940 - 11 Mar 1942:	Commander of Minesweepers, North
12 Mar 1942 - 16 Jun 1944:	Commander of Minesweepers, East
(10 Apr 1942:	Promoted to Kommodore)
(1 Feb 1943:	Promoted to Konteradmiral)
17 Jun 1944 - 1 Oct 1944:	Commander, 9. Security Division

Awards: *Knight's Cross*

Konteradmiral Reimar von **BONIN** (3 Oct 1890 - 18 May 1976)

29 Sep 1934 - 10 Jun 1937:	Chief of Staff, Naval Training Inspectorate
13 Jul 1936 - 17 Jul 1936:	Acting Inspector of Naval Training
1 Jul 1937 - 13 Sep 1944:	Naval Attaché, Helsinki, Riga, Tallinn & Kaunas
(1 Nov 1939:	Promoted to brevet Konteradmiral)
(1 Jan 1941:	Confirmed as Konteradmiral from brevet rank)
1 Nov 1944 - 31 Jan 1945:	Commander of Recruiting District Eutin
1 Feb 1945 - 4 Apr 1945:	Commander of Recruiting District Vienna III
1 May 1945 - 5 Aug 1945:	Inspector of Naval Training Units, St. Wolfgang

Verwaltungs Konteradmiral August **BÖNING** (15 Aug 1891 - 1 Jul 1964)

4 Apr 1939 - 26 Jan 1940:	Personnel Officer, North Sea Naval Station
27 Jan 1940 - 14 Jun 1943:	General Advisor, Naval Personnel Office, Naval High Command
15 Jun 1943 - 30 Jun 1945:	Chief of Commissary Office, Naval Group East
(1 Jan 1945:	Promoted to Verwaltungs Konteradmiral)
1944 - 30 Jun 1945:	Deputy Chief Intendant, Naval Group East

Kommodore Friedrich **BONTE** (19 Oct 1896 - 10 Apr 1940)

29 Jun 1937 - 31 Oct 1938:	Commander, 2. Destroyer Division
1 Nov 1938 - 25 Oct 1939:	Commander, 2. Destroyer Flotilla
26 Oct 1939 - 10 Apr 1940:	Flag Officer, Destroyers
(1 Nov 1939:	Promoted to Kommodore)
26 Oct 1939 - 29 Nov 1939:	Acting Flag Officer, Torpedo Boats
9 Apr 1940 - 10 Apr 1940:	Commander, Battle Group 1, Operation "Weserübung"

Awards: *Knight's Cross (posthumously)*

Marinegeneralstabsarzt (Konteradmiral) Dr. Paul **BONTE**
(12 Jul 1862 - 10 Mar 1940)

Sep 1914 - Apr 1916:	Recalled from retirement; Chief of Volunteer Nurses, Fortress Wilhelmshaven
25 May 1916 - 9 Jan 1917:	Deputy Chief Medical Officer, North Sea Naval Station
10 Jan 1917 - Nov 1918:	Attached to the Medical Service, North Sea Naval Station
Nov 1918:	Retired
(9 Mar 1920:	Promoted to brevet Marinegeneralstabsarzt)

Admiral Ludwig **BORCKENHAGEN** (15 Jul 1850 - 17 Jun 1917)
(18 Sep 1902:			Promoted to Konteradmiral)
(27 Jan 1907:			Promoted to Vizeadmiral)
(9 Nov 1909:			Promoted to brevet Admiral)
1 Aug 1914 - 17 Jun 1917:	Recalled from retirement; Commissioner, Berlin Prize Court

Admiral **BORIS III**, King of Bulgaria (30 Jan 1894 - 28 Aug 1943)
Admiral à la Suite (Honorary title)
Awards: *Order of the Black Eagle*

Vizeadmiral Kurt von dem **BORNE** (24 Nov 1885 - 31 Jan 1946)
1 Apr 1936 - 31 Jul 1944:	Chief of Defense Economics Office, Naval High Command
(1 Jul 1940:			Promoted to Konteradmiral)
(1 Sep 1942:			Promoted to Vizeadmiral)
1 Aug 1944 - 30 Sep 1944:	Attached to the Commander-in-Chief of the Navy
30 Sep 1944:			Retired
1 Oct 1944:			Recalled to reserve status; no appointment conferred

Awards: *German Cross in Silver*

Marinegeneralstabsarzt (Konteradmiral) Dr. Ernst **BÖSE**
(21 Mar 1868 - 12 Mar 1949)
3 Nov 1918 - 27 May 1919:	Attached to the Medical Service, North Sea Naval Station
28 May 1919 - 30 Jun 1923:	Chief Medical Officer, North Sea Naval Station
1 Jul 1923 - 31 Aug 1923:	Placed on inactive status
(31 Aug 1923:			Promoted to brevet Marinegeneralstabsarzt)
31 Aug 1923:			Retired
9 Mar 1939:			Recalled to reserve status as brevet Admiralarzt; no appointment conferred

Marinegeneraloberstabsarzt (Vizeadmiral) Dr. Johannes **BRACHMANN**
(29 Jan 1867 - 29 Apr 1941)
29 Nov 1918 - 30 Sep 1919:	Chief Medical Officer, Baltic Naval Station
1 Oct 1919 - 5 Apr 1922:	Station Medical Officer, Baltic Naval Station
6 Apr 1922 - 31 Dec 1927:	Chief Medical Officer of the Navy

(1 May 1922:   Promoted to Marinegeneralstabsarzt)
(31 Dec 1927:   Promoted to brevet Marinegeneralober-
                            stabsarzt)
31 Dec 1927:   Retired

Generalstabsintendant der Marine (Vizeadmiral) Walter **BRAEUER**
(2 Nov 1880 - 6 Jan 1955)
1 Jul 1934 31 Jan 1939:   Naval Intendant, Wilhelmshaven
(1 Jul 1936:   Promoted to Marinestationsintendant [Kon-
                            teradmiral])
31 Jan 1939:   Retired
21 Mar 1942 7 Apr 1942:   Recalled with Generalintendant der Marine
                            rank; attached to Armed Forces High
                            Command (OKW)
9 Apr 1942 18 Jun 1944:   Chief Intendant, Armed Forces Mission to
                            Romania
(1 Aug 1943:   Promoted to Generalstabsintendant
                            der Marine)
17 Aug 1944 7 Feb 1945:   Sick leave
8 Feb 1945 8 May 1945:   Attached to Armed Forces High Command
                            (OKW)

Awards: *German Cross in Silver*

Marinegeneralstabsarzt/Admiralarzt (Konteradmiral) Dr. Wilhelm **BRAHMS**
(14 Aug 1880 - 13 Dec 1966)
1 Jan 1928 - 30 Sep 1930:   Chief Medical Officer,
                            North Sea Naval Station
(30 Sep 1930:   Promoted to brevet Marinegeneralstabsarzt)
30 Sep 1930:   Retired
1 Sep 1939 - 31 May 1941:   Recalled as brevet Admiralarzt; Chief Medical
                            Officer, Bremen Naval Hospital
(1 Feb 1941:   Confirmed as Admiralarzt from brevet rank)
1 Jun 1941 - 31 Jan 1944:   Chief Medical Officer, Bedburg Hau Naval
                            Hospital
31 Jan 1944:   Retired

Ministerialdirektor (Vizeadmiral) Ferdinand **BRANDES**
(30 Apr 1879 - 19 Apr 1974)
27 Oct 1936 30 Nov 1944:   Chief of Group K II, Construction Office,
                            Naval High Command

(1 Jan 1937:   Promoted to Ministerialdirigent
                                [Konteradmiral])
(4 May 1942:   Promoted to Ministerialdirektor
                                [Vizeadmiral])
1 Dec 1944 31 Dec 1944:   Placed on inactive status
31 Dec 1944:   Retired
Awards: *German Cross in Silver*

Marineoberbaudirektor (Vizeadmiral) Prof. Dr. Friedrich **BRANDES**
(2 Dec 1879 - 11 Nov 1950)
29 Mar 1934 31 May 1944:   Chief of Naval Chemistry-Physics Research
                                Institute
(13 Oct 1941:   Promoted to Leitender Regierungsdirektor
                                [Konteradmiral])
(21 Feb 1944:   Rank changed to Marinebaudirektor)
1 Jun 1944 30 Apr 1946:   President of Naval Chemistry-Physics
                                Research Institute
(9 Nov 1944:   Promoted to Marineoberbaudirektor)

Konteradmiral Iwan **BRANDES** (5 Feb 1882 - 1 Mar 1935)
28 Sep 1926 - 24 Nov 1929:   Chief of Staff, Inspectorate of Naval Training
25 Nov 1929 - 28 Mar 1932:   Commandant, Kiel Naval Arsenal
(31 Mar 1932:   Promoted to brevet Konteradmiral)
31 Mar 1932:   Retired

Konteradmiral Friedrich **BRAUNE** (6 Oct 1889 - 29 Jun 1971)
4 Oct 1932 - 31 Mar 1935:   Commander, North Sea Naval Cadre Division
1 Apr 1935 - 22 Sep 1936:   Chief of Staff to the Deputy Commander,
                                North Sea Naval Station
1 Apr 1935 - 27 Jun 1935:   Acting Deputy Commander, North Sea Naval
                                Station
2 Oct 1936 - 30 Sep 1937:   Commander, Baltic Naval Cadre Regiment
1 Oct 1937 - 26 Oct 1938:   Commander, 1. Naval Cadre Regiment
2 Oct 1936 - 26 Oct 1938:   Commandant of Stralsund
27 Oct 1938 - 3 Nov 1938:   Attached to Labes Recruiting Office
10 Nov 1938 - 27 Dec 1939:   Commander of Recruiting Office, Kolberg
28 Dec 1939 - 30 Mar 1941:   Judge, Supreme Military Tribunal
(1 Feb 1940:   Promoted to brevet Konteradmiral)
(1 Jan 1941:   Confirmed as Konteradmiral from brevet rank)
31 Mar 1941 - 29 Apr 1941:   Attached to the Commander, Baltic Naval
                                Station

30 Apr 1941 - 8 May 1942:	Director of Bergen Shipyards
9 May 1942 - 14 Jun 1942:	Attached to the Commander, Baltic Naval Station
15 Jun 1942 - 31 Jul 1942:	Judge, Military Tribunal
31 Jul 1942:	Retired
1 Aug 1942:	Recalled to reserve status
1 Sep 1942 - 30 Apr 1945:	Judge, Berlin Prize Court
30 Apr 1945:	Retired

Konteradmiral Hasso von **BREDOW** (31 Mar 1883 - 16 Oct 1966)

6 Oct 1927 - 11 Oct 1929:	Commandant, Mürwik Naval School
16 Oct 1929 - 29 Sep 1931:	Commander, Baltic Naval Cadre Division
2 Jul 1930 - 5 Aug 1931:	At various times, Commandant & Harbor Captain of Kiel & Commissioner, Kaiser Wilhelm Canal
30 Sep 1931 - 27 Sep 1932:	Commandant & Harbor Captain of Kiel & Commissioner, Kaiser Wilhelm Canal
10 Jul 1932 - 2 Aug 1932:	Acting Commander, Baltic Naval Cadre Division
(30 Sep 1932:	Promoted to brevet Konteradmiral)
30 Sep 1932:	Retired
1 Oct 1933 - 3 Sep 1939:	Recalled; Chief of Psychological Testing Office, Kiel
4 Sep 1939 - 13 Oct 1939:	Commandant, Mürwik Naval School
18 Oct 1939 - 25 Jun 1940:	Chief of Fitness Testing Office, Kiel
26 Jun 1940 - 2 Mar 1943:	Coastal Commander, Pomeranian Coast
(1 Jan 1941:	Confirmed as Konteradmiral from brevet rank)
3 Mar 1943 - 31 May 1943:	Attached to the Commander-in-Chief of the Navy
31 May 1943:	Retired
1 Jun 1943:	Recalled to reserve status; no appointment conferred

Konteradmiral Hermann von **BREDOW** (4 Nov 1893 - 10 Mar 1954)

8 Feb 1936 - 19 Aug 1937:	Commandant, Artillery Training Ship *"Brummer"*
20 Aug 1937 - 31 Dec 1937:	Commander, I. Naval Reserve Detachment
1 Jan 1938 - 11 Apr 1939:	Commander, 5. Ships' Crew Detachment
12 Apr 1939 - 18 Jul 1940:	Fortress Commandant of Memel & Commander, VII. Naval Artillery Detachment

19 Jul 1940 - 30 Aug 1940:	Commander of Sea Defenses, Polar Coast
12 Sep 1940 - 6 Jan 1945:	Commander of Sea Defenses, Kristiansand
(1 Nov 1942:	Promoted to Konteradmiral)
1 Feb 1945 - 22 Jul 1945:	Inspector, Gas and Air Defense Naval Inspectorate

Ministerialdirigent (Konteradmiral) Charles **BREITENSTEIN**
(15 Jul 1898 - 31 Aug 1963)

31 Oct 1939 - 30 Nov 1944:	Chief of Electro-Technical Section, Naval Construction Department
30 Nov 1944 - 8 Oct 1945:	Chief of Engine & Electro-Technical Section, Naval Construction Department
(30 Jan 1945:	Promoted to Ministerialdirigent)

Konteradmiral Erich Alfred **BREUNING** (16 Oct 1897 - 28 Nov 1978)

16 Oct 1936 - 9 Sep 1942:	Advisor for Mines, Naval Operations Office, Naval High Command
21 Sep 1942 - 31 May 1943:	Commander, 3. Security Division
(1 Jun 1943:	Promoted to Konteradmiral)
1 Jun 1943 - 25 Sep 1944:	Commander of Naval Security Forces, West
28 Oct 1944 - 8 May 1945:	Chief of Staff of National Socialist Leadership Staff, Armed Forces High Command (OKW)

Awards: *German Cross in Gold*

Wirkliche Geheime Oberbaurat (Konteradmiral) Georg **BRINKMANN**
(31 May 1856 - 26 Sep 1937)

1 Apr 1913 - Nov 1919:	Chief of Ships Maintenance Section, Naval Construction Office
(3 Mar 1917:	Appointed Wirkliche Geheime Oberbaurat)
Nov 1919:	Retired

Vizeadmiral Helmuth **BRINKMANN** (12 Mar 1895 - 26 Sep 1983)

27 Oct 1938 - 24 Jul 1940:	Chief of Naval Defense Office, Naval High Command
1 Aug 1940 - 4 Aug 1942:	Commandant, Heavy Cruiser "*Prinz Eugen*"
5 Aug 1942 - 21 Nov 1943:	Chief of Staff, Naval Group South
(1 Sep 1942:	Promoted to Konteradmiral)
22 Nov 1943 - 9 Nov 1944:	Admiral Commanding, Black Sea
(1 Feb 1944:	Promoted to Vizeadmiral)
10 Oct 1944 - 21 Dec 1944:	Naval Liaison Officer to 20. Mountain Army

6 Jan 1945 - 31 May 1945:   Deputy Naval Commander, Baltic
20 Apr 1945 - 31 May 1945: Deputy Naval Commander, North Sea
Awards: *Knight's Cross; German Cross in Gold*

Ministerialdirigent (Konteradmiral) Fritz **BRÖKING**
(11 Mar 1877 - 29 Dec 1961)
1 Apr 1939 - 30 Oct 1939:   Advisor for Engine Construction,
                            Naval Construction Department
31 Oct 1939 - 14 Dec 1944: Chief of Engine Construction &
                            Electro-Technical Office for U Boats,
                            Naval Construction Department
(26 Sep 1941:   Promoted to Ministerialdirigent)
14 Dec 1944:   Retired
Awards: *German Cross in Silver*

Konteradmiral Ludwig **BRUCH** (2 Jul 1857 - 19 Jul 1943)
(8 Jun 1907:   Promoted to brevet Konteradmiral)
15 Sep 1914 - 2 Feb 1916:   Recalled from retirement; Commander, 2.
                            Shipyard Division
2 Feb 1916:   Retired

Konteradmiral Friedrich Willi **BRÜNINGHAUS** (22 Jan 1870 - 11 Oct 1951)
9 Aug 1914 - 13 Jul 1916:   Commandant, Battleship "*König*"
15 Jul 1916 - 9 Jul 1919:   Director of Supply Department, Naval High
                            Command
(9 Jul 1919:   Promoted to brevet Konteradmiral)
9 Jul 1919:   Retired)

Vizeadmiral Friedrich **BRUTZER** (25 Sep 1879 - 12 Jun 1958)
11 Jan 1919 - 20 Aug 1919: Staff Officer, North Sea Naval Station
21 Aug 1919 - 22 Jan 1921: Attached to Naval High Command
22 Jan 1921 - 31 Mar 1925: Chief of Naval Budget Office,
                            Ministry of Defense
4 Apr 1925 - 30 Sep 1925:   Commandant, Battleship "*Hannover*"
1 Oct 1925 - 29 Sep 1927:   Commandant, Battleship "*Elsaß*"
30 Sep 1927 - 14 Jan 1928: Attached to the Commander,
                            Baltic Naval Station
(1 Jan 1928:   Promoted to Konteradmiral)
14 Jan 1928 - 2 Apr 1928:   Acting Chief of Staff, Baltic Naval Station
3 Apr 1928 - 11 Jun 1928:   Attached to the Commander, Baltic Naval
                            Station

12 Jun 1928 - 30 Sep 1928:	Attached to the Ministry of Defense
1 Oct 1928 - 28 Sep 1930:	Chief of Naval Command Office, Naval High Command (Chief of Naval General Staff)
(1 Apr 1930:	Promoted to Vizeadmiral)
30 Sep 1930:	Retired

Admiralrichter (Konteradmiral) Dr. Wilhelm **BUCHHOLZ**
(16 Apr 1896 - 19 Aug 1955)

1934 - 2 Mar 1941:	Judge attached to Baltic Naval Station
3 Mar 1941 - 4 Feb 1945:	Chief Judge, North Sea Naval Station/ North Sea Naval Group
(1 Apr 1943:	Promoted to Marinechefrichter [Konteradmiral])
(1 May 1944:	Rank changed to Admiralrichter)
5 Feb 1945 - 8 Mar 1945:	Sick leave
9 Mar 1945 - 21 Mar 1945:	Attached to North Sea Naval Group
27 Mar 1945 - 8 May 1945:	Attached to Military Court, Torgau

Admiral Wilhelm **BÜCHSEL** (12 Apr 1848 - 7 Apr 1920)

(22 Mar 1897:	Promoted to Konteradmiral)
(1 May 1901:	Promoted to Vizeadmiral)
(23 Jun 1906:	Promoted to Admiral)
1 Nov 1915 - 15 Mar 1916:	Recalled from retirement; Director of Administration, Naval Office
15 Mar 1916:	Retired

Konteradmiral Friedrich von **BÜLOW** (10 Mar 1870 - 19 Dec 1929)

30 Jul 1914 - 19 Apr 1916:	Chief of Central Office, Naval General Staff
29 Apr 1916 - 15 Aug 1918:	Naval Representative to General Headquarters
16 Aug 1918 - 2 Jan 1919:	Deputy Chief of Naval General Staff
(9 Oct 1918:	Promoted to Konteradmiral)
9 Dec 1918 - 2 Jan 1919:	Acting Chief of Naval General Staff
3 Jan 1919 - 6 Mar 1919:	Chief of Naval Group, German Armistice Commission
7 Mar 1919 - 22 Nov 1919:	Attached to the Chief of the Naval Office
22 Nov 1919:	Retired

Admiral Theodor **BURCHARDI** (14 May 1892 - 12 Aug 1983)

5 Oct 1936 - 14 Oct 1937:	Director of Artillery, Kiel Naval Arsenal
15 Oct 1937 - 14 Jan 1940:	Commandant, Cruiser "*Köln*"

15 Jan 1940 - 3 Feb 1941:	Chief of Central Office, Kiel Shipyards
(1 Jan 1941:	Promoted to Konteradmiral)
4 Feb 1941 - 18 May 1941:	Chief of Staff, Kiel Shipyards
19 May 1941 - 5 Nov 1941:	Naval Commander "D"
6 Nov 1941 - 16 Jun 1944:	Naval Commander, Baltic
(1 Feb 1943:	Promoted to Vizeadmiral)
17 Jun 1944 - 18 Apr 1945:	Admiral Commanding Eastern Baltic
(1 Jan 1945:	Promoted to Admiral)

Awards: *Knight's Cross with Oakleaves; Knight's Cross; German Cross in Gold*

Marineoberbaudirektor (Vizeadmiral) Prof. Hermann **BURKHARDT**
(23 Jun 1881 - 20 Apr 1969)

3 Nov 1934 - 31 Aug 1937:	Chief of Shipbuilding Section, Naval Construction Department
(30 Dec 1936:	Promoted to Konteradmiral rank)
1 Sep 1937 - 30 Jun 1940:	Director of Shipbuilding, Wilhelmshaven Naval Shipyards
1 Jul 1940 - 31 Oct 1941:	Chief of Planning Office, Wilhelmshaven Naval Shipyards
31 Oct 1941:	Retired
(15 Jan 1942:	Promoted to Marineoberbaudirektor)

Geheime Oberbaurat (Konteradmiral) Dr. Hans **BÜRKNER**
(11 Jan 1864 - 29 Oct 1943)

28 Jun 1913 - 31 Mar 1919:	Chief of Shipbuilding Section, Naval Construction Office
1 Apr 1919 - 30 Sep 1919:	Acting Director of Naval Construction Office
30 Sep 1919:	Retired

Vizeadmiral Leopold **BÜRKNER** (29 Jan 1894 - 15 Jul 1975)

28 Jul 1937 - 15 Jun 1938:	Commandant, Training Cruiser "*Emden*"
14 Mar 1938 - 22 Mar 1938:	Acting Commander of Naval Forces, Spain
15 Jun 1938 - 30 Jun 1944:	Chief of Foreign Counterintelligence Section, Armed Forces High Command (OKW)
(1 Apr 1942:	Promoted to Konteradmiral)
(1 Oct 1943:	Promoted to Vizeadmiral)
1 Jul 1944 - 23 May 1945:	Chief of Counterintelligence Service (Abwehr), Armed Forces High Command (OKW)
3 May 1945 - 23 May 1945:	Chief of Protocol, Dönitz Government

Awards: *Knight's Cross of the War Merit Cross with Swords*

Admiralstabsintendant (Vizeadmiral) Fritz **BURMEISTER**
(21 Jun 1884 - 11 Jul 1956)
1 Oct 1934 - 15 Jun 1943:	Chief Intendant, Baltic Naval Station
(18 Dec 1936:	Promoted to Marinechefintendant [Konteradmiral])
(17 Nov 1941:	Rank changed to Marinegeneralintendant)
(11 Nov 1942:	Promoted to Marinegeneralstabsintendant)
15 Jun 1943 - 8 May 1945:	Chief of Administration Staff, Naval Group Baltic
(1 May 1944:	Rank changed to Admiralstabsintendant)

Konteradmiral Wilhelm **BUSSE** (20 Mar 1878 - 9 Dec 1965)
1 Sep 1939 - 8 May 1945:	Recalled from retirement; Attached to Naval Defense Office, Naval High Command
(1 Jun 1940:	Promoted to brevet Konteradmiral)
(1 Sep 1944:	Confirmed as Konteradmiral from brevet rank)
12 Oct 1940 - 8 May 1940:	Chief of Federation of German Naval Supremacy

Konteradmiral Hans **BÜTOW** (28 Dec 1894 - 9 May 1974)
8 Nov 1938 - 29 Nov 1939:	Commander, Danube Flotilla
30 Nov 1939 - 19 Apr 1942:	Flag Officer, Torpedo Boats
15 May 1942 - 21 Jun 1943:	Chief of Staff, Baltic Naval Station
(1 Jan 1943:	Promoted to Konteradmiral)
22 Jun 1943 - 1 May 1944:	Chief of Staff, Naval Group Baltic
8 Jun 1944 - 30 Nov 1944:	Commander of Naval Security Forces, Baltic
1 Dec 1944 - 21 Feb 1945:	Commander, 10. Security Division
23 Feb 1945 - 25 Feb 1946:	Admiral-in-Charge, Hamburg Naval Office

Awards: *Knight's Cross*

Admiralarzt (Konteradmiral) Dr. Hugo **CAANITZ** (9 May 1895 - 28 Feb 1968)
18 Oct 1937 - 14 Jan 1940:	Medical Officer, Baltic Naval Station
15 Jan 1940 - 8 Feb 1944:	Chief of MedicalScientific Section, Naval Medical Service
(1 Feb 1944:	Promoted to Admiralarzt)
9 Feb 1944 - 3 May 1945:	Chief Medical Officer, Stralsund Naval Hospital

Admiral Wilhelm **CANARIS** (1 Jan 1887 - 9 Apr 1945)
29 Sep 1930 - 23 Sep 1932:	Chief of Staff, North Sea Naval Station
1 Oct 1932 - 28 Sep 1934:	Commandant, Battleship "*Schlesien*"
29 Sep 1934 - 1 Jan 1935:	Commandant of Swinemünde

2 Jan 1935 - 12 Feb 1944:	Chief of Counter-Intelligence (Abwehr), Armed Forces High Command (OKW)
(1 May 1935:	Promoted to Konteradmiral)
(1 Apr 1938:	Promoted to Vizeadmiral)
(1 Jan 1940:	Promoted to Admiral)
13 Feb 1944 - 20 Mar 1944:	Attached to Armed Forces High Command (OKW)
21 Mar 1944 - 30 Jun 1944:	Attached to the Commander-in-Chief of the Navy
1 Jul 1944 - 23 Jul 1944:	Chief of Special Staff for Economic Warfare, Armed Forces High Command (OKW)
23 Jul 1944 - 9 Apr 1945:	Arrested, tried and executed for involvement in the July 20, 1944 plot to kill Hitler

Admiral Eduard von **CAPELLE** (10 Oct 1855 - 23 Feb 1931)

9 Jan 1904 - 31 Oct 1915:	Director of Administration, Naval Office
(7 Jul 1906:	Promoted to Konteradmiral)
(5 Sep 1909:	Promoted to Vizeadmiral)
(12 Apr 1913:	Promoted to Admiral)
31 Oct 1915:	Retired
15 Mar 1916 - 5 Oct 1918:	Recalled from retirement; State Secretary, Naval Office
5 Oct 1918:	Retired

Awards: *Pour le Mérite*

Admiral **CARL STEPHAN**, Erzherzog von Österreich
(5 Sep 1860 - 7 Apr 1933)
Admiral à la Suite (Honorary title)
Awards: *Order of the Black Eagle; Knight of the Royal Austrian Order of the Golden Fleece*

Generaladmiral Rolf **CARLS** (29 May 1885 - 15 Apr 1945)

1 Oct 1930 - 26 Sep 1932:	Chief of Staff, Naval High Command
3 Oct 1932 - 2 Oct 1933:	Commandant, Battleship "*Hessen*"
3 Oct 1933 - 28 Sep 1934:	Chief of Staff, High Seas Fleet
(1 Apr 1934:	Promoted to Konteradmiral)
29 Sep 1934 - 30 Sep 1936:	Flag Officer, Battleships
1 Oct 1936 - 23 Nov 1936:	Flag Officer, Pocket Battleships
21 Dec 1936 - 31 Oct 1938:	CinC, High Seas Fleet
(1 Jan 1937:	Promoted to Vizeadmiral)
(1 Jun 1937:	Promoted to Admiral)

1 Nov 1938 - 20 Sep 1940:	Commander, Baltic Naval Station
(19 Jul 1940:	Promoted to Generaladmiral)
31 Oct 1939 - 20 Sep 1940:	CinC, Naval Group East
21 Sep 1940 - 1 Mar 1943:	CinC, Naval Group North
2 Mar 1943 - 31 May 1943:	Attached to the Commander-in-Chief of the Navy
31 May 1943:	Retired
1 Jun 1943:	Recalled to reserve status; no appointment conferred

Awards: *Knight's Cross; German Cross in Gold*

Admiral **CHRISTIAN X**, King of Norway (26 Sep 1870 - 20 Apr 1947)
Admiral à la Suite (Honorary title)
Awards: *Order of the Black Eagle*

Admiral Otto **CILIAX** (30 Oct 1891 - 12 Dec 1964)
29 Sep 1934 - 21 Sep 1936:	Chief of Naval Operations
22 Sep 1936 - 30 Oct 1938:	Commandant, Battle Cruiser "*Admiral Scheer*"
22 Mar 1938 - 26 Jun 1938:	Acting Commander of German Naval Forces, Spain
1 Nov 1938 - 6 Jan 1939:	Attached to the Flag Officer, Pocket Battleships
7 Jan 1939 - 28 Sep 1939:	Commandant, Battleship "*Scharnhorst*"
29 Sep 1939 - 4 Dec 1939:	Attached to the Commander, North Sea Naval Station
(1 Nov 1939:	Promoted to Konteradmiral)
5 Dec 1939 - 5 Jun 1941:	Chief of Staff, Naval Group West
(1 Jun 1941:	Promoted to Vizeadmiral)
16 Jun 1941 - 2 Jun 1942:	Flag Officer, Battleships
21 Sep 1941 - 21 Oct 1941:	C-in-C, Baltic Fleet
26 Jun 1942 - 3 Mar 1943:	Inspector of Torpedoes
(1 Feb 1943:	Promoted to Admiral)
4 Mar 1943 - 25 Apr 1945:	C-in-C, Naval Group Norway

Awards: *Knight's Cross; German Cross in Gold*

Konteradmiral Franz **CLAASSEN** (15 Nov 1881 - 2 May 1945)
26 Sep 1925 - 29 Sep 1928:	Commandant of Swinemünde
30 Sep 1928:	Retired
(1 Dec 1928:	Promoted to brevet Konteradmiral)
2 Aug 1939 - Apr 1941:	Recalled; Commandant of Kolberg Sector
Apr 1941 - May 1941:	Attached to the Commander, Baltic Naval Station

May 1941 - 6 Nov 1941:	Naval Commander "C" (Riga-Libau)
7 Nov 1941 - 28 Feb 1942:	Attached to the Commander, Baltic Naval Station
(1 Jan 1942:	Confirmed as Konteradmiral from brevet rank)
28 Feb 1942:	Retired

Konteradmiral Siegfried **CLAASSEN** (5 Dec 1884 - 7 Jun 1951)

29 Sep 1928 - 20 Aug 1930:	Chief of Bremen Naval Office
25 Aug 1930 - 15 Oct 1930:	Attached to Wilhelmshaven Naval Shipyards
16 Oct 1930 - 30 Jun 1933:	Chief of Staff, Naval General Office, Naval General Staff & Chief of Shipyards Section
(30 Jun 1933:	Promoted to brevet Konteradmiral)
30 Jun 1933:	Retired
1 Jan 1939:	Recalled to reserve status
3 Sep 1939 - 15 Dec 1942:	Judge, Hamburg Prize Court
16 Dec 1942 - 31 Jan 1943:	Attached to the Commander, North Sea Naval Station
(1 Jan 1943:	Confirmed as Konteradmiral from brevet rank)
31 Jan 1943:	Retired

Konteradmiral Carl August **CLAUSSEN** (10 Mar 1881 - 11 Sep 1968)

13 Oct 1924 - 14 Oct 1926:	Chief of Stettin Naval Office
15 Oct 1926 - 30 Sep 1930:	Chief of Nautical Section, Naval High Command
(30 Sep 1930:	Promoted to brevet Konteradmiral)
30 Sep 1930:	Retired
1 Feb 1931 - 30 Sep 1933:	Recalled; Chief of Defense Economics, Military District (Wehrkreis) II
1 Oct 1933 - 31 Mar 1935:	Chief of Defense Economics, Military District X
1 Apr 1935 - 30 Sep 1937:	Inspector, Defense Economics Inspectorate X
30 Sep 1937:	Retired
17 Jun 1941 - 1 Jan 1942:	Recalled; Commissioner for Shipyards, Naval Mission to Romania
(1 Sep 1941:	Confirmed as Konteradmiral from brevet rank)
2 Jan 1942 - 1 Feb 1943:	Chief of Shipyards Staff, Admiral Commanding Black Sea
17 Feb 1943 - 9 May 1943:	Judge, Hamburg Prize Court
10 May 1943 - 30 Jun 1943:	Attached to the Commander-in-Chief of the Navy
30 Jun 1943:	Retired

Admiral Carl von **COERPER** (18 May 1854 - 20 Apr 1942)
(27 Jan 1906:	Promoted to Konteradmiral)
(27 Jan 1909:	Promoted to Vizeadmiral)
(6 May 1912:	Promoted to Admiral)
7 May 1912 - 22 Jul 1914:	Commander, Baltic Naval Station
23 Jul 1914 - 17 Sep 1914:	Placed on standby
17 Sep 1914:	Retired; Admiral à la Suite

Konteradmiral Dr. Fritz **CONRAD** (18 Apr 1883 - 1 Jan 1944)
21 Sep 1926 - 29 Sep 1928:	Commandant, Cruiser "*Nymphe*"
30 Sep 1928 - 27 Sep 1931:	Fortress Commandant of Swinemünde
(30 Sep 1931:	Promoted to brevet Konteradmiral)
30 Sep 1931:	Retired
1 Oct 1933 - 1 Nov 1939:	Recalled; Advisor, Nautical Office, Naval High Command
2 Nov 1939 - 1 Jan 1944:	Chief of Nautical-Scientific Office, Naval Meteorological Service
(1 Feb 1941:	Confirmed as Konteradmiral from brevet rank)

Ministerialdirigent (Konteradmiral) Ludwig **CORDES**
(25 Oct 1896 - 30 Mar 1958)
11 Dec 1939 - 31 Oct 1942:	Adviser, Naval Weapons Office, Naval High Command
1 Nov 1942 - 10 Nov 1942:	Chief of Electro-Artillery Section, Naval High Command
11 Nov 1942 - Jul 1945:	Chief of Artillery Construction Group, Naval High Command
(17 Mar 1944:	Promoted to Ministerialdirigent)

Konteradmiral Carl **COUPETTE** (31 Jul 1885 - 17 Feb 1964)
30 Sep 1931 - 31 Jan 1934:	Commander of Naval Cadre Division, Baltic
4 Apr 1932 - 17 Apr 1932:	Acting Commandant of Kiel & Naval Commissioner, Kaiser-Wilhelm Canal
1 Feb 1934 - 30 Sep 1935:	Chief of Staff to Deputy Commander, Baltic Naval Station
19 Jan 1934 - 19 Feb 1934:	Acting Commandant of Kiel & Naval Commissioner, Kaiser-Wilhelm Canal
13 Feb 1935 - 11 Mar 1935:	Acting Deputy Commander, Baltic Naval Station

29 Jul 1935 - 10 Aug 1935:	Acting Deputy Commander, Baltic Naval Station
15 Oct 1935 - 15 Mar 1938:	Chief of Navigation Office, Naval High Command
16 Mar 1938 - 31 Mar 1938:	Attached to the Ministry of Transport
(31 Mar 1938:	Promoted to brevet Konteradmiral)
31 Mar 1938:	Retired
24 May 1939:	Recalled to reserve status; no appointment conferred

Vizeadmiral Harald **DÄHNHARDT** (27 Oct 1863 - 21 May 1944)

(19 Nov 1910:	Promoted to Konteradmiral)
(31 Mar 1914:	Promoted to Vizeadmiral)
31 Mar 1914 - 15 Jan 1916:	Director of Supply Department, Naval Office
15 Jan 1916:	Retired

Konteradmiral Gottfried Freiherr von **DALWIGK zu Lichtenfels** (4 Jul 1868 - 23 May 1936)

1 Aug 1914 - 29 Aug 1914:	Commandant, Battleship "*Braunschweig*"
8 Nov 1914 - 11 Aug 1915:	Commandant, Battleship "*Kronprinz*"
20 Aug 1915 - 30 Nov 1916:	Deputy Commander, II. Squadron
(16 Nov 1915:	Promoted to Konteradmiral)
1 Dec 1916 - 27 May 1917:	Deputy Commander, IV. Squadron
18 Feb 1917 - 14 Mar 1917:	Acting Commander, IV. Squadron
28 May 1917 - 4 Dec 1917:	Deputy Commander, I. Squadron
6 Sep 1917 - 2 Nov 1917:	Acting Commander, I. Squadron
5 Dec 1917 - 15 Sep 1918:	Chief of Armistice Commission, Riga
16 Sep 1918 - 30 Sep 1919:	Chief of Construction Department, Naval Office
1 Feb 1919 - 31 Mar 1919:	Chief of Armistice Commission, Naval High Command
(30 Sep 1919:	Promoted to brevet Vizeadmiral)
30 Sep 1919:	Retired
(21 Apr 1920:	Confirmed as Vizeadmiral from brevet rank)

Vizeadmiral Hans von **DAMBROWSKI** (30 Mar 1861 - 31 May 1938)

(13 Jul 1909:	Promoted to Konteradmiral)
(6 May 1912:	Promoted to Vizeadmiral)
7 May 1912 - 14 Jul 1914:	Inspector of Naval Training
14 Jul 1914:	Retired

Wirkliche Geheime Rat (Konteradmiral) Dr. Fritz **DANNEEL**
(1851 - 13 Aug 1916)
3 Apr 1905 - 12 Mar 1916:	Director of Administration Section, Naval Office
(9 Feb 1915:	Appointed Wirkliche Geheime Rat)
12 Mar 1916:	Retired

Konteradmiral Hartwig von **DASSEL** (10 Apr 1861 - 6 Jun 1933)
(12 Dec 1908:	Promoted to brevet Konteradmiral)
1 Jan 1910 - 31 Dec 1931:	Reichskommissar, Stettin & Stralsund Naval Offices
18 Dec 1916 - 6 Dec 1918:	Reichskommissar, Lübeck & Rostock Naval Offices

Admiral Hermann **DENSCH** (15 Jun 1887 - 24 Aug 1963)
27 Sep 1930 - 25 Sep 1932:	Commandant, Cruiser "*Königsberg*"
27 Sep 1932 - 30 Sep 1936:	Chief of Staff, Naval High Command
(1 Oct 1935:	Promoted to Konteradmiral)
1 Oct 1936 - 31 Jan 1937:	Chairman, Ships Testing Commission
1 Feb 1937 - 27 Sep 1937:	Chief of Testing Command for New Ships
2 Oct 1937 - 20 Oct 1939:	Flag Officer, Reconnaissance Forces
(1 Apr 1938:	Promoted to Vizeadmiral)
21 Oct 1939 - 28 Nov 1939:	Attached to the Commander-in-Chief of the Navy
29 Nov 1939 - 28 Feb 1943:	Admiral Commanding, North Sea Naval Station
(1 Jan 1940:	Promoted to Admiral)
1 Mar 1943 - 31 May 1943:	Attached to the Commander-in-Chief of the Navy
31 May 1943:	Retired
1 Jun 1943:	Recalled to reserve status
1 Jul 1943 - 21 Apr 1945:	Commissioner, Berlin Prize Court
21 Apr 1945:	Retired

Awards: *German Cross in Silver*

Admiral Karl **DICK** (24 Apr 1858 - 30 Dec 1928)
(12 Sep 1908:	Promoted to Konteradmiral)
29 Aug 1910 - 4 Apr 1916:	Director of Shipyards, Naval Office
(22 Mar 1911:	Promoted to Vizeadmiral)
(17 Sep 1914:	Promoted to Admiral)
4 Apr 1916:	Retired

Marinegeneralstabsarzt (Konteradmiral) Dr. Eduard **DIRKSEN**
(31 Jul 1860 - 26 Nov 1927)
Aug 1914 - Nov 1918:	Recalled from retirement; Commissioner of Hospital Transport, Trier, Wirballen & Tilsit
(15 Feb 1918:	Promoted to brevet Marinegeneralstabsarzt)
Nov 1918:	Retired

Feldbischof (Konteradmiral/Generalmajor) Franz **DOHRMANN**
(4 Oct 1881 - 19 Apr 1969)
1 Apr 1934 - 22 Apr 1945:	Evangelical Field Bishop of the Armed Forces

Vizeadmiral Hugo **DOMINIK** (25 Oct 1871 - 15 Sep 1933)
8 Nov 1914 - 4 Jun 1918:	Commander, 5. Marine Regiment, Flanders Marine Corps
5 Jun 1918 - 10 Aug 1918:	Attached to the High Seas Fleet
11 Aug 1918 - 10 Dec 1918:	Commandant, Battleship *"Bayern"*
11 Dec 1918 - 25 Jan 1919:	Acting Commander of Interned Units
26 Jan 1919 - 1 Apr 1919:	Placed on inactive status
1 Apr 1919 - 16 Mar 1920:	Fortress Commandant, Wilhelmshaven
1 Apr 1919 - 29 Jul 1919:	Inspector, II. Naval Inspectorate
17 Mar 1920 - 10 Aug 1920:	Placed on inactive status
11 Aug 1920 - 20 Jul 1922:	Inspector of Naval Training
11 Jul 1921 - 14 Jul 1921:	Acting Commander, Baltic Naval Station
(11 Dec 1920:	Promoted to Konteradmiral)
(22 Nov 1921:	Promoted to Vizeadmiral)
31 Jul 1922:	Retired

Großadmiral Karl **DÖNITZ** (16 Sep 1891 - 24 Dec 1980)
29 Sep 1934 - 21 Sep 1935:	Commandant, Cruiser *"Emden"*
27 Sep 1935 - 13 Oct 1936:	Commander, U-Boat Flotilla *"Weddigen"*
1 Jan 1936 - 30 Jan 1943:	Flag Officer, Submarines
(1 Oct 1939:	Promoted to Konteradmiral)
(1 Sep 1940:	Promoted to Vizeadmiral)
(14 Mar 1942:	Promoted to Admiral)
(30 Jan 1943:	Promoted to Großadmiral, overstepping Generaladmiral rank)
30 Jan 1943 - 30 Apr 1945:	Commander-in-Chief of the Navy
17 Apr 1945 - 30 Apr 1945:	Armed Forces Commander, North
1 May 1945 - 23 may 1945:	Reich President, Minister of War, Supreme Commander of the Armed Forces

Awards: *Oakleaves to the Knight's Cross; Knight's Cross*

Konteradmiral Peter Christian **DONNER** (31 Mar 1881 - 12 Jun 1944)

12 Jan 1922 - 14 Oct 1923:	Chief of Staff to Commander of Baltic Naval Forces
15 Oct 1923 - 29 Feb 1924:	Attached to the Commander, Baltic Naval Station
1 Mar 1924 - 9 Sep 1925:	Chief of Training Group, Naval High Command
25 Sep 1925 - 26 Sep 1928:	Chief of Staff, Naval High Command
26 Sep 1928 - 31 Oct 1928:	Placed on inactive status
(31 Oct 1928:	Promoted to brevet Konteradmiral)
31 Oct 1928:	Retired
1 Oct 1929 - 30 Sep 1934:	Recalled; Director of Main Library, Baltic Naval Station
1 Oct 1934 - 12 Jun 1944:	Chief of Training Staff, Naval Training Inspectorate
(1 Jan 1941:	Confirmed as Konteradmiral from brevet rank)
12 Jun 1944:	Retired

Ministerialdirektor (Vizeadmiral), Obergruppenführer S.A. Xaver **DORSCH** (24 Dec 1899 - 8 Nov 1986)

16 May 1938 - Feb 1940:	Adviser, Central Office, Todt Organization
(Feb 1940:	Promoted to Ministerialdirektor)
Feb 1940 - 8 May 1945:	Chief of Central Office, Todt Organization
6 Apr 1944 - 8 May 1945:	Chief of Construction Department, Ministry of Armaments
(1 May 1944:	Promoted to Obergruppenführer S.A.)
1 May 1944 - 8 May 1945:	Chief of Luftwaffe Construction
1 May 1944 - 8 May 1945:	Deputy Minister of Armaments
25 Jul 1944 - 8 May 1945:	Chief of Naval Construction

Awards: *Knight's Cross of the War Merit Cross with Swords*

Konteradmiral Walther **DOSE** (14 Jun 1886 - 10 Nov 1970)

1 Apr 1935 - 31 Mar 1938:	Chief of Defense Economics Office, Bremen
1 Apr 1938 - 31 Dec 1939:	Section Chief, Defense Economics Staff, Armed Forces High Command (OKW)
1 Jan 1940 - 31 Aug 1942:	Chief of Defense Economics Office, Naval High Command
1 Sep 1942 - 5 May 1945:	Inspector, Armaments Inspectorate X
(1 Oct 1942:	Promoted to Konteradmiral)

Admiralarzt (Konteradmiral) Dr. Kurt **DÜTSCHKE**
(15 Oct 1892 - 21 May 1955)
19 Jun 1936 - 17 Dec 1939:	Chief Medical Officer, Kiel-Wik Naval Hospital & intermittently Acting Chief Medical Officer, Baltic Naval Station
18 Dec 1939 - 20 Dec 1940:	Medical Officer, High Seas Fleet
10 Jul 1940 - 20 Dec 1940:	Deputy Chief Medical Officer, Baltic Naval Station
21 Dec 1940 - 21 Jun 1943:	Chief Medical Officer, Naval Forces Baltic
(1 Feb 1941:	Promoted to Admiralarzt)
22 Jun 1943 - 31 Jan 1944:	Chief Medical Officer, Baltic Naval Group
31 Jan 1944:	Retired
1 Feb 1944 - 31 Jan 1945:	Recalled to reserve status; Chief Medical Officer, Bedburg-Hau Naval Hospital
31 Jan 1945:	Retired

Konteradmiral Hans **EBERIUS** (25 Nov 1870 - 30 Jan 1950)
1 Oct 1911 - 3 Aug 1916:	Director of Torpedoes, Wilhelmshaven Shipyards
4 Aug 1916 - 24 Sep 1916:	Attached to the High Seas Fleet
25 Sep 1916 - 4 Jun 1917:	Commandant, Battleship "*Westfalen*"
6 Jun 1917 - 28 Nov 1917:	Commodore of Torpedo Boats
30 Nov 1917 - 31 Jan 1918:	Commandant, Heavy Cruiser "*Hindenburg*"
5 Feb 1918 - 5 Jan 1919:	Section Chief, U-Boat Department, Naval Office
6 Jan 1919 - 30 Sep 1919:	Inspector of Torpedoes
25 May 1919 - 30 Sep 1919:	Inspector of U-Boats
1 Oct 1919 - 5 Jun 1920:	Inspector of Torpedoes & Mines
(8 Mar 1920:	Promoted to Konteradmiral)
6 Jun 1920 - 23 Oct 1920:	Placed on inactive status
23 Oct 1920:	Retired

Vizeadmiral Richard **ECKERMANN** (15 Jul 1862 - 13 Jan 1916)
(27 Jan 1911:	Promoted to Konteradmiral)
25 Feb 1914 - 11 Aug 1914:	Inspector of Torpedoes
30 Mar 1914 - 29 Apr 1914:	Commander, Training Squadron
12 Aug 1914 - 31 Aug 1914:	Acting Commander, VI. Squadron
2 Sep 1914 - 3 Feb 1915:	Chief of Staff, High Seas Fleet
(13 Oct 1914:	Promoted to Vizeadmiral)
16 Feb 1915 - 19 Jun 1915:	Commander, I. Squadron

20 Jun 1915 - 2 Jan 1916:   Sick leave
2 Jan 1916:   Retired

Ministerialdirektor (Admiral) Alfred **ECKHARDT** (30 May 1872 - 10 Feb 1960)
1 Oct 1936 - 31 Oct 1939:   Advisor for Shipyard & Harbor Construction, Naval High Command
(20 Apr 1938:   Promoted to Ministerialdirigent [Konteradmiral])
(14 Oct 1939:   Promoted to Ministerialdirigent with Vizeadmiral rank)
1 Nov 1939 - 31 Mar 1943:   Chief of Shipyard & Harbor Construction Group, Naval High Command
(20 Apr 1942:   Promoted to Ministerialdirektor [Vizeadmiral])
1 Apr 1943 - 13 Jul 1944:   Chief of Naval Construction, Naval General Office
14 Jul 1944 - 8 May 1945:   Attached to the Commander-in-Chief of the Navy
(4 Aug 1944:   Promoted to Ministerialdirektor with Admiral rank)

Awards: *German Cross in Silver*

Admiralrichter (Konteradmiral) Dr. Kurt **ECKHARDT**
(8 Aug 1887 - 28 Feb 1948)
20 Aug 1936 - 22 Jul 1945:   Advisor for Civil Rights, Naval Operations Department
(20 Apr 1944:   Promoted to Ministerialdirigent [Konteradmiral])
(1 May 1944:   Rank changed to Admiralrichter)

Konteradmiral Werner **EHRHARDT** (25 May 1898 - 23 Sep 1967)
25 Nov 1939 - 30 Jan 1943:   Section Chief, Personnel Office, Naval High Command
1 Nov 1942 - 5 Jan 1943:   Acting Chief of Naval Personnel
31 Jan 1943 - 14 Mar 1943:   Attached to the Chief of Naval Personnel
15 Mar 1943 - 4 Jan 1944:   Commandant, Heavy Cruiser "*Prinz Eugen*"
25 Jan 1944 - 25 May 1945:   Commandant, Schleswig Naval School
(1 Aug 1944:   Promoted to Konteradmiral)

Vizeadmiral Alfred **EHRLICH** (23 Sep 1854 - 20 Jan 1926)
(28 May 1906:	Promoted to Konteradmiral)
(13 Oct 1908:	Promoted to brevet Vizeadmiral)
2 Aug 1914 - 26 Oct 1914:	Recalled from retirement; attached to the Commander, North Sea Naval Station
27 Oct 1914 - 3 Jun 1916:	Fortress Commandant, Wilhelmshaven
3 Jun 1916:	Retired
(13 May 1916:	Confirmed as Vizeadmiral from brevet rank)

Vizeadmiral Eduard **EICHEL** (21 Dec 1880 - 3 May 1956)
15 Oct 1923 - 23 Mar 1925:	Chief of Staff to the Commander, High Seas Fleet
24 Mar 1925 - 23 Sep 1926:	Commandant, Cruiser "*Amazone*"
24 Sep 1926 - 4 Oct 1928:	Chief of Training Section, Naval High Command
5 Oct 1928 - 30 Sep 1932:	Director, Wilhelmshaven Naval Shipyards
(1 Nov 1928:	Promoted to Konteradmiral)
(30 Sep 1932:	Promoted to brevet Vizeadmiral)
30 Sep 1932:	Retired
24 May 1939:	Recalled to reserve status
6 Aug 1940 - 30 Apr 1943:	Director of Drontheim Shipyards
(1 Aug 1941:	Confirmed as Vizeadmiral from brevet rank)
30 Apr 1943:	Retired

Vizeadmiral (Wirkliche Geheime Rat) Carl von **EISENDECHER** (23 Jun 1841 - 19 Aug 1934)
1884 - 1919:	Prussian Ambassador to Baden
(12 Jan 1893:	Promoted to brevet Konteradmiral)
(27 Jan 1900:	Promoted to brevet Vizeadmiral)
8 Mar 1919:	Retired

Konteradmiral Hugo **EMSMANN** (26 Apr 1857 - 12 Dec 1933)
(7 Sep 1907:	Promoted to brevet Konteradmiral)
Aug 1914 - Nov 1918:	Recalled from retirement; Commander of Eilvese Radio Transmitting Station
Nov 1918:	Retired

Vizeadmiral Richard **ENGEL** (27 Jul 1866 - 22 Nov 1954)
1 Oct 1911 - 26 Aug 1915:	Commandant, Battleship "*Rheinland*"
29 Jun 1915 - 19 Feb 1916:	Deputy Commander, I. Squadron

(17 Oct 1915:	Promoted to Konteradmiral)
9 Mar 1916 - 2 Oct 1919:	Chief of Wilhelmshaven Shipyards
(29 Oct 1918:	Promoted to Vizeadmiral)
3 Oct 1919 - 24 Nov 1919:	Placed on inactive status
24 Nov 1919:	Retired

Konteradmiral Siegfried **ENGEL** (10 May 1892 - 12 Jul 1976)

26 Mar 1936 - 16 May 1938:	Chief of Foreign Navies Group, Naval High Command
17 May 1938 - 13 Apr 1943:	Chief of Staff to Deputy Commander, North Sea Naval Forces
(1 Apr 1943:	Promoted to Konteradmiral)
14 Apr 1943 - 19 Apr 1945:	Deputy Commander, North Sea Naval Forces

Konteradmiral Conrad **ENGELHARDT** (26 Mar 1898 - 28 Oct 1973)

25 May 1940 - 25 Jul 1940:	Chief of Staff to Naval Commander, North France
26 Jul 1940 - 14 Dec 1940:	Staff Officer to Naval Commander, Channel Coast
15 Dec 1940 - 15 Feb 1941:	Commander of Sea Defenses, Gascogne-Loire-Gironde
16 Feb 1941 - 15 May 1941:	Attached the Naval Liaison Staff, Rome
16 May 1941 - 3 Mar 1943:	Chief of Staff to Naval Commander, Baltic
5 Mar 1943 - 31 Dec 1943:	Chief of German Naval Transport, Italy
5 Jan 1944 - 23 May 1945:	Chief of Navigation Office, Naval High Command & Chief of Sea Transport of the Armed Forces
(16 Sep 1944:	Promoted to Konteradmiral)

Awards: *German Cross in Gold; Knight's Cross of the War Merit Cross with Swords*

Vizeadmiral Walter **ENGELHARDT** (22 Aug 1867 - 22 Sep 1943)

1 Aug 1911 - 23 Aug 1915:	Commandant, Battleship "*Ostfriesland*"
26 Aug 1915 - 10 Nov 1915:	Deputy Commander, IV. Squadron
11 Nov 1915 - 31 Jan 1916:	Commander of Stand-By Division
(27 Jan 1916:	Promoted to Konteradmiral)
1 Feb 1916 - 1 Mar 1916:	Commandant of Kiel
1 Mar 1916 - 27 May 1917:	Deputy Commander, I. Squadron
1 Jul 1916 - 10 Jul 1916:	Acting Commander, I. Squadron
3 Feb 1917 - 21 Feb 1917:	Acting Commander, I. Squadron
29 May 1917 - 21 Mar 1918:	Commandant of Kiel

22 Mar 1918 - 3 Dec 1918:	Inspector of Coastal Artillery, Fortress Commandant, Cuxhaven
12 Feb 1919:	Retired
(4 Sep 1919:	Promoted to brevet Vizeadmiral)
(21 Jun 1920:	Confirmed as Vizeadmiral from brevet rank)

Marinegeneralstabsarzt (Konteradmiral) Dr. Georg **ERDMANN**
(12 Nov 1860 - 28 Aug 1943)

Aug 1914 - Nov 1918:	Recalled from retirement; Inspector, IX. Military Medical Inspectorate
(10 Jun 1916:	Promoted to Marinegeneralstabsarzt)
Nov 1918:	Retired

Konteradmiral Hans **ERLER** (14 Oct 1874 - 28 Sep 1958)

23 Aug 1939:	Recalled from retirement to reserve status
(1 Jun 1940:	Promoted to brevet Konteradmiral)
21 Aug 1940 - 31 Mar 1943:	Attached to Naval Personnel Office, Naval High Command
31 Mar 1943:	Retired

Konteradmiral Theodor **ESCHENBURG** (14 Mar 1876 - 26 Feb 1968)

9 Apr 1919 - 5 Oct 1919:	Harbor Captain, Kiel
6 Oct 1919 - 31 Mar 1920:	Chief of Personnel, Baltic Naval Station
1 Apr 1920 - 15 Jul 1920:	Attached to the Commander, Baltic Naval Station
16 Jul 1920 - 30 Sep 1920:	Acting Inspector of Torpedoes & Mines
1 Oct 1920 - 31 Mar 1922:	Chief of Staff, Inspectorate of Torpedoes & Mines
1 Apr 1922 - 30 Sep 1923:	Inspector of Torpedoes & Mines
1 Oct 1923 - 26 Sep 1924:	Naval Commissioner, Kaiser-Wilhelm Canal
27 Sep 1924 - 31 Dec 1924:	Attached to the Commander, Baltic Naval Station
(31 Dec 1924:	Promoted to brevet Konteradmiral)
31 Dec 1924:	Retired

Admiralarzt (Konteradmiral) Dr. Alois **EVERS** (13 Mar 1893 - 31 Mar 1965)

28 Sep 1937 - 31 Dec 1939:	Chief Medical Officer, Swinemünde Naval Hospital
3 Jan 1940 - 31 Mar 1941:	Commandant, Naval Medical Academy
4 Apr 1941 - 29 Jun 1941:	Senior Medical Officer on staff of Admiral Southeast

30 Jun 1941 - 19 Aug 1942:	Senior Medical Officer, Naval Group South
20 Aug 1942 - 31 Oct 1942:	Attached to Medical Service, Baltic Naval Station
1 Nov 1942 - 8 Feb 1944:	Chief Medical Officer, Stralsund Naval Hospital
9 Feb 1944 - 8 May 1945:	Medical Officer, High Seas Fleet
(1 Jun 1944:	Promoted to Admiralarzt)

Konteradmiral Ernst **EWERS** (29 Sep 1873 - 14 Nov 1940)

2 Aug 1914 - 3 Jan 1915:	Commandant, Light Cruiser "*Nymphe*"
3 Jan 1915 - 28 Feb 1915:	Commandant, Light Cruiser "*Regensburg*"
1 Mar 1915 - 15 May 1915:	Commandant, Light Cruiser "*Kolberg*"
15 May 1915 - 6 Sep 1915:	Commandant, Light Cruiser "*Niobe*"
30 Sep 1915 - 2 Mar 1916:	Commandant, Coastal Defense Ship "*Heimdall*"
3 Mar 1916 - 9 Aug 1916:	Attached to the Commander, Baltic Naval Station
10 Aug 1916 - 31 Aug 1916:	Commandant, Battleship "*Preußen*"
1 Sep 1916 - 16 Sep 1916:	Commandant, Battleship "*Hessen*"
25 Sep 1916 - 3 Jun 1917:	Commandant, Battleship "*Schlesien*"
10 Jun 1917 - 23 Jul 1917:	Commandant, Battleship "*Westfalen*"
3 Aug 1917 - 24 Aug 1917:	Commandant, Battleship "*König Albert*"
25 Aug 1917 - 30 Nov 1917:	Attached to the Commander, Baltic Naval Station
1 Dec 1917 - 3 Dec 1918:	Commandant, Battleship "*König Albert*"
4 Dec 1918 - 31 Mar 1919:	Attached to Kiel Naval Personnel Group
1 Apr 1919 - 22 Jun 1919:	Attached to the Commander, Baltic Naval Station
23 Jun 1919 - 17 Mar 1920:	Commander of Security Forces, Baltic
(5 Mar 1920:	Promoted to Konteradmiral)
18 Mar 1920 - 23 Mar 1920:	Commander, Baltic Naval Station
24 Mar 1920 - 30 Sep 1920:	Attached to the Commander, Baltic Naval Station
30 Sep 1920:	Retired

Admiralarzt (Konteradmiral) Dr. Karl **EYERICH** (5 Feb 1886 - 17 Jul 1971)

1 Oct 1931 - 25 Oct 1938:	Chief Medical Officer, North Sea Naval Station
(1 Jan 1937:	Promoted to Admiralarzt)
1 Nov 1938 - 25 May 1941:	Attached to Naval Medical Service &

	Personnel Office, Naval High Command
26 May 1941 - 28 Feb 1944:	Chief Medical Officer, Bergen op Zoom Naval Hospital
29 Feb 1944 - 26 Aug 1944:	Chief Medical Officer, Marseille Naval Hospital
26 Aug 1944 - 1945:	Prisoner of war

Konteradmiral Robert **EYSSEN** (2 Apr 1892 - 31 Mar 1960)

26 Sep 1935 - 6 Oct 1937:	Commandant, Survey Ship *"Meteor"*
7 Oct 1937 - 30 Nov 1939:	Chief of Military Section, Naval Defense Office, Naval High Command
1 Dec 1939 - 20 Feb 1942:	Commandant, Auxiliary Cruiser *"Komet"*
(1 Jan 1941:	Promoted to Konteradmiral)
20 Mar 1942 - 9 Aug 1942:	Naval Liaison Officer to Luftflotte 4
18 Aug 1942 - 14 Jul 1944:	Chief of Oslo Naval Office
15 Jul 1944 - 31 Jan 1945:	Chief of Recruiting Office, Vienna III
1 Feb 1945 - 30 Apr 1945:	Attached to Vienna Recruitment Inspectorate
30 Apr 1945:	Retired

Awards: *Knight's Cross*

Konteradmiral Walther **FABER** (30 Aug 1888 - 18 Dec 1945)

21 Mar 1932 - 5 Oct 1934:	Chief of Staff, Inspectorate of Torpedoes & Mines
1 Jul 1934 - 2 Sep 1934:	Acting Inspector of Torpedoes & Mines
8 Oct 1934 - 8 Sep 1935:	Commander, Torpedo Testing Center, Eckernförde
9 Sep 1935 - 2 May 1936:	Attached to the Commander, Baltic Naval Station
24 Feb 1936 - 1 Mar 1936:	Naval Commissioner, Kaiser-Wilhelm Canal & Harbor Captain of Kiel
2 May 1936 - 27 Sep 1936:	Acting Chief of Staff to the Deputy Commander, Baltic Naval Station
29 Jun 1936 - 5 Jul 1936:	Acting Deputy Commander, Baltic Naval Station
26 Aug 1936 - 12 Sep 1936:	Acting Deputy Commander, Baltic Naval Station
28 Sep 1936 - 21 Aug 1938:	Chief of Bremen Naval Office
29 Aug 1938 - 8 Apr 1945:	Section Chief, Military Science Office, Naval High Command
(31 Mar 1940:	Promoted to brevet Konteradmiral)
8 Apr 1945:	Retired

Admiral Paul **FANGER** (11 Apr 1889 - 15 Apr 1945)
27 Mar 1933 - 25 Sep 1935:	Commandant, Ships Artillery School
30 Sep 1935 - 2 Sep 1937:	Commandant, Pocket Battleship *"Deutschland"*
3 Sep 1937 - 12 Jan 1940:	Commander, East Friesland Defenses
(1 Oct 1938:	Promoted to Konteradmiral)
17 Jan 1940 - 3 Mar 1943:	Chief of Artillery Office, Naval High Command
(1 Dec 1940:	Promoted to Vizeadmiral)
(1 Dec 1942:	Promoted to Admiral)
4 Mar 1943 - 31 May 1943:	Attached to the Commander-in-Chief of the Navy
31 May 1943:	Retired
1 Jun 1943:	Recalled to reserve status
15 Aug 1944 - 1 Apr 1945:	Inspector of Coastal and Ships Artillery, Naval Group Norway
Feb 1945 - Mar 1945:	Deputy Commander, Molde Sea Defenses

Awards: *German Cross in Silver*

Admiral (Ingeneur) Hans **FECHTER** (26 May 1885 - 4 Jul 1955)
19 Jun 1931 - 28 Sep 1933:	Chief Engineer, North Sea Naval Station
30 Sep 1933 - 30 Sep 1935:	Chief Engineer, High Seas Fleet
(1 Oct 1935:	Promoted to Konteradmiral Ingeneur)
1 Oct 1935 - 31 Dec 1939:	Inspector, Ships Equipment Inspectorate
(1 Nov 1937:	Promoted to Vizeadmiral Ingeneur)
(31 Dec 1939:	Promoted to brevet Admiral Ingeneur)
31 Dec 1939:	Retired
1 Jan 1940:	Recalled to reserve status; no appointment conferred

Admiral Otto **FEIGE** (21 Sep 1882 - 2 Jan 1951)
8 Oct 1927 - 26 Sep 1928:	Chief of Staff, Naval Artillery Inspectorate
27 Sep 1928 - 29 Sep 1930:	Commandant, Battleship *"Hessen"*
4 Oct 1930 - 29 Sep 1932:	Commander, Ships Artillery School
30 Sep 1932 - 26 Sep 1937:	Inspector of Naval Artillery
(1 Jan 1933:	Promoted to Konteradmiral)
(1 Oct 1935:	Promoted to Vizeadmiral)
1 Jan 1933 - 26 Sep 1937:	President, Artillery Testing Command
3 Aug 1933 - 16 Sep 1933:	Acting Commander, North Sea Naval Station
(30 Sep 1937:	Promoted to brevet Admiral)
30 Sep 1937:	Retired

24 May 1939:   Recalled to reserve status
May 1940 - Jun 1941:   Chief of Shipbuilding Staff for Heavy Cruiser
                                "*Petropavlovsk*", Leningrad
1 Jul 1941 - 13 Nov 1941:   Director-Designate, Leningrad Shipyards
(1 Sep 1941:   Confirmed as Admiral from brevet rank)
1 Dec 1941 - 30 Sep 1942:   Director, Nikolayev/Kherson Shipyards
1 Oct 1942 - 31 Dec 1942:   Placed on inactive status
31 Dec 1942:   Retired

Konteradmiral Otto **FEIN** (28 Mar 1895 - 9 Jan 1953)
1 Nov 1938 - 21 Aug 1939:   Acting Chief of Staff, Naval Group East
22 Aug 1939 -18 Sep 1939:   Staff Officer, Naval Group East
19 Sep 1939 - 12 Oct 1939:   Acting Chief of Staff, Naval Group East
13 Oct 1939 - 20 May 1940:   Staff Officer, Naval Group East
21 May 1940 - 9 Aug 1940:   Deputy Chief of Staff, Naval Group East
10 Aug 1940 - 19 Aug 1940:   Chief of Staff, Naval Group North
20 Aug 1940 - 14 Apr 1942:   Commandant, Battleship "*Gneisenau*"
(1 Apr 1942:   Promoted to Konteradmiral)
27 May 1942 - 31 Jan 1943:   Chief of Staff, Admiral Commanding Norway
1 Feb 1943 - 22 Nov 1944:   Chief of Staff, Naval Group Norway
12 Dec 1944 - 22 Jul 1945:   Chief of Nautical Office,
                                Naval High Command

Awards: *German Cross in Gold*

Konteradmiral Hans **FELDBAUSCH** (5 Oct 1891 - 20 Oct 1985)
24 Sep 1935 - 13 May 1937:   Chief of Königsberg Naval Office
15 May 1937 - 7 Jun 1938:   Commandant, Battleship "*Schleswig-Holstein*"
8 Jun 1938 - 21 Aug 1938:   Attached to Bremen Naval Office
22 Aug 1938 - 23 May 1940:   Chief of Bremen Naval Office
27 May 1940 - 23 Aug 1942:   Chief of Oslo Naval Office
(1 Jun 1940:   Promoted to Konteradmiral)
31 Aug 1942:   Retired
1 Sep 1942 - 30 Apr 1945:   Recalled to reserve status; Chief of Nautical &
                                Hydrographical Department,
                                Naval Observatory
30 Apr 1945:   Retired

Konteradmiral Carl **FELDMANN** (12 Aug 1875 - 8 Jul 1963)
22 May 1917 - 9 Jul 1918:   Commandant, Light Cruiser "*Königsberg*"
13 Jul 1918 - 15 Dec 1918:   Commandant, Heavy Cruiser "*Von der Tann*"

15 Aug 1918 - 4 Dec 1918:	Acting Deputy Commander, I. Reconnaissance Group
16 Dec 1918 - 31 Mar 1919:	Chief of Demobilization Group for Reconnaissance Forces
1 Apr 1919 - 30 Jun 1919:	Attached to Naval Office
1 Jul 1919 - 31 Mar 1920:	Chief of Wilhelmshaven Welfare Office
31 Mar 1920:	Retired
(8 Aug 1940:	Promoted to brevet Konteradmiral)

Konteradmiral Constanz **FELDT** (16 Oct 1867 - 22 May 1942)

1 Oct 1912 - 11 Aug 1915:	Commandant, Battleship "*Preussen*"
12 Aug 1915 - 24 Nov 1916:	Commandant, Battleship "*Kronprinz*"
22 Dec 1916 - 28 Jul 1918:	Chief of Staff, North Sea Naval Station
(14 Oct 1917:	Promoted to Konteradmiral)
19 Aug 1918 - 30 Nov 1918:	Deputy Commander, III. Squadron
1 Dec 1918 - 17 Jan 1919:	Attached to the Commander, North Sea Naval Station
17 Jan 1919:	Retired

Wirkliche Geheime Admiralitätsrat (Konteradmiral) Dr. Paul **FELISCH** (18 May 1855 - 25 Dec 1933)

27 May 1907 - 30 Jun 1920:	Director of Justice Department, Naval Office
(10 Jan 1914:	Appointed Wirkliche Geheime Admiralitätsrat)
30 Jun 1920:	Retired

Admiraloberstabsarzt (Admiral) Prof. Dr. Alfred **FICKENTSCHER** (30 Apr 1888 - 10 Jan 1979)

30 Mar 1932 - 18 Jun 1936:	Chief Medical Officer, Kiel-Wik Naval Hospital
19 Jun 1936 - 28 Oct 1938:	Medical Officer, High Seas Fleet
31 Oct 1938 - 26 Nov 1939:	Chief Medical Officer, North Sea Naval Station
(1 Nov 1938:	Promoted to Admiralarzt [Konteradmiral])
(1 Nov 1939:	Promoted to Admiralstabsarzt [Vizeadmiral])
27 Nov 1939 - 30 Nov 1943:	Chief of Naval Medical Service, Naval High Command
(1 Sep 1942:	Promoted to Admiraloberstabsarzt [Admiral])
30 Nov 1943:	Retired
1 Dec 1943:	Recalled to reserve status; no appointment conferred

Awards: *German Cross in Silver*

Admiral Hermann von **FISCHEL** (13 Jan 1887 - 13 May 1950)

23 Sep 1930 - 14 Mar 1933:	Chief of Naval Training Office, Naval High Command
15 Mar 1933 - 31 Mar 1933:	Attached to the staff of Pocket Battleship "*Deutschland*"
1 Apr 1933 - 29 Sep 1935:	Commandant, Pocket Battleship "*Deutschland*"
30 Sep 1935 - 30 Sep 1936:	Chairman, Ships Testing Commission
(1 Oct 1935:	Promoted to Konteradmiral)
25 Nov 1936 - 8 Feb 1938:	Flag Officer, Battleships
8 Sep 1937 - 7 Oct 1937:	Commander of Naval Forces, Spain
8 Feb 1938 - 13 Mar 1938:	Commander of Naval Forces, Spain
14 Mar 1938 - 31 Mar 1938:	Attached to the Commander-in-Chief of the Navy
(1 Apr 1938:	Promoted to Vizeadmiral)
2 Apr 1938 - 31 Dec 1939:	Chief of Naval General Office, Naval High Command
1 Jan 1940 - 8 Jan 1941:	Chief of Testing Command for New Ships
29 Aug 1940 - 27 Oct 1940:	Commander-Designate, Transport Fleet "B" for Operation "Sealion"
9 Jan 1941 - 16 Feb 1941:	Commander, Naval Security Forces, West
20 Feb 1941 - 31 Jan 1943:	Naval Commander, Channel Coast
(1 Sep 1941:	Promoted to Admiral)
1 Feb 1943 - 10 May 1943:	Admiral Commanding, Channel Coast
11 May 1943 - 18 Jun 1943:	Attached to Luftwaffe Training Staff
19 Jun 1943 - 30 Jun 1943:	Chief of Luftwaffe Training Staff
30 Jun 1943:	Retired
1 Jul 1943 - 14 Sep 1944:	Recalled to reserve status; Chief of Luftwaffe Training Staff
15 Sep 1944 - 30 Nov 1944:	Attached to the Commander, Naval Group North
30 Nov 1944:	Retired

Awards: *German Cross in Gold*

Konteradmiral Andreas **FISCHER** (29 Feb 1872 - 6 Dec 1946)

18 Oct 1914 - 11 Nov 1914:	Commander, Ships Training Division
15 Nov 1914 - Mar 1916:	Commander, 1. Marine Artillery Regiment, Flanders Marine Corps
Mar 1916 - Oct 1918:	Commandant of Ostende
Oct 1918 - 30 Nov 1918:	Commander of Special Group, Flanders Marine Corps

1 Dec 1918 - 16 Mar 1919:	Reserve status; no appointment conferred
16 Mar 1919:	Retired
(23 Dec 1919:	Promoted to brevet Konteradmiral)

Konteradmiral Reinhard von **FISCHER-LOSZAINEN**
(30 Jun 1870 - 12 Sep 1940)

25 Apr 1913 - 10 Apr 1918:	Naval Attaché, Sweden & Denmark
11 Apr 1918 - 11 Jan 1919:	Naval Attaché, Stockholm
11 Jan 1919:	Retired
(30 Aug 1919:	Promoted to brevet Konteradmiral)

Admiralintendant (Konteradmiral) Dr. Ernst **FITZLER**
(16 Aug 1893 - 24 Jun 1971)

15 Nov 1939 - 4 Jun 1943:	Chief of Accommodations Section, Naval Administration Department
(1 Apr 1942:	Promoted to Ministerialdirigent [Konteradmiral])
(5 Jun 1943:	Rank changed to Marinegeneralintendant)
5 Jun 1943 - 15 Jun 1943:	Chief Intendant, Wilhelmshaven
15 Jun 1943 - 8 May 1945:	Chief of Administration, Naval Group North Sea
(1 May 1944:	Rank changed to Admiralintendant)

Reichskriegsgerichtsrat (Vizeadmiral) Dr. Max **FLEGEL**
(24 Mar 1878 - 4 May 1956)

(1 Oct 1936:	Promoted to Reichskriegsgerichtsrat [Konteradmiral])
1 Oct 1936 - 30 Sep 1942:	Judge-Advocate-General, Armed Forces High Command (OKW)
(30 Sep 1942:	Promoted to Vizeadmiral rank)
30 Sep 1942:	Retired

Admiral Friedrich Wilhelm **FLEISCHER** (14 Sep 1890 - 13 Feb 1952)

29 Sep 1934 - 29 Sep 1937:	Chief of Organization Office, Naval High Command
1 Oct 1937 - 3 Aug 1938:	Commandant, Battleship *"Schlesien"*
4 Aug 1938 - 11 Apr 1939:	Fortress Commandant of Pillau
(1 Apr 1939:	Promoted to Konteradmiral)
27 Feb 1939 - 6 May 1939:	Chief of Königsberg Naval Office
22 Mar 1939 - 11 Apr 1939:	Fortress Commandant of Memel
12 Apr 1939 - 12 Jan 1940:	Coastal Commander, Eastern Baltic

13 Jan 1940 - 25 Jul 1940:	Coastal Commander, East Friesland
26 Jul 1940 - 19 Feb 1941:	Naval Commander, Channel Coast
21 Feb 1941 - 4 Apr 1941:	Naval Commander "B"
(1 Apr 1941:	Promoted to Vizeadmiral)
5 Apr 1941 - 30 Jun 1941:	Chief of Naval Mission to Romania
1 Jul 1941 - 2 May 1942:	Admiral Commanding, Black Sea
23 Jun 1942 - 31 Aug 1942:	Attached to Wilhelmshaven Shipyards
(1 Sep 1942:	Promoted to Admiral)
1 Sep 1942 - 22 Oct 1944:	Director of Wilhelmshaven Shipyards
23 Oct 1944 - 31 Dec 1944:	Attached to the Commander, Naval Group North Sea
31 Dec 1944:	Retired

Awards: *German Cross in Silver*

Marinegeneralstabsarzt (Konteradmiral) Dr. Günther von **FOERSTER**
(16 Mar 1864 - 13 Jan 1938)

10 Jan 1917 - 27 May 1919:	Chief Medical Officer, North Sea Naval Station
(9 Mar 1919:	Promoted to brevet Marinegeneralstabsarzt)
27 May 1919:	Retired

Admiral Richard **FOERSTER** (31 Mar 1879 - 9 Apr 1952)

11 Jul 1923 - 24 Sep 1925:	Chief of Staff, Naval High Command
15 Oct 1925 - 23 Sep 1928:	Commandant, Cruiser "*Emden*"
1 Oct 1928 - 26 Feb 1930:	Inspector of Naval Training
21 May 1929 - 22 Jun 1929:	Inspector of Torpedoes and Mines
(1 Dec 1928:	Promoted to Konteradmiral)
27 Feb 1930 - 27 Sep 1932:	Flag Officer, Battleships
28 Sep 1932 - 21 Sep 1933:	Commander, North Sea Naval Station
(1 Oct 1932:	Promoted to Vizeadmiral)
22 Sep 1933 - 20 Dec 1936:	C-in-C, High Seas Fleet
(1 Dec 1935:	Promoted to Admiral)
31 Dec 1936:	Retired
15 Feb 1939:	Placed on reserve status; no appointment conferred

Konteradmiral Günther von der **FORST** (17 Dec 1897 - 24 Mar 1982)

7 May 1938 - 7 Mar 1940:	Commandant, Station Tender "*Grille*"
8 Mar 1940 - 5 May 1940:	Naval Liaison Officer to 18. Army
6 May 1940 - 9 Jun 1940:	Commandant, Station Tender "*Grille*"

20 Jun 1940 - 18 Jul 1940:	Chief of Staff to Admiral, South Norway
19 Jul 1940 - 31 May 1941:	Commander of Sea Defenses, Stavanger
1 Jun 1941 - 10 Dec 1941:	Sea Commandant "T"
11 Dec 1941 - 6 Nov 1942:	Quartermaster to Admiral Commanding, Norway
7 Nov 1942 - 31 Jan 1943:	Attached to the Commander, Baltic Naval Station
1 Feb 1943 - 3 Nov 1943:	Chief of Staff to Admiral Commanding, Aegean
4 Nov 1943 - 1 May 1944:	Attached to the Commander, Baltic Naval Group
(1 Apr 1944:	Promoted to Konteradmiral)
2 May 1944 - 23 Jul 1945:	Chief of Staff, Baltic Naval Group

Admiral Erich **FÖRSTE** (11 Feb 1892 - 10 Jul 1963)

25 Sep 1934 - 1 Sep 1937:	Chief of Budget Office, Naval High Command
29 Sep 1937 - 20 May 1938:	Commandant, Cruiser "*Karlsruhe*"
21 May 1938 - 25 Nov 1939:	Commandant, Battleship "*Gneisenau*"
(1 Nov 1939:	Promoted to Konteradmiral)
6 Dec 1939 - 3 Feb 1941:	Chief of Central Office, Wilhelmshaven Shipyards
4 Feb 1941 - 21 Sep 1941:	Chief of Staff, Wilhelmshaven Shipyards
(1 Sep 1941:	Promoted to Vizeadmiral)
27 Sep 1941 - 22 Feb 1943:	Admiral Commanding, Aegean
(1 Mar 1943:	Promoted to Admiral)
1 Mar 1943 - 21 Jun 1943:	Admiral Commanding, North Sea Naval Station
22 Jun 1943 - 10 Jul 1945:	C-in-C, Naval Group North Sea

Awards: *German Cross in Gold*

Vizeadmiral Walther **FRANZ** (7 Aug 1880 - 19 Jan 1956)

3 Sep 1918 - 5 Mar 1919:	Commandant, Light Cruiser "*Königsberg*"
6 Mar 1919 - 30 Sep 1919:	Battalion Commander, Kiel Volunteer Regiment
1 Oct 1919 - 18 May 1923:	Director of Artillery and Navigation, Wilhelmshaven Shipyards
19 May 1923 - 3 Oct 1928:	Director of Wilhelmshaven Shipyards
(1 Apr 1927:	Promoted to Konteradmiral)
11 Oct 1928 - 31 Dec 1929:	Commander of North Sea Forces, Deputy Commander, Battleship Division

(1 Dec 1928:	Promoted to Vizeadmiral)
1 Jan 1930 - 27 Feb 1930:	Flag Officer, Battleships
31 Mar 1930:	Retired
24 May 1939:	Recalled to reserve status
3 Sep 1939 - 28 Sep 1941:	Commissioner, Wilhelmshaven Prize Court
29 Sep 1941 - 17 May 1944:	Chief of Naval Printing Office
31 May 1944:	Retired

Marineoberbaudirektor (Vizeadmiral) Georg **FREDE**
(23 Feb 1882 - 22 Apr 1970)

(27 May 1936:	Promoted to Strombaudirektor [Konteradmiral])
1 Jun 1936 - 14 Oct 1939:	Director of Section VII, Wilhelmshaven Naval Shipyards
15 Oct 1939 - 31 Jan 1943:	Director of Harbor Construction, Wilhelmshaven Naval Shipyards
1 Feb 1943 - Oct 1944:	Chief of Construction, Wilhelmshaven
(1 Apr 1944:	Promoted to Marineoberbaudirektor)
Oct 1944 - Apr 1945:	Senior Engineer Liaison Officer, Naval Group North Sea
Apr 1945:	Retired

Ministerialrat (Konteradmiral) Frerich **FRERICHS** (6 Feb 1874 - 7 Dec 1946)

1 Apr 1933 - 28 Feb 1939:	General Advisor, Air Defense Office, Naval High Command
(28 Feb 1939:	Promoted to Ministerialrat with Konteradmiral rank)
28 Feb 1939:	Retired

Konteradmiral Theodor **FREY** (8 Jul 1869 - 7 Apr 1945)

15 Aug 1914 - 2 Feb 1915:	Deputy Director, Nautical Department, Naval Office
4 Feb 1915 - 30 Jun 1915:	Commandant, Battleship "*Kaiser Wilhelm der Große*"
12 Aug 1915 - 22 Dec 1916:	Commandant, Battleship "*Preußen*"
1916:	At various time, Senior Naval Officer, Sund
23 Dec 1916 - 23 Jan 1919:	Chief of Central Office, Wilhelmshaven Shipyards
23 Jan 1919:	Retired
(30 Aug 1919:	Promoted to brevet Konteradmiral)

Vizeadmiral Albrecht Freiherr von **FREYBERG-EISENBERG-ALLMENDINGEN**
(4 Feb 1876 - 13 Sep 1943)

15 Oct 1914 - 1 Jan 1914:	Attached to the Commander of Naval Aviation
2 Jan 1915 - 6 Feb 1920:	Naval Attaché, Vienna
1 Mar 1920 - 31 Mar 1920:	Attached to the Embassy in Den Haag
1 Apr 1920 - 20 May 1920:	Attached to Naval High Command
21 May 1920 - 30 Sep 1922:	Chief of Naval Personnel, Naval High Command
1 Oct 1922 - 30 Sep 1923:	Naval Commissioner, Kaiser-Wilhelm Canal
13 Feb 1923 - 30 Sep 1923:	Harbor Captain, Kiel
1 Oct 1923 - 31 Mar 1925:	Commandant, Battleship "*Hannover*"
8 Apr 1925 - 21 Sep 1926:	Inspector, Naval Depot Inspectorate
(1 Oct 1925:	Promoted to Konteradmiral)
22 Sep 1926 - 14 Oct 1933:	Chief of League of Nations Navy Group, Naval High Command
(1 Oct 1928:	Promoted to brevet Vizeadmiral)
(1 Aug 1933:	Confirmed as Vizeadmiral from brevet rank)
15 Oct 1933 - 28 Sep 1934:	Chief of Naval Conferences Group, Naval High Command
30 Sep 1934:	Retired
19 Jul 1939:	Placed on reserve status; no appointment conferred

Marinegeneralstabsarzt (Konteradmiral) Dr. Josef **FREYMADL**
(17 Jan 1864 - 15 Mar 1951)

13 Apr 1914:	Retired
(14 Jan 1922:	Promoted to brevet Marinegeneralstabsarzt)

Admiral Kurt **FRICKE** (8 Nov 1889 - 2 May 1945)

25 Sep 1933 - 5 Oct 1934:	Flag Officer, Torpedo Boats
6 Oct 1934 - 30 Sep 1936:	Chief of Staff, Inspectorate of Torpedoes & Mines
6 Oct 1936 - 30 Sep 1937:	Transferred to the Naval Academy
1 Oct 1937 - 12 Jun 1941:	Chief of Naval Operations
(1 Nov 1939:	Promoted to Konteradmiral)
(1 Jun 1941:	Promoted to Vizeadmiral)
30 Apr 1939 - 12 Jun 1941:	Naval Liaison Officer to the Commander-in-Chief of the Luftwaffe
13 Jun 1941 - 20 Feb 1943:	Chief of Naval General Staff
(1 Apr 1942:	Promoted to Admiral)

21 Mar 1943 - 11 Dec 1944: C-in-C, Naval Group South
12 Dec 1944 - 2 May 1945: Transferred to the Führer Reserve
Awards: *Knight's Cross*

Konteradmiral Otto **FRICKE** (29 May 1894 - 26 Nov 1966)
1 Oct 1937 - 30 Apr 1940: Chief of Staff, Naval Artillery Inspectorate & Commander, 11. Naval Artillery Regiment
7 Jul 1938 - 6 Aug 1938: Acting Inspector of Naval Artillery
1 May 1940 - 18 Jul 1940: Harbor Commandant, Stavanger
19 Jul 1940 - 17 Apr 1942: Chief of Staff to Naval Commander, Channel Coast
18 Apr 1942 - 15 Nov 1942: Chief of Staff to Admiral Commanding, France
(1 Sep 1942: Promoted to Konteradmiral)
16 Nov 1942 - 31 Mar 1943: Quartermaster, Naval Group West
1 Apr 1943 - 22 Jul 1945: Inspector of Naval Artillery

Generaladmiral Hans-Georg von **FRIEDEBURG** (15 Jul 1895 - 23 May 1945)
2 Nov 1938 - 5 Feb 1939: Staff Officer to Commander of Security Forces, North Sea
6 Feb 1939 - 5 Jun 1939: Attached to the Flag Officer, U-Boats
6 Jun 1939 - 8 Jul 1939: Commandant, U-Boat "U 27"
9 Jul 1939 - 24 Sep 1939: Acting Flag Officer, UBoats
25 Sep 1939 - 11 Sep 1941: Chief of Organization Office, U-Boat Command
12 Sep 1941 - 31 Jan 1943: Deputy Flag Officer, UBoats
(1 Sep 1942: Promoted to Konteradmiral)
(1 Feb 1943: Promoted to Vizeadmiral)
1 Feb 1943 - 30 Apr 1945: Flag Officer, U-Boats
(1 Apr 1943: Promoted to Admiral)
(1 May 1945: Promoted to Generaladmiral)
1 May 1945 - 23 May 1945: Commander-in-Chief of the Navy
Awards: *German Cross in Silver; Knight's Cross of the War Merit Cross with Swords*

Vizeadmiral (Ingeneur) Ernst **FRIEDRICH** (10 Oct 1874 - 17 May 1957)
15 Feb 1917 - 21 Jun 1919: Chief Engineer, Light Cruiser "*Nürnberg*"
22 Jun 1919 - 2 Jul 1920: Prisoner-of-War
3 Jul 1920 - 31 Mar 1921: Engineer-Inspector, Naval Training Inspectorate
1 Apr 1921 - 31 Jan 1922: Commandant, Kiel-Wik Naval School
6 May 1921 - 21 May 1921: Chief Engineer, Baltic Naval Station

21 Sep 1921 - 5 Oct 1921:	Chief Engineer, Baltic Naval Station
15 Feb 1922 - 3 Mar 1922:	Placed on inactive status
4 Mar 1922 - 31 Dec 1927:	Engineer-Officer, Naval High Command
(1 Apr 1923:	Promoted to Konteradmiral Ingeneur)
(31 Dec 1927:	Promoted to Vizeadmiral Ingeneur)
31 Dec 1927:	Retired
25 Jul 1939:	Recalled to reserve status; no appointment conferred

Vizeadmiral Friedrich **FRISIUS** (17 Jan 1895 - 30 Aug 1970)

21 Sep 1935 - 4 Dec 1938:	Section Chief, Counterintelligence Service, Ministry of War
5 Dec 1938 - 5 Aug 1940:	Staff Officer, Hamburg Naval Office
6 Aug 1940 - 15 Jan 1941:	Chief of Boulogne Naval Office
26 Jan 1941 - 15 Dec 1941:	Commander of Boulogne Sea Defenses
16 Dec 1941 - 28 Oct 1944:	Commander of Pas de Calais Sea Defenses
(1 Dec 1942:	Promoted to Konteradmiral)
(30 Sep 1944:	Promoted to Vizeadmiral)
15 Sep 1944 - 9 May 1945:	Fortress Commandant of Dunkirk

Awards: *German Cross in Gold*

Vizeadmiral (Ingeneur) Walter **FRÖHLICH** (5 Aug 1893 - 12 Dec 1969)

25 Sep 1936 - 7 Nov 1938:	Engineer Officer attached to the Flag Officer, Battleships
8 Nov 1938 - 10 Dec 1939:	Chief of Staff, Ships Equipment Inspectorate
11 Dec 1939 - 7 Jan 1941:	Chief Engineer, High Seas Fleet
8 Jan 1941 - 28 Mar 1943:	Chief of Staff, Testing Command for New Ships
(1 Apr 1942:	Promoted to Konteradmiral Ingeneur)
29 Mar 1943 - 14 Jul 1945:	Inspector of Ships Equipment
(1 Apr 1943:	Promoted to Vizeadmiral Ingeneur)

Konteradmiral Theodor **FUCHS** (23 May 1868 - 28 Aug 1942)

15 Oct 1912 - 10 Jun 1917:	Commandant, Battleship *"Friedrich der Grosse"*
11 Jun 1917 - 24 Jul 1917:	On leave
25 Jul 1917 - 16 Aug 1917:	Commandant, Battleship *"Friedrich der Grosse"*
17 Aug 1917 - 18 Sep 1917:	Attached to the Commander, Baltic Naval Station
19 Sep 1917 - 30 Sep 1917:	Commander of Transport Fleet to capture the Baltic Islands

1 Oct 1917 - 15 Nov 1917:	Attached to the Commander, Baltic Naval Station
16 Nov 1917 - 8 Nov 1918:	Commandant, Kiel Defenses
(18 Sep 1918:	Promoted to brevet Konteradmiral)
9 Nov 1918 - 5 Dec 1918:	Attached to the Commander, Baltic Naval Station
28 Jan 1919:	Retired

Admiral Werner **FUCHS** (18 Jan 1891 - 30 Jun 1976)

20 Mar 1934 - 30 Sep 1935:	Commandant, Cruiser "*Köln*"
1 Oct 1935 - 27 Mar 1938:	Chief of Naval Training Office, Naval High Command
28 Mar 1938 - 30 Jun 1939:	Chief of Fleet Office, Naval High Command
(1 Oct 1938:	Promoted to Konteradmiral)
1 Jul 1939 - 31 Oct 1944:	Chief of Shipbuilding Directorate, Naval High Command
(1 Dec 1940:	Promoted to Vizeadmiral)
(1 Apr 1942:	Promoted to Admiral)
1 Nov 1944 - 23 May 1945:	Transferred to the Führer Reserve

Awards: *German Cross in Silver; Knight's Cross of the War Merit Cross with Swords*

Marineoberbaudirektor (Vizeadmiral) Albert **FUHRMANN** (28 May 1887 - 7 Dec 1941)

1 Oct 1936 - 31 Mar 1939:	Chief of Ships & Engine Construction Section, Kiel Naval Shipyards
(1937:	Promoted to Marinebaudirektor [Konteradmiral])
1 Apr 1939 - 28 Feb 1941:	Director of Engine Construction, Kiel Naval Shipyards
(6 Feb 1941:	Rank changed to Ministerialrat)
1 Mar 1941 - 7 Dec 1941:	Chief of Research & Development Section, Naval High Command
(23 Dec 1941:	Posthumously promoted to Marineoberbaudirektor)

Vizeadmiral Felix **FUNKE** (3 Jan 1865 - 22 Jul 1932)

(18 Nov 1912:	Promoted to Konteradmiral)
1 Mar 1914 - 26 Dec 1914:	Acting Commander, III. Squadron
27 Dec 1914 - 11 Aug 1915:	Commander, II. Squadron

11 Aug 1915 - 18 Sep 1915: Sick leave
(18 Sep 1915: Promoted to brevet Vizeadmiral)
18 Sep 1915: Retired

Konteradmiral Werner **FÜRBRINGER** (2 Oct 1888 - 8 Feb 1982)
29 Sep 1937 - 5 Dec 1937: Acting Commandant, U-Boat School
6 Dec 1937 - 16 Feb 1938: Attached to Naval High Command
17 Feb 1938 - 9 Nov 1938: Chief of Statistical Section, Naval General Office, Naval High Command
10 Nov 1938 - 31 Oct 1939: Chief of Embargo Apparatus Section, Naval General Office, Naval High Command
1 Nov 1939 - 31 Oct 1942: Chief of AntiSubmarine Section, U-Boat Directorate, Naval High Command
1 Nov 1942 - 30 Jun 1943: Inspector, Armaments Inspectorate Baltic
(1 Dec 1942: Promoted to Konteradmiral)
30 Jun 1943: Retired
1 Jul 1943: Recalled to reserve status; no appointment conferred

Vizeadmiral Friedrich **GÄDEKE** (15 May 1866 - 26 May 1935)
(18 Nov 1912: Promoted to Konteradmiral)
1 Oct 1913 - 27 Aug 1915: Deputy Commander, I. Squadron
20 Jun 1915 - 25 Aug 1915: Acting Commander, I. Squadron
18 Sep 1915 - 17 Dec 1916: Director of Nautical Department, Naval Office
(17 Oct 1915: Promoted to Vizeadmiral)
17 Dec 1916: Retired

Konteradmiral Hans-Joachim **GADOW** (6 Sep 1898 - 4 Aug 1978)
16 May 1938 - 20 Oct 1939: Staff Officer to Flag Officer, Torpedo Boats
21 Oct 1939 - 30 Nov 1939: Staff Officer to Flag Officer, Destroyers
1 Dec 1939 - 13 Apr 1940: Commander, 3. Destroyer Flotilla
14 Apr 1940 - 9 Aug 1940: Naval Commissioner, Narvik
30 Aug 1940 - 31 Oct 1940: Chief of Staff-Designate, Transport Fleet B
1 Nov 1940 - 18 Feb 1941: Commander of Transport Fleet, France
19 Feb 1941 - 7 Mar 1941: Chief of Antwerp Naval Office
5 Apr 1941 - 25 Mar 1943: Chief of Naval Training Command, Romania & Chief of Staff, Romanian Fleet & Commander of Escorts, Black Sea
8 Apr 1943 - 21 Jun 1943: Chief of Staff, North Sea Naval Station
22 Jun 1943 - 10 Jul 1945: Chief of Staff, Naval Group North Sea

(1 Feb 1944: Promoted to Konteradmiral)
Awards: *German Cross in Gold*

Konteradmiral Reinhard **GADOW** (25 Apr 1882 - 1946)
7 Sep 1927 - 23 Sep 1929:	Chief of Budget Office, Ministry of Defense
24 Sep 1929 - 30 Jun 1930:	Attached to the Commander-in-Chief of the Navy
(30 Jun 1930:	Promoted to brevet Konteradmiral)
30 Jun 1930:	Retired
22 Mar 1939:	Recalled to reserve status
Sep 1940 - 31 Mar 1945:	Director of Libraries, Armed Forces High Command
(1 Jul 1942:	Confirmed as Konteradmiral from brevet rank)
31 Mar 1945:	Retired

Admiral Ernst Freiherr von **GAGERN** (6 Jul 1878 - 14 Sep 1954)
11 Nov 1918 - 12 Jan 1920:	Member of Navy Group, German Permanent Peace Commission
13 Jan 1920 - 30 May 1920:	President, Naval Peace Commission
3 Jun 1920 - 9 Jan 1925:	Commander, Baltic Naval Station
(1 Apr 1921:	Promoted to Konteradmiral)
(1 Oct 1924:	Promoted to Vizeadmiral)
31 Jan 1925:	Retired
13 Sep 1939 - 3 Oct 1942:	Recalled; Deputy Commissioner, Berlin Prize Court
(1 Sep 1942:	Promoted to Admiral)
4 Oct 1942 - 31 Oct 1942:	Attached to the Commander-in-Chief of the Navy
31 Oct 1942:	Retired

Konteradmiral Albert **GAYER** (2 Dec 1881 - 9 Sep 1930)
17 Nov 1918 - 19 May 1920:	Commandant, Light Cruiser "*Regensburg*"
30 May 1920 - 31 Mar 1923:	Department Head, Fleet Office, Naval High Command
1 Apr 1923 - 18 Jan 1930:	Chief of Naval Office, Hamburg
(1 Mar 1929:	Promoted to brevet Konteradmiral)
19 Jan 1930 - 31 Jan 1930:	Attached to the Commander, North Sea Naval Station
31 Jan 1930:	Retired

Konteradmiral Heinrich **GEBHARDT** (17 Apr 1885 - 22 Jul 1939)
30 Sep 1930 - 25 Sep 1931:	Commandant, Battleship "*Hannover*"
9 Oct 1931 - 30 Sep 1934:	Chairman, Testing Committee for New Ships
1934:	Acting Inspector, Naval Depot Inspectorate
(30 Sep 1934:	Promoted to brevet Konteradmiral)
30 Sep 1934:	Retired
22 Mar 1939:	Recalled to reserve status; no appointment conferred

Admiral Thomas, Principe di Savoia, Duca di **GENOVA**
(6 Feb 1854 - 15 Apr 1931)
Admiral à la Suite (Honorary title)
Awards: *Order of the Black Eagle; Royal Bavarian St.Hubertus Order*

Konteradmiral (Ingeneur) Wilhelm **GENSKE** (31 Oct 1885 - 27 Aug 1958)
1 Oct 1933 - 7 Jun 1938:	Chief of Welfare, Baltic Naval Station
8 Jun 1938 - 31 Mar 1944:	Chief of Welfare, Military District (Wehrkreis) X
(1 Dec 1942:	Promoted to Konteradmiral Ingeneur)
1 Apr 1944 - 31 Jul 1944:	Attached to Military District X and Baltic Naval Station
31 Jul 1944:	Retired

Großadmiral (Generalfeldmarschall) **GEORGE V**, King of Great Britain & Ireland (3 Jun 1865 - 20 Jan 1936)
Großadmiral à la Suite (Honorary title)
Awards: *Order of the Black Eagle; Royal Bavarian St.Hubertus Order; Royal Saxon Order of the Diamond Crown*

Admiral Gerhard **GERDES** (13 Feb 1861 - 1 Mar 1841)
(5 Sep 1909:	Promoted to Konteradmiral)
26 Mar 1910 - 2 Oct 1917:	Director of Weapons Department, Naval Office
(27 Jan 1913:	Promoted to Vizeadmiral)
3 Oct 1917 - 14 Oct 1917:	Placed on reserve status
14 Oct 1917:	Retired
(30 Apr 1918:	Promoted to brevet Admiral)

Konteradmiral (Ingeneur) Arthur **GERLACH** (7 Mar 1890 - 24 Nov 1968)
1 Jan 1940 - 31 May 1942:	Recalled from retirement; attached to Shipbuilding Directorate, Naval High Command
2 Jun 1942 - 8 May 1945:	Director of Naval Armaments & Repair Works, Swinemünde
(1 Feb 1943:	Promoted to Konteradmiral Ingeneur)

Konteradmiral Joachim von **GERLACH** (22 Nov 1895 - 19 Mar 1979)
1 Oct 1937 - 1 Nov 1938:	Chief of Staff, Inspectorate of Torpedoes
2 May 1938 - 29 May 1938:	Acting Inspector of Torpedoes
2 Nov 1938 - 15 Apr 1940:	Chief of Torpedo Section, Naval Weapons Office, Naval High Command
16 Apr 1940 - 26 Jun 1940:	Attached to the Admiral Commanding, Norway
27 Jun 1940 - 9 Jul 1940:	Attached to Naval High Command
10 Jul 1940 - 9 Jun 1942:	Commandant, Wesermünde District
10 Jun 1942 - 20 Sep 1942:	Chief of Staff to the Naval Commander, Denmark
21 Sep 1942 - 5 Apr 1945:	Commander of Sea Defenses, Narvik
(1 Feb 1943:	Promoted to Konteradmiral)
6 Apr 1945 - 8 May 1945:	Attached to the C-in-C, Baltic Naval Group

Admiral Walter **GLADISCH** (2 Jan 1882 - 23 Mar 1954)
10 Jan 1919 - 28 Feb 1919:	Attached to the High Seas Fleet
1 Mar 1919 - 30 Sep 1919:	Staff Officer, Political Office, Naval High Command
1 Oct 1919 - 26 Sep 1922:	Department Head, Naval High Command
27 Sep 1922 - 28 Jun 1923:	Chief of Fleet Office, Naval High Command (Chief of Naval Operations)
3 Jul 1923 - 1 Dec 1923:	Commandant, Cruiser "*Arcona*"
1 Dec 1923 - 23 Mar 1925:	Commandant, Cruiser "*Amazone*"
24 Mar 1925 - 14 Oct 1928:	Chief of Staff, High Seas Fleet
(1 Oct 1928:	Promoted to Konteradmiral)
15 Oct 1928 - 31 Dec 1929:	Commander, Baltic Naval Forces
1 Jan 1930 - 28 Sep 1930:	Flag Officer, Reconnaissance Forces
29 Sep 1930 - 27 Sep 1931:	Chief of Naval Command Office, Naval High Command (Chief of Naval General Staff)
(1 Oct 1931:	Promoted to Vizeadmiral)
1 Oct 1931 - 30 Sep 1933:	C-in-C, High Seas Fleet
(30 Sep 1933:	Promoted to brevet Admiral)

30 Sep 1933:	Retired
22 Mar 1939 - 12 Sep 1939:	Placed on reserve status
13 Sep 1939 - 30 Jun 1943:	Commissioner, Berlin Prize Court
(1 Feb 1941:	Confirmed as Admiral from brevet rank)
30 Jun 1943:	Retired

Konteradmiral Eberhard **GODT** (5 Aug 1900 - 13 Sep 1995)

4 Jan 1938 - 30 Sep 1939:	Staff Officer to Flag Officer, Submarines
1 Oct 1939 - 28 Feb 1943:	Chief of Operations to Flag Officer, Submarines
(1 Mar 1943:	Promoted to Konteradmiral)
1 Mar 1943 - 31 May 1945:	Chief of Submarine Operations Office, Naval High Command

Awards: *German Cross in Gold*

Konteradmiral Herbert **GOEHLE** (4 Mar 1878 - 12 Mar 1947)

1 Oct 1933 - 31 Mar 1936:	Chief of Economics Office, Naval High Command
31 Mar 1936:	Retired
(1 May 1936:	Promoted to brevet Konteradmiral)
7 Jul 1941 - 31 Nov 1941:	Recalled; Chief of Shipbuilding Staff, Baltic
1 Dec 1941 - 29 Feb 1944:	Director of La Pallice/La Rochelle Shipyards
(1 Jul 1942:	Confirmed as Konteradmiral from brevet rank)
29 Feb 1944:	Retired

Konteradmiral Ernst **GOETTE** (26 Jan 1869 - 3 Feb 1945)

30 Jul 1914 - 14 Nov 1917:	Commandant, Battleship "*Grosser Kurfürst*"
15 Nov 1917 - 18 Aug 1918:	Deputy Commander, III. Squadron
(27 Jan 1918:	Promoted to Konteradmiral)
19 Aug 1918 - 16 Dec 1918:	Deputy Commander, IV. Squadron
4 Oct 1918 - 10 Oct 1918:	Acting Commander, IV. Squadron
13 Nov 1918 - 16 Dec 1918:	Acting Commander, IV. Squadron
17 Dec 1918 - 6 Mar 1919:	President, Wilhelmshaven Armistice Commission
7 Mar 1919 - 10 Aug 1919:	President, Naval Peace Commission, Wilhelmshaven
11 Aug 1919 - 26 Nov 1919:	Attached to the Commander, North Sea Naval Station
26 Nov 1919:	Retired

Admiralarzt (Konteradmiral) Dr. Walther **GOETTE**
(11 Mar 1894 - 26 Aug 1959)

26 Sep 1936 - 8 Jan 1940:	Medical Officer attached to the Deputy Naval Commander, North Sea & Unit Medical Officer, North Sea Naval Forces
9 Jan 1940 - 27 Apr 1941:	Chief Medical Officer, Naval Training Inspectorate
1 May 1941 - 23 Feb 1944:	Chief Medical Officer, Wesermünde Naval Hospital
(1 Apr 1943:	Promoted to Admiralarzt)
24 Feb 1944 - 21 Jan 1945:	Attached to Armed Forces Medical Service
22 Jan 1945 - 30 Apr 1945:	Attached to the Medical Service, Naval Group North
30 Apr 1945:	Retired

Konteradmiral Eberhard von **GOETZE** (13 Aug 1893 - 16 Oct 1977)

7 Oct 1938 - 28 Oct 1938:	Chief of Staff, Inspectorate of Naval Artillery
10 Oct 1938 - 22 Oct 1938:	Acting Inspector of Naval Artillery
29 Oct 1938 - 30 Apr 1940:	Chief of Artillery Testing Command for Ships
1 May 1940 - 30 Jun 1940:	Chief of Staff, Inspectorate of Naval Artillery
1 Jul 1940 - 2 Aug 1943:	Chief of Mechanized Artillery Section, Naval High Command
(1 Mar 1942:	Promoted to Konteradmiral)
1 Oct 1940 - 31 Mar 1941:	Chief of Ships Artillery Testing Command
3 Aug 1943 - 28 Feb 1945:	Chief of Artillery Development Office, Naval High Command
28 Feb 1945:	Retired

Konteradmiral Wilhelm **GOETZE** (3 Oct 1873 - 26 Sep 1954)

2 Aug 1914 - 11 Nov 1914:	Chief of Central Welfare Office, Elbe
12 Nov 1914 - 13 Aug 1915:	Commander, Ships Training Division
13 Aug 1915 - 30 Jun 1917:	Commandant, Heavy Cruiser "*Freya*"
1 Jul 1917 - 20 Dec 1918:	Commander, II. Torpedo Division
21 Dec 1918 - 30 Jan 1919:	Attached to the Commander, North Sea Naval Station
(23 Dec 1919:	Promoted to brevet Konteradmiral)
30 Jan 1919:	Retired

Konteradmiral Lothar von **GOHREN** (16 Mar 1874 - 31 Mar 1923)

1 Apr 1914 - 2 Aug 1915:	First Officer, Battleship "*Thüringen*"

3 Aug 1915 - 16 Feb 1916:	Commandant, Light Cruiser "*Stuttgart*"
17 Feb 1916 - 10 Jul 1919:	Attached to Budget Department, Naval High Command
10 Jul 1919 - 30 Sep 1919:	Director of Budget Department, Naval High Command
1 Oct 1919 - 31 Jan 1921:	Chief of Naval Budget Office, Ministry of Defense
1 Feb 1921 - 21 Feb 1921:	Attached to the Commander-in-Chief of the Navy
22 Feb 1921 - 31 Mar 1923:	Chief of Naval Office, Hamburg
(1 Oct 1921:	Promoted to Konteradmiral)

Vizeadmiral Friedrich **GÖTTING** (7 Feb 1886 - 3 Jan 1946)

1 Jun 1929 - 4 Oct 1931:	Chief of Armed Forces Office, Ministry of Defense
5 Oct 1931 - 26 Sep 1933:	Commandant, Battleshiip "*Schleswig-Holstein*"
29 Sep 1933 - 28 Sep 1934:	Commandant of Swinemünde
(1 Oct 1934:	Promoted to Konteradmiral)
3 Oct 1934 - 30 Sep 1936:	Inspector of Torpedoes & Mines
9 Jul 1935 - 10 Aug 1935:	Acting Inspector of Naval Training
19 Jul 1936 - 15 Aug 1936:	Acting Inspector of Naval Training
1 Oct 1936 - 20 Dec 1939:	Inspector of Torpedoes
(1 Oct 1937:	Promoted to Vizeadmiral)
1 Oct 1936 - 20 May 1937:	Acting Inspector of Mines
1 Oct 1937 - 31 Oct 1938:	Acting Inspector of Naval Communications
1 Oct 1937 - 20 Dec 1939:	President of Torpedo Testing Commission
1 Oct 1937 - 31 Oct 1938:	President of Naval Communications Equipment Testing Commission
3 Jan 1939 - 15 Jan 1939:	Acting Commander, Baltic Naval Station
28 Dec 1939 - 23 Jun 1940:	Chief of Torpedo Office, Naval High Command
24 Jun 1940 - 31 Aug 1942:	Attached to the Commander-in-Chief of the Navy
1 Sep 1942 - 28 Feb 1943:	Commander of Coastal Defenses, Eastern Baltic & Fortress, Commandant of Gotenhafen
2 Mar 1943 - 31 May 1943:	Attached to Baltic Naval Group
31 May 1943:	Retired

Admiral Max von **GRAPOW** (18 Apr 1861 - 4 Mar 1924)

(27 Jan 1909:	Promoted to Konteradmiral)

(10 Apr 1911:	Promoted to Vizeadmiral)
11 Apr 1911 - 18 Sep 1915:	Director of Nautical Department, Naval Office
5 Aug 1914 - 23 Feb 1915:	Commander, V. Squadron
(23 Mar 1915:	Promoted to brevet Admiral)
18 Sep 1915:	Retired

Konteradmiral Kurt **GRAßHOFF** (29 May 1869 - 4 Jul 1952)

4 Nov 1911 - 9 Jun 1917:	Section Chief, Admiralty
11 Jun 1917 - 24 Jul 1917:	Acting Commandant, Battleship "*Friedrich der Große*"
26 Jul 1917 - 5 Jan 1918:	Commandant, Battleship "*Kaiserin*"
12 Aug 1917 - 7 Sep 1917:	Acting Deputy Commander, IV. Squadron
6 Jan 1918 - 28 Aug 1918:	Attached to the U-Boat Training School
29 Aug 1918 - 9 Oct 1918:	Commander of U-Boats, Mediterranean Sea
10 Oct 1918 - 4 Dec 1918:	Sick leave
5 Dec 1918 - 4 Nov 1919:	Attached to the Commander, North Sea Naval Station
5 Nov 1919 - 4 Mar 1920:	Attached to Naval High Command
(29 Nov 1919:	Promoted to brevet Konteradmiral)
4 Mar 1920:	Retired

Vizeadmiral Werner **GRASSMANN** (9 Mar 1888 - 20 Oct 1943)

1 Jul 1933 - 30 Sep 1934:	Chief of Shipyards Office, Naval High Command
1 Oct 1934 - 13 Sep 1935:	Chief of General Artillery Office, Naval High Command
26 Sep 1935 - 27 Sep 1937:	Commandant, Ships Artillery School
30 Sep 1937 - 22 Jan 1939:	Inspector of Naval Artillery & President of Ships & Land Artillery Testing Commission
(1 Oct 1937:	Promoted to Konteradmiral)
23 Jan 1939 - 2 Apr 1939:	Attached to the Commander-in-Chief of the Navy
3 Apr 1939 - 30 Jun 1939:	Chief of Shipbuilding Office, Naval High Command
1 Jul 1939 - 22 Aug 1939:	Attached to the Commander-in-Chief of the Navy
23 Aug 1939 - 3 Jun 1941:	Chief of Naval Command Office, Naval High Command
(1 Jan 1940:	Promoted to Vizeadmiral)
7 Jun 1941 - 28 Feb 1943:	Commander of Coastal Defenses, Western Baltic

4 Jun 1941 - 7 Sep 1941:	Acting Inspector of Naval Artillery
1 Mar 1943 - 31 May 1943:	Attached to the C-in-C, Baltic Naval Group
31 May 1943:	Retired
1 Jun 1943:	Recalled to reserve status; no appointment conferred

Konteradmiral Willibald **GRAUER** (3 Jun 1869 - 21 Oct 1925)

1 Apr 1907 - 12 May 1915:	Attached to the Pensions Office, Naval Office
13 May 1915 - 22 Jun 1919:	Director of Pensions Office, Naval Office
23 Jun 1919 - 4 Mar 1920:	Attached to the Ministry of Labor
(4 Mar 1920:	Promoted to brevet Konteradmiral)
4 Mar 1920:	Retired

Admiralstabsarzt (Vizeadmiral) Dr. Emil **GREUL** (29 Dec 1895 - ?)

2 Oct 1935 - 31 Mar 1939:	Chief Medical Officer, Cuxhaven Naval Hospital & Garrison
1 Apr 1939 - 15 Apr 1941:	Chief Medical Officer, Wesermünde Naval Hospital
16 Apr 1941 - 30 Sep 1943:	Commandant, Naval Medical Academy
(1 Sep 1942:	Promoted to Admiralarzt)
(1 Oct 1943:	Promoted to Admiralstabsarzt)
1 Oct 1943 - 23 May 1945:	Chief of Naval Medical Service

Awards: *Knight's Cross of the War Merit Cross with Swords*

Admiral Dr. Otto **GROOS** (17 Jul 1882 - 29 May 1970)

10 Jan 1926 - 30 Jun 1927:	Commandant, Cruiser "*Hamburg*"
1 Jul 1927 - 5 Oct 1927:	Attached to the Commander-in-Chief of the Navy
6 Oct 1927 - 31 Mar 1929:	Instructor, NCO Training Course
1 Apr 1929 - 8 Apr 1931:	Chief of NCO Training Course
(1 Dec 1930:	Promoted to Konteradmiral)
9 Apr 1931 - 25 Sep 1931:	Chief of Staff, Baltic Naval Station
28 Sep 1931 - 28 Sep 1934:	Chief of Naval Command Office, Naval High Command (Chief of Naval General Staff)
(1 Apr 1934:	Promoted to Vizeadmiral)
30 Sep 1934:	Retired
22 Mar 1939:	Recalled to reserve status
25 Jun 1940 - 30 Jun 1944:	Chief of Special Staff for Economic Warfare, Armed Forces High Command (OKW)
(1 Sep 1941:	Promoted to Admiral)

16 Oct 1944 - 3 May 1945:	Chief of Special Staff for Economic Warfare, Armed Forces High Command (OKW)

Konteradmiral (Ingeneur) Helmut **GRUBE** (7 May 1893 - 5 Dec 1978)
3 Oct 1935 - 30 Sep 1938:	Advisor, Ships Equipment Inspectorate
10 Oct 1938 - 13 Nov 1939:	Advisor, Testing Command for New Ships
14 Nov 1939 - 7 Jan 1941:	Chief of Staff, Testing Command for New Ships
8 Jan 1941 - 19 Jan 1943:	Section Chief, Shipbuilding Directorate, Naval High Command
(1 Feb 1942:	Promoted to Konteradmiral Ingeneur)
20 Jan 1943 - 31 Dec 1944:	Engineer Officer, Naval Group West & Director of Supply Office, Wilhelmshaven Shipyards
1 Feb 1945 - 8 May 1945:	Chief of Testing Commission for New Ships

Awards: *German Cross in Silver*

Konteradmiral Ferdinand von **GRUMME-DOUGLAS**
(5 Jun 1860 - 18 Jul 1937)
(27 Jan 1910:	Promoted to Brevet Konteradmiral)
Aug 1914 - 14 May 1917:	Reserve status, no appointment conferred
14 May 1917:	Retired

Marinegeneralstabsarzt (Konteradmiral) Dr. Oscar **GUDDEN**
(20 Nov 1862 - 24 Jan 1944)
17 Nov 1916:	Retired
(28 Apr 1922:	Promoted to brevet Marinegeneralstabsarzt)

Admiral Günther **GUSE** (30 Aug 1886 - 6 May 1953)
27 Sep 1930 - 26 Sep 1932:	Chief of Staff, High Seas Fleet
27 Sep 1932 - 28 Sep 1934:	Chief of Fleet Office, Naval High Command (Chief of Naval Operations)
29 Sep 1934 - 31 Oct 1938:	Chief of Naval Command Office, Naval High Command (Chief of Naval General Staff)
(1 Apr 1935:	Promoted to Konteradmiral)
(1 Nov 1937:	Promoted to Vizeadmiral)
1 Nov 1938 - 15 Jun 1941:	Inspector, Naval Communications Inspectorate
(1 Jan 1940:	Promoted to Admiral)
28 Jan 1939 - 5 Mar 1939:	Acting Inspector of Naval Training
15 May 1939 - 27 May 1939:	Acting Admiral Commanding, Baltic Naval Station

1 Jan 1940 - 15 Feb 1940:	Deputy Admiral Commanding, Baltic Naval Station
16 Feb 1940 - 20 Sep 1940:	Acting Admiral Commanding, Baltic Naval Station
21 Sep 1940 - 8 Mar 1943:	Admiral Commanding, Baltic Naval Station
9 Mar 1943 - 31 May 1943:	Attached to the Commander-in-Chief of the Navy
31 May 1943:	Retired
1 Jun 1943:	Recalled to reserve status; no appointment conferred

Awards: *German Cross in Silver*

Admiral **GUSTAV V**, King of Sweden (16 Jun 1858 - 29 Oct 1950)
Admiral à la Suite (Honorary title)
Awards: *Order of the Black Eagle; Royal Bavarian St.Hubertus Order; Royal Saxon Order of the Diamond Crown*

Konteradmiral Karl-Otto **GUTJAHR** (29 Jun 1895 - 21 Jun 1975)

1 Oct 1938 - 6 Nov 1939:	Advisor, Naval Personnel Office
7 Nov 1939 - 8 Mar 1943:	Section Chief, Naval Weapons Office, Naval High Command & Chief of Torpedo Development Commission, Ministry of Armaments
24 Jun 1940 - 7 Aug 1940:	Acting Chief of Torpedo Office, Naval High Command
9 Mar 1943 - 31 May 1945:	Chief of Torpedo Office, Naval High Command
(1 Apr 1943:	Promoted to Konteradmiral)

Awards: *German Cross in Silver*

Konteradmiral Hans **GYGAS** (27 May 1872 - 31 May 1963)

17 Feb 1919 - 23 May 1919:	Commander, 1. Marine Regiment, Kiel Marine Division
24 May 1919 - 12 Sep 1919:	Commandant of Kiel
13 Sep 1919 - 22 Nov 1919:	Attached to the Commander, Baltic Naval Station
22 Nov 1919:	Retired
(28 Feb 1920:	Promoted to brevet Konteradmiral)

Admiral **HAAKON VII**, King of Norway (3 Aug 1872 - 21 Sep 1957)
Admiral à la Suite (Honorary title)
Awards: *Order of the Black Eagle*

Generalmajor der Marinefestungspionere Franz **HABICHT**
(6 Oct 1891 - 28 Dec 1972)
26 Sep 1938 - 14 May 1940:	Advisor, Naval Weapons Office, Naval High Command
15 May 1940 - 1 Jun 1944:	Chief of Naval Pioneers Staff to Admiral Commanding, France
1 Jun 1944 - 23 Jul 1945:	Chief of Pioneer & Fortress Office, Naval High Command & Inspector of Naval Pioneers
(1 Jul 1944:	Promoted to Generalmajor der Marinefestungspionere)

Awards: *German Cross in Silver*

Konteradmiral Erich **HAEKER** (30 Jun 1886 - 27 Apr 1958)
15 Jan 1935 - 28 Feb 1937:	Recalled from retirement; Naval Economics Officer, Economics Inspectorate VI
1 Mar 1937 - 27 Mar 1938:	Advisor, Naval Defense Office, Naval High Command
28 Mar 1938 - 21 Jul 1940:	Commander, Swinemünde Recruiting Command
22 Jul 1940 - 27 May 1942:	Director of Armaments & Navigation Office, Wilhelmshaven Shipyards
(1 Feb 1942:	Promoted to Konteradmiral)
28 May 1942 - 23 Aug 1942:	Director of Nikolayev Shipyards
24 Aug 1942 - 17 Oct 1944:	Director of Armaments & Navigation Office, Wilhelmshaven Shipyards
18 Oct 1944 - 31 Jan 1945:	Attached to the C-in-C, North Sea Naval Group
31 Jan 1945:	Retired

Konteradmiral Max **HAHN** (23 Jan 1870 - 9 May 1944)
21 Sep 1912 - 5 Feb 1916:	Commandant, Heavy Cruiser "*Von der Tann*"
18 Mar 1916 - 23 Dec 1916:	Commandant, Battleship "*Bayern*"
25 Dec 1916 - 30 Nov 1917:	Commander, IV. Reconnaissance Group
(14 Oct 1917:	Promoted to Konteradmiral)
2 Dec 1917 - 13 May 1919:	Inspector of Ships Artillery
14 May 1919 - 30 Sep 1919:	Placed on inactive status
30 Sep 1919:	Retired

Konteradmiral (Ingeneur) Ernst **HALWE** (17 Jan 1886 - 6 Feb 1961)
1 Oct 1934 - 9 Sep 1935:	Station Engineer, Baltic Naval Station
10 Sep 1935 - 27 Sep 1937:	Chief of Staff, Ships Equipment Inspectorate
15 Nov 1935 - 2 Jun 1936:	Chief Engineer, North Sea Naval Station
1 Oct 1937 - 2 Nov 1942:	Commander of Defense Economics Office, Kiel
(1 Apr 1942:	Promoted to Konteradmiral Ingeneur)
14 Nov 1942 - 16 May 1943:	Director of Naval Armaments & Repair Works, Salamis
25 May 1943 - 31 Jan 1945:	Chief of Liaison Office, Armaments Inspectorate Prague
1 Feb 1945 - 8 May 1945:	Plenipotentiary for Motor Vehicle Procurement, Protectorate of Bohemia-Moravia

Waffen Konteradmiral Hans **HAMELAU** (13 Jun 1886 - 7 Dec 1961)
7 Nov 1939 - 5 Oct 1941:	General Advisor, Naval Weapons Office, Naval High Command
6 Oct 1941 - 4 Oct 1943:	Commandant of Naval Artillery Office, Naval Artillery Arsenal Kiel-Dietrichsdorf
5 Oct 1943 - 8 May 1945:	Inspector of Naval Testing
(1 Jun 1944:	Promoted to Waffen Konteradmiral)

Awards: *German Cross in Silver*

Vizeadmiral Heinrich **HANKE** (16 Dec 1890 - 23 Apr 1945)
14 Oct 1936 - 2 Aug 1943:	Chief of Artillery Development & Construction Office, Naval High Command
(1 Nov 1939:	Promoted to Konteradmiral)
(1 Feb 1942:	Promoted to Vizeadmiral)
25 Dec 1939 - 16 Jan 1940:	Acting Chief of Artillery Office, Naval High Command
3 Aug 1943 - 30 Sep 1943:	Attached to the Commander-in-Chief of the Navy
30 Sep 1943:	Retired
1 Oct 1943:	Recalled to reserve status; no appointment conferred

Admiral Gottfried **HANSEN** (8 Nov 1881 - 16 Jul 1976)
15 Mar 1921 - 5 Jan 1925:	Chief of Naval Weapons Office, Naval High Command

8 Jan 1925 - 31 Jan 1926:	Commandant, Battleship *"Braunschweig"*
1 Feb 1926 - 30 Sep 1926:	Commandant, Battleship *"Schleswig-Holstein"*
1 Oct 1926 - 30 Sep 1928:	Inspector of Naval Artillery
(1 Jan 1928:	Promoted to Konteradmiral)
1 Oct 1928 - 30 Sep 1932:	Commander, Baltic Naval Station
(1 Oct 1930:	Promoted to Vizeadmiral)
(30 Sep 1932:	Promoted to brevet Admiral)
30 Sep 1932:	Retired
24 May 1939:	Recalled to reserve status
17 Nov 1941 - 30 Jun 1943:	Chief of Luftwaffe Training Staff
(1 Sep 1942:	Confirmed as Admiral from brevet rank)
1 Jul 1943 - 31 Jul 1943:	Attached to the C-in-C, Baltic Naval Group
31 Jul 1943:	Retired

Konteradmiral Victor **HARDER** (21 Nov 1870 - 19 Sep 1933)

6 Jan 1913 - 28 Jul 1915:	Commandant, Light Cruiser *"Stralsund"*
8 Aug 1915 - 1 Jun 1916:	Commandant, Heavy Cruiser *"Lützow"*
25 Aug 1916 - 22 Sep 1916:	Acting Commandant, Battleship *"Prinzregent Luitpold"*
19 Oct 1916 - 5 Aug 1918:	Commandant, Battleship *"Baden"*
6 Aug 1918 - 28 Nov 1918:	Commander, II. Reconnaissance Group
30 Nov 1918 - 30 Jun 1919:	Commander of Security Forces, North Sea
6 Jan 1919 - 30 Jun 1919:	C-in-C, High Seas Fleet
1 Jul 1919 - 22 Nov 1919:	Attached to the Commander, North Sea Naval Station
22 Nov 1919:	Retired
(26 Jan 1920:	Promoted to brevet Konteradmiral)

Admiralarzt (Konteradmiral) Dr. Werner d'**HARGUES**
(28 Nov 1890 - 2 Aug 1972)

26 Sep 1935 - 24 Oct 1938:	Chief Medical Officer, Inspectorate of Naval Training
26 Sep 1935 - 5 Apr 1936:	Chief Medical Officer, Inspectorate of Torpedoes & Mines
11 Aug 1937 - 11 Sep 1937:	Chief Medical Officer, Baltic Naval Station
11 Feb 1938 - 22 Feb 1938:	Chief Medical Officer, Baltic Naval Station
25 Oct 1938 - 9 Feb 1941:	Chief Medical Officer, Wilhelmshaven Naval Hospital
(1 Jan 1941:	Promoted to Admiralarzt)
31 Jul 1939 - 20 Aug 1939:	Chief Medical Officer, North Sea Naval Forces

13 Feb 1941 - 31 Aug 1942:	Chief Medical Officer, Admiral Commanding, France
1 Sep 1942 - 21 Jun 1943:	Chief Medical Officer, North Sea Naval Station
22 Jun 1943 - 31 Mar 1944:	Chief Medical Officer, North Sea Naval Group
1 Apr 1944 - 31 May 1944:	Attached to the North Sea Naval Group
1 Jun 1944 - 17 Oct 1944:	Chief Medical Officer, Eindhoven Naval Hospital
18 Oct 1944 - 8 May 1945:	Chief Medical Officer, Arendsee Naval Hospital

Wirkliche Geheime Admiralitätsrat (Konteradmiral) Theodor **HARMS** (24 May 1853 - 27 Nov 1931)

1 Jun 1906 - 23 Aug 1919:	Chief of Section B VII, Naval Office
(16 Oct 1916:	Appointed Wirkliche Geheime Admiralitätsrat)
4 Dec 1918 - 6 Feb 1919:	Acting Director of Construction Administration Section, Naval Office
23 Aug 1919:	Retired

Konteradmiral Hans **HARTMANN** (16 Jan 1897 - 9 Mar 1976)

29 Aug 1938 - 30 Nov 1939:	Commander, 5. Destroyer Division
1 Dec 1939 - 4 Apr 1940:	Staff Officer to Flag Officer, Battleships
5 Apr 1940 - 19 Jun 1940:	Chief of Staff to Naval Commander South Norway
20 Jun 1940 - 3 Dec 1941:	Staff Officer to Admiral Commanding, Norway
4 Dec 1941 - 9 Sep 1942:	Commander, 3. Security Division
12 Sep 1942 - 15 Nov 1942:	Attached to the Flag Officer, Cruisers
16 Nov 1942 - 1 Feb 1943:	Commandant, Heavy Cruiser *"Admiral Hipper"*
22 Feb 1943 - 15 Mar 1943:	Chief of Military Office, Shipbuilding Directorate, Naval High Command
16 Mar 1943 - 6 Jun 1943:	Chief of Staff, High Seas Fleet
(1 Jun 1943:	Promoted to Konteradmiral)
7 Jun 1943 - 14 Mar 1944:	Special Advisor for Personnel Savings
15 Mar 1944 - 16 Oct 1944:	Commander of Sea Defenses, Attika
7 Nov 1944 - 30 Jan 1945:	Commander, 1. Naval Rifle Brigade
31 Jan 1945 - 28 Feb 1945:	Commander, 1. Naval Division
9 Mar 1945 - 24 Mar 1945:	Special Advisor for Personnel Savings
4 Apr 1945 - 31 Aug 1945:	Commander of Sea Defenses, Oslo Fjord

Awards: *German Cross in Gold*

Konteradmiral Johannes **HARTOG** (22 Apr 1867 - 8 Jan 1947)
1 Oct 1911 - 1 Aug 1914:	Commander, 1. Torpedo Division
1 Aug 1914 - 6 Sep 1914:	Deputy Commander of Torpedo Boats
7 Sep 1914 - 3 Apr 1916:	Commander of Torpedo Boats
3 Apr 1916 - 3 Dec 1917:	Commandant, Heavy Cruiser "*Derfflinger*"
5 Dec 1917 - 30 Nov 1918:	Deputy Commander, I. Squadron
3 Aug 1918 - 8 Sep 1918:	Acting Commander, I. Squadron
23 Sep 1918 - 2 Oct 1918:	Acting Commander, I. Squadron
(27 Jan 1918:	Promoted to Konteradmiral)
1 Dec 1918 - 7 Apr 1919:	Attached to the Commander, Baltic Naval Station
7 Apr 1919:	Retired

Konteradmiral Gustav **HASS** (11 Mar 1872 - 1 Mar 1932)
5 Jun 1913 - 7 Nov 1914:	Chief of Marine Artillery Section, Tsingtau
7 Nov 1914 - 25 Jan 1920:	Prisoner of war
26 Jan 1920 - 15 Jul 1920:	Attached to the Commander, North Sea Naval Station
(15 Jul 1920:	Promoted to brevet Konteradmiral)
15 Jul 1920:	Retired

Konteradmiral Wilhelm von **HAXTHAUSEN** (30 Aug 1874 - 1 Mar 1936)
14 Mar 1919 - 29 Feb 1920:	Battalion Commander, III. Marine Brigade
5 Mar 1920 - 23 Mar 1920:	Commander, Baltic Standing Naval Force Division
24 Mar 1920:	Retired
15 Jun 1920 - 27 Mar 1923:	Recalled; Commandant, Kiel Arsenal
(9 Sep 1922:	Promoted to Konteradmiral)
31 Mar 1923:	Retired

Vizeadmiral Georg **HEBBINGHAUS** (12 Oct 1866 - 11 Jun 1944)
1 Oct 1912 - 25 Dec 1914:	Chief of Staff, Baltic Naval Station
(15 Nov 1913:	Promoted to Konteradmiral)
26 Dec 1914 - 27 Aug 1915:	Commander, II. Reconnaissance Group
28 Aug 1915 - 30 Sep 1918:	Director of General Naval Department, Naval Office
(25 Nov 1916:	Promoted to Vizeadmiral)
1 Oct 1918 - 28 Nov 1918:	Attached to the Secretary of State, Naval Office
28 Nov 1918 - 27 Jun 1919:	Placed on inactive status
27 Jun 1919:	Retired

Admiral August von **HEERINGEN** (26 Nov 1855 - 29 Sep 1927)
(7 Jul 1906:	Promoted to Konteradmiral)
(5 Sep 1909:	Promoted to Vizeadmiral)
(27 Jan 1913:	Promoted to Admiral)
13 Apr 1913 - 15 Jul 1914:	Commander, North Sea Naval Station
15 Jul 1914:	Retired; Admiral à la Suite

Admiralarzt (Konteradmiral) Dr. Hellmut **HEIM** (13 Jan 1900 - 20 Aug 1986)
30 Sep 1935 - 23 May 1940:	Chief Surgeon, Kiel-Wik Naval Hospital
24 May 1940 - 24 Jun 1940:	Attached to the Army Medical Inspectorate
24 Jun 1940 - 19 Sep 1943:	Chief Medical Officer, Hardinghen Naval Hospital
20 Sep 1943 - 17 Sep 1944:	Chief Medical Officer, Paris Naval Hospital
18 Sep 1944 - 1 Oct 1944:	Chief Medical Officer, Hospital Ship "*Monte Rosa*"
2 Oct 1944 - 2 Nov 1944:	Chief Medical Officer, Ambulance Ship "*General Steuben*"
3 Nov 1944 - Aug 1946:	Chief Medical Officer, Malente Naval Hospital
(1 Dec 1944:	Promoted to Admiralarzt)
1943 - 1945:	Consultant Surgeon of the Navy

Konteradmiral (Ingeneur) Julius **HEIMBERG** (19 Sep 1897 - 22 Feb 1975)
1 Dec 1938 - 20 Jan 1941:	Section Chief, Shipbuilding Directorate, Naval High Command
22 Jan 1941 - 12 Jun 1941:	Fleet Engineer attached to Deputy C-in-C, High Seas Fleet
13 Jun 1941 - 31 Jul 1943:	Fleet Engineer, High Seas Fleet
16 Aug 1943 - 31 Oct 1944:	Member of Shipbuilding Commission, Naval High Command
(1 Nov 1944:	Promoted to Konteradmiral Ingeneur)
1 Nov 1944 - 10 Jul 1945:	Chief of Shipbuilding Office, Naval High Command

Vizeadmiral Heino von **HEIMBURG** (24 Oct 1889 - Oct 1945)
29 Sep 1933 - 3 Oct 1937:	Commander of Elbe & Weser Estuaries Defenses
6 Oct 1937 - 31 Dec 1939:	Judge, Supreme Military Tribunal
(1 Aug 1939:	Promoted to Konteradmiral)
1 Jan 1940 - 29 Aug 1942:	Inspector, Bremen Recruiting Inspectorate

(1 Apr 1942:   Promoted to Vizeadmiral)
31 Aug 1942:   Retired
1 Sep 1942:   Recalled to reserve status; no appointment conferred
31 May 1943:   Retired

Awards: *Pour le Mérite*

Admiral Oskar **HEINECKE** (13 Jul 1878 - 25 Jan 1945)
3 Oct 1919 - 10 Mar 1920:   Commandant, Cruiser "*Königsberg*"
11 Mar 1920 - 31 May 1920: Placed on inactive status
1 Jun 1920 - 18 Oct 1922:   Fortress Commandant, Cuxhaven
19 Oct 1922 - 29 Mar 1925: Inspector, Naval Depot Inspectorate
30 Mar 1925 - 3 Oct 1927:   Inspector of Torpedoes & Mines
1 Jul 1925 - 18 Aug 1925:   Acting Inspector of Naval Training
5 Jan 1927 - 21 Feb 1927:   Acting Inspector of Naval Training
1 Aug 1927 - 11 Aug 1927:   Acting Inspector of Naval Training
(1 Oct 1926:   Promoted to Konteradmiral)
4 Oct 1927 - 31 Dec 1927:   Attached to the Commander, Baltic Naval Station
31 Dec 1927:   Retired
(25 Jan 1937:   Promoted to brevet Vizeadmiral)
(19 Aug 1939:   Promoted to brevet Admiral)

Awards: *Pour le Mérite*

Konteradmiral Paul **HEINRICH** (6 Apr 1871 - 6 Oct 1927)
1 Aug 1914 - 25 Aug 1915:   Chief of Staff, C-in-C Baltic Fleet
3 Sep 1915 - 1 Apr 1916:   Commandant, Heavy Cruiser "*Derfflinger*"
4 Apr 1916 - 4 Jun 1917:   Commodore, Deputy Commander of Torpedo Boats
26 Jun 1916 - 6 Jul 1916:   Acting Commander of Torpedo Boats
5 Jun 1917 - 30 Nov 1918:   Commodore, Commander of Torpedo Boats
1 Dec 1918 - 14 Dec 1918:   Attached to the Secretary of State, Naval Office
15 Dec 1918 - 12 Feb 1919: Acting Inspector of U-Boats
13 Feb 1919 - 30 Mar 1919: Attached to the Naval Office
31 Mar 1919 - 12 Jan 1920: President, Navy Peace Commission
(29 Nov 1919:   Promoted to Konteradmiral)
13 Jan 1920 - 5 Mar 1920:   Attached to the Commander-in-Chief of the Navy
5 Mar 1920:   Retired

Konteradmiral (Ingeneur) Walter **HEINZE** (6 Nov 1878 - 5 Jan 1948)
1 Feb 1922 - 11 Oct 1925:	Commandant, Kiel-Wik Naval School
15 Oct 1925 - 7 Oct 1928:	Chief Engineer, Baltic Naval Station
8 Oct 1928 - 31 Oct 1928:	Attached to the Commander, Baltic Naval Station
(31 Oct 1928:	Promoted to brevet Konteradmiral Ingeneur)
31 Oct 1928:	Retired

Marineobergeneralarzt (Konteradmiral) Prof.Dr. Heinrich **HELFERICH** (4 May 1851 - 18 Dec 1945)
(10 Mar 1906:	Promoted to Marineobergeneralarzt)
1914 - Nov 1918:	Recalled from retirement; Consulting Surgeon, XI. Military District Military Hospital
Nov 1918:	Retired

Admiral Konrad von **HENKEL-GEBHARDI** (4 Jun 1860 - 16 Jun 1923)
(19 Nov 1910:	Promoted to Konteradmiral)
1 Jul 1910 - 16 Oct 1918:	Chief of Kiel Shipyards
(14 Jul 1914:	Promoted to Vizeadmiral)
(11 Jun 1918:	Promoted to brevet Admiral)
17 Oct 1918 - 13 Dec 1918:	Attached to the Commander, Baltic Naval Station
13 Dec 1918:	Retired

Konteradmiral Walter **HENNECKE** (23 May 1898 - 1 Jan 1984)
7 Nov 1938 - 29 Jul 1940:	First Officer, Light Cruiser "*Nürnberg*"
11 Nov 1938 - 19 Nov 1938:	Acting Commandant, Light Cruiser "*Nürnberg*"
30 Jul 1940 - 4 Apr 1943:	Commandant, Ships Artillery School
Aug 1940 - Nov 1940:	Commander of Towing Units, Transport Fleet B
24 May 1941 - 14 Oct 1941:	Commandant, Battleship "*Schleswig-Holstein*"
6 May 1943 - 26 Jun 1944:	Commander of Sea Defenses, Normandy
(1 Mar 1944:	Promoted to Konteradmiral)
26 Jun 1944:	Captured in Normandy; prisoner of war

Awards: *Knight's Cross*

Konteradmiral Heinz von **HENNIG** (10 May 1883 - 29 Nov 1947)
28 Sep 1927 - 10 Nov 1929:	Commandant, Ems Estuary Defenses
18 Nov 1929 - 28 Sep 1931:	Chief of Staff, Naval Training Inspectorate

(30 Sep 1931: Promoted to brevet Konteradmiral)
30 Sep 1931: Retired
7 Apr 1940 - 31 Mar 1946: Recalled; Chief of Station Library, Baltic Naval Command

Konteradmiral Hans **HENNING** (27 Jun 1895 - 16 Jan 1948)
12 Apr 1939 -3 Sep 1939: Naval Attaché, Paris
4 Sep 1939 - 10 Oct 1939: Attached to the Commander-in-Chief of the Army
11 Oct 1939 - 11 Jan 1943: Naval Attaché, Copenhagen
(1 Sep 1942: Promoted to Konteradmiral)
8 Apr 1940 - 9 Jun 1942: Chief of Staff to Naval Commander, Denmark
16 Apr 1941 - 3 Jun 1941: Deputy Naval Commander, Denmark
12 Jan 1943 - 8 May 1945: Naval Attaché, Lisbon

Konteradmiral Dr. Reinhold **HENRICI** (9 Apr 1890 - 2 Jun 1948)
1 Aug 1939 - 20 Jul 1940: Chief of Production Section for Industrial Armaments, Naval High Command
21 Jul 1940 - 4 Dec 1942: Inspector, Armaments Inspectorate Southwest France
15 Dec 1942 - 30 Apr 1945: Group Chief, Ministry of Armaments
(1 Feb 1944: Promoted to Konteradmiral)
30 Apr 1945: Retired

Vizeadmiral **HENRIK**, Prince of the Netherlands (19 Apr 1876 - 3 Jul 1934)
Vizeadmiral à la Suite (Honorary title)
Awards: *Order of the Black Eagle with Chain; Royal Bavarian St. Hubertus Order; Grand Cross of the Mecklenburg Griffin Order*

Konteradmiral Carl **HERING** (7 Apr 1868 - 25 Aug 1948)
8 Oct 1912 - 5 Nov 1918: Director of Friedrichsort Torpedo Works
12 Aug 1914 - 2 Nov 1914: Inspector of Torpedoes
(18 Sep 1918: Promoted to Konteradmiral)
6 Nov 1918 - 9 Dec 1918: Attached to the Inspectorate of Torpedoes
10 Dec 1918 - 4 Aug 1919: Attached to the Commander, Baltic Naval Station
4 Aug 1919: Retired

Konteradmiral Friedrich **HERMANN** (12 Sep 1880 - 24 Dec 1937)
25 May 1921 - 1 Jul 1923: Commandant, Cruiser *"Arcona"*

3 Jul 1923 - 19 Sep 1926:	Commandant of Pillau
30 May 1925 - 7 Oct 1925:	Commander, Coastal Defense Detachment V
18 Oct 1926 - 3 Oct 1927:	Harbor Captain of Kiel, Naval Commissioner, Kaiser-Wilhelm Canal
4 Oct 1927 - 31 Dec 1927:	Attached to the Commander, Baltic Naval Station
(31 Dec 1927:	Promoted to brevet Konteradmiral)
31 Dec 1927:	Retired

Konteradmiral Willy **HERMANN** (8 Apr 1881 - 30 Dec 1944)

3 Apr 1927 - 29 Feb 1928:	Attached to Wilhelmshaven Shipyards
1 Mar 1928 - 4 Dec 1929:	Commandant, Kiel Naval Arsenal
4 Dec 1929 - 31 Dec 1929:	Attached to the Commander, Baltic Naval Station
(31 Dec 1929:	Promoted to brevet Konteradmiral)
31 Dec 1929:	Retired

Konteradmiral Hans **HERR** (16 Sep 1871 - 7 Feb 1936)

3 Sep 1914 - 21 Dec 1914:	Commander, Marine Artillery Brigade
22 Dec 1914 - 30 Sep 1917:	Commander of Aviation, Flanders Marine Corps
26 Oct 1917 - 24 Mar 1918:	Commandant, Battleship "*Thüringen*"
25 Mar 1918 - 30 Nov 1918:	Commandant, Battleship "*Ostfriesland*"
1 Dec 1918 - 15 Apr 1919:	Attached to the Commander, North Sea Naval Station
16 Apr 1919 - 19 Oct 1919:	Commander, Weser Estuary Defenses
20 Oct 1919 - 24 Nov 1919:	Attached to the Commander, North Sea Naval Station
24 Nov 1919:	Retired
(26 Jan 1920:	Promoted to brevet Konteradmiral)

Wirkliche Geheime Rat (Konteradmiral) Dr. Paul **HERZ**
(21 Apr 1854 - Sep 1930)

(1 Oct 1900:	Appointed Wirkliche Geheime Rat)
13 Oct 1900 - 1916:	Senate President, Imperial Military Court
1916:	Retired

Konteradmiral Carl **HEUSER** (13 Mar 1867 - 6 Jul 1942)

19 Aug 1913 - 17 Feb 1917:	Commandant, Battleship "*Prinzregent Luitpold*"

18 Feb 1917 - 23 May 1918:	Director of Ship Construction Bureau, Naval Office
(14 Oct 1917:	Promoted to Konteradmiral)
24 May 1918 - 31 Jul 1919:	Director of Nautical Department, Naval Office
1 Aug 1919 - 5 Sep 1919:	Attached to the Commander-in-Chief of the Navy
5 Sep 1919 - 5 Nov 1919:	Placed on inactive status
5 Nov 1919:	Retired

Admiral Emil **HEUSINGER von Waldegg** (22 Oct 1880 - 8 Dec 1966)

8 Sep 1927 - 26 Sep 1928:	Commandant, Battleship "*Hessen*"
28 Sep 1928 - 30 Sep 1930:	Chief of Naval General Staff
(1 Oct 1930:	Promoted to Konteradmiral)
1 Oct 1930 - 14 Nov 1930:	Attached to the Commander-in-Chief of the Navy
15 Nov 1930 - 26 Sep 1935:	Chief of General Office, Naval High Command
(1 Oct 1933:	Promoted to Vizeadmiral)
(30 Sep 1935:	Promoted to brevet Admiral)
30 Sep 1935:	Retired
15 Feb 1939:	Recalled on reserve status; no appointment conferred

Konteradmiral Eberhard **HEYDEL** (23 Mar 1872 - 21 Feb 1926)

1 Oct 1911 - Dec 1917:	Staff Officer, Naval General Staff
Dec 1917 - 29 Jun 1918:	Western Theater of Operations Section Chief, Naval General Staff
30 Jun 1918 - 12 Aug 1918:	Commandant, Battleship "*Oldenburg*"
13 Aug 1918 - 12 Sep 1918:	Commandant, Battleship "*Helgoland*"
13 Sep 1918 - 21 Nov 1918:	Commandant, Battleship "*Oldenburg*"
22 Nov 1918 - 4 Mar 1920:	Attached to Naval General Staff
(4 Mar 1920:	Promoted to brevet Konteradmiral)
4 Mar 1920:	Retired

Konteradmiral Erich **HEYDEN** (24 Sep 1879 - 11 Jan 1948)

23 Sep 1922 - 26 Sep 1924:	Commandant, Cruiser "*Hamburg*"
27 Sep 1924 - 30 Nov 1924:	Attached to Naval Personnel Office
1 Dec 1924 - 30 Nov 1928:	Chief of Naval Personnel
(30 Nov 1928:	Promoted to brevet Konteradmiral)
30 Nov 1928:	Retired

27 Apr 1940 - 1 May 1943:	Recalled; Director of Horten Shipyards
(1 Feb 1941:	Confirmed as Konteradmiral from brevet rank)
2 May 1943 - 30 Jun 1943:	Attached to the Commander, Baltic Naval Station
30 Jun 1943:	Placed on inactive status
31 Jul 1944:	Retired

Vizeadmiral Hellmuth **HEYE** (9 Aug 1895 - 10 Nov 1970)

29 Apr 1939 - 4 Sep 1940:	Commandant, Heavy Cruiser "*Admiral Hipper*" & Commander of 2. Naval Group, Operation "Weserübung"
5 Sep 1940 - 18 Oct 1940:	Chief of Staff, Commander of Naval Security, East
19 Oct 1940 - 13 Feb 1941:	Chief of Staff, Commander of Naval Security, West
14 Feb 1941 - 30 Jun 1941:	Chief of Staff, Admiral Southeast
1 Jul 1941 - 14 Sep 1942:	Chief of Staff, Naval Group South
(1 Sep 1942:	Promoted to Konteradmiral)
15 Sep 1942 - 9 Nov 1942:	Acting Admiral Commanding, Black Sea
3 Dec 1942 - 4 Apr 1944:	Chief of Staff, Naval Group North
7 Jun 1943 - 4 Apr 1944:	Chief of Staff, High Seas Fleet
20 Apr 1944 - 10 Sep 1945:	Flag Officer, Midget Weapons
(1 Aug 1944:	Promoted to Vizeadmiral)

Awards: *Knight's Cross*

Konteradmiral (Ingeneur) Friedrich **HILBIG** (13 Dec 1874 - 20 Oct 1960)

1 Apr 1922 - 30 Sep 1925:	Chief Engineer, North Sea Naval Station
1 Oct 1925 - 31 Oct 1925:	Attached to the Commander, North Sea Naval Station
(31 Oct 1925:	Promoted to brevet Konteradmiral Ingeneur)
31 Oct 1925:	Retired
1 Jun 1941 - 29 Jun 1941:	Recalled; attached to Wilhelmshaven Naval Dockyards
30 Jun 1941 - 9 Dec 1942:	Chief of Naval Armaments Office, Cherbourg
(1 Jul 1942:	Confirmed as Konteradmiral Ingeneur from brevet rank)
10 Dec 1942 - 31 Jan 1943:	Attached to the Commander, North Sea Naval Station
31 Jan 1943:	Retired

Konteradmiral Walter **HILDEBRAND** (1 May 1873 - 27 Feb 1923)

22 Nov 1914 - 3 Sep 1915:	Commandant, Light Cruiser "*Thetis*"
4 Sep 1915 - 4 Jan 1916:	Attached to the Commander, Baltic Naval Station
5 Jan 1916 - 11 Feb 1917:	Commandant, Light Cruiser "*Berlin*"
15 Feb 1917 - 31 Dec 1917:	Commandant, Light Cruiser "*Nürnberg*"
6 Jan 1918 - 24 Jan 1918:	Commandant, Battleship "*Kaiserin*"
2 Feb 1918 - 9 Nov 1918:	Commandant, Heavy Cruiser "*Hindenburg*"
10 Nov 1918 - 3 Dec 1918:	Commandant, Heavy Cruiser "*Derfflinger*"
4 Dec 1918 - 15 Feb 1919:	Attached to the Naval Office
16 Feb 1919 - 24 Jun 1919:	Section Chief, Naval Office
25 Jun 1919 - 31 Mar 1921:	Chief of Personnel, North Sea Naval Office
25 Nov 1920 - 1 Apr 1921:	Acting Commander, North Sea Naval Forces
2 Apr 1921 - 25 Sep 1921:	Attached to the Commander-in-Chief of the Navy
26 Sep 1921 - 27 Feb 1923:	Chief of Naval General Office
(1 Dec 1921:	Promoted to Konteradmiral)

Konteradmiral Paul von **HINTZE** (13 Feb 1864 - 19 Aug 1941)

(10 Apr 1911:	Promoted to brevet Konteradmiral)
1914 - 1917:	Ambassador-Extraordinary, Peking
1917 - 9 Jul 1918:	Ambassador, Norway
9 Jul 1918 - 7 Oct 1918:	State Secretary, Foreign Ministry
8 Oct 1918 - 10 Nov 1918:	Foreign Ministry Representative to the Army High Command

Konteradmiral Ernst **HINTZMANN** (23 Jun 1880 - 17 Jan 1951)

27 Sep 1937 - 3 Sep 1939:	Section Chief, Military Science Office, Naval High Command
(31 Oct 1938:	Promoted to brevet Konteradmiral)
4 Sep 1939 - 30 Sep 1939:	Preparation for Naval Attaché posting
1 Oct 1939 - 10 May 1940:	Naval Attaché, The Hague
11 May 1940 - 31 Jan 1943:	Navy Commissioner for Shipyards, Netherlands & Belgium
(1 Feb 1941:	Confirmed as Konteradmiral from brevet rank)
1 Feb 1943 - 5 Dec 1943:	Chief of Shipyards Staff, Netherlands
6 Dec 1943 - 31 Jan 1944:	Placed on reserve status
31 Jan 1944:	Retired

Konteradmiral Horst von **HIPPEL** (25 Jan 1865 - 9 Jun 1920)
(12 Apr 1913:	Promoted to brevet Konteradmiral)
29 Aug 1914 - Jan 1916:	Recalled from retirement; Commander, 1. Sailor Division
Jan 1916 - Nov 1917:	Deputy Commissioner, Kiel Prize Court
Nov 1917:	Retired

Admiral Franz Ritter von **HIPPER** (13 Sep 1863 - 25 May 1932)
(27 Jan 1912:	Promoted to Konteradmiral)
1 Oct 1913 - 12 Aug 1918:	Commander of Reconnaissance Forces
(17 Jun 1915:	Promoted to Vizeadmiral)
(11 Aug 1918:	Promoted to Admiral)
13 Aug 1918 - 30 Nov 1918:	C-in-C, High Seas Fleet
13 Dec 1918:	Retired

Awards: *Pour le Mérite, Bavarian Military Max Joseph Order*

Konteradmiral Waldemar **HIRTH** (25 Dec 1884 - 28 Nov 1963)
1 May 1925 - 30 Jun 1934:	Chief of Torpedo Testing Office
(1 Apr 1934:	Promoted to brevet Konteradmiral)
2 Feb 1934 - 28 Feb 1934:	Acting Inspector of Torpedoes & Mines
30 Jun 1934:	Retired

Konteradmiral Otto **HOEPNER** (23 Dec 1856 - 7 Apr 1927)
(16 Oct 1909:	Promoted to brevet Konteradmiral)
3 Aug 1914 - Nov 1918:	Recalled from retirement; Judge, Hamburg Prize Court
Nov 1918:	Retired

Konteradmiral Karl **HOFFMANN** (26 Oct 1895 - 6 May 1945)
2 May 1938 - 14 Aug 1940:	Staff Officer to Flag Officer, Reconnaissance Forces
15 Aug 1940 - 14 Sep 1940:	Attached to the Commander-in-Chief of the Navy
15 Sep 1940 - 14 Feb 1941:	Chief of Colonial Matters Group, Naval High Command
15 Feb 1941 - 31 Aug 1942:	Chief of Naval Control Commission, Armistice Commission, Africa
1 Sep 1941 - 31 Aug 1942:	Chief of Staff, Armistice Commission, Africa
1 Sep 1942 - 5 Jan 1943:	Attached to the Flag Officer, U-Boats
6 Jan 1943 - 5 Feb 1943:	Chief of Staff to Flag Officer, U-Boats

11 Feb 1943 - 2 Dec 1944:	Chief of Staff, Naval Group West
(1 Apr 1943:	Promoted to Konteradmiral)
3 Dec 1944 - 6 May 1945:	Admiral-Quartermaster, Naval High Command

Awards: *German Cross in Gold*

Vizeadmiral Kurt Caesar **HOFFMANN** (26 Aug 1895 - 19 May 1988)

28 Sep 1936 - 30 Sep 1937:	Commandant, Coastal Artillery School
1 Oct 1937 - 26 Jun 1939:	Commandant, Coastal Artillery & Flak School
27 Jun 1939 - 15 Sep 1939:	Commandant, Light Cruiser "*Königsberg*"
21 Sep 1939 - 28 Mar 1942:	Commandant, Battleship "*Scharnhorst*"
29 Mar 1942 - 30 Jun 1942:	Attached to the Commander, Baltic Naval Station
(1 Apr 1942:	Promoted to Konteradmiral)
1 Jul 1942 - 4 Mar 1943:	Naval Commander, Netherlands
5 Mar 1943 - 22 Jul 1945:	Chief of Artillery Armaments Office, Naval High Command
(1 Apr 1943:	Promoted to Vizeadmiral)

Awards: *Knight's Cross; German Cross in Gold*

Großadmiral (*Generalfeldmarschall; Marshal of Turkey [Mushir]; British Admiral of the Fleet & Field Marshal*) Wilhelm II von **HOHENZOLLERN**, Kaiser von Deutsches Reich (27 Jan 1859 - 4 Jun 1941)

Awards*: Order of the Black Eagle, with Chain; Pour le Mérite with Oakleaves; Royal Bavarian St.Hubertus Order; Grand Cross of the Royal Saxon Military St.Heinrich Order; Royal Saxon Order of the Diamond Crown; Grand Cross of the Royal Bavarian MilitaryMaxJoseph Order; Grand Cross of the Iron Cross; Royal Austrian Order of the Golden Fleece; Grand Cross of the Royal Austrian MilitaryMaria-Theresia Order; British Knight of the Garter; Grand Cross of the Royal Hungarian Stephan Order; Royal Bulgarian Order of the Holy Kyrill & Method; Grand Cross of the Royal Bulgarian Military Order; Royal Bulgarian Order of Valor 1st Class with Diamonds; Grand Diamond Star of the Imperial Ottoman Iftichar Order; Royal Russian St. Andreas Order; Royal Italian Annunziata Order; Royal Norwegian Order of the Lion; Royal Swedish Seraphin Order; Royal Danish Order of the Elephant*

Konteradmiral Ludolf von **HOHNHORST** (13 Aug 1899 - 14 May 1978)

16 Feb 1939 - 30 Jun 1940:	Advisor, Naval Intelligence Office, Naval High Command
1 Jul 1940 - 18 Apr 1941:	Advisor for Naval Matters, Armistice Commission, France
23 Apr 1941 - 22 Sep 1942:	Chief of Staff to Admiral Commanding, Norwegian West Coast

23 Sep 1942 - 6 Nov 1942:	Attached to Staff of Admiral Commanding, Norway
7 Nov 1942 - 12 May 1944:	Quartermaster, Naval Group Norway
24 Apr 1944 - 21 Aug 1944:	Acting Commander of Sea Defenses, Bergen
30 Aug 1944 - 20 Nov 1944:	Commander of Sea Defenses, Arctic Ocean
(1 Oct 1944:	Promoted to Konteradmiral)
8 Dec 1944 - 31 May 1945:	Chief of Staff, Naval Group Norway

Vizeadmiral Franz von **HOLLEBEN** (25 Feb 1863 - 18 Feb 1938)

(19 Nov 1910:	Promoted to Konteradmiral)
19 Nov 1910 - 31 Aug 1917:	Chief of Danzig Shipyards
(13 Oct 1914:	Promoted to brevet Vizeadmiral)
1 Sep 1917 - 14 Oct 1917:	Attached to the Commander, Baltic Naval Station
14 Oct 1917:	Retired

Vizeadmiral Carl **HOLLWEG** (12 Dec 1867 - 22 Feb 1932)

1 Oct 1912 - 14 Mar 1915:	Commandant, Battleship "*Schlesien*"
8 Apr 1915 - 31 Mar 1917:	Director of Military Bureau, Naval Office
(25 Nov 1916:	Promoted to Konteradmiral)
1 Apr 1917 - 31 Aug 1917:	Attached to the Danzig Shipyards
1 Sep 1917 - 27 Aug 1918:	Director of Danzig Shipyards
28 Aug 1918 - 23 Jan 1919:	Director of Shipyard Department, Naval Office
23 Jan 1919:	Retired
(4 Sep 1919:	Promoted to brevet Vizeadmiral)

Großadmiral Henning von **HOLTZENDORF** (9 Jan 1853 - 6 Jun 1919)

(27 Jan 1904:	Promoted to Konteradmiral)
(27 Apr 1907:	Promoted to Vizeadmiral)
(27 Jan 1910:	Promoted to Admiral)
5 Sep 1915 - 10 Aug 1918:	Recalled from retirement; Chief of Naval General Staff
(31 May 1918:	Promoted to Großadmiral)
10 Aug 1918:	Retired; for services rendered, retained on Naval List.

Awards: *Order of the Black Eagle, Pour le Mérite, Oakleaves to the Pour le Mérite*

Vizeadmiral Eduard **HOLZHAUER** (7 Sep 1852 - 4 Jan 1936)

(10 Dec 1904:	Promoted to brevet Konteradmiral)

Aug 1914 - Nov 1918:	Recalled from retirement; Naval General Staff Representative for Prize Matters and Judge, Berlin Prize Court
(22 Mar 1916:	Confirmed as Konteradmiral from brevet rank)
Nov 1918:	Retired
(4 Feb 1920:	Promoted to brevet Vizeadmiral)

Konteradmiral Paul **HÖNICKE** (13 Sep 1883 - 14 Mar 1963)

13 Nov 1924 - 4 Oct 1926:	Commander, Coastal Defense Detachment IV
13 Oct 1926 - 25 Sep 1931:	Director of Artillery & Mines, Wilhelmshaven Shipyards
(30 Sep 1931:	Promoted to brevet Konteradmiral)
30 Sep 1931:	Retired
1 Jan 1939:	Recalled on reserve status
1 Sep 1939 - 1 May 1943:	Naval Weapons Office Representative to the Army Weapons Office
(1 Apr 1941:	Confirmed as Konteradmiral from brevet rank)
2 May 1943 - 30 Jun 1943:	Placed on inactive status
30 Jun 1943:	Retired

Konteradmiral Wilhelm **HÖPFNER** (22 Aug 1868 - 16 Apr 1951)

22 Sep 1913 - 1 Jun 1916:	Commandant, Battleship *"Oldenburg"*
2 Jun 1916 - 31 Mar 1917:	Badly wounded in action; medical leave
1 Apr 1917 - 24 Aug 1917:	Director of Military Bureau, Naval Office
25 Aug 1917 - 10 Dec 1917:	Sick leave
11 Dec 1917 - 9 Nov 1918:	Inspector, II. Naval Inspectorate
(28 Apr 1918:	Promoted to Konteradmiral)
10 Nov 1918 - 31 Jan 1919:	Placed on inactive status
1 Feb 1919 - 7 Nov 1919:	Naval Commissioner for the Kaiser Wilhelm Canal
7 Nov 1919 - 24 Nov 1919:	Placed on inactive status
24 Nov 1919:	Retired

Vizeadmiral Albert **HOPMAN** (30 Apr 1865 - 14 Mar 1942)

1 Oct 1911 - 18 Apr 1915:	Chief of Central Bureau, Naval Office
(22 Mar 1915:	Promoted to Konteradmiral)
20 Apr 1915 - 15 Jan 1916:	Chief of Reconnaissance Forces, Baltic
21 Jan 1916 - 20 May 1916:	Advisor to the Turkish Ministry of the Navy
22 May 1916 - 15 Sep 1916:	Attached to the Naval General Staff
16 Sep 1916 - 6 Oct 1916:	Acting Deputy Chief of Naval General Staff

7 Oct 1916 - 9 Dec 1916:	Chief of Naval Operations
11 Dec 1916 - 7 Dec 1917:	Chief of Reconnaissance Forces, Eastern Baltic
(14 Oct 1917:	Promoted to Vizeadmiral)
15 Dec 1917 - 16 Dec 1917:	Chief of Staff, Baltic Fleet
25 Dec 1917 - 1 Jul 1919:	Chief of Armistice Commission, Black Sea & Mediterranean
2 Jul 1919 - 29 Oct 1919:	Attached to the Commander-in-Chief of the Navy
30 Oct 1919 - 15 Jan 1920:	Chief of German Delegation, Inter-Allied Commission for the evacuation of the Baltic
16 Jan 1920 - 9 Mar 1920:	Attached to the Commander-in-Chief of the Navy
9 Mar 1920:	Retired

Admiral Otto **HORMEL** (13 Sep 1886 - 22 Apr 1971)

21 Nov 1932 - 1 Oct 1933:	Chief of Hamburg Naval Office
5 Oct 1933 - 29 Sep 1935:	Commandant, Cruiser "*Leipzig*"
30 Sep 1935 - 3 Oct 1937:	Chief of Central Office, Wilhelmshaven Shipyards
30 Nov 1937 - 31 Mar 1939:	Commandant, Kiel Naval Arsenal
(1 Apr 1938:	Promoted to Konteradmiral)
1 Apr 1939 - 5 May 1943:	Director, Kiel Shipyards
(1 Jan 1940:	Promoted to Vizeadmiral)
(1 Apr 1942:	Promoted to Admiral)
6 May 1943 - 31 Aug 1943:	Attached to the Commander-in-Chief of the Navy
31 Aug 1943:	Retired
1 Sep 1943:	Recalled to reserve status
12 Jun 1944 - 31 Mar 1945:	Attached to Naval Training Staff
31 Mar 1945:	Retired

Konteradmiral Johannes **HORN** (1 May 1872 - 21 Dec 1945)

2 Aug 1914 - 30 Sep 1914:	Commandant, Light Cruiser "*Amazone*"
1 Oct 1914 - 14 Jan 1917:	Commandant, Light Cruiser "*Augsburg*"
23 Jan 1917 - 21 Dec 1917:	1st Staff Officer to the C-in-C, Baltic Fleet
22 Dec 1917 - 31 Mar 1918:	Liaison Officer to the Armed Forces High Command
1 Apr 1918 - 12 Aug 1918:	Naval Delegate to the Armistice Negotiations, Brest-Litovsk
13 Aug 1918 - 29 Nov 1918:	Section Chief, Naval General Staff

30 Nov 1918 - 24 Nov 1919: Chief of Military Political Office, Naval High Command
25 Nov 1919 - 31 May 1922: Naval Commissioner, Kaiser-Wilhelm Canal
(31 May 1922: Promoted to brevet Konteradmiral)
31 May 1922: Retired

Konteradmiral Karl von **HORNHARDT** (30 Apr 1872 - 17 Feb 1958)
1 Apr 1914 - 16 Nov 1914: Commandant, Heavy Cruiser "*Hansa*"
17 Nov 1914 - 6 Feb 1917: Commander, 3. Marine Regiment, Flanders Marine Corps
18 Feb 1917 - 13 Dec 1918: Commandant, Battleship "*Prinzregent Luitpold*"
14 Dec 1918 - 15 Jan 1919: Attached to the Commander, Baltic Naval Station
16 Jan 1919 - 31 Oct 1919: Inspector, I. Naval Inspectorate
8 Nov 1919 - 23 Mar 1920: Inspector of Naval Training
(8 Mar 1920: Promoted to Konteradmiral)
24 Mar 1920 - 18 Jun 1920: Attached to the Commander, Baltic Naval Station
19 Jun 1920 - 29 Sep 1920: Attached to the Commander-in-Chief of the Navy
29 Sep 1920: Retired

Konteradmiral Günther **HORSTMANN** (25 Mar 1894 - ?)
19 Feb 1937 - 16 Nov 1939: Chief of Stettin Naval Office
17 Nov 1939 - 30 Jul 1940: Commandant, Battleship "*Schlesien*"
31 Jul 1940 - 19 Jan 1941: Chief of Antwerp Naval Office
20 Jan 1941 - 4 Mar 1943: Chief of German Naval Transport, Italy
(1 Sep 1942: Promoted to Konteradmiral)
19 Mar 1943 - 4 Dec 1944: Commander, 5. Security Division
5 Dec 1944 - 31 Dec 1944: Commander, Hamburg IV Recruiting Office
1 Jan 1945 - 4 Feb 1945: Commander, Hamburg IV/VI Recruiting Office
5 Feb 1945 - 3 May 1945: Inspector of Recruiting, Stettin
Awards: *German Cross in Gold*

Marineoberbaudirektor (Vizeadmiral) Hans **HORSTMANN** (15 Dec 1885 - 11 Jan 1972)
1 Aug 1939 - 26 Jul 1940: Deputy Director of Engine Construction, Wilhelmshaven Naval Dockyards
(19 Sep 1939: Promoted to Marinemaschinenbaudirektor [Konteradmiral])

27 Jul 1940 - 30 Jun 1942:	Director of Engine Construction, Wilhelmshaven Naval Dockyards
(20 Apr 1942:	Promoted to Marineoberbaudirektor)
1 Sep 1941 - 31 Oct 1942:	Chief of Factory & Planning Office, Wilhelmshaven Naval Dockyards
1 Nov 1942 - 9 Jul 1945:	Director of Construction & Chief of Technical Office, Wilhelmshaven Naval Dockyards:

Awards: *German Cross in Silver*

Vizeadmiral Martin **HOSEMANN** (3 Nov 1876 - 13 Mar 1928)

21 Sep 1919 - 4 Jan 1921:	Chief of Nautical Office, Naval High Command
5 Jan 1921 - 22 Feb 1922:	Attached to the Commander-in-Chief of the Navy
23 Feb 1922 - 20 Sep 1924:	Chief of Defense Office, Naval High Command
21 Sep 1924 - 11 Oct 1927:	Inspector of Naval Training
(1 Apr 1925:	Promoted to Konteradmiral)
31 Aug 1925 - 19 Sep 1925:	Acting Inspector of Torpedoes & Mines
28 Oct 1925 - 10 Nov 1925:	Acting Commander, Baltic Naval Station
1 Jun 1926 - 30 Jun 1926:	Acting Inspector of Torpedoes & Mines
7 Mar 1927 - 28 Mar 1927:	Acting Inspector of Torpedoes & Mines
17 Oct 1927 - 17 Dec 1927:	Deputy Commander, Baltic Naval Station
18 Dec 1927 - 31 Dec 1927:	Attached to the Commander, Baltic Naval Station
(31 Dec 1927:	Promoted to brevet Vizeadmiral)
31 Dec 1927:	Retired

Vizeadmiral Friedrich **HÜFFMEIER** (14 Jun 1898 - 13 Jan 1972)

26 Aug 1939 - 12 Sep 1939:	Naval Liaison Officer, Army High Command (OKH)
13 Sep 1939 - 28 May 1941:	Chief of U-Boat Construction Office, Naval High Command
29 May 1941 - 28 Mar 1942:	Commandant, Light Cruiser "*Köln*"
29 Mar 1942 - 17 Oct 1943:	Commandant, Battleship "*Scharnhorst*"
(1 Oct 1943:	Promoted to Konteradmiral)
18 Oct 1943 - 21 Jun 1944:	Section Chief, Naval High Command
22 Jun 1944 - 24 Jul 1944:	Transferred to Naval Group West
25 Jul 1944 - 9 May 1945:	Naval Commander, Channel Islands
(1 Jan 1945:	Promoted to Vizeadmiral)

25 Jul 1944 - 26 Feb 1945:	Deputy Fortress Commandant of Guernsey
1 Oct 1944 - 26 Feb 1945:	Chief of Staff, Armed Forces Commander, Channel Islands
27 Feb 1945 - 9 May 1945:	Armed Forces Commander, Channel Islands & Fortress Commandant of Guernsey

Admiral Friedrich von **INGENOHL** (30 Jun 1857 - 19 Dec 1933)

(7 Sep 1907:	Promoted to Konteradmiral)
(27 Jan 1910:	Promoted to Vizeadmiral)
(15 Nov 1913:	Promoted to Admiral)
15 Nov 1913 - 2 Feb 1915:	C-in-C, High Seas Fleet
16 Feb 1915 - 13 Aug 1915:	Commander, Baltic Naval Station
13 Aug 1915:	Retired; Admiral à la Suite

Konteradmiral Walter **ISENDAHL** (10 Sep 1872 - 30 Apr 1945)

1 May 1914 - 24 Apr 1918:	Chief of Naval Signals, Naval General Staff
28 Apr 1918 - 14 Sep 1918:	Member of Nautical Technical Commission
15 Sep 1918 - 21 Nov 1918:	Commandant, former Russian Battleship "*Wolja*"
22 Nov 1918 - 5 Jan 1919:	Attached to the Naval High Command
6 Jan 1919 - 14 May 1919:	Attached to Army Corps Lüttwitz
15 May 1919 - 30 Sep 1919:	Chief of Baltic Flotilla Service Works Office, Naval High Command
1 Oct 1919 - 29 Jan 1920:	Chief of Water Police
29 Jan 1920:	Retired
(7 Apr 1920:	Promoted to brevet Konteradmiral)
1 Aug 1940 - 26 Jul 1941:	Recalled to reserve status
26 Jul 1941 - 31 Jan 1943:	Special Purposes Officer in Southern Russia to the Commander-in-Chief of the Navy
31 Jan 1943:	Retired

Konteradmiral Siegfried von **JACHMANN** (28 Mar 1867 - 12 May 1945)

17 Mar 1914 - 28 Feb 1918:	Coastal Inspector, Pomerania & Mecklenburg
(28 Feb 1918:	Promoted to brevet Konteradmiral)
28 Feb 1918:	Retired

Admiral Hermann **JACOBSEN** (23 Apr 1859 - 14 Nov 1943)

(9 Nov 1907:	Promoted to Konteradmiral)
(27 Jan 1911:	Promoted to Vizeadmiral)
3 Nov 1914 - 10 Jan 1918:	Recalled from retirement; Commander, 1. Marine Division, Flanders Marine Corps

(10 Jan 1918:   Promoted to brevet Admiral)
10 Jan 1918:   Retired

Vizeadmiral Leo **JACOBSON** (21 Oct 1862 - 19 Feb 1954)
(27 Jan 1911:   Promoted to Konteradmiral)
1 Oct 1912 - 27 Jan 1919:   Commandant of Helgoland
(13 Oct 1914:   Promoted to brevet Vizeadmiral)
(27 Jan 1916:   Confirmed as Vizeadmiral from brevet rank)
20 Feb 1917 - 12 Apr 1917: Fortress Commandant, Wilhelmshaven
28 Jan 1919 - 17 Mar 1919: Attached to the Secretary of State, Naval Office
17 Mar 1919:   Retired

Vizeadmiral Gisbert **JASPER** (28 Aug 1865 - 9 Feb 1953)
(12 Apr 1913:   Promoted to Konteradmiral)
2 Aug 1914 - 16 Nov 1914:   Deputy Commander of Reconnaissance Ships
12 Aug 1914 - 16 Nov 1914: Commander, V. Reconnaissance Group
17 Nov 1914 - 19 Aug 1915: Commander, II. Marine Brigade,
                         Flanders Marine Corps
20 Aug 1915 - 11 Nov 1918: Commander, 2. Marine Division,
                         Flanders Marine Corps
(25 Nov 1916:   Promoted to Vizeadmiral)
12 Nov 1918 - 18 Oct 1919: Attached to the Commander,
                         Baltic Naval Station
18 Oct 1919:   Retired

Waffen Konteradmiral Richard **JEWINSKI** (5 Apr 1887 - 28 May 1984)
15 Nov 1936 - 1 May 1942:   Chief of Mines Offices Group,
                         Inspectorate of Mines
12 May 1942 - 30 Sep 1943: Commander of Swinemünde Mines Office
(1 Feb 1943:   Promoted to Waffen Konteradmiral)
1 Oct 1943 - 5 May 1945:   Commandant, Swinemünde Mines Arsenal

Konteradmiral Rolf **JOHANNESSON** (22 Jul 1900 - 6 Dec 1889)
8 Jun 1938 - 27 Jan 1942:   Commandant, Destroyer "*Erich Steinbrinck*"
8 Feb 1942 - 2 Apr 1943:   Commandant, Destroyer ZG 3 "*Hermes*"
6 Apr 1943 - 8 Nov 1944:   Commander, 4. Destroyer Flotilla
27 Dec 1943 - 15 Jan 1944: Acting Commander, Battle Group Norway
13 Nov 1944 - 31 Dec 1945: Commander of Sea Defenses,
                         Elbe & Weser Estuaries
(30 Jan 1945:   Promoted to Konteradmiral)

11 Feb 1945 - 14 Mar 1945:	Acting Admiral Commanding, Heligoland Bight

Awards: *Knight's Cross; German Cross in Gold*

Konteradmiral (Ingeneur) Wilhelm **JOHANNSEN** (27 Jan 1894 - 6 Nov 1956)

28 Sep 1937 - 30 Jul 1940:	Chief of Naval Armaments Office, Swinemünde
1 Aug 1940 - 19 Sep 1942:	Chief Engineer, Baltic Naval Station
20 Sep 1942 - 4 Feb 1944:	Director of Naval Armaments & Repair Works, Narvik
(1 Jan 1943:	Promoted to Konteradmiral Ingeneur)
5 Feb 1944 - 20 Feb 1945:	Commandant, Drontheim Naval Arsenal
21 Feb 1945 - 8 May 1945:	Attached to the C-in-C, Baltic Naval Group

Marinepropst (Konteradmiral) Dr. Heinrich **JÖPPEN** (9 Mar 1853 - 22 Feb 1927)

27 Oct 1913 - 30 Apr 1920:	Catholic Field Bishop of the Army & Navy
30 Apr 1920:	Retired

Konteradmiral Adolph **JOSEPHI** (28 Oct 1859 - 5 Sep 1919)

(27 Jan 1913:	Promoted to brevet Konteradmiral)
2 Aug 1914 - 15 Oct 1914:	Judge, Hamburg Prize Court
16 Oct 1914 - 27 Jul 1915:	Commander of Wannsee Station, Volunteer Motor Boat Corps
27 Jul 1915 - 18 Feb 1916:	Placed on inactive status
18 Feb 1916:	Retired

Konteradmiral Rudolf **JUNKER** (12 Mar 1895 - 21 Jun 1980)

1 Oct 1937 - 2 Nov 1938:	Chief of Underwater Weapons Section, Naval Weapons Office, Naval High Command
3 Nov 1938 - 17 Feb 1943:	Chief of Staff, Inspectorate of Torpedoes
(1 Dec 1942:	Promoted to Konteradmiral)
20 Mar 1939 - 25 Mar 1939:	Acting Inspector of Torpedoes
5 Jun 1939 - 17 Jun 1939:	Acting Inspector of Torpedoes
18 Feb 1943 - 3 Dec 1944:	Commander of Torpedo Testing Center, Eckernförde
4 Dec 1944 - 21 Sep 1945:	Inspector of Torpedoes

Awards: *German Cross in Silver*

Vizeadmiral Ernst **JUNKERMANN** (25 Jun 1881 - 5 Mar 1944)
6 Oct 1924 - 2 May 1925:	Commander, Baltic Standing Naval Division
3 May 1925 - 18 Jul 1925:	Commandant, Cruiser *"Hamburg"*
19 Jul 1925 - 6 Apr 1926:	Commandant, Cruiser *"Berlin"*
7 Apr 1926 - 7 Sep 1927:	Commandant, Battleship *"Hessen"*
10 Sep 1927 - 4 Oct 1928:	Chief of Naval Defense Section, Naval High Command
5 Oct 1928 - 31 Mar 1931:	Inspector of Torpedoes & Mines
(1 Mar 1929:	Promoted to Konteradmiral)
(31 Mar 1931:	Promoted to brevet Vizeadmiral)
5 Oct 1928 - 13 Oct 1928:	Acting Inspector of Naval Training
16 Sep 1929 - 12 Oct 1929:	Acting Inspector of Naval Training
10 Jul 1930 - 2 Aug 1930:	Acting Inspector of Naval Training
26 Sep 1930 - 7 Oct 1930:	Acting Inspector of Naval Training
10 Oct 1930 - 23 Oct 1930:	Acting Commander, Baltic Naval Station
31 Mar 1931:	Retired
1 Jan 1939:	Recalled to reserve status
26 May 1940 - 28 Feb 1941:	Deputy Commissioner, Hamburg Prize Court
1 Mar 1941 - Aug 1941:	Commissioner, Southeast Berlin Prize Court
Aug 1941 - 31 Aug 1942:	Judge, Berlin Prize Court
(1 Apr 1942:	Confirmed as Vizeadmiral from brevet rank)
31 Aug 1942:	Retired

Ministerialdirektor (Vizeadmiral) Curt **JUST** (31 Dec 1878 - 2 Aug 1961)
1 Apr 1938 - 29 Oct 1939:	Chief of Technical Dockyards Section, Naval General Office, Naval High Command
(1939:	Promoted to Ministerialdirigent [Konteradmiral])
30 Oct 1939 - 28 Feb 1943:	Chief of Dockyards Group, Naval Construction Office, Naval High Command
(1 Jun 1942:	Promoted to Ministerialdirektor)
1 Mar 1943:	Retired

Konteradmiral Otto **KÄHLER** (3 Mar 1894 - 2 Nov 1967)
6 Sep 1939 - 15 Oct 1939:	Chief of Patrol Boat Units, West
16 Oct 1939 - 14 Mar 1940:	Construction Advisor, Ship 10
15 Mar 1940 - 20 Jul 1941:	Commandant, Auxiliary Cruiser *"Thor"*
21 Jul 1941 - 30 Jun 1942:	Section Chief, Sea Navigation Office, Ministry of Transport
1 Jul 1942 - 15 Oct 1942:	Naval Liaison Officer to the Commissioner for Sea Navigation

16 Oct 1942 - 4 Jan 1944: Chief of Navigation Office, Naval High Command
(1 Feb 1943: Promoted to Konteradmiral)
5 Jan 1944 - 18 Sep 1944: Commander of Sea Defenses, Brittany
18 Sep 1944: Captured; POW
Awards: *Knight's Cross with Oakleaves; Knight's Cross*

Vizeadmiral Wilhelm **KAHLERT** (23 Feb 1877 - 28 Jan 1932)
1 Apr 1918 - 14 Sep 1920: Attached to the Naval General Staff
15 Sep 1920 - 28 Feb 1921: Chief of Special Questions Section, Naval High Command
1 Mar 1921 - 31 Mar 1921: Attached to V. Military District
1 Apr 1921 - 2 Jul 1923: Commandant of Pillau
3 Jul 1923 - 30 Sep 1923: Chief of Staff, Naval General Office, Naval High Command
1 Oct 1923 - 27 Sep 1925: Chief of Naval General Office, Naval High Command
(1 Oct 1924: Promoted to Konteradmiral)
(30 Sep 1925: Promoted to brevet Vizeadmiral)
30 Sep 1925: Retired
1 Jul 1930 - 28 Jan 1932: Commissioner, Emden & Brake Sea Offices

Konteradmiral Friedrich von **KAMEKE** (2 Jun 1870 - 29 Sep 1921)
8 Aug 1914 - 22 Oct 1915: Commandant, Battleship "*Schwaben*"
26 Oct 1915 - 11 Aug 1918: Commandant, Battleship "*Helgoland*"
3 Aug 1918 - 7 Aug 1918: Deputy Commander, I. Squadron
10 Aug 1918 - 11 Aug 1918: Deputy Commander, I. Squadron
12 Aug 1918 - 21 Dec 1918: Chief of Staff, North Sea Naval Station
22 Dec 1918 - 15 Feb 1919: Attached to the Commander, North Sea Naval Station
16 Feb 1919 - 17 Mar 1919: Attached to the Commander, Baltic Naval Station
17 Mar 1919: Retired
(8 Mar 1920: Promoted to brevet Konteradmiral)

Ministerialdirigent (Konteradmiral) Theodor **KAMPFFMEYER**
(5 Aug 1887 - 9 Apr 1968)
30 Oct 1939 - 18 Aug 1943: Chief of Section K I G, Naval Construction Office, Naval High Command
18 Aug 1943 - 30 Nov 1944: Chief of New Ships Section, Naval Construction Office, Naval High Command

30 Nov 1944 - 9 May 1945:	Chief of Section K I A, Naval Construction Office, Naval High Command
(1 Jan 1945:	Promoted to Ministerialdirigent)

Großadmiral (Generalfeldmarschall, Marshal of Turkey [Mushir]) **KARL I**, König von Österreich
(17 Aug 1887 - 1 Apr 1922)
Großadmiral à la Suite (Honorary title)
Awards: *Order of the Black Eagle; Pour le Mérite with Oakleaves; Royal Bavarian St.Hubertus Order; Royal Saxon Order of the Diamond Crown; Royal Austrian Order of the Golden Fleece; Grand Cross of the Royal Austrian MilitaryMaria-Theresia Order*

Konteradmiral Johannes von **KARPF** (17 Oct 1867 - 16 Dec 1941)
2 Aug 1914 - 22 Apr 1915:	Commandant, Heavy Cruiser "*Roon*"
25 Apr 1915 - 17 Sep 1915:	Deputy Commander, Baltic Reconnaissance Forces
11 Oct 1915 - 24 Jan 1916:	Commander, 1. Torpedo Division
26 Jan 1916 - 29 Sep 1916:	Commandant, Heavy Cruiser "*Moltke*"
30 Sep 1916 - 7 Nov 1916:	Attached to the Commander, Baltic Naval Station
8 Nov 1916 - 21 Dec 1916:	Inspector of Naval Training
22 Dec 1916 - 7 May 1917:	Seconded to the Heavy Cruiser "*Hindenburg*"
8 May 1917 - 1 Dec 1917:	Commandant, Heavy Cruiser "*Hindenburg*"
2 Dec 1917 - 8 Nov 1918:	Commander, IV. Reconnaissance Group
(18 Sep 1918:	Promoted to Konteradmiral)
9 Nov 1918 - 5 Nov 1919:	Attached to the Commander, Baltic Naval Station
5 Nov 1919:	Retired

Vizeadmiral (Ingeneur) Karl **KAUFMANN** (24 Aug 1893 - 4 Oct 1975)
29 Sep 1936 - 23 Nov 1939:	Section Chief, Naval Personnel Office
24 Nov 1939 - 26 Aug 1942:	Commandant, Wesermünde Naval School
(1 Dec 1940:	Promoted to Konteradmiral Ingeneur)
27 Aug 1942 - 25 Apr 1945:	Commandant, Kiel Naval School
(1 Apr 1945:	Promoted to Vizeadmiral Ingeneur)
26 Apr 1945 - 11 Aug 1945:	Commandant, Kiel Naval Arsenal

Vizeadmiral Ludwig **KAULHAUSEN** (30 Jan 1875 - 19 Jul 1957)
17 Feb 1919 - 23 May 1919:	Deputy Commandant of Kiel

23 May 1919 - 2 Jul 1919:	Commander, 3. Regiment, Kiel Marine Division
3 Jul 1919 - 30 Nov 1919:	Commander, Kiel Coastal Defense Regiment
1 Dec 1919 - 31 Mar 1920:	Inspector of Coastal Defense, Kiel
1 Apr 1920 - 12 Apr 1920:	Commander, Kiel Marine Detachment
13 Apr 1920 - 7 Sep 1920:	Commander, III. Marine Brigade
8 Sep 1920 - 17 Nov 1920:	Attached to the Commander, Baltic Naval Station
18 Nov 1920 - 28 Feb 1922:	Chief of Personnel Office, Baltic Naval Station
1 Mar 1922 - 31 Mar 1922:	Attached to Baltic Standing Naval Force Division
1 Apr 1922 - 30 Sep 1923:	Commander, Baltic Standing Naval Force Division
(1 Oct 1923:	Promoted to Konteradmiral)
1 Oct 1923 - 31 Mar 1925:	Inspector of Torpedoes & Mines
(31 Mar 1925:	Promoted to brevet Vizeadmiral)
31 Mar 1925:	Retired

Konteradmiral Heinrich **KEHRHAHN** (17 Jul 1881 - 14 May 1962)

9 Nov 1925 - 1 Jan 1928:	Commandant of Wilhelmshaven
1 Jan 1928 - 26 Sep 1928:	Commander, North Sea Naval Division
5 Oct 1928 - 28 Sep 1930:	Chief of Naval Defense Office, Naval High Command
(30 Sep 1930:	Promoted to brevet Konteradmiral)
30 Sep 1930:	Retired
24 May 1939:	Recalled to reserve status
4 Sep 1939 - 20 Jan 1940:	Deputy Commissioner, Hamburg Prize Court
24 May 1940 - 31 Jan 1944:	Chief of Naval Office, Bremen
(1 Feb 1941:	Confirmed as Konteradmiral from brevet rank)
1 Feb 1944 - 31 Mar 1944:	Attached to the Commander, North Sea Naval Group
31 Mar 1944:	Retired

Ministerialdirigent (Konteradmiral) Walter **KELM** (21 Aug 1883 - 12 Oct 1954)

15 Nov 1939 - 31 Mar 1943:	Chief of Section C III, Naval Administration Office, Naval High Command
(19 Jul 1940:	Promoted to Ministerialdirigent)
1 Apr 1943 - 24 Jul 1944:	Chief of Surface Engineering Group, General Naval Office, Naval High Command
25 Jul 1944 - 8 May 1945:	General Advisor of Construction Technology to the Chief of Naval Armaments

Konteradmiral Paul **KETTNER** (15 Jan 1872 - 28 Nov 1959)

1 Oct 1913 - 23 Jan 1915:	Commandant, Light Cruiser "*Breslau*"
24 Jan 1915 - 29 Mar 1915:	Attached to the Commander, Baltic Naval Station
30 Mar 1915 - 26 Mar 1917:	Commandant, Battleship "*Preußen*"
27 Mar 1917 - 21 Sep 1917:	Commandant of Bruges
28 Sep 1917 - 3 Nov 1918:	Chief of Staff, Special Command Turkey
1 Dec 1918 - 31 Mar 1919:	Chief of Demobilization Office, Special Command Turkey
1 Apr 1919 - 8 Jun 1919:	Attached to the Commander, Baltic Naval Station
8 Jun 1919:	Retired
(9 Mar 1920:	Promoted to brevet Konteradmiral)

Vizeadmiral Walter Freiherr von **KEYSERLINGK** (27 Jun 1869 - 10 Dec 1946)

1 Oct 1912 - 27 Jan 1916:	Commandant, Battleship "*Lothringen*"
28 Jan 1916 - 1 Jun 1917:	Commandant, Battleship "*Kaiser*"
(31 May 1917:	Promoted to Konteradmiral)
18 Feb 1917 - 14 Mar 1917:	Deputy Commander, IV. Squadron
28 Apr 1917 - 2 May 1917:	Deputy Commander, IV. Squadron
30 Jun 1917 - 4 Aug 1918:	Chief of Naval Operations
5 Aug 1918 - 1 Oct 1918:	Attached to the Commander, Baltic Naval Station
2 Oct 1918 - 31 Jul 1919:	Commander of Baltic Security Forces
1 Aug 1919 - 24 Nov 1919:	Attached to the Commander-in-Chief of the Navy
24 Nov 1919:	Retired
(12 May 1920:	Promoted to brevet Vizeadmiral)

Konteradmiral Harald **KIENAST** (28 Sep 1894 - 8 Mar 1986)

20 Apr 1938 - 23 Apr 1939:	Director of Communications Office, Wilhelmshaven Shipyards
24 Apr 1939 - 18 Nov 1939:	Chief of Technical Communications Section, Naval High Command
19 Nov 1939 - 15 Jun 1941:	Section Chief, Technical Communications Office, Naval High Command
16 Jun 1941 - 31 May 1943:	Chief of Technical Communications Office, Naval High Command
(1 Oct 1942:	Promoted to Konteradmiral)
3 Jun 1943 - 8 Jun 1943:	Commandant, Kaiser-Wilhelm Canal

9 Jun 1943 - 13 Nov 1944:	Senior Commander of Naval Communications Schools
8 Dec 1944 - 24 Jan 1945:	Commander, Upper Silesia Recruiting Command & Battle Commander, Kattowitz
25 Jan 1945 - 15 Mar 1945:	Sick leave
16 Mar 1945 - 29 May 1945:	Senior Commander of Naval Communications Schools

Konteradmiral Hellmut **KIENAST** (14 Feb 1892 - 18 Aug 1987)

23 Sep 1935 - 30 Sep 1937:	Chief of Staff, Inspectorate of Naval Artillery
17 Mar 1937 - 15 Apr 1937:	Acting Inspector of Naval Artillery
6 Oct 1937 - 10 May 1940:	Commandant of Wesermünde
6 Oct 1937 - 4 Nov 1939:	Commander, 2. Ships' Crew Regiment
14 May 1940 - 18 Jun 1940:	Commander, 21. Naval Artillery Regiment & Commander of Defense District Holland
19 Jun 1940 - 30 Jun 1942:	Naval Commander, Netherlands
(1 Aug 1940:	Promoted to brevet Konteradmiral)
(1 Jan 1941:	Confirmed as Konteradmiral from brevet rank)
1 Jul 1942 - 29 Sep 1942:	Attached to the Commander, North Sea Naval Station
30 Sep 1942 - 5 Dec 1944:	Inspector, Bremen Recruiting Inspectorate
6 Dec 1944 - 31 Jan 1945:	Attached to the C-in-C, North Sea Naval Group
31 Jan 1945:	Retired
1 Feb 1945:	Recalled to reserve status
10 Feb 1945 - 3 May 1945:	Judge, Hamburg Prize Court

Vizeadmiral Günther **KIESERITZKY** (22 Sep 1893 - 19 Nov 1943)

24 Mar 1936 - 12 Jun 1938:	Chief of Inland Office, Ministry of War
13 Jun 1938 - 25 Apr 1939:	Commandant, Battleship *"Schleswig-Holstein"*
27 Apr 1939 - 20 Jun 1940:	Chief of Staff, Naval Communications Inspectorate
5 Aug 1939 - 25 Aug 1939:	Acting Inspector of Naval Communications
21 Jun 1940 - 2 Dec 1940:	Sea Commandant, Brest
3 Dec 1940 - 15 Jun 1942:	Commandant of Sea Defenses, Brittany
(1 Sep 1941:	Promoted to Konteradmiral)
23 Jun 1942 - 12 Jan 1943:	Commander of Coastal Defenses, Heligoland Bight
7 Feb 1943 - 19 Nov 1943:	Admiral Commanding, Black Sea
(1 Mar 1943:	Promoted to Vizeadmiral)

Awards: *Knight's Cross (posthumously); German Cross in Gold*

Vizeadmiral Hugo **KINDERLING** (26 Mar 1860 - 1 Dec 1943)
(11 Dec 1909:	Promoted to Konteradmiral)
17 Sep 1914 - 16 Feb 1916:	Recalled from retirement; Commandant of Kiel
(16 Feb 1916:	Promoted to brevet Vizeadmiral)
16 Feb 1916:	Retired

Vizeadmiral Walther **KINZEL** (17 Aug 1880 - 3 Oct 1964)
2 Apr 1922 - 30 Sep 1923:	Commandant, Cruiser "*Thetis*"
4 Oct 1923 - 4 Jan 1925:	Chief of Staff, Naval General Office, Naval High Command
6 Jan 1925 - 30 Sep 1928:	Chief of Weapons Office, Naval High Command
1 Oct 1928 - 29 Sep 1932:	Inspector of Naval Artillery
(1 Jan 1929:	Promoted to Konteradmiral)
25 Jul 1929 - 10 Aug 1929:	Inspector, Naval Depot Inspectorate
(30 Sep 1932:	Promoted to brevet Vizeadmiral)
30 Sep 1932:	Retired
1 Jan 1939:	Recalled to reserve status
10 Oct 1940 - 19 Oct 1940:	Attached to Naval High Command
20 Oct 1940 - 31 Mar 1944:	Chief of Main Shipyard Staff, France
(1 Sep 1941:	Confirmed as Vizeadmiral from brevet rank)
1 Apr 1944 - 30 Apr 1944:	Placed on inactive status
30 Apr 1944:	Retired

Awards: *German Cross in Silver*

Konteradmiral Gustav **KIRCHHOFF** (21 Jun 1863 - 5 Mar 1945)
2 Aug 1914 - Sep 1914:	Recalled from retirement; Commander, I. Marine Artillery Detachment
Sep 1914 - 30 Nov 1918:	Commander of Coastal Artillery, Kiel Naval Harbor
1 Dec 1918 - 30 Aug 1919:	Placed on inactive status
(30 Aug 1919:	Promoted to brevet Konteradmiral)
30 Aug 1919:	Retired

Vizeadmiral Gustav **KLEIKAMP** (8 Mar 1896 - 13 Sep 1952)
1 Jun 1937 - 23 Apr 1939:	Chief of Technical Communications Office, Naval High Command
26 Apr 1939 - 28 Aug 1940:	Commandant, Battleship "*Schleswig-Holstein*"
Apr 1940:	Commander of 7. Naval Group, Operation "Weserübung"

29 Aug 1940 - 27 Oct 1940: Chief of Calais Naval Office
29 Aug 1940 - 10 Dec 1940: Commander-Designate, Transport Fleet C
28 Oct 1940 - 30 Dec 1940: Attached to the Commander-in-Chief of the Navy
31 Dec 1940 - 21 Feb 1943: Chief of Military Office, Shipbuilding Directorate, Naval High Command
(1 Apr 1942: Promoted to Konteradmiral)
4 Mar 1943 - 31 Dec 1944: Admiral Commanding, Netherlands
(1 Oct 1943: Promoted to Vizeadmiral)
1 Jan 1945 - 14 Mar 1945: Attached to the C-in-C, Naval Group North
15 Mar 1945 - 7 May 1945: Admiral Commanding, Heligoland Bight
Awards: *German Cross in Gold*

Konteradmiral Georg **KLEINE** (13 Dec 1881 - 15 Jul 1944)
18 Oct 1922 - 8 Jan 1925: Chief of Staff, Naval Artillery Inspectorate
19 Jan 1925 - 19 Sep 1926: Commandant, Cruiser "*Nymphe*"
22 Sep 1926 - 29 Sep 1930: Commandant, Ships Artillery School
(30 Sep 1930: Promoted to brevet Konteradmiral)
30 Sep 1930: Retired
24 May 1939: Recalled to reserve status
7 Apr 1941 - 29 Oct 1941: Commandant, Kaiser-Wilhelm Canal
30 Oct 1941 - 26 Jul 1943: Commandant of Rügen Island
(1 Jul 1943: Confirmed as Konteradmiral from brevet rank)
27 Jul 1943 - 31 Aug 1943: Attached to the C-in-C, Naval Group Baltic
31 Aug 1943: Retired

Marineoberbaudirektor (Vizeadmiral) Otto **KLETTE**
(22 Jun 1875 - 29 Dec 1964)
1 Feb 1927 - 27 Jul 1940: Director of Engine Construction, Wilhelmshaven Naval Dockyards
(6 Mar 1936: Promoted to Werftdirektor with Konteradmiral rank)
28 Jul 1940 - 31 Dec 1940: Leave
31 Dec 1940: Retired
10 Jan 1942 - 12 Sep 1944: Recalled; Chief of Naval Inspection Office, Paris
(17 Mar 1942: Promoted to Marineoberbaudirektor)
30 Sep 1944: Retired

Konteradmiral (Ingeneur) Otto **KLIMPT** (11 Dec 1858 - 25 May 1928)
1 Apr 1914 - 20 Aug 1919:	Chief Engineer, Baltic Naval Station
(20 Aug 1919:	Promoted to Konteradmiral Ingeneur)
20 Aug 1919:	Retired

\

Konteradmiral Lebrecht von **KLITZING** (4 Nov 1872 - 12 May 1945)
12 Aug 1914 - 6 Nov 1914:	Commandant, Coastal Defense Ship "*Hagen*"
14 Dec 1914 - 29 Jan 1915:	Commandant, Light Cruiser "*Pillau*"
18 Feb 1915 - 30 Aug 1915:	Commandant, Light Cruiser "*Breslau*"
31 Aug 1915 - 30 Sep 1915:	Attached to the Commander, Baltic Naval Station
1 Oct 1915 - 28 Jan 1917:	Member, Technical Research Commission
29 Jan 1917 - 22 Aug 1918:	President, Technical Research Commission
23 Aug 1918 - 19 Nov 1918:	Commander of Naval Installations, Kurland and Livland
20 Nov 1918 - 28 Feb 1919:	Deputy Commander, Baltic Waters
1 Mar 1919 - 22 Nov 1919:	Attached to the Commander, Baltic Naval Station
22 Nov 1919:	Retired
(26 Jan 1920:	Promoted to brevet Konteradmiral)

Konteradmiral Friedrich **KLOEBE** (29 Jan 1869 - 17 Sep 1932)
1 Aug 1914 - Oct 1915:	Recalled from retirement; Attached to Naval Intelligence
Oct 1915 - 22 Mar 1916:	Attached to the German Embassy, Athens
23 Mar 1916 - 16 Aug 1916:	Attached to Naval Intelligence
17 Aug 1916 - Oct 1918:	Director of Armaments, Danzig Naval Shipyards
Oct 1918 - 30 Dec 1918:	Attached to the Commander, Baltic Naval Station
30 Dec 1918:	Retired
(30 Aug 1919:	Promoted to brevet Konteradmiral)

Konteradmiral Otto **KLÜBER** (19 Jan 1895 - 27 Aug 1953)
27 Sep 1937 - 12 Sep 1938:	Staff Officer attached to High Seas Fleet
13 Sep 1938 - 23 Nov 1938:	Attached to the Commander, North Sea Naval Station
24 Nov 1938 - 7 Aug 1940:	Commandant, Light Cruiser "*Nürnberg*"
20 Aug 1940 - 27 Aug 1942:	Chief of Staff, Naval Group North
(1 Apr 1942:	Promoted to Konteradmiral)

1 Sep 1942 - 14 Mar 1944:	Admiral Commanding, Northern Waters
17 Apr 1944 - 20 Apr 1945:	Group Chief, Naval Armaments Directorate, Naval High Command

Awards: *German Cross in Gold*

Konteradmiral Karl **KLÜPFEL** (11 Apr 1878 - 27 Jan 1962)

30 Nov 1918 - 30 Sep 1922:	Member, Navy Peace Commission
1 Oct 1922 - 26 Sep 1924:	Chief of Naval Personnel
27 Sep 1924 - 5 Jan 1925:	Attached to the Battleship *"Hessen"*
6 Jan 1925 - 6 Apr 1926:	Commandant, Battleship *"Hessen"*
7 Apr 1926 - 30 Sep 1926:	Attached to the Commander, Baltic Naval Station
(30 Sep 1926:	Promoted to brevet Konteradmiral)
30 Sep 1926:	Retired
23 Aug 1939:	Recalled to reserve status; no appointment conferred

Konteradmiral Reinhold **KNOBLOCH** (13 Mar 1883 - 27 Mar 1962)

29 Sep 1928 - 27 Sep 1929:	Chief of Staff, Inspectorate of Naval Artillery
28 Sep 1929 - 25 Feb 1930:	Commandant, Battleship *"Elsaß"*
26 Feb 1930 - 29 Sep 1931:	Commandant, Battleship *"Schleswig-Holstein"*
30 Sep 1931 - 28 Sep 1933:	Commander of Defenses, Elbe & Weser Estuaries
30 Sep 1933:	Retired
1 Oct 1933 - 30 Apr 1936:	Recalled; Instructor, Inspectorate of Naval Artillery
(30 Apr 1936:	Promoted to brevet Konteradmiral)
30 Apr 1936:	Retired
15 Feb 1939:	Recalled to reserve status; no appointment conferred

Konteradmiral (Ingeneur) Waldemar **KOBER** (14 Dec 1898 - 3 Oct 1955)

27 May 1937 - 6 Nov 1939:	Advisor, Military Office, Naval High Command
7 Nov 1939 - 5 Mar 1940:	Unit Engineer to Flag Officer, Battleships
6 Mar 1940 - 31 Dec 1940:	Unit Engineer to Flag Officer, Reconnaissance Forces
8 Jan 1941 - 4 Feb 1943:	Section Chief, Shipbuilding Directorate, Naval High Command
5 Feb 1943 - 5 Jun 1943:	Director of Naval Armaments & Repair Works, Liepaja

6 Jun 1943 - 17 Aug 1943:	Attached to the C-in-C, Baltic Naval Group
18 Aug 1943 - 22 nov 1943:	Liaison Officer to Main Shipbuilding Committee, Naval High Command
23 Nov 1943 - 15 Dec 1944:	Commandant, La Pallice Shipyards
(1 Feb 1944:	Promoted to Konteradmiral Ingeneur)
4 Jan 1945 - 8 May 1945:	Chief of Finished Ships Group, Shipbuilding Directorate, Naval High Command

Admiral Reinhard **KOCH** (31 Oct 1861 - 26 Jun 1939)

(27 Jan 1910:	Promoted to Konteradmiral)
(15 Nov 1913:	Promoted to Vizeadmiral)
15 Jul 1914 - 1 Aug 1914:	Inspector of Naval Training
2 Aug 1914 - 3 Sep 1915:	Commandant, Fortress Kiel
7 Feb 1915 - 15 Feb 1915:	Acting Commander, Baltic Naval Station
14 Aug 1915 - 3 Sep 1915:	Acting Commander, Baltic Naval Station
4 Sep 1915 - 15 Aug 1918:	Deputy Chief of Naval General Staff
(17 Jan 1918:	Promoted to Admiral)
16 Aug 1918 - 6 Nov 1918:	Placed on inactive status
6 Nov 1918:	Retired

Konteradmiral Richard **KOCH** (28 May 1863 - 9 Jul 1927)

25 Jul 1914 - Apr 1918:	Recalled from retirement; Inspector, V. Coastal Inspectorate
Apr 1918 - 13 Sep 1919:	Attached to the Commander, North Sea Naval Station
(13 Sep 1919:	Promoted to brevet Konteradmiral)
13 Sep 1919:	Retired

Konteradmiral Walther **KOEHLER** (2 Sep 1882 - 17 Mar 1970)

8 Mar 1927 - 30 Sep 1928:	Naval Liaison Officer, Military District (Wehrkreis) I
1 Oct 1928 - 28 Sep 1930:	Chief of Staff, North Sea Naval Station
1 Oct 1930 - 27 Sep 1932:	Chief of Nautical Office, Naval High Command
(30 Sep 1932:	Promoted to brevet Konteradmiral)
30 Sep 1932:	Retired
1 Jan 1939:	Recalled to reserve status
23 Jun 1941 - 31 Mar 1942:	Commissioner, Berlin - Riga Prize Court
1 Nov 1941 - 31 Mar 1943:	Commissioner, Berlin - Southeast Prize Court
(1 Apr 1942:	Confirmed as Konteradmiral from brevet rank)

1 Apr 1942 - 28 Feb 1943:	Commissioner, Berlin Prize Court
1 Mar 1943 - 31 Dec 1944:	Judge, Hamburg Prize Court
31 Dec 1944:	Retired

Marinegeneralstabsarzt (Konteradmiral) Harry **KOENIG**
(11 Jun 1858 - 25 Jan 1946)

Oct 1914 - 27 Dec 1914:	Recalled from retirement; Member, Hospital Transport Commission, Posen
28 Dec 1914 - Aug 1916:	Chief Medical Officer, XXXXI. Reserve Corps
(24 Apr 1916:	Promoted to brevet Marinegeneralstabsarzt)
Aug 1916 - Nov 1918:	Chief Medical Officer, Army Detachment Gronau
Nov 1918:	Retired

Großadmiral Hans von **KOESTER** (29 Apr 1844 - 21 Feb 1928)

(1 Apr 1889:	Promoted to Konteradmiral)
(10 Oct 1892:	Promoted to Vizeadmiral)
(22 Mar 1897:	Promoted to Admiral)
(28 Jun 1905:	Promoted to Großadmiral)
29 Dec 1906:	Retired; for services rendered, retained on Naval List
1914 - 1918:	Naval Delegate for War Wounded

Awards: *Order of the Black Eagle, Diamonds to the Order of the Black Eagle*

Admiralintendant (Konteradmiral) Dr. Alfred **KÖHLER**
(27 Jul 1899 - 1 Mar 1957)

1 Nov 1939 - 1 Mar 1944:	Chief of General Section, Naval High Command
(1 Apr 1942:	Promoted to Ministerialdirigent)
(1 May 1944:	Rank redesignated as Admiralintendant)
15 Jul 1944 - 21 Apr 1945:	Chief of Special Staff for Inland Accommodations
22 Apr 1945 - 21 May 1945:	Chief Naval Intendant, Naval Hospital Administration South

Vizeadmiral Hans **KOLBE** (11 May 1882 - 8 Sep 1957)

1 Jul 1920 - 4 Aug 1920:	Commander, Baltic Training Flotilla
23 Aug 1920 - 8 Sep 1921:	Commander, III. Flotilla
9 Sep 1921 - 26 Sep 1924:	Commander, III. Coastal Defense Detachment
27 Sep 1924 - 24 Sep 1926:	Chief of Staff, Inspectorate of Torpedoes & Mines

25 Sep 1926 - 27 Mar 1929:   Commandant, Cruiser *Berlin*
28 Mar 1929 - 19 Sep 1929:   Commander, Baltic Naval Division
20 Sep 1929 - 31 Mar 1931:   Chief of Staff, Baltic Naval Station
1 Apr 1931 - 30 Sep 1932:   Inspector of Mines & Torpedoes
(1 Oct 1931:   Promoted to Konteradmiral)
6 Jun 1931 - 22 Jun 1931:   Acting Inspector of Naval Training
1 Sep 1931 - 14 Sep 1931:   Acting Inspector of Naval Training
15 Feb 1932 - 8 Mar 1932:   Acting Inspector of Naval Training
1 Oct 1932 - 24 Sep 1934:   Flag Officer, Reconnaissance Forces
(30 Sep 1934:   Promoted to brevet Vizeadmiral)
30 Sep 1934:   Retired

Konteradmiral Wilhelm **KOPP** (22 Mar 1882 - 17 Sep 1963)
1 Oct 1936 - 30 Sep 1939:   Recalled from retirement; Commander of Recruiting Command Stade
1 Oct 1939 - 2 May 1941:   Commander of Recruiting Command Hamburg IV
3 May 1941 - 13 Jun 1941:   Fortress Commandant of Memel
5 Jul 1941 - 2 Nov 1941:   Commander of Sea Defenses, North Russia
3 Nov 1941 - 8 Jan 1943:   Commander of Sea Defenses, Ukraine
(1 Feb 1942:   Promoted to Konteradmiral)
9 Jan 1943 - 8 Apr 1943:   Commander of Sea Defenses, Loire
9 Apr 1943 - 30 Jun 1943:   Placed on inactive status
30 Jun 1943:   Retired
1 Jul 1943:   Recalled to reserve status; no appointment conferred

Konteradmiral (Ingeneur) Wilhelm **KORRENG** (20 Mar 1880 - 30 Dec 1967)
26 Sep 1927 - 26 Sep 1930:   Chief Engineer, North Sea Naval Station
(30 Sep 1930:   Promoted to brevet Konteradmiral Ingeneur)
30 Sep 1930:   Retired
28 Mar 1939:   Recalled to reserve status; no appointment conferred

Konteradmiral Max **KÖTHNER** (20 Jul 1870 - 17 Jan 1933)
16 Feb 1914 - 25 Aug 1915:   Commander, II. Torpedo Division
26 Aug 1915 - 11 Nov 1915:   Commandant, Battleship *Nassau*
12 Nov 1915 - 3 Apr 1916:   Commodore & Deputy Commander of Torpedo Boats
4 Apr 1916 - 3 Aug 1916:   Acting Commander, I. Torpedo Division

4 Aug 1916 - 8 Jan 1919:	Director of Torpedoes, Wilhelmshaven Shipyards
8 Jan 1919:	Retired
(18 Nov 1919:	Promoted to brevet Konteradmiral)

Konteradmiral Ernst **KRAFFT** (28 Feb 1885 - 27 Jul 1954)

29 Sep 1930 - 27 Sep 1934:	Commandant of Pillau
1 Oct 1934 - 18 Mar 1940:	Library Director, Baltic Naval Station & temporarily Commander of Rügen District
19 Mar 1940 - 26 Jun 1940:	Fortress Commandant, Pomeranian Coast
(1 Jun 1940:	Promoted to brevet Konteradmiral)
27 Jun 1940 - 31 Aug 1942:	Coastal Commander, Eastern Baltic & Fortress Commandant of Gotenhafen
(1 Jan 1941:	Confirmed as Konteradmiral from brevet rank)
31 Aug 1942:	Retired
1 Sep 1942:	Recalled to reserve status
31 May 1943:	Retired

Vizeadmiral Hugo **KRAFT** (10 Feb 1866 - 15 Nov 1925)

9 Mar 1914 - 8 Mar 1916:	Chief of Wilhelmshaven Shipyards
(14 Jul 1914:	Promoted to Konteradmiral)
9 Mar 1916 - 4 Dec 1917:	Director of Shipyard Department, Naval Office
(25 Nov 1916:	Promoted to Vizeadmiral)
5 Dec 1917 - 19 Jan 1918:	Attached to the High Seas Fleet
19 Jan 1918 - 13 Feb 1918:	Acting Commander, IV. Squadron
14 Feb 1918 - 14 Apr 1918:	Attached to the High Seas Fleet
15 Apr 1918 - 9 May 1918:	Acting Commander, III. Squadron
10 May 1918 - 3 Jun 1918:	Attached to the High Seas Fleet
4 Jun 1918 - 22 Jul 1918:	Acting Commander, IV. Squadron
23 Jul 1918 - 11 Aug 1918:	Attached to the High Seas Fleet
12 Aug 1918 - 4 Nov 1918:	Commander, III. Squadron
5 Nov 1918 - 8 Jan 1919:	Attached to the Secretary of State, Naval Office
8 Jan 1919:	Retired

Admiralarzt (Konteradmiral) Dr. Karl-Adalbert **KRAFT**
(24 Dec 1892 - 9 Feb 1943)

7 Oct 1936 - 21 Oct 1938:	Unit Medical Officer to Flag Officer, Reconnaissance Forces
22 Oct 1938 - 25 Oct 1939:	Medical Officer to Deputy Commander, Baltic Naval Station

22 Oct 1938 - 22 May 1940:	Unit Medical Officer to Commander of Naval Security Forces, Baltic
23 May 1940 - 21 Jan 1941:	Senior Medical Officer to Admiral Commanding, Norway
22 Jan 1941 - 23 Aug 1942:	Chief Medical Officer, La Baule Naval Hospital
(1 Sep 1942:	Promoted to Admiralarzt)
10 Sep 1942 - 16 Nov 1942:	Senior Medical Officer to Admiral Commanding, France
16 Nov 1942 - 9 Feb 1943:	Senior Medical Officer, Naval Group West

Admiral Theodor **KRANCKE** (30 Mar 1893 - 18 Jun 1973)

4 Oct 1937 - 21 Aug 1939:	Commandant, Naval Academy
22 Aug 1939 - 27 Oct 1939:	Chief of Staff, North Sea Security Forces
31 Oct 1939 - 4 Feb 1940:	Commandant, Heavy Cruiser *"Admiral Scheer"*
5 Feb 1940 - 11 Apr 1940:	Naval Representative in Special Staff for Operation "Weserübung", Armed Forces High Command (OKW)
12 Apr 1940 - 16 Jun 1940:	Chief of Staff to Admiral Commanding, Norway
17 Jun 1940 - 3 Jun 1941:	Commandant, Heavy Cruiser *"Admiral Scheer"*
(1 Apr 1941:	Promoted to Konteradmiral)
4 Jun 1941 - 19 Apr 1943:	Chief of Naval Command Office, Naval High Command
(1 Apr 1942:	Promoted to Vizeadmiral)
(1 Mar 1943:	Promoted to Admiral)
1 Jan 1942 - 28 Feb 1943:	Naval Representative, Führer Headquarters
20 Apr 1943 - 18 Apr 1945:	C-in-C, Naval Group West
26 Apr 1945 - 26 Aug 1945:	C-in-C, Naval Group Norway

Awards: *Knight's Cross with Oakleaves; Knight's Cross*

Konteradmiral Otto **KRANZBÜHLER** (17 Jan 1871 - 8 Apr 1932)

5 Aug 1914 - 9 Jul 1915:	Commandant, Battleship *"Kaiser Wilhelm II"*
10 Jul 1915 - 29 Mar 1917:	Attached to the Naval Aviation Section, Naval Office
30 Mar 1917 - 13 Feb 1919:	Chief of Naval Aviation
14 Feb 1919 - 6 Jun 1919:	Chief of Naval Aviation Section, Naval Office
7 Jun 1919 - 4 Mar 1920:	Attached to the Naval Office
(29 Nov 1919:	Promoted to brevet Konteradmiral)
4 Mar 1920:	Retired

Vizeadmiral Walter **KRASTEL** (29 Jan 1892 - 15 Sep 1966)
1 Oct 1934 - 30 Sep 1937:	Chief of Underwater Weapons Group, Naval Weapons Office, Naval High Command
9 Oct 1937 - 15 Nov 1938:	Commandant, Cruiser "*Nürnberg*"
16 Nov 1938 - 6 Sep 1942:	Commandant, Explosives School
(1 Dec 1940:	Promoted to Konteradmiral)
Sep 1940 - Nov 1940:	Deputy Commander of Minelayers
3 Aug 1941 - 27 Oct 1941:	Acting Naval Commander, Norwegian Polar Coast
30 Apr 1942 - 7 Jun 1942:	Simultaneously, Acting Naval Commander, Norwegian North Coast
7 Sep 1942 - 31 Mar 1943:	Chief of Explosives Office, Naval High Command
(1 Feb 1943:	Promoted to Vizeadmiral)
1 Apr 1943 - 30 Apr 1943:	Transferred to Armaments Inspectorate X
1 May 1943 - 31 May 1943:	Transferred to Armaments Inspectorate XX
1 Jun 1943 - 8 May 1945:	Inspector, Armaments Inspectorate XX

Konteradmiral Ernst **KRATZENBERG** (25 Jan 1896 - 16 Jul 1984)
1 Oct 1935 - 14 Jan 1940:	Advisor, Naval Defense Office, Naval High Command
15 Jan 1940 - 28 May 1941:	Commandant, Light Cruiser "*Köln*"
29 May 1941 - 17 May 1943:	Chief of Construction Section, U-Boat Directorate, Naval High Command
(1 Feb 1943:	Promoted to Konteradmiral)
22 Feb 1943 - 17 May 1943:	Chief of U-Boat Directorate, Naval High Command
18 May 1943 - 19 Apr 1945:	Chief of Staff to Flag Officer, Submarines
20 Apr 1945 - 8 May 1945:	Deputy Commander-Designate, North Sea Naval Forces

Awards: *German Cross in Silver*

Vizeadmiral Günther **KRAUSE** (25 Jan 1890 - 12 Oct 1983)
3 Oct 1933 - 6 Oct 1935:	Chief of Stettin Naval Office
7 Oct 1935 - 2 May 1937:	Commandant, Battleship "*Schleswig-Holstein*"
7 May 1937 - 15 Apr 1943:	Inspector of Naval Artillery Equipment
(1 Aug 1939:	Promoted to Konteradmiral)
(1 Feb 1942:	Promoted to Vizeadmiral)
16 Apr 1943 - 30 Jun 1943:	Attached to the Commander, North Sea Naval Station

1 Jul 1943 - 10 Feb 1945:	Director of Horten Shipyards
6 Sep 1943 - 25 Oct 1943:	Acting Commander of Sea Defenses, Arctic Ocean Coast
11 Feb 1945 - 31 Mar 1945:	Attached to the C-in-C, North Sea Naval Group
31 Mar 1945:	Retired

Awards: *German Cross in Silver*

Admiralarzt (Konteradmiral) Dr. Emil **KRAUSS** (29 Mar 1883 - 20 Apr 1949)

21 Mar 1930 - 29 Mar 1932:	Chief Medical Officer, Kiel-Wik Naval Hospital
30 Mar 1932 - 28 Sep 1934:	Medical Officer, High Seas Fleet
(30 Sep 1934:	Promoted to brevet Admiralarzt)
30 Sep 1934:	Retired

Konteradmiral Fritz **KRAUSS** (20 Mar 1898 - 13 Jul 1978)

4 Apr 1938 - 10 Jan 1940:	Navigational Officer, Pocket Battleship "*Lützow*"
11 jan 1940 - 18 Apr 1940:	First Officer, Pocket Battleship "*Lützow*"
19 Apr 1940 - 23 Jun 1940:	Acting Commandant, Pocket Battleship "*Lützow*"
24 Jun 1940 - 30 Nov 1940:	Chief of Staff to Naval Commander, West France
1 Dec 1940 - 4 Apr 1941:	Attached to Naval High Command
5 Apr 1941 - 1 Feb 1943:	First Officer, Heavy Cruiser "*Admiral Hipper*"
2 Feb 1943 - 1 Apr 1943:	Acting Commandant, Heavy Cruiser "*Admiral Hipper*"
2 Apr 1943 - 31 Aug 1943:	Chief of Naval Communications, Italy
1 Oct 1943 - 16 Aug 1944:	Section Chief, Technical Communications Office, Naval High Command
17 Aug 1944 - 22 Jul 1945:	Chief of Naval Intelligence
(16 Sep 1944:	Promoted to Konteradmiral)

Vizeadmiral Leo **KREISCH** (25 Jun 1895 - 22 Feb 1977)

29 Sep 1937 - 30 Sep 1939:	Staff Officer, Baltic Naval Station
21 Jun 1939 - 12 Jul 1939:	Acting Chief of Staff, Baltic Naval Station
1 Oct 1939 - 7 Aug 1940:	Chief of Military Office, U-Boat Directorate, Naval High Command
8 Aug 1940 - 25 Mar 1941:	Commandant, Light Cruiser "*Nürnberg*"
28 Mar 1941 - 3 Jul 1941:	Commandant, Pocket Battleship "*Lützow*"

4 Jul 1941 - 17 Nov 1941:	Chief of Naval Training Command, Romania
18 Nov 1941 - 26 Jan 1942:	Acting Commandant, Pocket Battleship "*Lützow*"
27 Jan 1942 - 12 Aug 1943:	Commander of U-Boats, Italy
(1 Jan 1943:	Promoted to Konteradmiral)
13 Aug 1943 - 25 Jan 1944:	Commander of U-Boats, Mediterranean
(1 Jan 1945:	Promoted to Vizeadmiral)
26 Jan 1944 - 29 May 1945:	Flag Officer, Destroyers

Awards: *German Cross in Gold*

Admiral Günther von **KROSIGK** (13 Sep 1860 - 16 Jun 1938)

(3 Apr 1909:	Promoted to Konteradmiral)
(5 Sep 1911:	Promoted to Vizeadmiral)
16 Jul 1914 - 29 Dec 1918:	Commander, North Sea Naval Station
(22 Mar 1915:	Promoted to Admiral)
8 Jan 1919:	Retired

Konteradmiral Wilhelm von **KROSIGK** (20 Nov 1871 - 12 Aug 1953)

5 Aug 1914 - 27 Nov 1915:	Commandant, Heavy Cruiser "*Prinz Heinrich*"
28 Nov 1915 - 19 Dec 1915:	Placed on inactive status
20 Dec 1915 - 27 Mar 1916:	Commandant, Heavy Cruiser "*Prinz Heinrich*"
28 Mar 1916 - 31 May 1917:	Commander, I. Seaman Division
2 Jun 1917 - 8 Nov 1918:	Commandant, Battleship "*Posen*"
12 Aug 1918 - 23 Aug 1918:	Acting Deputy Commander, I. Squadron
11 Sep 1918 - 22 Sep 1918:	Acting Deputy Commander, I. Squadron
9 Nov 1918 - 27 May 1919:	Attached to the Commander, North Sea Naval Station
27 May 1919:	Retired
(22 Feb 1920:	Promoted to brevet Konteradmiral)

Ministerialdirigent (Konteradmiral) Dr. Walter **KRÜGER** (22 Sep 1883 - 19 Nov 1942)

7 Nov 1939 - 31 Oct 1942:	Chief of Weapons Construction Technical Section, Naval Weapons Office, Naval High Command
(1942:	Promoted to Ministerialdirigent)
1 Nov 1942 - 19 Nov 1942:	Chief of Artillery Construction Group, Naval Artillery Office, Naval High Command

Marinehafenbaudirektor (Konteradmiral) Dr. Wilhelm **KRÜGER**
(15 Feb 1871 - 29 Feb 1940)

1 Apr 1933 - 1 Feb 1936:	Director of Harbor Construction, Wilhelmshaven Naval Dockyards
1 Feb 1936:	Retired
(21 Jul 1936:	Accorded Konteradmiral rank)

Ministerialdirigent (Konteradmiral) Paul **KÜCHLER**
(13 Mar 1885 - 9 Jan 1967)

1 Oct 1939 - 31 Mar 1943:	Chief of Technical Personnel Section, Naval Construction Office, Naval High Command
(20 Apr 1942:	Promoted to Ministerialdirigent)
1 Apr 1943 - 30 Apr 1944:	Chief of Personnel Section, Naval Construction Office, Naval High Command
1 May 1944 - 31 Oct 1944:	Chief of Central Personal Section for Technical Officers, Naval Armaments Directorate, Naval High Command
31 Oct 1944:	Retired

Konteradmiral Karl **KÜHLENTHAL** (26 Oct 1872 - 5 May 1969)

1 Oct 1911 - Nov 1917:	Chief of Installation of Coastal Defenses & Artillery Depots
Nov 1917 - 12 Dec 1918:	Artillery Commander, 1. Marine Division, Flanders Marine Corps
8 Jul 1918 - 6 Aug 1918:	Acting Commander, I. Marine Brigade
2 Jan 1919 - 30 Sep 1920:	Inspector, Naval Depot Inspectorate
(16 Sep 1920:	Promoted to brevet Konteradmiral)
30 Sep 1920:	Retired

Konteradmiral Friedrich von **KÜHLWETTER** (20 Nov 1865 - 9 Jan 1931)

3 Aug 1914 - 18 Aug 1914:	Recalled from retirement; Judge, Kiel Prize Court
19 Aug 1914 - Sep 1914:	Attached to the Special Mission to Turkey
Sep 1914 - Mar 1915:	Commandant of Bosphorus Fortifications, Chief of Staff to the C-in-C, Bosphorus Straits
Mar 1915 - 8 Nov 1916:	Attached to the Naval General Staff
8 Nov 1916:	Retired
(18 Dec 1919:	Promoted to brevet Konteradmiral)

Konteradmiral (Ingeneur) Walter **KÜHN** (27 Jul 1890 - 24 Apr 1944)
2 Oct 1934 - 14 Oct 1936:	Unit Engineer to Flag Officer, Reconnaissance Forces
15 Oct 1936 - 7 Feb 1937:	Attached to the Ships Equipment Inspectorate
8 Feb 1937 - 4 Aug 1940:	Station Engineer, Baltic Naval Station
5 Aug 1940 - 30 Apr 1943:	Group Engineer, Naval Group North
(1 Sep 1940:	Promoted to Konteradmiral Ingeneur)
1 May 1943 - 30 Sep 1943:	Attached to the C-in-C, Baltic Naval Group
30 Sep 1943:	Retired

Konteradmiral Max **KÜHNE** (19 May 1872 - 12 Jan 1961)
1 Mar 1941 - 10 Feb 1942:	Recalled from retirement; Judge, Berlin Prize Court
11 Feb 1942 - 30 Sep 1942:	Commissioner, Hamburg Prize Court
(1 Sep 1942:	Promoted to Konteradmiral)
1 Oct 1942 - 31 Oct 1942:	Attached to the Commander, North Sea Naval Station
31 Oct 1942:	Retired

Vizeadmiral Robert **KÜHNE** (19 Apr 1868 - 30 Jan 1947)
5 Aug 1914 - 3 Feb 1915:	Commandant, Battleship *"Kaiser Wilhelm der Grosse"*
4 Feb 1915 - 8 Nov 1915:	Commandant, Battleship *"Elsaß"*
11 Nov 1915 - 9 Feb 1916:	Commandant, Battleship *"Nassau"*
10 Feb 1916 - 23 Feb 1916:	Attached to the Commander, North Sea Naval Station
24 Feb 1916 - 18 Jan 1918:	Inspector, II. Naval Inspectorate
(24 Apr 1916:	Promoted to Konteradmiral)
18 Jan 1918 - 1 Aug 1918:	Placed on inactive status
1 Aug 1918 - 25 Nov 1918:	Chairman of Commission on Personnel Matters
25 Nov 1918:	Retired
(24 Nov 1919:	Promoted to brevet Vizeadmiral)

Ministerialdirigent (Konteradmiral) Dr. Wilhelm **KULLMANN** (27 Jan 1900 - 13 Oct 1973)
1 Mar 1939 - 2 Jul 1944:	Director of Administration, Wilhelmshaven Naval Dockyards
(14 Feb 1944:	Promoted to Generalintendant der Marine)
(5 Jun 1944:	Rank redesignated as Ministerialdirigent)

3 Jul 1944 - Jul 1945: Chief of Dockyards & Arsenals Administration Section, Naval High Command

Generaladmiral Oskar **KUMMETZ** (21 Jul 1891 - 17 Dec 1980)
4 Oct 1934 - 28 Sep 1937: Flag Officer, Torpedo Boats
30 Sep 1937 - 30 Oct 1938: Chief of Staff, Baltic Naval Station
31 Oct 1938 - 20 Oct 1939: Chief of Staff, High Seas Fleet
21 Oct 1939 - 20 Dec 1939: Attached to the Commander, Baltic Naval Station
21 Dec 1939 - 29 May 1942: Inspector of Torpedoes
(1 Jan 1940: Promoted to Konteradmiral)
(1 Apr 1942: Promoted to Vizeadmiral)
5 Apr 1940 - 11 Apr 1940: Commander, Battle Group V
3 Jun 1942 - 18 Feb 1943: Flag Officer, Cruisers
19 Feb 1943 - 29 Feb 1944: Flag Officer, Battleships
(1 Mar 1943: Promoted to Admiral)
1 Mar 1944 - 23 Jul 1945: C-in-C, Naval Group Baltic
(16 Sep 1944: Promoted to Generaladmiral)
Awards: *Knight's Cross*

Konteradmiral Prof. Dr. Karl **KÜPFMÜLLER** (6 Oct 1897 - 26 Dec 1977)
12 Jan 1944 - 8 May 1945: Chief of Scientific Command Staff, Naval High Command
(1944: Accorded Konteradmiral rank)
Awards: *Knight's Cross of the War Merit Cross with Swords*

Vizeadmiral FriedrichWilhelm **KURZE** (5 Jul 1891 - 23 Dec 1945)
24 Sep 1931 - 25 Sep 1935: Commandant, Survey Ship "*Meteor*"
28 Sep 1935 - 11 Dec 1944: Chief of Nautical Department, Naval High Command
(1 Jan 1940: Promoted to Konteradmiral)
(1 Mar 1942: Promoted to Vizeadmiral)
12 Dec 1944 - 28 Feb 1945: Attached to the C-in-C, Baltic Naval Group
28 Feb 1945: Retired
1 Mar 1945: Recalled to reserve status; no appointment conferred
Awards: *German Cross in Silver*

Konteradmiral Hans **KÜSEL** (28 Feb 1870 - 14 Jun 1951)
17 Jan 1912 - 22 Sep 1915: Commandant, Battleship "*Hessen*"
28 Sep 1915 - 17 Nov 1916: Commandant, Battleship "*Thüringen*"

15 Dec 1916 - 8 Nov 1918:	Chief of Staff, Baltic Naval Station
(18 Sep 1918:	Promoted to Konteradmiral)
8 Nov 1918 - 10 Mar 1919:	Acting Commander, Baltic Naval Station
11 Mar 1919 - 24 Nov 1919:	Attached to the Commander, Baltic Naval Station
24 Nov 1919:	Retired
23 Aug 1939:	Recalled to reserve status; no appointment conferred

Konteradmiral William **KUTTER** (25 Apr 1863 - 8 Oct 1941)

2 Aug 1914 - 15 Jan 1916:	Recalled from retirement; Commander, 1. Construction Division
(15 Jan 1916:	Promoted to brevet Konteradmiral)
15 Jan 1916:	Retired

Marinegeneralstabsarzt (Konteradmiral) Prof. Dr. Hermann **KÜTTNER** (10 Oct 1870 - 10 Oct 1932)

2 Aug 1914 - 5 Aug 1918:	Consultant Surgeon, Fortress Hospital Breslau, Silesia & Posen Reserve Hospitals and Flanders Marine Corps
5 Aug 1918:	Retired
(26 Jan 1920:	Promoted to brevet Marinegeneralstabsarzt)

Konteradmiral **KYRILL VLADIMIROVICH**, Grand Duke of Russia (12 Oct 1876 - 13 Oct 1938)
Konteradmiral à la Suite (Honorary title)
Awards: *Order of the Black Eagle*

Marineoberbaudirektor der Reserve (Vizeadmiral) Prof. Walter **LAAS** (7 Feb 1870 - 16 Oct 1951)

1 Nov 1941 - 30 Jun 1943:	Entry into the Navy; Chief of Technical Section, Dockyards Staff Aegean
(1 Jan 1943:	Promoted to Marineoberbaudirektor der Reserve)
1 Jul 1943 - 31 Jul 1943:	Attached to Naval High Command
31 Jul 1943:	Retired

Konteradmiral Rudolf **LAHS** (3 Jan 1880 - 16 Nov 1954)

22 Nov 1927 - 31 Mar 1928:	Chief of Naval Transport Office, Naval High Command

1 Apr 1928 - 29 Mar 1929:	Chief of Naval Air Defense Office, Naval High Command
(31 Mar 1929:	Promoted to brevet Konteradmiral)
31 Mar 1929:	Retired

Konteradmiral Heinrich **LAMPE** (24 Jun 1877 - 1 Jan 1928)

27 Dec 1919 - 16 Mar 1920:	Liaison Officer, Navy Peace Commission, Flensburg
17 Mar 1920 - 22 May 1920:	Inspector, Coastal Defense Inspectorate V
23 May 1920 - 31 Mar 1922:	Commandant of Wilhelmshaven
1 Apr 1922 - 30 Sep 1023:	Commander, North Sea Naval Division
1 Oct 1923 - 31 Dec 1923:	Attached to the Commander, North Sea Naval Station
(31 Dec 1923:	Promoted to brevet Konteradmiral)
31 Dec 1923:	Retired

Vizeadmiral Fritz **LAMPRECHT** (9 Aug 1893 - 23 Jul 1961)

6 Oct 1933 - 15 Nov 1938:	Commandant, Explosives School
18 Nov 1938 - 29 Aug 1942:	Chief of Explosives Office, Naval High Command
(1 Dec 1940:	Promoted to Konteradmiral)
4 Sep 1942 - 13 Nov 1942:	Acting Commander, Sea Defenses, Crimea
14 Nov 1942 - 30 Nov 1942:	Acting Commander, Sea Defenses Ukraine
7 Dec 1942 - 31 Jul 1944:	Inspector, Armaments Inspectorate Netherlands
(1 Feb 1943:	Promoted to Vizeadmiral)
29 Aug 1944 - 8 May 1945:	Commander, Naval Ship-Borne Flak Brigade North

Konteradmiral Richard **LANGE** (27 Feb 1868 - 18 Feb 1939)

1 Oct 1912 - 2 Jun 1917:	Commandant, Battleship *"Posen"*
(31 May 1917:	Promoted to Konteradmiral)
2 Feb 1916 - 29 Feb 1916:	Acting Deputy Commander, I. Squadron
17 Jul 1916 - 7 Sep 1916:	Acting Deputy Commander, I. Squadron
1 Feb 1917 - 2 Feb 1917:	Acting Deputy Commander, I. Squadron
3 Jun 1917 - 1 Jan 1919:	Inspector, Naval Depot Inspectorate
2 Jan 1919 - 23 Jan 1919:	Attached to the Secretary of State, Naval Office
23 Jan 1919:	Retired

Admiralarzt (Konteradmiral) Dr. Walter **LANGE** (12 Jul 1882 - 27 Oct 1961)
29 Sep 1930 - 28 Sep 1933:	Chief Medical Officer, Baltic Naval Station
(30 Sep 1933:	Promoted to brevet Marinegeneralstabsarzt [Konteradmiral])
30 Sep 1933:	Retired
15 Sep 1939 - 9 Apr 1940:	Recalled; attached to the Medical Service, Baltic Naval Station
10 Apr 1940 - 31 Oct 1943:	Chief Medical Officer, Malente Naval Hospital
(1 Aug 1941:	Confirmed as Admiralarzt from brevet rank)
1 Nov 1943 - 31 Dec 1943:	Attached to the Chief Medical Officer, Baltic Naval Group
31 Dec 1943:	Retired

Vizeadmiral Werner **LANGE** (18 Jul 1893 - 19 Nov 1965)
22 Sep 1936 - 2 Apr 1939:	Naval Attaché, Rome
8 May 1939 - 28 Aug 1940:	Commandant, Light Cruiser "*Emden*"
29 Aug 1940 - 19 Dec 1940:	Chief of Military Office, U-Boat Directorate, Naval High Command
20 Dec 1940 - 22 Feb 1943:	Chief of U-Boat Directorate, Naval High Command
(1 Apr 1941:	Promoted to Konteradmiral)
23 Feb 1943 - 28 Nov 1944:	Admiral Commanding, Aegean
(1 Apr 1943:	Promoted to Vizeadmiral)
29 Nov 1944 - 30 Mar 1945:	Admiral Commanding, Western Baltic
31 Mar 1945 - 8 May 1945:	Attached to the C-in-C, Baltic Naval Group

Awards: *Knight's Cross; German Cross in Gold*

Vizeadmiral Hugo **LANGEMAK** (4 May 1869 - 1 Jul 1937)
23 Sep 1913 - 30 Jul 1914:	Chief of Staff, Torpedo Inspectorate
31 Jul 1914 - 3 Feb 1915:	Commandant, Battleship "*Elsaß*"
4 Feb 1915 - 27 Sep 1915:	Commandant, Battleship "*Thüringen*"
30 Sep 1915 - 14 Jan 1916:	Deputy Commander of Reconnaissance Forces, Baltic
15 Jan 1916 - 9 Feb 1916:	Commodore & Acting Commander of Reconnaissance Forces, Eastern Baltic
15 Jan 1916 - 23 Apr 1916:	Commodore & Acting Commander, VI. Reconnaissance Group and Commander of Torpedo Boats, Baltic
(24 Apr 1916:	Promoted to Konteradmiral)
24 Apr 1916 - 3 Jun 1916:	Commander, VI. Reconnaissance Group and Commander of Torpedo Boats, Baltic

4 Jun 1916 - 10 Dec 1916:	Commander of Reconaissance Forces, Eastern Baltic
11 Dec 1916 - 14 Feb 1917:	Attached to the Commander, Baltic Naval Station
15 Feb 1917 - 12 Apr 1917:	Acting Commandant, Helgoland
13 Apr 1917 - 2 May 1917:	Attached to the C-in-C, High Seas Fleet
3 May 1917 - 19 May 1917:	Acting Deputy Commander, IV. Squadron
20 May 1917 - 9 Jul 1917:	Attached to the Secretary of State, Naval Office
10 Jul 1917 - 17 Jan 1919:	Inspector of Mines and Explosive Weapons
18 Jan 1919 - 8 Jun 1919:	Attached to the Naval Office
8 Jun 1919:	Retired
(4 Sep 1919:	Promoted to brevet Vizeadmiral)

Konteradmiral Max **LANS** (4 Nov 1868 - 3 Aug 1928)

30 Aug 1914 - 12 Jul 1916:	Commandant, Battleship *"Braunschweig"*
15 Jul 1916 - 18 Jan 1917:	Commandant, Battleship *"Hessen"*
23 Jul 1916 - 15 Aug 1916:	Senior Naval Commander, Sund
29 Jan 1917 - 6 Sep 1917:	Director of Libau Naval Works
29 Apr 1917 - 11 Jun 1917:	Commander of Naval Installations, Kurland
7 Sep 1917 - 11 Oct 1917:	Harbor Captain, Riga - Dunaburg
12 Oct 1917 - 17 May 1918:	Commander of Naval Installations & Deputy Governor, Baltic Islands
18 May 1918 - 31 May 1918:	Commander of Naval Installations, Kurland
1 Jun 1918 - 22 Aug 1918:	Commander of Naval Installations, Kurland & Livland
3 Sep 1918 - 16 Nov 1918:	Commander, II. Marine Brigade, Flanders Marine Corps
17 Nov 1918 - 17 Mar 1919:	Attached to the Commander, North Sea Naval Station
17 Mar 1919:	Retired
(30 Aug 1919:	Promoted to brevet Konteradmiral)

Konteradmiral Otto **LANS** (28 Jun 1870 - 17 Mar 1942)

9 Aug 1914 - 11 Nov 1915:	Recalled from retirement; Section Chief, Naval Cabinet
12 Nov 1915 - 30 Jun 1918:	Deputy Section Chief, Naval Cabinet
30 Jun 1918:	Retired
(20 Dec 1920:	Promoted to brevet Konteradmiral)

Admiral Wilhelm von **LANS** (5 Mar 1861 - 21 Mar 1947)
(5 Sep 1909:	Promoted to Konteradmiral)
(27 Jan 1913:	Promoted to Vizeadmiral)
27 Jan 1913 - 14 Feb 1915:	Commander, I. Squadron
15 Feb 1915 - 18 Sep 1915:	Attached to the Commander, North Sea Naval Station
(18 Sep 1915:	Promoted to brevet Admiral)
18 Sep 1915:	Retired; Admiral à la Suite
1916 - 1917:	Reserve C-in-C, High Seas Fleet

Awards: *Pour le Mérite*

Konteradmiral Hans Paul **LEITHÄUSER** (25 Jun 1895 - 22 Jul 1943)
31 Oct 1938 - 28 Nov 1939:	Commandant, Artillery Training Ship "*Brummer*"
29 Nov 1939 - 14 Mar 1943:	Chief of Artillery Fire Control Section, Naval Weapons Office, Naval High Command
15 Mar 1943 - 22 Jul 1943:	Commandant of Sea Defenses, Attika
(23 Jul 1943:	Promoted to Konteradmiral, posthumously)

Konteradmiral (Ingeneur) Franz **LEMKE** (31 Jan 1862 - 10 Nov 1925)
3 Apr 1918 - 7 Jan 1919:	Chief Engineer, High Seas Fleet
8 Jan 1919 - 26 May 1920:	Chief Engineer, Baltic Naval Station
27 May 1920 - 3 Mar 1922:	Chief Engineer, Naval High Command
4 Mar 1922 - 31 Mar 1922:	Attached to the Commander-in-Chief of the Navy
(31 Mar 1922:	Promoted to brevet Konteradmiral Ingeneur)
31 Mar 1922:	Retired

Konteradmiral Magnus von **LEVETZOW** (8 Jan 1871 - 13 Mar 1939)
9 Jan 1913 - 26 Jan 1916:	Commandant, Heavy Cruiser "*Moltke*"
26 Jan 1916 - 20 Jan 1918:	Chief of Operations, High Seas Fleet
21 Jan 1918 - 5 Aug 1918:	Commodore & Commander, II. Reconaissance Group
28 Aug 1918 - 17 Dec 1918:	Chief of Staff, Naval General Staff
18 Dec 1918 - 7 Jan 1920:	Attached to the Naval Office
8 Jan 1920 - 18 Mar 1920:	Commander, Baltic Naval Station
(21 Jan 1920:	Promoted to Konteradmiral)
19 Mar 1920 - 29 Oct 1920:	Placed on inactive status
29 Oct 1920:	Retired

Awards: *Pour le Mérite*

Konteradmiral Bernhard **LIEBETANZ** (31 Jul 1894 - 10 Jan 1966)
30 Sep 1937 - 6 May 1939:	Advisor, Organization Section, Naval General Staff
7 May 1939 - 15 Mar 1940:	Chief of Königsberg Naval Office
16 Mar 1940 - 9 May 1940:	Deputy Fortress Commandant of Gotenhafen & Deputy Coastal Commander, Eastern Baltic
24 May 1940 - 13 Jun 1940:	Harbor Commandant of Den Helder
14 Jun 1940 - 22 Jul 1940:	Naval Liaisons Officer, 4. Army
23 Jul 1940 - 2 Sep 1940:	Chief of Bordeaux Naval Office
3 Sep 1940 - 2 Feb 1941:	Chief of Le Havre Naval Office
3 Feb 1941 - 14 Aug 1942:	Commander of Sea Defenses, Seine-Somme
23 Sep 1942 - 10 Apr 1943:	Chief of Staff to Admiral Commanding, Norwegian West Coast
(1 Dec 1942:	Promoted to Konteradmiral)
16 Apr 1943 - 20 Apr 1945:	Inspector of Naval Arsenals

Vizeadmiral Joachim **LIETZMANN** (1 Sep 1894 - 19 Sep 1959)
24 Aug 1937 - 30 Mar 1940:	Naval Attaché, Tokyo
28 May 1940 - 21 Jun 1940:	Chief of Staff to Admiral Commanding, West
22 Jun 1940 - 7 Apr 1942:	Chief of Staff to Admiral Commanding, France
(1 Jan 1941:	Promoted to Konteradmiral)
8 Apr 1942 - 2 Mar 1943:	Commander of Fleet Training Units
3 Mar 1943 - 9 Sep 1943:	Coastal Defense Commander, Pommeranian Coast
10 Sep 1943 - 3 Jul 1944:	Admiral Commanding, Adriatic
(1 Oct 1943:	Promoted to Vizeadmiral)
4 Jul 1944 - 16 Jul 1944:	Placed on inactive status
17 Jul 1944 - 7 Dec 1944:	Admiral Commanding, Adriatic
10 Jan 1945 - 5 May 1945:	Special Purposes Admiral, Southeast

Awards: *German Cross in Gold*

Admiral Eugen **LINDAU** (3 May 1883 - 10 May 1960)
6 Nov 1929 - 25 Sep 1931:	Commandant, Cruiser "*Karlsruhe*"
28 Sep 1931 - 28 Sep 1933:	Commandant of Swinemünde
(1 Oct 1933:	Promoted to Konteradmiral)
2 Oct 1933 - 31 Jan 1935:	Chief of Hamburg Naval Office
1 Feb 1935 - 5 Oct 1936:	Admiral-in-Charge Hamburg Naval Office
6 Oct 1936 - 14 Aug 1938:	Inspector of Elbing Recruiting Inspectorate
(20 Apr 1937:	Promoted to brevet Vizeadmiral)
(1 Oct 1937:	Confirmed as Vizeadmiral from brevet rank)

22 Aug 1938 - 31 Dec 1939:	Inspector of Bremen Recruiting Inspectorate
1 Jan 1940 - 25 May 1940:	Deputy Commissioner, Hamburg Prize Court
26 May 1940 - 19 Feb 1941:	Naval Commander, North France
20 Feb 1941 - 7 Aug 1942:	Naval Commander, West France
(1 Mar 1942:	Promoted to Admiral)
8 Aug 1942 - 31 Aug 1942:	Attached to the Commander, North Sea Naval Station
31 Aug 1942:	Retired

Konteradmiral Werner **LINDENAU** (21 Sep 1892 - 21 Aug 1975)

4 Aug 1938 - 4 Apr 1939:	Commandant, Battleship *"Schlesien"*
18 Apr 1939 - 28 Feb 1943:	Commandant of Torpedo School
(1 Feb 1942:	Promoted to Konteradmiral)
29 Aug 1940 - 27 Oct 1940:	Chief of Boulogne Naval Office & Commander-Designate, Transport Fleet D
27 May 1941 - 8 Oct 1941:	Commandant, Battleship *"Schlesien"*
1 Mar 1943 - 14 Jun 1943:	Commandant of Torpedo Arsenal West
15 Jun 1943 - 16 Aug 1944:	Senior Naval Commander, Paris
17 Aug 1944 - 9 Jan 1945:	Senior Naval Commander, West
11 Jan 1945 - 8 May 1945:	Commandant of Kaiser-Wilhelm Canal

Vizeadmiral Wilfried von **LOEWENFELD** (25 Sep 1879 - 5 Jul 1946)

17 Nov 1918 - 8 Apr 1919:	Commander, 5. Marine Regiment, Kiel Marine Division
9 Apr 1919 - 2 May 1919:	Commander, von Loewenfeld Marine Brigade
3 May 1919 - 30 Jun 1920:	Commander, III. Marine Brigade
1 Jul 1920 - 23 Mar 1921:	Attached to the Commander-in-Chief of the Navy
24 Mar 1921 - 31 Mar 1922:	Commander, Baltic Standing Naval Force Division
1 Apr 1922 - 1 Jul 1922:	Attached to the Cruiser *"Berlin"*
2 Jul 1922 - 30 Sep 1923:	Commandant, Cruiser *"Berlin"*
1 Oct 1923 - 5 Oct 1924:	Commander, Baltic Standing Naval Force Division
6 Oct 1924 - 11 Sep 1925:	Chief of Staff, Baltic Naval Station
2 Oct 1925 - 10 Mar 1927:	Chief of Fleet Office, Naval High Command (Chief of Naval Operations)
16 Mar 1927 - 14 Oct 1928:	Commander of Baltic Naval Forces & Flag Officer, Reconnaissance Forces
(1 Jan 1928:	Promoted to Konteradmiral)

(31 Oct 1928:   Promoted to brevet Vizeadmiral)
31 Oct 1928:   Retired
25 Jul 1939:   Recalled to reserve status;
                          no appointment conferred

Vizeadmiral Heinrich **LÖHLEIN** (1 Feb 1871 - 2 Mar 1960)
11 Nov 1911 - 31 May 1915: Chief of Naval Intelligence, Naval Office
1 Jun 1915 - 30 Jan 1916:   Chief of Central Section, Naval Office
31 Jan 1916 - 19 May 1916: Director of Supply Department, Naval Office
4 Jun 1916 - 30 Jun 1916:   Commandant, Battleship "*Oldenburg*"
1 Jul 1916 - 13 Jul 1916:   Commandant, Battleship "*König Albert*"
14 Jul 1916 - 12 Aug 1918: Commandant, Battleship "*Oldenburg*"
16 Aug 1918 - 7 Oct 1918:   Chief of Security, North Sea
8 Oct 1918 - 6 Feb 1919:   Chief of U-Boat Office, Naval High Command
7 Feb 1919 - 30 Sep 1919:   Director of Shipyard Department,
                            Naval High Command
1 Oct 1919 - 26 Sep 1921:   Chief of Naval General Office,
                            Naval High Command
(22 Nov 1919:   Promoted to Konteradmiral)
(20 Dec 1920:   Promoted to Vizeadmiral)
5 Aug 1920 - 18 Aug 1920:   Acting Commander-in-Chief of the Navy
26 Sep 1921:   Retired

Vizeadmiral Walter Georg **LOHMANN** (11 Dec 1891 - 13 Apr 1955)
26 Aug 1936 - 19 Jun 1937: Commandant, Cruiser "*Emden*"
20 Jun 1937 - 28 Sep 1937: Chief of Königsberg Naval Office
29 Sep 1937 - 12 Oct 1939: Chief of Budget Office, Naval High Command
13 Oct 1939 - 30 Sep 1942: Commandant, Mürwik Naval School
(1 Jan 1940:   Promoted to Konteradmiral)
(1 Mar 1942:   Promoted to Vizeadmiral)
1 Oct 1942 - 22 Feb 1945:   Admiral-in-Charge, Hamburg Naval Office &
                            Commander, Naval Flak Brigade North
23 Feb 1945 - 30 Apr 1945: Attached to the C-in-C, Naval Group North
30 Apr 1945:   Retired
Awards: *German Cross in Silver*

Vizeadmiral Max **LOOFF** (2 May 1874 - 20 Sep 1954)
1 Apr 1914 - 11 Jul 1915:   Commandant, Light Cruiser "*Königsberg*"
12 Jul 1915 - 21 Nov 1917: Commander of Naval Troops,
                            German East Africa

22 Nov 1917 - 26 Feb 1919:	Prisoner of War
27 Feb 1919 - 20 Jun 1919:	Attached to the Commander, Baltic Naval Station
21 Jun 1919 - 2 Sep 1919:	Attached to Inspectorate of Mines & Explosives
3 Sep 1919 - 12 Sep 1919:	Attached to the Commandant of Kiel
13 Sep 1919 - 31 May 1920:	Commandant of Kiel
1 Jun 1920 - 30 Sep 1920:	Attached to the Commander, Baltic Naval Station
1 Oct 1920 - 31 Mar 1922:	Inspector of Torpedoes & Mines
(10 Jan 1921:	Promoted to Konteradmiral)
(31 Mar 1922:	Promoted to brevet Vizeadmiral)
31 Mar 1922:	Retired
24 May 1939:	Recalled to reserve status; no appointment conferred

Admiralrichter (Konteradmiral) Dr. Erich **LORENZEN**
(19 Jun 1896 - 5 May 1945)

15 Oct 1936 - 31 Mar 1940:	Supervising Judge, North Sea Naval Station
1 Apr 1940 - 28 Feb 1941:	Staff officer to the Commander, North Sea Naval Station
3 Mar 1941 - 30 Jun 1941:	Attached to Naval High Command
1 Jul 1941 - 19 Sep 1943:	Military Advocate, Reich Military Court
(1 Oct 1942:	Promoted to Reichskriegsgerichtsrat [Konteradmiral])
20 Sep 1943 - 5 May 1945:	Supervising Judge, Baltic Naval Group
(1 Oct 1943:	Rank redesignated as Marinechefrichter)
(1 May 1944:	Rank redesignated as Admiralrichter)

Konteradmiral Hermann **LOREY** (25 Sep 1877 - 15 Oct 1954)

13 Mar 1918 - 5 Oct 1920:	Advisor, Naval Transport Office, Naval High Command
6 Oct 1920 - 27 May 1924:	Commander, Ems Estuary Defenses
28 May 1924 - 30 Jun 1924:	Commander, Coastal Defense Detachment VI
(30 Jun 1924:	Promoted to brevet Konteradmiral)
30 Jun 1924:	Retired
22 Mar 1939:	Recalled to reserve status
Jun 1940 - 8 May 1945:	Director of Navy Museum
(1 Feb 1941:	Confirmed as Konteradmiral from brevet rank)

Ministerialdirektor (Vizeadmiral) Hermann **LOTTMANN**
(23 Mar 1881 - 8 Jul 1943)
1 May 1934 - 21 Aug 1937:	Director of Shipbuilding, Wilhelmshaven Naval Dockyards
(1 Jan 1937:	Promoted to Werftdirektor [Konteradmiral])
1 Sep 1937 - 31 Oct 1939:	Chief of Shipbuilding Section, Naval High Command
(1 Jan 1939:	Rank redesignated as Ministerialdirigent)
(9 Oct 1939:	Promoted to Ministerialdirektor)
1 Nov 1939 - 8 Jul 1943:	Chief of Design & Shipbuilding Group, Naval High Command

Vizeadmiral Hugo **LOURAN** (27 Feb 1865 - 18 May 1931)
(11 Nov 1911:	Retired as brevet Konteradmiral)
20 Oct 1914 - 28 May 1918:	Recalled from retirement; Harbor Captain of Antwerp & Commandant, Schelde Estuary Defenses
(27 Jan 1916:	Confirmed as Konteradmiral from brevet rank)
28 May 1918:	Retired
(28 Jan 1921:	Promoted to brevet Vizeadmiral)

Vizeadmiral Werner **LÖWISCH** (22 Feb 1894 - 6 Jun 1971)
2 Oct 1937 - 6 Mar 1939:	Commandant, Light Cruiser "*Leipzig*"
3 Apr 1939 - 13 Sep 1943:	Naval Attaché, Rome
(1 Apr 1941:	Promoted to Konteradmiral)
14 Sep 1943 - 2 Oct 1943:	Attached to the German Naval Commander, Italy
3 Oct 1943 - 30 Jun 1944:	Chief of Naval Liaison Staff, Croatia
(1 Jul 1944:	Promoted to Vizeadmiral)
4 Jul 1944 - 16 Jul 1944:	Admiral Commanding, Adriatic
17 Jul 1944 - 31 Dec 1944:	Commander, German Naval Command, Italy
1 Jan 1945 - 2 May 1945:	C-in-C, Naval Group South

Konteradmiral Ulrich **LÜBBERT** (28 Feb 1867 - 7 Aug 1945)
1 Oct 1913 - 25 Oct 1915:	Commandant, Battleship "*Helgoland*"
26 Oct 1915 - 30 Jun 1917:	Commander, 2. Torpedo Division
1 Jul 1917 - 16 Jul 1917:	Attached to the Commander, North Sea Naval Station
(16 Jul 1917:	Promoted to brevet Konteradmiral)
16 Jul 1917:	Retired

Konteradmiral Ernst **LUCHT** (27 Feb 1896 - 2 Nov 1975)
2 Oct 1937 - 29 Jan 1940:	Advisor, Inspectorate of Mines
30 Jan 1940 - 5 Aug 1940:	Chief of Technical Development Section, Naval Weapons Office, Naval High Command
6 Aug 1940 - 31 Mar 1943:	Chief of Military-Technical Section, Naval Weapons Office, Naval High Command
(1 Apr 1943:	Promoted to Konteradmiral)
4 Apr 1943 - 14 Jan 1945:	Commander of Naval Security Forces, North Sea
15 Jan 1945 - 22 Jun 1945:	Flag Officer, Naval Security Forces

Awards: *Knight's Cross; German Cross in Gold*

Konteradmiral Fritz **LÜDECKE** (5 Feb 1873 - 22 Feb 1931)
27 Jul 1914 - 14 Mar 1915:	Commandant, Light Cruiser "*Dresden*"
15 Mar 1915 - 1919:	Interned in Chile
1919 - 9 Mar 1920:	Chief of Cruiser Squadron Decommissioning Office
(8 Mar 1920:	Promoted to brevet Konteradmiral)
9 Mar 1920:	Retired

Admiral Günther **LÜTJENS** (25 May 1889 - 27 May 1941)
26 Sep 1932 - 15 Sep 1934:	Chief of Officer Personnel Office, Naval High Command
16 Sep 1934 - 23 Sep 1935:	Commandant, Cruiser "*Karlsruhe*"
24 Sep 1935 - 15 Mar 1936:	Chief of Staff, North Sea Naval Station
16 Mar 1936 - 3 Oct 1937:	Chief of Naval Personnel
(1 Oct 1937:	Promoted to Konteradmiral)
8 Oct 1937 - 20 Oct 1939:	Flag Officer, Torpedo Boats
21 Oct 1939 - 17 Jun 1940:	Flag Officer, Reconnaissance Forces
(1 Jan 1940:	Promoted to Vizeadmiral)
11 Mar 1940 - 23 Apr 1940:	Acting C-in-C, High Seas Fleet
18 Jun 1940 - 27 May 1941:	C-in-C, High Seas Fleet
(1 Sep 1940:	Promoted to Admiral)
3 Aug 1940 - 19 Oct 1940:	Acting Commander of Security Forces, West
3 Aug 1940 - 26 Oct 1940:	Naval Commander, West

Awards: *Knight's Cross*

Vizeadmiral (Ingeneur) Dr. Gustav **LÜTTGE** (26 Dec 1890 - 25 Dec 1963)
1 Nov 1938 - 7 Nov 1939:	Chief of Military-Technical Office, Shipyards Directorate, Naval High Command

8 Nov 1939 - 31 Mar 1942:	Chief of Reinforcements Office, Naval High Command
(1 Apr 1941:	Promoted to Konteradmiral Ingeneur)
1 Apr 1942 - 14 Apr 1944:	Chief of Reinforcements & Fuel Management Office, Naval Quartermaster's Office
15 Apr 1944 - 31 Jul 1944:	Attached to the Chief of Naval Armaments
1 Aug 1944 - Jan 1945:	Chief of Armaments and Defense Economics Office, Naval High Command
Jan 1945 - 8 May 1945:	Coal Commissioner of the Navy
(1 Apr 1945:	Promoted to Vizeadmiral Ingeneur)

Vizeadmiral Friedrich **LÜTZOW** (31 Aug 1881 - 1 Nov 1964)

6 Apr 1919 - 2 Jun 1920:	Chief of Counterintelligence Service, Naval High Command
3 Jun 1920 - 3 Sep 1920:	Chief of Staff, Inspectorate of Torpedoes & Mines
6 Jun 1920 - 15 Jul 1920:	Acting Inspector of Torpedoes & Mines
4 Sep 1920 - 20 Feb 1922:	Advisor, Naval Archives
21 Feb 1922 - 26 Sep 1924:	Chief of Staff, North Sea Naval Station
27 Sep 1924 - 2 May 1925:	Commandant, Cruiser "*Hamburg*"
3 May 1925 - 9 Sep 1925:	Sick leave
10 Sep 1925 - 27 Sep 1927:	Commander, North Sea Naval Division
28 Sep 1927 - 31 Mar 1929:	Chief of Officer Training Courses
(1 Dec 1928:	Promoted to brevet Konteradmiral)
1 Apr 1929 - 31 Mar 1931:	Chief of Naval Printing Office, Naval High Command
31 Mar 1931:	Retired
24 Dec 1939:	Recalled to reserve status
24 Dec 1939 - 23 May 1945:	Attached to the Commander-in-Chief of the Navy
(1 Feb 1941:	Confirmed as Konteradmiral from brevet rank)
(1 Feb 1943:	Promoted to Vizeadmiral)

Konteradmiral Leberecht **MAASS** (24 Nov 1863 - 28 Aug 1914)

(9 Dec 1913:	Promoted to Konteradmiral)
1 Mar 1914 - 28 Aug 1914:	Deputy Commander of Reconnaissance Forces & Commander of Torpedo Boats

Vizeadmiral Bruno **MACHENS** (25 Jul 1895 - 20 Nov 1976)

6 Sep 1937 - 10 Mar 1940:	Staff Officer, North Sea Naval Station

9 Apr 1940 - 16 Jun 1940:	Staff Officer, Admiral Commanding, Norway
17 Jun 1940 - 26 May 1942:	Chief of Staff to Admiral Commanding, Norway
8 Jun 1942 - 19 Apr 1943:	Deputy Naval Quartermaster
(1 Sep 1942:	Promoted to Konteradmiral)
4 Oct 1942 - 31 Jan 1943:	Chief of Naval Command Office, Naval High Command
20 Apr 1943 - 2 Dec 1944:	Quartermaster-Admiral of the Navy
(1 Dec 1944:	Promoted to Vizeadmiral)
8 Jan 1945 - 21 Jul 1945:	Admiral Commanding, Polar Coast

Vizeadmiral Erhard **MAERTENS** (26 Feb 1891 - 5 May 1945)

1 Oct 1934 - 30 Sep 1936:	Commandant, Naval Communications School
1 Oct 1936 - 30 Sep 1937:	Chief of Staff, Inspectorate of Torpedoes
3 May 1937 - 3 Jun 1937:	Acting Inspector of Torpedoes
21 Jul 1937 - 3 Aug 1937:	Acting Inspector of Torpedoes
1 Oct 1937 - 27 Apr 1939:	Chief of Staff, Naval Communications Inspectorate
2 May 1938 - 29 May 1938:	Acting Inspector of Naval Communications
7 Mar 1939 - 18 Mar 1939:	Acting Inspector of Naval Communications
28 Apr 1939 - 18 Nov 1939:	Chief of Naval Intelligence
19 Nov 1939 - 15 Jun 1941:	Chief of Technical Communications Office, Naval High Command
(1 Jul 1940:	Promoted to Konteradmiral)
16 Jun 1941 - 5 May 1943:	Chief of Naval Communications
(1 Sep 1942:	Promoted to Vizeadmiral)
6 May 1943 - 30 Jun 1943:	Acting Director, Kiel Shipyards
1 Jul 1943 - 27 Nov 1944:	Commandant, Kiel Naval Arsenal
28 Nov 1944 - 28 Feb 1945:	Attached to the C-in-C, Baltic Naval Group
28 Feb 1945:	Retired

Konteradmiral Erich **MAHRHOLZ** (9 Nov 1879 - 29 Dec 1969)

1 Apr 1922 - 30 Sep 1923:	Commander, Coastal Defense Detachment I
1 Oct 1923 - 8 Sep 1925:	Commandant of Swinemünde
12 Sep 1925 - 29 Feb 1928:	Commandant, Kiel Naval Arsenal
1 Mar 1928 - 31 Mar 1928:	Attached to the Commander, Baltic Naval Station
(31 Mar 1928:	Promoted to brevet Konteradmiral)
31 Mar 1928:	Retired
1 Sep 1933 - 31 Mar 1935:	Recalled; Training Officer, Baltic Naval Station

1 Apr 1935 - 31 Mar 1936:	Training Officer, Naval Artillery Inspectorate
1 Apr 1936 - 30 Sep 1937:	Training Officer, Baltic Naval Station
1 Oct 1937 - 31 Aug 1939:	Commissioner, Kaiser Wilhelm Canal
1 Sep 1939 - 6 Apr 1941:	Commandant, Kaiser Wilhelm Canal
(1 Sep 1940:	Confirmed as Konteradmiral from brevet rank)
15 Apr 1941 - 22 May 1941:	Acting Commander of Defenses, Pomeranian Coast
23 May 1941 - 29 Oct 1941:	Attached to the Commander, Baltic Naval Station
30 Oct 1941 - 2 Jun 1943:	Commandant of Kaiser Wilhelm Canal
3 Jun 1943 - 31 Jul 1943:	Attached to the Commander, Baltic Naval Group
31 Jul 1943:	Retired

Konteradmiral Otto **MANDT** (7 Jun 1858 - 2 Jan 1919)

Aug 1914 - 30 Jun 1916:	Recalled from retirement; Director of Brüsterort Communications Station
(30 Jun 1916:	Promoted to brevet Konteradmiral)
30 Jun 1916:	Retired

Vizeadmiral Ernst Ritter von **MANN**, Edler von Tiechler
(11 Apr 1864 - 2 Oct 1934)

20 Sep 1913 - 1 Sep 1914:	Chief of Staff, High Seas Fleet
2 Sep 1914 - 2 Nov 1914:	Sick leave
3 Nov 1914 - 10 Dec 1917:	Inspector of Torpedoes
(22 Mar 1915:	Promoted to Konteradmiral)
11 Dec 1917 - 4 Oct 1918:	Director of U-Boat Bureau, Naval Office
(27 Jan 1918:	Promoted to Vizeadmiral)
22 Sep 1918 - 13 Feb 1919:	State Secretary, Naval Office
13 Feb 1919:	Retired

Vizeadmiral Dr. Eberhard von **MANTEY** (15 Aug 1869 - 7 Dec 1940)

23 Jun 1914 - 26 Jan 1916:	Commandant, Battleship "*Wittelsbach*"
27 Jan 1916 - 14 Feb 1916:	Attached to the Naval General Staff
15 Feb 1916 - 8 Jun 1919:	Director of Military Science Office, Naval General Staff
(18 Sep 1918:	Promoted to Konteradmiral)
8 Jun 1919 - 31 Mar 1933:	Director of Naval Archives
(16 Sep 1920:	Promoted to brevet Vizeadmiral)
31 Mar 1933:	Retired

Generaladmiral Wilhelm **MARSCHALL** (30 Sep 1886 - 20 Mar 1976)
26 Sep 1931 - 24 Sep 1934:	Chief of Staff, Baltic Naval Station
25 Sep 1934 - 12 Nov 1934:	Commandant, Battleship "*Hessen*"
12 Nov 1934 - 21 Sep 1936:	Commandant, Pocket Battleship "*Admiral Scheer*"
22 Sep 1936 - 1 Oct 1937:	Chief of Naval Operations
(1 Oct 1936:	Promoted to Konteradmiral)
8 Oct 1937 - 8 Feb 1938:	Commander of Naval Forces, Spain
9 Feb 1938 - 20 Oct 1939:	Flag Officer, Battleships
(1 Nov 1938:	Promoted to Vizeadmiral)
21 Oct 1939 - 7 Jul 1940:	C-in-C, High Seas Fleet
(1 Dec 1939:	Promoted to Admiral)
26 Aug 1940 - 8 Aug 1942:	Inspector of Naval Training
Dec 1941 - Mar 1942:	Acting C-in-C, Naval Group South
10 Apr 1942 - 2 May 1942:	Commander, Baltic Naval Station
12 Aug 1942 - 30 Nov 1942:	Admiral Commanding, France
21 Sep 1942 - 19 Apr 1943:	C-in-C, Naval Group West
(1 Feb 1943:	Promoted to Generaladmiral)
20 Apr 1943 - 30 Jun 1943:	Attached to the Commander-in-Chief of the Navy
30 Jun 1943:	Retired
1 Jul 1943:	Recalled to reserve status
4 Jun 1944 - 23 Nov 1944:	Special Plenipotentiary for the Danube
24 Nov 1944 - 30 Nov 1944:	Attached to the Commander-in-Chief of the Navy
30 nov 1944 - 19 Apr 1945:	Placed on inactive status
19 Apr 1945 - 8 May 1945:	C-in-C, Naval Group West

Awards: *Pour le Mérite; German Cross in Gold*

Marinegeneralstabsarzt (Konteradmiral) Dr. Robert **MARTIN** (25 Jan 1864 - 23 Oct 1929)
25 Feb 1914 - 17 Nov 1916:	Chief Medical Officer, Torpedo Inspectorate
15 Mar 1914 - 17 Nov 1916:	Chief Medical Officer, U-Boat Inspectorate
31 Jul 1914 - 17 Nov 1916:	Medical Officer, High Seas Fleet
17 Nov 1916:	Retired
(7 Oct 1921:	Promoted to brevet Marinegeneralstabsarzt)

Vizeadmiral Ralf von der **MARWITZ** (29 Oct 1888 - 29 Sep 1966)
28 Sep 1932 - 6 Oct 1935:	Commander of Ems Estuary Defenses
7 Oct 1935 - 9 Jul 1937:	Commandant of Wesermünde

10 Jul 1937 - 11 Apr 1939:	Naval Attaché, Paris, Lisbon
(1 Apr 1939:	Promoted to brevet Konteradmiral)
19 May 1939 - 31 Aug 1944:	Naval Attaché, Ankara & Sofia
(1 Nov 1939:	Confirmed as Konteradmiral from brevet rank)
(1 Feb 1942:	Promoted to Vizeadmiral)
19 May 1939 - 6 Apr 1941:	Naval Attaché, Athens
19 May 1939 - 23 Aug 1944:	Naval Attaché, Bucharest

Vizeadmiral Siegfried **MAßMANN** (2 Apr 1882 - 15 Feb 1944)

20 Sep 1926 - 28 Sep 1928:	Chief of Staff, North Sea Naval Station
29 Sep 1928 - 25 Feb 1930:	Commandant, Battleship "*Schleswig-Holstein*"
26 Feb 1930 - 29 Sep 1930:	Commandant, Battleship "*Hannover*"
30 Sep 1930 - 30 Sep 1932:	Chief of Central Office, Wilhelmshaven Shipyards
(1 Oct 1932:	Promoted to Konteradmiral)
1 Oct 1932 - 29 Sep 1935:	Director of Wilhelmshaven Shipyards
(30 Sep 1935:	Promoted to brevet Vizeadmiral)
30 Sep 1935:	Retired
15 Feb 1939 - 16 Nov 1941:	Recalled; Training Officer for Aviation Matters
(1 Sep 1940:	Confirmed as Vizeadmiral from brevet rank)
Jun 1940 - 21 Aug 1940:	Chief of Special Staff to Commanding Admiral, West
5 Jun 1941 - 20 Aug 1941:	Chief of Naval Mission to Romania
20 Nov 1941 - 15 Feb 1944:	Chief of Naval Construction Staff, Aegean

Awards: *German Cross in Silver*

Waffen Konteradmiral Friedrich **MATTHES** (17 Oct 1881 - 11 Dec 1950)

4 Oct 1937 - 6 Nov 1939:	General Advisor, Naval Weapons Office, Naval High Command
7 Nov 1939 - 4 May 1943:	Chief of Artillery Administration Section, Naval Weapons Office, Naval High Command
13 Jan 1943 - 16 Apr 1944:	Group Chief for Artillery & Munitions Administration, Smoke & Gas Protection Equipment & Artillery Arsenals, Naval Weapons Office, Naval High Command
(1 Feb 1943:	Promoted to Waffen Konteradmiral)
17 Apr 1944 - 31 Jul 1944:	Attached to the Commander-in-Chief of the Navy
31 Jul 1944:	Retired

Awards: *German Cross in Silver*

Vizeadmiral Walter **MATTHIAE** (3 Aug 1880 - 27 Jun 1960)
1 Oct 1924 - 23 Oct 1927:	Press Officer, Ministry of Defense
24 Oct 1927 - 9 Feb 1928:	Attached to Wilhelmshaven Shipyards
10 Feb 1928 - 29 Sep 1930:	Chief of Central Office, Wilhelmshaven Shipyards
30 Sep 1930 - 31 Oct 1930:	Attached to the Commander, North Sea Naval Station
(31 Oct 1930:	Promoted to brevet Konteradmiral)
31 Oct 1930:	Retired
1 Apr 1931 - 30 Mar 1932:	Recalled; Director of Printing Office, Naval High Command
31 Mar 1932 - 14 Sep 1940:	Director of Armed Forces High Command (OKW) Library
15 Sep 1940 - 10 May 1945:	Chief of Naval Shipyards, Lorient
(1 Jan 1941:	Confirmed as Konteradmiral from brevet rank)
(1 Nov 1944:	Promoted to Vizeadmiral)
20 Aug 1944 - 10 May 1945:	Commander of Naval Defenses, Lorient

Konteradmiral Wilhelm **MATTHIES** (27 Sep 1896 - 7 Jul 1980)
28 Sep 1936 - 3 Sep 1939:	Commander, V. Naval Artillery Detachment
1 Apr 1938 - 22 Jul 1939:	At various times, simultaneously Commandant of Pillau
4 Sep 1939 - 6 Sep 1939:	Commander, Naval Flak Regiment
7 Sep 1939 - 30 Sep 1939:	Commander, Naval Flak Regiment Pillau
1 Oct 1939 - 3 Jan 1940:	Commander, 5. Naval Artillery Regiment
4 Jan 1940 - 30 Apr 1942:	Commander, 1. Naval Flak Regiment
5 Feb 1941 - 15 Apr 1941:	Acting Coastal Commander, Western Baltic
1 May 1942 - 14 Nov 1943:	Commander, I. Naval Flak Brigade
(1 Feb 1943:	Promoted to Konteradmiral)
1 Mar 1943 - 14 Nov 1943:	Coastal Commander, Western Baltic
15 Nov 1943 - 31 Mar 1944:	Chief of Coastal & Air Defense Group, Naval High Command
1 Apr 1944 - 9 Jul 1944:	Chief of Coastal Defense Office, Naval High Command
10 Jul 1944 - 7 May 1945:	Section Chief, Naval General Office, Naval High Command

Awards: *German Cross in Gold*

Vizeadmiral Franz **MAUVE** (11 Nov 1864 - 12 Dec 1931)
1 Oct 1913 - 10 Aug 1915:	Deputy Commander, II. Squadron

(22 Mar 1914: Promoted to Konteradmiral)
10 Aug 1915 - 30 Nov 1916: Commander, II. Squadron
(25 Nov 1916: Promoted to Vizeadmiral)
1 Dec 1916 - 12 Aug 1917: Commander, IV. Squadron
13 Aug 1917 - 25 Sep 1917: Attached to the Commander, North Sea Naval Station
25 Sep 1917: Retired

Vizeadmiral Wilhelm **MEENDSEN-BOHLKEN** (25 Jun 1897 - 20 Aug 1985)
16 May 1938 - 11 Jun 1941: Chief of Armaments Economics Office, Armed Forces High Command (OKW)
12 Jun 1941 - 28 Nov 1942: Commandant, Heavy Cruiser "*Admiral Scheer*"
29 Nov 1942 - 4 Mar 1943: Naval Commander, Tunisia
(1 Feb 1943: Promoted to Konteradmiral)
5 Mar 1943 - 17 May 1943: Commander, German Naval Command, Italy
18 May 1943 - 12 Aug 1943: Attached to the Commander-in-Chief of the Navy
13 Aug 1943 - 16 Jul 1944: Commander, German Naval Command, Italy
(1 Jun 1944: Promoted to Vizeadmiral)
31 Jul 1944 - 23 May 1945: C-in-C, High Seas Fleet
Awards: *Knight's Cross; German Cross in Gold*

Konteradmiral Johannes **MEIER** (13 Sep 1860 - 14 Sep 1939)
(19 Nov 1910: Promoted to brevet Konteradmiral)
16 Jan 1915 - 31 Dec 1918: Recalled from retirement; Director of Central Information Bureau, Naval Office
31 Dec 1918: Retired

Admiral Wilhelm **MEISEL** (4 Nov 1893 - 7 Sep 1974)
6 Dec 1937 - 16 Feb 1938: Deputy Commandant, U-Boat School
17 Feb 1938 - 13 Apr 1938: Commandant, U-Boat School
14 Apr 1938 - 5 Sep 1938: Attached to the Flag Officer, Torpedo Boats
6 Sep 1938 - 25 Oct 1938: Attached to Staff of Flag Officer, Battleships
26 Oct 1938 - 27 Oct 1939: Commander, 1. Destroyer Flotilla
28 Oct 1939 - 3 Sep 1940: Chief of Staff, Baltic Naval Security Forces
6 Aug 1940 - 15 Aug 1940: Acting Commander, Baltic Naval Security Forces
4 Sep 1940 - 8 Nov 1942: Commandant, Heavy Cruiser, "*Admiral Hipper*"
(1 Sep 1942: Promoted to Konteradmiral)

16 Nov 1942 - 10 Feb 1943:	Chief of Staff, Naval Group West
(1 Feb 1943:	Promoted to Vizeadmiral)
21 Feb 1943 - 22 Jul 1945:	Chief of Naval General Staff
(1 Apr 1944:	Promoted to Admiral)

Awards: *Knight's Cross*

Konteradmiral Albrecht **MEISSNER** (14 Oct 1883 - 21 Jul 1962)

1 Apr 1925 - 31 Aug 1925:	Deputy Chief of Staff, High Seas Fleet
1 Sep 1925 - 27 Sep 1927:	Chief of Staff, Inspectorate of Naval Artillery
28 Sep 1927 - 9 Oct 1929:	Commandant, Cruiser "*Amazone*"
12 Oct 1929 - 30 Sep 1932:	Commandant, Mürwik Naval School
(30 Sep 1932:	Promoted to brevet Konteradmiral)
30 Sep 1932:	Retired
1 Jan 1939:	Recalled to reserve status; no appointment conferred
31 May 1943:	Retired

Konteradmiral Dr. Paul **MEIXNER** (4 Jun 1891 - 8 Jun 1950)

27 Jan 1941 - 7 Dec 1942:	Chief of Tripoli Naval Transport Office
18 Oct 1941 - 5 Mar 1943:	Naval Liaison Officer to the Staff of Generalfeldmarschall Rommel
18 Oct 1941 - 5 Mar 1943:	Chief of Naval Transport Office, North Africa
Oct 1942 - 28 Feb 1943:	Commander, German Naval Command, North Africa
5 Mar 1943 - 11 May 1943:	Commander, German Naval Command, Tunisia & Chief of Staff, Italian Naval Command, Tunisia
11 May 1943:	Captured; POW
(12 Jun 1944:	Promoted to Konteradmiral)

Awards: *German Cross in Gold; German Cross in Silver*

Konteradmiral Heinz-Eduard **MENCHE** (6 Mar 1886 - 25 Dec 1961)

3 Nov 1928 - 9 Oct 1929:	Commandant, Torpedo & Communications School
10 Oct 1929 - 18 Jan 1930:	Attached to the Commander, Baltic Naval Station
19 Jan 1930 - 20 Nov 1932:	Chief of Naval Office, Hamburg
(30 Nov 1932:	Promoted to brevet Konteradmiral)
30 Nov 1932:	Retired
19 Jul 1939:	Recalled to reserve status
27 Jan 1941 - 30 Apr 1943:	Chief of Naval Office, Bordeaux

(1 Feb 1942:	Confirmed as Konteradmiral from brevet rank)
26 Nov 1942 - 30 Apr 1943:	Chief of Naval Transport, Marseille
1 May 1943 - 31 Jul 1944:	Chief of Naval Office, Marseille
1 Aug 1944 - 31 Aug 1944:	Attached to the Commander, Naval Group West
31 Aug 1944:	Retired

Awards: *German Cross in Silver*

Vizeadmiral (Turkish General of Artillery) Johannes **MERTEN**
(15 Dec 1857 - 8 Apr 1926)

(27 Jan 1908:	Promoted to Konteradmiral)
(19 Nov 1910:	Promoted to brevet Vizeadmiral; retired)
21 Aug 1914 - 28 Aug 1914:	Recalled from retirement; attached to the Chief of the Special Mission to Turkey
29 Aug 1914 - 1 Nov 1918:	Commandant of Dardanelles Defenses
(27 Jan 1916:	Confirmed as Vizeadmiral from brevet rank)
2 Nov 1918 - 25 Jul 1919:	Placed on inactive status
25 Jul 1919:	Retired

Ministerialdirigent (Konteradmiral) Hans **METHLING**
(2 Jan 1872 - 7 Mar 1943)

7 Nov 1939 - 4 Dec 1942:	Reactivated from reserve status; Chief Engineer, Naval Weapons Office, Naval High Command
(7 Nov 1939:	Promoted to Ministerialdirigent)
4 Dec 1942:	Retired

Vizeadmiral Alexander **MEURER** (15 Aug 1862 - 3 Feb 1948)

(10 Apr 1911:	Promoted to brevet Konteradmiral)
11 Apr 1911 - 18 Sep 1918:	President, Ship Planning Commission
(16 Sep 1916:	Confirmed as Konteradmiral from brevet rank)
19 Sep 1918 - 17 Nov 1918:	Attached to the Commander, Baltic Naval Station
17 Nov 1918:	Retired
(24 Nov 1919:	Promoted to brevet Vizeadmiral)

Vizeadmiral Hugo **MEURER** (28 May 1869 - 4 Jan 1960)

1 Oct 1912 - 12 Jul 1916:	Commandant, Battleship "*Deutschland*"
14 Jul 1916 - 23 May 1917:	Commandant, Battleship "*König*"
28 May 1917 - 13 Oct 1917:	Commodore & Acting Deputy Commander, IV. Squadron

13 Aug 1917 - 4 Sep 1917:	Acting Commander, IV. Squadron
(14 Oct 1917:	Promoted to Konteradmiral)
14 Oct 1917 - 12 Aug 1918:	Deputy Commander, IV. Squadron
21 Feb 1918 - 30 Apr 1918:	Chief of Baltic Special Group
30 Jul 1918 - 12 Aug 1918:	Acting Commander, IV. Squadron
13 Aug 1918 - 12 Nov 1918:	Commander, IV. Squadron
29 Nov 1918 - 5 Jan 1919:	Acting C-in-C, High Seas Fleet
6 Jan 1919 - 11 Mar 1919:	Placed on inactive status
12 Mar 1919 - 8 Jan 1920:	Commander, Baltic Naval Station
(8 Jan 1920:	Promoted to brevet Vizeadmiral)
8 Jan 1920:	Retired

Konteradmiral Ernst **MEUSEL** (12 Jan 1881 - 15 Nov 1933)

31 May 1920 - 29 Sep 1922:	Chief of Staff, Baltic Naval Station
30 Sep 1922 - 26 Sep 1924:	Commandant, Cruiser "*Medusa*"
27 Sep 1924 - 19 Sep 1926:	Chief of Staff, North Sea Naval Station
29 Sep 1926 - 25 Sep 1930:	Commandant of Pillau
(30 Sep 1930:	Promoted to brevet Konteradmiral)
30 Sep 1930:	Retired

Admiral Raul **MEWIS** (3 Jun 1886 - 23 Feb 1972)

30 Sep 1931 - 5 Jun 1933:	Chief of Staff, Inspectorate of Naval Training
7 Jun 1933 - 26 Mar 1935:	Commandant, Training Sail Ship "*Gorch Fock*"
27 Mar 1935 - 30 Sep 1937:	Fortress Commandant & Harbor Captain of Kiel
(1 Apr 1937:	Promoted to Konteradmiral)
1 Oct 1937 - 6 Apr 1940:	Commander of Western Baltic Defenses
(1 Nov 1939:	Promoted to Vizeadmiral)
15 Jan 1938 - 15 Feb 1938:	Deputy Commander, Baltic Naval Station
19 Aug 1938 - 31 Aug 1938:	Deputy Commander, Baltic Naval Station & Commander of Baltic Naval Security Forces
28 Oct 1938 - 4 Jan 1939:	Deputy Commander, Baltic Naval Station & Commander of Baltic Naval Security Forces
21 May 1939 - 14 Jun 1939:	Acting Chief of Testing Commission for New Ships
16 Jun 1939 - 15 Jul 1939:	Deputy Commander, Baltic Naval Station & Commander of Baltic Naval Security Forces
8 Apr 1940 - 31 May 1940:	Coastal Commander, Denmark
1 Jun 1940 - 31 Jan 1943:	Naval Commander, Denmark
(1 Mar 1942:	Promoted to Admiral)

16 Apr 1941 - 3 Jun 1941:	Acting Coastal Commander, Western Baltic
1 Feb 1943 - 18 Mar 1943:	Admiral Commanding, Denmark
19 Mar 1943 - 31 May 1943:	Attached to the Commander, Baltic Naval Station
31 May 1943:	Retired
1 Jun 1943:	Recalled to reserve status; no appointment conferred

Awards: *German Cross in Silver*

Ministerialdirigent (Konteradmiral) Dr. Georg **MEYER**
(16 May 1880 - 10 May 1943)

11 Jan 1936 - 14 Nov 1939:	Official in Administration Office, Naval High Command
(1 Nov 1939:	Promoted to Ministerialdirigent)
15 Nov 1939 - 10 May 1943:	Chief of Personnel Section, Naval General Office, Naval High Command & standing member, Naval Quartermaster's Office

Konteradmiral Hans **MEYER** (8 Nov 1855 - 17 Jan 1918)

(25 Apr 1904:	Promoted to brevet Konteradmiral; retired)
2 Sep 1914 - 15 Sep 1915:	Recalled from retirement; Inspector, Naval Depot Inspectorate
16 Sep 1915 - 17 Oct 1915:	Attached to the Commander, North Sea Naval Station
17 Oct 1915:	Retired

Konteradmiral Hans Karl **MEYER** (1 Dec 1898 - 23 Jan 1989

16 Jul 1939 - 5 Jun 1941:	Staff Officer, Naval Group West
6 Jun 1941 - 15 Nov 1942:	Chief of Staff, Naval Group West
13 Dec 1942 - 17 Feb 1943:	Commandant, Light Cruiser "*Köln*"
25 Feb 1943 - 30 Apr 1944:	Commandant, Battleship "*Tirpitz*"
16 Jan 1944 - 30 Apr 1944:	Acting Flag Officer, Battleships
1 May 1944 - 28 Jun 1944:	Attached to Naval High Command
(1 Jun 1944:	Promoted to Konteradmiral)
29 Jun 1944 - 22 Jul 1945:	Chief of Naval Operations

Awards: *German Cross in Gold*

Vizeadmiral Alfred **MEYER-WALDECK** (27 Nov 1864 - 25 Aug 1928)

20 Aug 1911 - 7 Nov 1914:	Governor & Land Forces Commander, Kiautschou

8 Nov 1914 - 31 Aug 1920:   Prisoner of War
(30 Jan 1920:   Promoted to Konteradmiral, effective 22 March 1915)
(30 Jan 1920:   Promoted to Vizeadmiral, effective 27 January 1918)
31 Aug 1920:   Retired

Vizeadmiral William **MICHAELIS** (19 Jul 1871 - 5 Jan 1948)
1 Oct 1913 - 3 Feb 1915:   Commandant, Battleship "*Thüringen*"
4 Feb 1915 - 28 Jan 1916:   Chief of Staff, High Seas Fleet
6 Feb 1916 - 30 Sep 1918:   Chief of Mobilization Section, Naval Office
1 Oct 1918 - 30 Sep 1919:   Director of General Naval Department, Naval Office
1 Oct 1919 - 1 Jul 1920:   Chief of Naval Command Office, Naval High Command (Chief of Naval General Staff)
(17 Dec 1919:   Promoted to Konteradmiral)
22 Mar 1920 - 30 Aug 1920:   Acting Commander-in-Chief of the Navy
31 Aug 1920 - 31 Dec 1920:   Attached to the Commander-in-Chief of the Navy
(31 Dec 1920:   Promoted to brevet Vizeadmiral)
31 Dec 1920:   Retired

Konteradmiral Hans **MICHAHELLES** (18 May 1899 - 14 Jun 1975)
6 May 1938 - 23 Aug 1943:   General Advisor, Naval Defense Office
May 1941 - Jul 1941:   Naval Liaison Officer, 12. Army
28 Aug 1943 - 17 Apr 1945:   Commander of Sea Defenses, Gascony
(1 Oct 1944:   Promoted to Konteradmiral)
29 Sep 1944 - 8 Oct 1944:   Fortress Commandant, South Gironde Estuary
9 Oct 1944 - 17 Apr 1945:   Fortress Commandant, North Gironde Estuary
17 Apr 1945:   Captured; POW
Awards: *Knight's Cross*

Vizeadmiral Alexander **MICHELS** (17 Mar 1891 - 26 Jun 1968)
3 Oct 1936 - 22 Feb 1943:   Chief of Staff, Inspectorate of Mines
(1 Jan 1941:   Promoted to Konteradmiral)
(1 Feb 1943:   Promoted to Vizeadmiral)
1937 - 1943:   At various times, simultaneously Acting Inspector of Mines
23 Feb 1943 - 10 Sep 1945:   Inspector of Mines
Awards: *German Cross in Silver*

Vizeadmiral Andreas **MICHELSEN** (19 Feb 1869 - 8 Apr 1932)
2 Aug 1914 - 23 Aug 1915:	Commandant, Heavy Cruiser *"Prinz Adalbert"*
20 Apr 1915 - 3 Jul 1915:	Chief of Staff, Baltic Reconaissance Forces
25 Aug 1915 - 10 Jan 1916:	Chief of Staff to the Commander, Eastern Baltic
11 Jan 1916 - 13 Apr 1916:	Chief of Staff to the Commander, Eastern Baltic Reconnaissance Forces
14 Apr 1916 - 4 Jun 1917:	Commodore & Commander, Torpedo Boats
5 Jun 1917 - 11 Nov 1918:	Commodore & Commander of U-Boats
12 Nov 1918 - 21 Dec 1918:	Chief of Staff, High Seas Fleet
22 Dec 1918 - 2 Jan 1919:	Chief of Staff, North Sea Naval Station
2 Jan 1919 - 16 Mar 1920:	Commander, North Sea Naval Station
(29 Nov 1919:	Promoted to Konteradmiral)
(21 Jan 1920:	Promoted to Vizeadmiral)
17 Mar 1920 - 20 Dec 1920:	Attached to the Commander-in-Chief of the Navy
20 Dec 1920:	Retired

Awards: *Pour le Mérite*

Vizeadmiral **MIKHAIL ALEXANDROVICH**, Grand Duke of Russia (4 Dec 1878 - Jul 1918)
Vizeadmiral à la Suite (Honorary title)
Awards: *Order of the Black Eagle*

Konteradmiral Hans **MIROW** (30 Aug 1895 - 9 Jun 1986)
29 Nov 1938 - 28 Aug 1940:	Chief of Attaché Group, Naval High Command
29 Aug 1940 - 19 Jul 1942:	Commandant, Light Cruiser *"Emden"*
23 Jul 1942 - 20 Nov 1942:	Chief of Naval Control Commission, Africa
21 Nov 1942 - 9 Dec 1942:	Interned in Spain and Morocco
10 Dec 1942 - 28 Jan 1943:	Naval Liaison Officer, Toulon
(1 Feb 1943:	Promoted to Konteradmiral)
1 Feb 1943 - 31 Jan 1944:	Chief of Command Section, Quartermaster's Office, Naval High Command
4 Feb 1944 - 11 May 1945:	Commander of Sea Defenses, Loire & St. Nazaire

Vizeadmiral Robert **MISCHKE** (10 Mar 1865 - 27 Mar 1932)
(14 Dec 1912:	Promoted to Konteradmiral)
15 Dec 1912 - 31 Jul 1914:	Inspector, I. Naval Inspectorate

1 Aug 1914 - 2 Jan 1917:	Commander, Baltic Coastal Defense Division
(27 Jan 1916:	Promoted to Vizeadmiral)
3 Jan 1917 - 4 Feb 1917:	Attached to the Commander, Baltic Naval Station
4 Feb 1917:	Retired

Admiralintendant (Konteradmiral) Dr. Adolf **MÖLLER**
(10 May 1897 - 17 Nov 1983)

1 Jan 1939 - 31 Oct 1939:	Chief of Administration Section, Naval General Office, Naval High Command
1 Nov 1939 - 30 Jun 1944:	Chief of Dockyards & Arsenals Administration Section, Naval High Command
(20 Apr 1942:	Promoted to Ministerialdirigent)
(1 May 1944:	Rank redesignated as Admiralintendant)
1 Jul 1944 - 20 Apr 1945:	Chief of Personnel & Pay Section, Naval Administration Office, Naval High Command
24 Apr 1945 - Jul 1945:	Chief Intendant, Armed Forces Commander Norway

Admiralarzt (Konteradmiral) Dr. Hans-Hinrich **MÖLLER**
(3 Aug 1898 - 4 Oct 1974)

16 Oct 1937 13 Feb 1941:	Medical Officer, Baltic Naval Station
14 Feb 1941 - 4 Apr 1941:	Senior Medical Officer to Admiral "Z"
28 Apr 1941 - 30 Sep 1943:	Chief Medical Officer, Inspectorate of Naval Training
1 Oct 1943 - 31 Mar 1945:	Commandant, Naval Medical Academy
(1 Sep 1944:	Promoted to Admiralarzt)
1 Apr 1945 - Jul 1945:	Chief Medical Officer, Tübingen Naval Hospital

Admiral Conrad **MOMMSEN** (10 May 1871 - 4 Nov 1946)

2 Aug 1914 - 27 Jan 1915:	Commandant, Light Cruiser "*Frauenlob*"
30 Jan 1915 - 5 Apr 1917:	Commandant, Light Cruiser "*Pillau*"
27 Apr 1917 - 13 Jul 1918:	Commandant, Heavy Cruiser "*Von der Tann*"
14 Jul 1918 - 30 Sep 1919:	Director of Onboard Artillery Materials Office, Naval High Command
1 Oct 1919 - 21 Feb 1921:	Chief of Weapons Office, Naval High Command
(24 Mar 1921:	Promoted to Konteradmiral)
2 Apr 1921 - 10 Apr 1922:	Commander of North Sea Naval Forces
11 Apr 1922 - 21 Sep 1924:	Chief of Naval Command Office, Naval High Command (Chief of Naval General Staff)

(1 Nov 1923:   Promoted to Vizeadmiral)
26 Sep 1924 - 29 Sep 1927:   C-in-C, High Seas Fleet
30 Sep 1927 - 31 Dec 1927:   Attached to the Commander-in-Chief
                                of the Navy
(31 Dec 1927:   Promoted to brevet Admiral)
31 Dec 1927:   Retired

Admiraloberstabsarzt (Admiral) Prof. Dr. Sigmund **MOOSAUER**
(13 Mar 1877 - 20 Apr 1944)
14 Jul 1920 - 31 Mar 1923:   Chief Medical Officer, Kiel-Wik Naval Hospital
1 Apr 1923 - 31 Mar 1924:   Chief Medical Officer, Baltic Naval Station
1 Apr 1924 - 31 Mar 1925:   Medical Officer, High Seas Fleet
1 Apr 1925 - 31 Mar 1926:   Chief Medical Officer, High Seas Fleet
1 Apr 1926 - 12 Sep 1927:   Chief Medical Officer, Baltic Naval Station
13 Sep 1927 - 31 Dec 1927:   Attached to the Commander-in-Chief
                                of the Navy
(1 Jan 1928:   Promoted to Marinegeneralstabsarzt
                                [Konteradmiral])
1 Jan 1928 - 31 Dec 1939:   Chief of Naval Medical Service
(1 Apr 1934:   Promoted to brevet Admiralstabsarzt
                                [Vizeadmiral])
(1 Jan 1936:   Confirmed as Admiralstabsarzt from brevet
                                rank)
(1 Oct 1938:   Promoted to Admiraloberstabsarzt [Admiral])
31 Dec 1939:   Retired
1 Jan 1940:   Recalled to reserve status; no appointment
                                conferred

Admiral Hermann **MOOTZ** (12 Jul 1889 - 4 Jan 1962)
27 Sep 1933 - 30 Sep 1936:   Chief of Naval Defense Office,
                                Naval High Command
1 Oct 1936 - 4 Jan 1939:   Chief of Staff, Naval High Command
(1 Oct 1937:   Promoted to Konteradmiral)
5 Jan 1939 - 13 Oct 1940:   Commander of Baltic Naval Security Forces
(1 Nov 1939:   Promoted to Vizeadmiral)
5 Jan 1939 - 21 Aug 1939:   Acting Deputy Commander,
                                Baltic Naval Station
3 Apr 1939 - 13 Apr 1939:   Acting Commander of Western Baltic Defenses
19 Jul 1939 - 12 Aug 1939:   Acting Commander of Western Baltic Defenses
14 Oct 1940 - 8 Jan 1941:   Commander of Naval Security Forces, West

9 Jan 1941 - 30 Sep 1942:	Chief of Testing Command for New Ships
(1 Apr 1942:	Promoted to Admiral)
1 Oct 1942 - 28 Feb 1943:	Inspector of Naval Training
1 Mar 1943 - 31 May 1943:	Attached to the Commander-in-Chief of the Navy
31 May 1943:	Retired
1 Jun 1943:	Recalled to reserve status
12 Jun 1944 - 31 Mar 1945:	Attached to Naval Training Staff, Naval High Command
31 Mar 1945:	Retired

Awards: *German Cross in Silver*

Konteradmiral Hermann **MÖRSBERGER** (12 Aug 1872 - 29 Feb 1940)

Sep 1914 - Jul 1917:	Commander of Heavy Artillery, Flanders Marine Corps
Jul 1917 - 14 Aug 1917:	Commander of Artillery, 2. Marine Division, Flanders Marine Corps
15 Aug 1917 - 27 Aug 1917:	Attached to the Battleship "*Markgraf*"
28 Aug 1917 - 14 Nov 1918:	Commandant, Battleship "*Markgraf*"
15 Nov 1918 - 19 Dec 1918:	Attached to the Commander, Baltic Naval Station
20 Dec 1918 - 2 Aug 1919:	Chief of II. Demobilization Office
3 Aug 1919 - 31 Aug 1919:	Acting Inspector, I. Naval Inspectorate
1 Sep 1919 - 22 Nov 1919:	Attached to the Commander, Baltic Naval Station
22 Nov 1919:	Retired
(27 Jan 1920:	Promoted to brevet Konteradmiral)

Konteradmiral Wilhelm **MÖSSEL** (20 Oct 1897 - 5 Sep 1986)

1 Feb 1937 - 25 Aug 1939:	Attached to Luftwaffe General Staff
26 Aug 1939 - 11 May 1945:	Naval Liaison Officer to the C-in-C of the Luftwaffe
(1 Oct 1944:	Promoted to Konteradmiral)

Admiralarzt (Konteradmiral) Dr. Willy **MÜCKE** (20 Jul 1888 - 2 Nov 1968)

12 Oct 1934 - Jan 1942:	Chief Medical Officer, Wilhelmshaven Shipyards
(1 Apr 1939:	Promoted to brevet Admiralarzt)
(1 Jun 1941:	Confirmed as Admiralarzt from brevet rank)
21 Aug 1939 - 3 Sep 1939:	Acting Chief Medical Officer, North Sea Naval Station

Jan 1942 - 31 Mar 1945: Chief of Naval Works Medical Department, Naval High Command
31 Mar 1945: Retired

Konteradmiral Erich **MÜLLER** (3 Apr 1895 - 7 Mar 1967)
6 Oct 1937 - 12 Sep 1939: Advisor, Underwater Weapons Group, Naval High Command
13 Sep 1939 - 31 Mar 1943: Commander, Mines Testing Command
(1 Apr 1943: Promoted to Konteradmiral)
1 Apr 1943 - 15 Jul 1945: Chief of Mines Directorate, Naval High Command
Awards: *German Cross in Silver*

Admiral Georg Alexander von **MÜLLER** (24 Mar 1854 - 18 Apr 1940)
(27 Jan 1905: Promoted to Konteradmiral)
8 Jul 1906 - 28 Oct 1918: Chief of the Naval Cabinet
(17 Sep 1907: Promoted to Vizeadmiral)
(29 Aug 1910: Promoted to Admiral)
29 Oct 1918 - 28 Nov 1918: Placed on inactive status
28 Nov 1918: Retired
Awards: *Order of the Black Eagle; Pour le Mérite*

Admiralarzt (Konteradmiral) Dr. Gerhard **MÜLLER** (11 Apr 1894 - 9 Nov 1981)
27 Sep 1932 - 27 Sep 1937: Chief Medical Officer, Swinemünde Naval Hospital
4 Oct 1937 - 19 Feb 1941: Attached to Wilhelmshaven Medical Office
20 Feb 1941 - 12 Jun 1941: Chief Medical Officer, Wilhelmshaven Naval Hospital
13 Jun 1941 - 31 Mar 1943: Medical Officer, High Seas Fleet
(1 Jan 1943: Promoted to Admiralarzt)
1 Apr 1943 - 31 Mar 1944: Senior Medical Officer, Naval Group Norway
1 Apr 1944 - 30 Jun 1944: Placed on inactive status
30 Jun 1944: Retired

Geheime Marineoberbaurat (Vizeadmiral) Richard **MÜLLER** (16 Aug 1865 - ?)
Jun 1913 - 10 Apr 1917: Section Chief, Construction Department, Naval Office
11 Apr 1917 - 9 Sep 1919: Chief of Technical Bureau, Inspectorate of Submarines

10 Sep 1919 - 1 Jan 1920: Chief of Technical Section, Admiralty
(23 Dec 1919: Promoted to Geheime Marineoberbaurat)
2 Jan 1920 - 23 Aug 1923: Chief of Naval Construction, Naval High Command
23 Aug 1923: Retired

Konteradmiral Harry **MÜNDEL** (31 Aug 1876 - 27 Apr 1946)
20 Oct 1920 - 30 Sep 1921: Inspector, Coastal Inspectorate III, Harbor Captain of Kiel
1 Oct 1921 - 20 Mar 1923: Chief of Naval Office, Lübeck
21 Mar 1923 - 30 Apr 1923: Attached to the Commander, Baltic Naval Station
(30 Apr 1923: Promoted to brevet Konteradmiral)
30 Apr 1923: Retired

Konteradmiral Friedrich **MUSCULUS** (12 Dec 1862 - 4 Dec 1942)
(19 Nov 1910: Promoted to brevet Konteradmiral; retired)
25 Nov 1914 - 16 Jun 1918: Recalled from retirement; Deputy Chief of Danzig Shipyards
25 Nov 1914 - 16 Aug 1916: Director of Armaments, Danzig Shipyards
17 Jun 1918 - 31 Jul 1918: Attached to the Commander, Baltic Naval Station
31 Jul 1918: Retired

Admiralarzt (Konteradmiral) Dr. Fritz **NADLER** (6 Aug 1895 - 30 Mar 1985)
1 Jun 1938 - 30 Apr 1941: Chief Medical Officer, Stralsund Naval Hospital
1 May 1941 - 31 Jan 1943: Chief Medical Officer, Hospital Ship "*Straßburg*"
1 Mar 1943 - 31 Mar 1944: Senior Medical Officer, Naval Group West
(1 Apr 1943: Promoted to Admiralarzt)
1 Apr 1944 - 31 Dec 1944: Chief Medical Officer, North Sea Naval Group
1 Jan 1945 - 31 Mar 1945: Attached to the Chief Medical Officer, North Sea Naval Group
31 Mar 1945: Retired

Konteradmiral Ernst-Oldwig von **NATZMER** (15 Oct 1868 - 21 Aug 1942)
5 Aug 1914 - 29 Mar 1915: Commandant, Battleship "*Kaiser Barbarossa*"
1 Apr 1915 - 13 Aug 1915: Commandant, Heavy Cruiser "*Freya*"
24 Aug 1915 - 25 Mar 1918: Commandant, Battleship "*Ostfriesland*"
26 Mar 1918 - 9 May 1918: Attached to the Commander, Baltic Naval Station

10 May 1918 - 2 Aug 1918:	Commander of Ships Training Division
7 Aug 1918 - 7 Dec 1918:	Commander, I. Marine Brigade, Flanders Marine Corps
20 Jan 1919 - 22 Nov 1919:	Inspector, Coastal Inspectorate II
22 Nov 1919:	Retired
(4 Feb 1920:	Promoted to brevet Konteradmiral)

Konteradmiral Dr. Karl-August **NERGER** (25 Feb 1875 - 12 Jan 1947)

1 Jul 1914 - 24 Mar 1916:	Commandant, Light Cruiser "*Stettin*"
31 Mar 1916 - 4 May 1918:	Commandant, Auxiliary Cruiser "*Wolf*"
10 Jun 1918 - 15 Dec 1918:	Commander of Mine Units, High Seas Fleet
16 Dec 1918 - 25 Jul 1919:	Attached to the Commander, Baltic Naval Station
25 Jul 1919:	Retired
(19 Aug 1939:	Promoted to brevet Konteradmiral)

Konteradmiral (Ingeneur) Fritz **NIEMAND** (27 Jul 1892 - 12 Feb 1943)

1 Oct 1936 - 31 Mar 1939:	Director of Armaments Office, Kiel Naval Arsenal
1 Apr 1939 - 31 Mar 1940:	Director of Armaments Office, Kiel Shipyards
1 Apr 1940 - 3 Dec 1942:	Director of Supplies Office, Kiel Shipyards
(1 Sep 1941:	Promoted to Konteradmiral Ingeneur)
4 Dec 1942 - 12 Feb 1943:	Attached to the Commander, Baltic Naval Station

Admiralstabsintendant (Vizeadmiral) Fritz **NOBE** (24 Oct 1880 - 2 May 1945)

1 Feb 1939 - 4 Jun 1943:	Chief Intendant, North Sea Naval Station
(11 Mar 1939:	Promoted to Stationsintendant [Konteradmiral])
(14 Nov 1942:	Promoted to Generalstabsintendant der Marine [Vizeadmiral])
12 Jul 1943 - 2 May 1945:	Chief Intendant, Armed Forces Commander Norway
(1 May 1944:	Rank redesignated as Admiralstabsintendant)

Admiralarzt (Konteradmiral) Dr. Heinrich **NÖLDECKE**
(16 Aug 1896 - 17 Jun 1955)

2 Oct 1934 - 1 Jul 1940:	Medical Advisor, North Sea Naval Station
2 Jul 1940 - 20 May 1941:	Chief Medical Officer, Kiel-Hassee Naval Hospital
21 May 1941 - 30 Sep 1942:	Chief Medical Officer, Stralsund Naval Hospital

1 Oct 1942 - 28 Jan 1944:	Chief Medical Officer, Kiel-Hassee & Kiel-Wik Naval Hospitals
29 Jan 1944 - 14 Jul 1945:	Chief of Medical Service, Baltic Naval Group
(1 Mar 1944:	Promoted to Admiralarzt)

Admiral Willy von **NORDECK** (26 Jan 1888 - 12 Oct 1956)

4 Oct 1930 - 2 Oct 1932:	Commandant, Battleship "*Hessen*"
5 Oct 1932 - 29 Sep 1935:	Chief of Central Office, Wilhelmshaven Shipyards
(1 Apr 1935:	Promoted to Konteradmiral)
30 Sep 1935 - 22 Jun 1942:	Director of Wilhelmshaven Shipyards
(1 Oct 1937:	Promoted to Vizeadmiral)
(1 Jan 1940:	Promoted to Admiral)
23 Jun 1942 - 31 Aug 1942:	Attached to the Commander-in-Chief of the Navy
31 Aug 1942:	Retired
1 Sep 1942:	Recalled to reserve status; no appointment conferred
31 May 1943:	Retired

Awards: *German Cross in Silver*

Vizeadmiral Heinz **NORDMANN** (28 May 1893 - 23 Dec 1945)

30 Sep 1937 - 2 Apr 1939:	Chief of Organization Office, Naval High Command
3 Apr 1939 - 27 Feb 1940:	Commandant, Light Cruiser "*Leipzig*"
28 Feb 1940 - 27 Jul 1941:	Chief of Naval Transport Office, Ministry of Transport
(1 Apr 1941:	Promoted to Konteradmiral)
28 Jul 1941 - 18 Jan 1942:	Chief of Staff, Kiel Shipyards
9 Apr 1942 - 17 Sep 1942:	Commander of Sea Defenses, Arctic Ocean
18 Sep 1942 - 19 Jan 1945:	Admiral Commanding, Norwegian Polar Coast
(1 Apr 1943:	Promoted to Vizeadmiral)
20 Jan 1945 - 30 Apr 1945:	Attached to the Commander-in-Chief of the Navy
30 Apr 1945:	Retired

Vizeadmiral Hermann **NORDMANN** (19 Jan 1868 - 11 Feb 1933)

15 Mar 1914 - 8 Sep 1914:	Inspector of U-Boats
1 Oct 1914 - 28 Aug 1915:	Commandant, Battleship "*Markgraf*"
12 Aug 1915 - 28 Aug 1915:	Acting Deputy Commander, III. Squadron

29 Aug 1915 - 8 Dec 1916:   Deputy Commander, III. Squadron
(18 Sep 1915:   Promoted to Konteradmiral)
12 Jun 1916 - 20 Aug 1916:   Acting Commander, III. Squadron
26 Dec 1916 - 29 Jun 1917:   Chief of Naval Operations
20 Aug 1917 - 24 Jan 1918:   Commander of Security, Western Baltic
25 Jan 1918 - 27 Oct 1918:   Commander of Security Forces, Baltic
(18 Sep 1918:   Promoted to Vizeadmiral)
2 Nov 1918 - 14 Nov 1918:   Acting Inspector of U-Boats
15 Nov 1918 - 12 Feb 1919:   Attached to the Commander, Baltic Naval Station
12 Feb 1919:   Retired

Konteradmiral Moritz von **OBERNITZ** (9 Aug 1869 - 4 Apr 1958)
1 Jun 1913 - 30 Oct 1917:   Recalled from retirement; Special Purposes Officer, Baltic Naval Station
31 Oct 1917 - Dec 1917:   Harbor Captain of Riga-Daugavpils
Dec 1917 - 31 Jan 1919:   Special Purposes Officer, Baltic Naval Station
31 Jan 1919:   Retired
(18 Nov 1919:   Promoted to brevet Konteradmiral)

Konteradmiral Walther **OEHLER** (3 Jan 1888 - 6 Jul 1968)
21 Oct 1938 - 6 Sep 1939:   Naval Advisor, Recruiting Inspectorate Königsberg
7 Sep 1939 - 13 Sep 1939:   Commander, 5. Replacement Naval Artillery Detachment
14 Sep 1939 - 13 Oct 1939:   Attached to the Fortress Commandant, Gotenhafen
14 Oct 1939 - 21 Jan 1940:   Commander, Wilhelmshaven Flak Group
22 Jan 1940 - 2 Mar 1940:   Attached to the Coastal Defense Commander, East Friesland
3 Mar 1940 - 14 Mar 1940:   Commandant, Nordeney District
15 Mar 1940 - 2 Apr 1940:   Commandant, Helgoland District
3 Apr 1940 - 10 May 1940:   Commandant, Wilhelmshaven District
26 May 1940 - 30 Apr 1942:   Commander, 2. Naval Flak Regiment
1 May 1942 - 13 Dec 1943:   Commander, II. Naval Flak Brigade
(1 Oct 1942:   Promoted to Konteradmiral)
14 Dec 1943 - 20 Apr 1944:   Commander of Sea Defenses, Bergen
21 Apr 1944 - 29 Aug 1944:   Sick leave
29 Aug 1944 - 31 Jan 1945:   Attached to the C-in-C, Baltic Naval Group
31 Jan 1945:   Retired
Awards: *German Cross in Gold*

Admiral Iwan Christian Hermann **OLDEKOP** (8 Feb 1878 - 13 May 1942)
10 Sep 1920 - 26 Sep 1922:	Chief of Fleet Office, Naval High Command (Chief of Naval Operations)
26 Feb 1921 - 26 Sep 1922:	Acting Chief of Naval Command Office, Naval High Command (Chief of Naval General Staff)
27 Sep 1922 - 30 Sep 1923:	Commandant, Battleship "*Hannover*"
1 Oct 1923 - 31 Mar 1925:	Commander of Light Forces, Baltic
(1 Nov 1923:	Promoted to Konteradmiral)
1 Apr 1925 - 24 Sep 1925:	Commander of Baltic Naval Forces & Flag Officer, Reconnaissance Forces
28 Sep 1925 - 28 Sep 1927:	Chief of General Naval Office, Naval High Command
30 Sep 1927 - 30 Sep 1931:	C-in-C, High Seas Fleet
30 Sep 1927 - 31 Dec 1929:	Commander, Battleship Division
(1 Jan 1928:	Promoted to Vizeadmiral)
(30 Sep 1931:	Promoted to brevet Admiral)
30 Sep 1931:	Retired

Admiral (*General der Kavallerie*) Friedrich August, Großherzog von **OLDENBURG** (16 Nov 1852 - 24 Feb 1931)
Admiral à la Suite (Honorary title)

Konteradmiral Ernst **ORTH** (4 Mar 1870 - 11 Jul 1941)
16 Jul 1913 - 4 Apr 1919:	Director of Armaments, Wilhelmshaven Shipyards
5 Apr 1919 - 18 Nov 1919:	Chief of Printing Office, Naval High Command
18 Nov 1919:	Retired
(18 Dec 1919:	Promoted to brevet Konteradmiral)

Vizeadmiral (Ingeneur) Karl **PACKROß** (17 Jan 1891 - 6 Jan 1946)
20 Feb 1933 - 24 Nov 1935:	Member, Ships Testing Commission
25 Nov 1935 - 30 Sep 1937:	Advisor, Armed Forces Office, Ministry of War
1 Oct 1937 - 3 Jun 1940:	Chief of Defense Economics Office, Berlin III
4 Jun 1940 - Jun 1941:	Inspector, Armaments Inspectorate II
(1 Jan 1941:	Promoted to Konteradmiral Ingeneur)
Jun 1941 - Jan 1942:	Inspector, Armaments Inspectorate III
Jan 1942 - 26 Apr 1945:	Inspector, Armaments Inspectorate II
(1 Jun 1944:	Promoted to Vizeadmiral Ingeneur)

Admiral Conrad **PATZIG** (24 May 1888 - 1 Dec 1975)
6 Jun 1932 - 2 Jan 1935:	Chief of CounterIntelligence Service (Abwehr)
28 Feb 1935 - 6 Oct 1935:	Commandant, Battleship *"Schleswig-Holstein"*
7 Oct 1935 - 5 Jan 1936:	Attached to the Pocket Battleship *"Admiral Graf Spee"*
6 Jan 1936 - 1 Oct 1937:	Commandant, Pocket Battleship *"Admiral Graf Spee"*
4 Oct 1937 - 31 Oct 1942:	Chief of Naval Personnel
(1 Nov 1937:	Promoted to Konteradmiral)
(1 Jan 1940:	Promoted to Vizeadmiral)
(1 Apr 1942:	Promoted to Admiral)
1 Nov 1942 - 31 Mar 1943:	Attached to the Commander-in-Chief of the Navy
31 Mar 1943:	Retired
1 Apr 1943:	Recalled to reserve status; no appointment conferred

Awards: *German Cross in Silver*

Konteradmiral Oswald **PAUL** (1 Aug 1883 - 11 May 1949)
1 Dec 1930 - 31 Oct 1936:	Recalled from retirement; Naval Advisor, Military District (Wehrkreis) III
1 Nov 1936 - 31 Mar 1937:	Chief of Naval Section, Inspectorate of Recruiting, Berlin
1 Apr 1937 - 30 Jun 1938:	Commander, Recruiting Command Berlin I
1 Jul 1938 - 9 Jan 1940:	Commander, Recruiting Command Berlin IX
10 Jan 1940 - 31 May 1944:	Commander, Recruiting Command Vienna
(1 Jan 1941:	Promoted to Konteradmiral)
1 Jun 1944 - 31 Jul 1944:	Attached to the C-in-C, Baltic Naval Group
31 Jul 1944:	Retired

Ministerialdirigent (Konteradmiral) Richard **PEIN** (23 Nov 1883 - 29 Jun 1965)
1 Nov 1939 - 24 Jul 1944:	Chief of Personnel Section, Harbor Construction Group, Naval High Command
(1 Sep 1943:	Promoted to Ministerialdirigent)
25 Jul 1944 - 8 May 1945:	Chief Liaison Officer to Todt Organization

Ministerialdirigent (Konteradmiral) Hans **PELTE** (4 Dec 1873 - 8 Apr 1943)
11 Jan 1936 - 31 Dec 1938:	Director of Dockyards Administration Section, Naval General Office, Naval High Command
(1 Jul 1936:	Promoted to Ministerialdirigent)

31 Dec 1938: Retired
Sep 1939 - 7 Apr 1940: Attached to Germania Shipyards, Kiel
8 Apr 1940 - 8 Apr 1943: Chief of Accommodations & Building Construction, North Sea Naval Station Intendant's Office

Vizeadmiral (Ingeneur) Hans **PETERS** (23 Dec 1884 - 29 Nov 1947)
14 Oct 1929 - 28 Sep 1933: Chief Engineer, High Seas Fleet
29 Sep 1933 - 30 Sep 1936: Engineer, Naval General Staff & Chief of Military Section for Ships Equipment
(1 Oct 1933: Promoted to Konteradmiral Ingeneur)
(30 Sep 1936: Promoted to brevet Vizeadmiral Ingeneur)
30 Sep 1936: Retired
24 May 1939: Recalled to reserve status; no appointment conferred

Konteradmiral (Ingeneur) Max **PETERS** (6 Jun 1888 - 11 Apr 1961)
25 Sep 1937 - 12 Nov 1939: Advisor to Deputy Commander, North Sea Naval Station
15 Nov 1939 - 19 Sep 1940: Commander, 14. Ships' Crew Detachment
20 Sep 1940 - 23 Mar 1943: Commander, 18. Ships' Crew Detachment
24 Mar 1943 - 9 Jan 1944: Director of Naval Armaments & Repair Works, Pillau
10 Jan 1944 - 28 Mar 1945: Commandant of Gotenhafen Naval Arsenal
(1 Aug 1944: Promoted to Konteradmiral Ingeneur)

Konteradmiral Rudolf **PETERS** (9 Aug 1899 - 14 Sep 1990)
4 Nov 1938 - 14 Aug 1940: Advisor, Inspectorate of Naval Training
24 Sep 1939 - 27 Oct 1939: Acting Chief of Staff, Inspectorate of Naval Training
15 Aug 1940 - 26 Dec 1940: Staff Officer to Flag Officer, Cruisers
27 Dec 1940 - 15 Apr 1942: First Officer, Battleship "*Gneisenau*"
15 Apr 1942 - 17 Apr 1942: Acting Commandant, Battleship "*Gneisenau*"
18 Apr 1942 - 22 Jul 1942: Attached to the Commander, Baltic Naval Station
23 Jul 1942 - 1 Jan 1943: Commander, 24. U-Boat Flotilla
2 Jan 1943 - 4 Jun 1944: Commander of U-Boats, Norway
15 Mar 1944 - 4 Jun 1944: Admiral Commanding, Northern Waters
5 Jun 1944 - 20 Oct 1944: Commander, 1. Battle Group
(1 Jul 1944: Promoted to Konteradmiral)
21 Oct 1944 -23 Jan 1945: Attached to the Naval Armaments Directorate

24 Jan 1945 - 28 Feb 1945:	Attached to the Inspectorate of Torpedoes
1 Mar 1945 - 28 Mar 1945:	Attached to the C-in-C, Baltic Naval Group
29 Mar 1945 - 30 Apr 1945:	Attached to the Torpedo Office, Naval High Command
30 Apr 1945:	Retired

Awards: *German Cross in Gold*

Kommodore Rudolf **PETERSEN** (15 Jun 1905 - 2 Feb 1983)

12 Aug 1938 - 19 Oct 1941:	Commander, 2. Torpedo Boat Flotilla
26 Oct 1941 - 26 Nov 1941:	Attached to Staff of Flag Officer, Torpedo Boats
27 Nov 1941 - 19 Apr 1942:	Attached to Commander, Baltic Naval Station
20 Apr 1942 - 22 Jul 1945:	Flag Officer, Torpedo Boats
(23 Sep 1944:	Promoted to Kommodore)

Awards: *Knight's Cross with Oakleaves; Knight's Cross*

Konteradmiral Albertus **PETRUSCHKY** (3 Mar 1866 - 23 Jan 1943)

(11 Jan 1913:	Promoted to brevet Konteradmiral; retired)
5 Aug 1914 - 12 Aug 1914:	Recalled from retirement; Commander, 2. Sailor Division
15 Aug 1914 - 27 Aug 1914:	Attached to Friedrichsort Command Station
3 Sep 1914 - 16 Feb 1916:	Commander, II. Sailor Artillery Group & Commandant of Seafront Defenses, Wilhelmshaven
Apr 1916 - Dec 1917:	Commissioner, Kiel Prize Court
Dec 1917:	Retired

Vizeadmiral Adolf **PFEIFFER** (29 Oct 1876 - 14 May 1961)

14 Jan 1919 - 22 Feb 1922:	Chief of Military Office, Naval High Command
1 Mar 1922 - 14 Oct 1923:	Commandant, Battleship *"Braunschweig"*
15 Oct 1923 - 19 Sep 1924:	Commander of Light Naval Forces, North Sea
22 Sep 1924 - 30 Sep 1928:	Chief of Naval Command Office, Naval High Command (Chief of Naval General Staff)
(1 Feb 1925:	Promoted to Konteradmiral)
(30 Sep 1928:	Promoted to brevet Vizeadmiral)
30 Sep 1928:	Retired
22 Mar 1939:	Recalled to reserve status
3 Sep 1939 - 2 Oct 1942:	Judge, Berlin Prize Court
(1 Sep 1942:	Confirmed as Vizeadmiral from brevet rank)
31 Oct 1942:	Retired

Konteradmiral Hans **PFUNDHELLER** (3 Jul 1869 - 25 Dec 1940)
14 Apr 1914 - 15 Sep 1914:	Responsible for trial runs, Construction Department, Naval Office
16 Sep 1914 - 18 Nov 1914:	Commandant, Auxiliary Cruiser "*Berlin*"
19 Nov 1914 - Jun 1915:	Interned in Norway
Jun 1915 - 27 Mar 1919:	Attached to the Construction Department, Naval Office
27 Mar 1919:	Retired
(30 Aug 1919:	Promoted to brevet Konteradmiral)

Konteradmiral Otto **PHILIPP** (21 Oct 1867 - 11 May 1941)
(22 Jun 1914:	Promoted to brevet Konteradmiral; retired)
20 Aug 1914 - 20 May 1917:	Recalled; Chief of Naval Aviation
(22 Mar 1916:	Confirmed as Konteradmiral from brevet rank)
21 May 1917 - 9 Nov 1918:	Attached to the staff of the C-in-C, Marches
9 Nov 1918:	Retired

Konteradmiral (Turkish Major-General) Waldemar **PIEPER** (14 Aug 1871 - 24 Feb 1945)
12 Aug 1914 - 4 Nov 1914:	Commandant, Heavy Cruiser "*Yorck*"
5 Nov 1914 - 2 Feb 1915:	Attached to the Commander, North Sea Naval Station
3 Feb 1915 - 30 Jul 1917:	Inspector of Weapons, Turkish Weapons Office
31 Jul 1917 - 2 Oct 1917:	Attached to the Naval Office
3 Oct 1917 - 30 Sep 1919:	Director of Artillery and Hand Weapons Construction Bureau, Naval Office
(18 Sep 1918:	Promoted to Konteradmiral)
29 Dec 1918 - 30 Sep 1919:	Deputy Director of Weapons Department
1 Oct 1919 - 24 Nov 1919:	Attached to the Commander-in-Chief of the Navy
24 Nov 1919:	Retired

Marinegeneralstabsarzt/Admiralarzt (Konteradmiral) Edgar **PILLET** (20 Sep 1877 - 12 May 1959)
1 Apr 1922 - 25 Mar 1926:	Senior Medical Officer, Flensburg-Mürwik Naval Hospital
29 Mar 1926 - 30 Mar 1927:	Chief Medical Officer, Kiel-Wik Naval Hospital
2 Apr 1927 - 11 Sep 1927:	Chief Medical Officer, Naval Training Inspectorate & Chief Medical Officer, Inspectorate of Torpedoes & Mines

12 Sep 1927 - 29 Sep 1930:	Chief Medical Officer, Baltic Naval Station
(30 Sep 1930:	Promoted to brevet Marinegeneralstabsarzt)
30 Sep 1930:	Retired
9 Mar 1939:	Recalled to reserve status as brevet Admiralarzt; no appointment conferred

Marinegeneralstabsarzt (Konteradmiral) Dr. Friedrich **PINGGÉRA**
(26 Jan 1876 - 18 Jan 1940)

1 Jan 1923 - 30 Jun 1927:	Attached to the Medical Section, Naval Office
1 Jul 1927 - 30 Sep 1928:	Chief Medical Officer, High Seas Fleet
(30 Sep 1928:	Promoted to brevet Marinegeneralstabsarzt)
30 Sep 1927:	Retired

Konteradmiral Max **PIRALY** (18 Sep 1848 - 15 Aug 1917)

1895 - 1917:	Recalled from retirement; Superintendant, Kasier-Wilhelm Canal
(24 Jun 1914:	Promoted to brevet Konteradmiral)

Konteradmiral Hugo **PLACHTE** (7 Dec 1853 - 14 Jul 1930)

(9 Jan 1904:	Promoted to brevet Konteradmiral; retired)
3 Aug 1914 - Dec 1918:	Recalled from retirement; Reichskommissar, Hamburg Prize Court
Dec 1918:	Retired

Vizeadmiral Oskar Graf von **PLATEN-HALLERMUND**
(18 Mar 1865 - 14 Apr 1957)

(10 Oct 1911:	Promoted to brevet Konteradmiral)
11 Oct 1911 - 1 Apr 1935:	Marshal of the Kaiser's Court
(22 Mar 1916:	Promoted to brevet Vizeadmiral)
1 Apr 1935:	Retired

Konteradmiral Joachim **PLATH** (3 Jun 1893 - 28 Jun 1971)

29 Sep 1937 - 3 Apr 1939:	Staff Officer to Flag Officer, Battleships
4 Apr 1939 - 11 Nov 1941:	Chief of Organization Office, Naval High Command
16 Nov 1941 - 24 Feb 1943:	Commander, 1. Security Division
(1 Sep 1942:	Promoted to Konteradmiral)
1 Mar 1943 - 30 Sep 1943:	Coastal Commander, Eastern Baltic
1 Oct 1943 - 11 Dec 1944:	Coastal Commander, Central Baltic
1 Mar 1943 - 11 Dec 1944:	Fortress Commandant of Gotenhafen

12 Dec 1944 - 3 May 1945:	Admiral attached to Army Group H
4 May 1945 - 22 Jul 1945:	Commander, Naval Division Group 317

Konteradmiral Friedrich **POHL** (4 Aug 1868 - 3 Jun 1950)
15 Oct 1911 - 27 Oct 1914:	Member of Ships Oversight Commission
16 Oct 1914 - 27 Oct 1914:	Member of Hamburg Prize Court
28 Oct 1914 - Oct 1918:	Director of Bruges Naval Shipyards
Oct 1918 - 16 Mar 1919:	Attached to the Commander, North Sea Naval Station
16 Mar 1919:	Retired
(30 Aug 1919:	Promoted to brevet Konteradmiral)

Admiral Hugo von **POHL** (25 Aug 1855 - 23 Feb 1916)
(7 Jul 1906:	Promoted to Konteradmiral)
(5 Sep 1909:	Promoted to Vizeadmiral)
(27 Jan 1913:	Promoted to Admiral)
1 Apr 1913 - 1 Feb 1915:	Chief of Naval General Staff
2 Feb 1915 - 23 Jan 1916:	C-in-C, High Seas Fleet
24 Jan 1916:	Retired; Admiral à la Suite

Konteradmiral Harry Graf von **POSADOWSKY-WEHNER**
(17 Aug 1869 - 5 Nov 1923)
Aug 1914 - Oct 1914:	Recalled from retirement; Chief of Wannsee Group, Volunteer Motor Boat Corps
Oct 1914 - Jun 1917:	Commander of Vistula Flotilla, Volunteer Motor Boat Corps
Jun 1917 - 31 Jul 1917:	Attached to the Commander, Baltic Naval Station
1 Aug 1917 - 26 Apr 1918:	Director of Engineer & Deck Officer School
27 Apr 1918 - 31 Jan 1919:	Attached to Army Group Eichhorn & the Commander, North Sea Naval Station
31 Jan 1919:	Retired
(17 Oct 1919:	Promoted to brevet Konteradmiral)

Marinegeneralstabsarzt/Admiralarzt (Konteradmiral) Victor **PRAEFCKE**
(25 Oct 1872 - 19 Nov 1962)
1 Oct 1919 - 30 Jun 1923:	Chief Medical Officer, Kiel-Wik Naval Hospital
5 Sep 1920 - 14 Oct 1920:	Acting Chief Medical Officer, Baltic Naval Station
1 Jul 1923 - 31 Oct 1925:	Chief Medical Officer, North Sea Naval Station
31 Oct 1925:	Retired

(21 Nov 1925:	Promoted to brevet Marinegeneralstabsarzt)
9 Mar 1939:	Recalled to reserve status as brevet Admiralarzt; no appointment conferred

Admiral Wilhelm **PRENTZEL** (28 Jul 1878 - 2 May 1945)

31 May 1920 - 30 Sep 1921:	Chief of Staff, North Sea Naval Station
1 Oct 1921 - 14 Feb 1924:	Chief of Nautical Office, Naval High Command
1 Mar 1923 - 5 Jun 1923:	Acting Chief of Naval General Office, Naval High Command
15 Feb 1924 - 22 Sep 1925:	Commandant, Battleship "*Elsaß*"
23 Sep 1925 - 10 Sep 1927:	Commander, North Sea Naval Forces & Deputy Commander, Battleship Division
(1 Oct 1926:	Promoted to Konteradmiral)
4 Oct 1927 - 14 Nov 1930:	Chief of Naval General Office, Naval High Command
(1 Oct 1928:	Promoted to Vizeadmiral)
15 Nov 1930 - 30 Nov 1930:	Attached to the Commander-in-Chief of the Navy
(30 Nov 1930:	Promoted to brevet Admiral)
30 Nov 1930:	Retired
1 Jan 1939:	Recalled to reserve status
25 Aug 1939 - 9 Sep 1939:	Naval Representative for East Prussia
10 Sep 1939 - 30 Nov 1944:	Attached to the Commander-in-Chief of the Navy
(1 Feb 1941:	Confirmed as Admiral from brevet rank)
30 Nov 1944:	Retired

Ministerialdirektor (*Vizeadmiral*) Dr. Paul **PRESZE** (20 Jan 1868 - 28 Jan 1948)

15 Sep 1920 - 23 Aug 1923:	Head of Ships Construction Design Service, Construction Section, Naval General Office, Naval High Command
24 Aug 1923 - 31 Dec 1924:	Director of Construction Section, Naval General Office, Naval High Command
1 Jan 1925 - 20 Jan 1934:	Chief of Naval Construction
(1 May 1927:	Promoted to Ministerialdirektor)
21 Jan 1934 - 30 Apr 1934:	Placed on inactive status
30 Apr 1934:	Retired

Großadmiral (*Generaloberst m.d.R.e. GFM, k.u.k. Großadmiral, British Admiral of the Fleet*) Heinrich Albert Wilhelm Prinz von **PREUSSEN**
(14 Aug 1862 - 20 Apr 1929)
(15 Sep 1895:	Promoted to Konteradmiral)
(5 Dec 1899:	Promoted to Vizeadmiral)
(13 Sep 1901:	Promoted to Admiral)
(4 Sep 1909:	Promoted to Großadmiral)
1 Oct 1909 - 10 Aug 1919:	Inspector-General of the Navy
31 Jul 1914 - 24 Jan 1918:	C-in-C, Baltic Naval Forces
10 Aug 1919:	Resigned
Awards: *Order of the Black Eagle, Pour le Mérite, Oakleaves to the Pour le Mérite*

Vizeadmiral Theodor **PÜLLEN** (25 Nov 1871 - 5 Jun 1931)
1 Aug 1914 - 28 Aug 1914:	Commandant, Auxiliary Cruiser "*C*"
8 Sep 1914 - 30 Apr 1916:	Commandant, Light Cruiser "*Graudenz*"
1 May 1916 - 3 Jun 1916:	Attached to the Commander, North Sea Naval Station
4 Jun 1916 - 10 Apr 1917:	Attached to the Commander of Coastal Defenses, Hamburg
9 Jun 1917 - 28 Jan 1918:	Commodore & Commander of U-Boats, Mediterranean & Commander of Pola U-Boat Flotilla
29 Jan 1918 - 3 Dec 1918:	Attached to the Naval Cabinet
4 Dec 1918 - 12 Dec 1918:	Section Chief, Naval Cabinet
13 Dec 1918 - 1 Jul 1920:	Chief of Naval Personnel
2 Jul 1920 - 10 Apr 1922:	Chief of Naval Command Office, Naval High Command (Chief of Naval General Staff)
(20 Dec 1920:	Promoted to Konteradmiral)
11 Apr 1922 - 19 Sep 1923:	Commander, North Sea Naval Forces
(1 Aug 1922:	Promoted to Vizeadmiral)
20 Sep 1923 - 31 Oct 1923:	Attached to the Commander, North Sea Naval Station
31 Oct 1923:	Retired

Konteradmiral Siegfried **PUNT** (26 Feb 1881 - 5 Oct 1960)
10 Jul 1920 - 21 Sep 1926:	Commander, Ships Artillery School
22 Sep 1926 - 11 Oct 1928:	Inspector, Naval Depot Inspectorate
12 Oct 1928 - 30 Nov 1928:	Attached to the Commander, North Sea Naval Station
(30 Nov 1928:	Promoted to brevet Konteradmiral)

30 Nov 1928:	Retired
24 May 1939:	Recalled to reserve status
12 Mar 1941 - 30 Jun 1942:	Commissioner, Kongsberg State Weapons Factory, Norway
1 Jul 1942 - 22 Nov 1942:	Director of Bordeaux Naval Shipyards
(1 Oct 1942:	Confirmed as Konteradmiral from brevet rank)
23 Nov 1942 - 31 Jan 1943:	Transferred to the Führer Reserve
31 Jan 1943:	Retired

Konteradmiral Karl-Jesko von **PUTTKAMER** (24 Mar 1900 - 4 Mar 1981)

17 Sep 1938 - 22 Aug 1939:	Commandant, Destroyer "*Hans Lody*" & Flag Captain, 4. Destroyer Flotilla
23 Aug 1939 - 30 Sep 1939:	Naval Liaison Officer to Führer Headquarters
1 Oct 1939 - 30 Apr 1945:	Naval Adjutant to the Führer & Naval Liaison Officer to the Commander-in-Chief of the Army
(1 Sep 1943:	Promoted to Konteradmiral)
1 May 1945 - 8 May 1945:	Dismantling of Naval Adjutant's Office

Konteradmiral Hans **QUAET-FASLEM** (3 Dec 1874 - 11 Dec 1941)

1 Dec 1918 - 31 Jul 1919:	Acting Flag Officer, Torpedo Boats
1 Mar 1919 - 17 Mar 1920:	Chief of Staff, North Sea Naval Station
18 Mar 1920 - 14 Sep 1920:	Placed on inactive status
15 Sep 1920 - 4 Jan 1921:	Attached to Naval Archives
5 Jan 1921 - 30 Sep 1921:	Chief of Nautical Office, Naval High Command
1 Oct 1921 - 31 Dec 1921:	Attached to the Commander-in-Chief of the Navy
(31 Dec 1921:	Promoted to brevet Konteradmiral)
31 Dec 1921:	Retired

Großadmiral Dr. Erich **RAEDER** (24 Apr 1876 - 6 Nov 1960)

15 Jul 1919 - 30 Jun 1920:	Chief of Central Office, Naval High Command
1 Jul 1920 - 19 Jul 1922:	Director of Naval Archives
20 Jul 1922 - 18 Sep 1924:	Inspector of Naval Training
(1 Aug 1922:	Promoted to Konteradmiral)
19 Sep 1924 - 9 Jan 1925:	Commander of Light Forces, North Sea
10 Jan 1925 - 24 Sep 1928:	Commander, Baltic Naval Station
(10 Sep 1925:	Promoted to Vizeadmiral)

24 Sep 1928 - 30 Jan 1943: Commander-in-Chief of the Navy
(1 Oct 1928: Promoted to Admiral)
(20 Apr 1936: Promoted to Generaladmiral & appointed Reichs Minister)
(1 Apr 1939: Promoted to Großadmiral)
30 Jan 1943 - 8 May 1945: Admiral-Inspector of the Navy
Awards: *Knight's Cross*

Konteradmiral Kurt **RAMIEN** (3 Oct 1889 - 8 Sep 1939)
2 Oct 1933 - 31 May 1937: Flag Officer, Minesweepers
1 Jun 1937 - 8 Sep 1939: Commander, Mines Testing Command
(1 Apr 1938: Promoted to Konteradmiral)

Feldbischof (Konteradmiral) Franz Justus **RARKOWSKI** (8 Jun 1873 - 9 Feb 1950)
20 Feb 1938 - 6 Feb 1945: Catholic Field Bishop of the Armed Forces
6 Feb 1945: Retired

Konteradmiral Ulrich **RASMUS** (4 Feb 1887 - 24 Oct 1943)
2 Oct 1934 - 26 Sep 1936: Chief of Shipyards Section, Naval High Command
1 Oct 1936 - 6 May 1941: Naval Liaison Officer to Military District (Wehrkreis) XII
7 May 1941 - 30 Dec 1942: Naval Liaison Officer to 11. Army
(1 Feb 1942: Promoted to Konteradmiral)
31 Dec 1942 - 30 Apr 1943: Naval Liaison Officer to Army Group South
30 Apr 1943: Retired

Admiral Hubert von **REBEUR-PASCHWITZ** (14 Aug 1863 - 16 Feb 1933)
(22 Mar 1912: Promoted to Konteradmiral)
2 Aug 1914 - 17 Apr 1915: Deputy Commander of Reconnaissance Forces
17 Apr 1915 - 7 Nov 1916: Inspector of Naval Training
(18 Sep 1915: Promoted to Vizeadmiral)
12 Aug 1916 - 30 Aug 1916: Acting Commander, Baltic Naval Station
9 Nov 1916 - 18 Nov 1916: Transferred to II. Squadron
19 Nov 1916 - 21 Nov 1916: Acting Commander, II. Squadron
22 Nov 1916 - 30 Nov 1916: Attached to II. Squadron
1 Dec 1916 - 15 Aug 1917: Commander, II. Squadron
16 Aug 1917 - 30 Aug 1917: Attached to the Commander, Baltic Naval Station

4 Sep 1917 - 2 Nov 1918:	Commander, Mediterranean Division & C-in-C, Turkish and Bulgarian Fleets
3 Nov 1918 - 12 Feb 1919:	Attached to the Secretary of State, Naval Office
12 Feb 1919:	Retired
(4 Sep 1919:	Promoted to brevet Admiral)

Konteradmiral Johannes **RECKE** (7 Jul 1862 - 22 Jun 1946)

(2 Sep 1909:	Promoted to brevet Konteradmiral; retired)
20 Jul 1915 - 11 Sep 1915:	Recalled from retirement; attached to the Secretary of State, Naval Office
11 Sep 1915:	Retired

Konteradmiral (Turkish Major-General) Victor **RECLAM** (7 Jan 1871 - 26 Oct 1946)

2 Aug 1914 - 6 Dec 1914:	Commandant, Cuxhaven Seafront
26 Dec 1914 - 7 Sep 1915:	German Commander, Bosphorus
8 Sep 1915 - 11 Dec 1916:	Inspector, Coastal Inspectorate, Turkey
12 Dec 1916 - 11 Jan 1917:	Attached to the Secretary of State, Naval Office
12 Jan 1917 - 10 Nov 1918:	Commandant, Battleship "*Nassau*"
11 Nov 1918 - 7 Apr 1919:	Attached to the Secretary of State, Naval Office
8 Apr 1919 - 8 May 1919:	Transferred to Coastal Inspectorate III
9 May 1919 - 1 Dec 1919:	Inspector, Coastal Inspectorate III
15 Aug 1919 - 1 Dec 1919:	Chief of Ships Oversight Commission, Kiel
2 Dec 1919 - 29 Jan 1920:	Attached to the Commander, Baltic Naval Station
(29 Jan 1920:	Promoted to brevet Konteradmiral)
29 Jan 1920:	Retired

Konteradmiral Johannes **REDLICH** (14 Dec 1866 - 14 Nov 1925)

4 Oct 1913 - 25 Sep 1916:	Commandant, Battleship "*Westfalen*"
1 Nov 1916 - 18 Sep 1918:	Director of Sea Transport Bureau, Naval Office
(18 Sep 1918:	Promoted to Konteradmiral)
19 Sep 1918 - 30 Dec 1918:	President, Ship Oversight Commission
31 Dec 1918 - 30 Jan 1919:	Attached to the Commander, North Sea Naval Station
30 Jan 1919:	Retired

Ministerialdirigent (Konteradmiral) Franz **REICH** (30 Mar 1885 - 21 Dec 1943)

1 Nov 1939 - 8 Jul 1943:	Chief of Design Section, Naval Construction Office, Naval High Command
(12 Jun 1942:	Promoted to Marineoberbaudirektor [Konteradmiral])

9 Jul 1943 - 21 Dec 1943: Chief of Design & Construction Group, Naval Construction Office, Naval High Command
(15 Dec 1943: Rank redesignated as Ministerialdirigent)

Vizeadmiral Georg **REIMER** (21 Jul 1888 - 25 Jun 1974)
24 Mar 1932 - 5 Jun 1933: Commander, Torpedo & Signals School
6 Jun 1933 - 28 Sep 1934: Chief of Staff, Inspectorate of Naval Training
29 Sep 1934 - 30 Sep 1935: Inspector, Naval Depot Inspectorate
1 Oct 1935 - 6 May 1937: Inspector of Naval Ordnance
(1 Apr 1937: Promoted to brevet Konteradmiral)
7 May 1937 - 7 Jun 1940: Inspector, Defense Economics Inspectorate II
(1 Nov 1939: Confirmed as Konteradmiral from brevet rank)
8 Jun 1940 - 30 Nov 1942: Inspector of Armaments, Netherlands
(1 Apr 1942: Promoted to Vizeadmiral)
1 Dec 1942 - 28 Feb 1943: Attached to the Commander, North Sea Naval Station
28 Feb 1943: Retired
1 Sep 1942: Recalled to reserve status; no appointment conferred
28 Feb 1943: Retired

Konteradmiral Karl von **RESTORFF** (18 Jun 1871 - 9 Feb 1946)
10 Aug 1914 - 29 Aug 1914: Commandant, Light Cruiser "*Graudenz*"
29 Aug 1914 - 28 Oct 1915: Commodore & Deputy Commander of Torpedo Boats
1 Jan 1915 - 25 Jan 1915: Acting Commander, IV. Reconnaissance Group
12 Nov 1915 - 4 Dec 1918: Section Chief, Naval Cabinet
30 Oct 1918 - 27 Nov 1918: Acting Chief of the Naval Cabinet
5 Dec 1918 - 11 Aug 1919: Attached to the Commander, Baltic Naval Station
(11 Aug 1919: Promoted to brevet Konteradmiral)
11 Aug 1919: Retired

Konteradmiral Heinrich **RETZMANN** (27 Apr 1872 - 4 Nov 1959)
26 Nov 1913 - 14 Dec 1915: Commandant, Light Cruiser "*Straßburg*"
20 Jan 1916 - 25 Mar 1916: Chief of Section for Ships Construction & Weapons, Naval General Department, Naval Office
26 Mar 1916 - 11 Aug 1918: Chief of Central Section, Naval General Staff

24 Aug 1918 - 30 Nov 1918:	Commandant, Battleship *"Baden"*
1 Dec 1918 - 14 Jan 1919:	Attached to the Commander, North Sea Naval Station
15 Jan 1919 - 27 Jul 1919:	Attached to Berlin Prize Court
28 Jul 1919 - 26 Nov 1919:	Commissioner, Berlin Prize Court
(26 Nov 1919:	Promoted to brevet Konteradmiral)
26 Nov 1919:	Retired

Ministerialdirektor (*Vizeadmiral*) Hermann **REUTER** (6 Jul 1870 - 2 Apr 1934)

23 Aug 1914 - 14 Nov 1914:	Chief Intendant, Mobile Marine Division
15 Nov 1914 - 30 Sep 1916:	Field Intendant, Flanders Marine Corps
(28 May 1915:	Promoted to Geheime Admiralitätsrat II. Klasse [Konteradmiral])
9 Oct 1916 - 2 Mar 1917:	Attached to the Director of Naval Administration
3 Mar 1917 - 10 Dec 1918:	Chief of Administrative Questions Section, Directorate of Naval Administration
11 Dec 1918 - 2 Apr 1934:	Director of Administration, Admiralty
(1 Nov 1919:	Appointed Wirkliche Geheime Admiralitätsrat [Vizeadmiral])
(1 Apr 1920:	Rank redesignated as Ministerialdirektor)

Admiral Ludwig von **REUTER** (9 Feb 1869 - 18 Dec 1943)

1 Sep 1914 - 2 Sep 1915:	Commandant, Heavy Cruiser *"Derfflinger"*
3 Sep 1915 - 10 Sep 1916:	Commander, IV. Reconnaissance Group
28 Mar 1916 - 12 May 1916:	Commander, II. Reconnaissance Group
11 Sep 1916 - 21 Jan 1918:	Commodore & Commander, II. Reconnaissance Group
(25 Nov 1916:	Promoted to Konteradmiral)
22 Jan 1918 - 10 Aug 1918:	Deputy Commander, I. Reconnaissance Group
5 Feb 1918 - 9 Feb 1918:	Acting Commander of Reconnaissance Forces & Acting Commander, I. Reconnaissance Group
6 Aug 1918 - 10 Aug 1918:	Acting Commander of Reconnaissance Forces & Acting Commander, I. Reconnaissance Group
11 Aug 1918 - 17 Nov 1918:	Commander of Reconnaissance Forces & Commander, I. Reconnaissance Group
18 Nov 1918 - 21 Jun 1919:	Chief of Transfer Forces (Scapa Flow)
22 Jun 1919 - 29 Aug 1920:	Attached to the Commander-in-Chief of the Navy
(28 Jan 1920:	Promoted to Vizeadmiral)

29 Aug 1920:   Retired
(19 Aug 1939:   Promoted to brevet Admiral)

Vizeadmiral Max **REYMANN** (8 Mar 1872 - 10 Jul 1948)
2 Aug 1914 - 26 Aug 1914:   Commandant, Auxiliary Cruiser
                                 "*Kaiser Wilhelm der Große*"
27 Aug 1914 - Oct 1918:   Interned in Spain
Oct 1918 - 9 Aug 1919:   Interned in Switzerland
10 Aug 1919 - 25 Sep 1919:   Attached to the Commander,
                                 Baltic Naval Station
26 Sep 1919 - 16 Mar 1920:   Chief of Staff, Baltic Naval Station
17 Mar 1920 - 9 Sep 1920:   Placed on inactive status
10 Sep 1920 - 16 Jan 1923:   President, Navy Peace Commission
(1 Jan 1921:   Promoted to Konteradmiral)
17 Jan 1923 - 27 Apr 1923:   Placed on inactive status
(27 Apr 1923:   Promoted to brevet Vizeadmiral)
27 Apr 1923:   Retired

Konteradmiral Wilhelm **RHEIN** (10 Mar 1887 - 24 Jul 1964)
26 Sep 1931 - 8 Mar 1933:   Chief of Staff, Inspectorate of Naval Artillery
9 Mar 1933 - 30 Jun 1935:   Chief of Training Section,
                                 Naval High Command
30 Jun 1935:   Retired
24 Aug 1939 - 25 Sep 1939:   Recalled from retirement; Chief of Staff to
                                 Coastal Commander, East Prussia
26 Sep 1939 - 17 Dec 1939:   Chief of Staff to Naval Commissioner, Danzig
18 Dec 1939 - Jun 1940:   Chief of Staff, Naval Weapons Office,
                                 Naval High Command
22 Aug 1940 - 19 Oct 1940:   Commissioner for Shipyards, France
20 Oct 1940 - 31 Aug 1942:   Chief of Staff, Naval Weapons Office,
                                 Naval High Command
(1 Sep 1942:   Promoted to Konteradmiral)
1 Sep 1942 - 8 May 1945:   Chief of Research, Inventions & Patents
                                 Group, Naval High Command

Marinegeneralstabsarzt (Konteradmiral) Dr. Claudius **RICHELOT**
(11 Sep 1863 - 23 Jan 1929)
3 Aug 1914 - 16 Apr 1915:   Ship's Doctor, Hospital Ship "*Sierra Ventana*"
17 Apr 1915 - 10 Apr 1916:   Chief Medical Officer, Inspectorate
                                 of Naval Training

26 Jul 1915 - 9 Aug 1915:	Acting Chief Medical Officer, Baltic Naval Station
25 Oct 1915 - 5 Jan 1916:	Acting Chief Medical Officer, Baltic Naval Station
11 Apr 1916 - 23 Apr 1916:	Chief Medical Officer, Kiel Garrison
25 Apr 1916 - 15 Jan 1917:	Deputy Chief Medical Officer, Baltic Naval Station
16 Jan 1917 - 28 Nov 1918:	Chief Medical Officer, Baltic Naval Station
28 Nov 1918:	Retired
(7 Oct 1921:	Promoted to brevet Marinegeneralstabsarzt)

Vizeadmiral (Turkish Major-General & Rear-Admiral) Friedrich **RICHTER** (17 Feb 1873 - 6 Jan 1922)

1 Oct 1913 - 3 Aug 1915:	Commandant, Light Cruiser *"Elbing"*
13 Oct 1915 - 27 Sep 1917:	Chief of Staff, Special Mission to Turkey
28 Sep 1917 - 3 Nov 1918:	Chief of Staff, Mediterranean Division & Chief of Staff, Turkish Fleet
21 Nov 1918 - 6 Feb 1919:	Chief of Demobilization Command, Mediterranean Division
7 Feb 1919 - 7 Nov 1919:	Inspector of Naval Training
15 Nov 1919 - 29 Feb 1920:	Commodore & Acting Commander, Baltic Security Forces
1 Mar 1920 - 16 Mar 1920:	Commander, North Sea Naval Forces
(8 Mar 1920:	Promoted to Konteradmiral)
16 Mar 1920 - 24 May 1920:	Placed on inactive status
25 May 1920 - 31 Mar 1921:	Commander, North Sea Naval Forces
1 Apr 1921 - 19 May 1921:	Attached to the Commander, North Sea Naval Station
20 May 1921 - 30 Nov 1921:	Inspector of Naval Artillery
(30 Nov 1921:	Promoted to brevet Vizeadmiral)
30 Nov 1921:	Retired

Konteradmiral Leo **RIEDEL** (8 Jun 1884 - 5 Oct 1946)

27 Sep 1928 - 29 Sep 1930:	Commander North Sea Naval Division
1 Apr 1930 - 31 Dec 1932:	Commandant of Wilhelmshaven
(31 Dec 1932:	Promoted to brevet Konteradmiral)
31 Dec 1932:	Retired
1 Oct 1940:	Recalled to reserve status; no appointment conferred

Konteradmiral Theodor Heinrich **RIEDEL** (17 Sep 1889 - 24 Dec 1939)

1 Oct 1934 - 13 Oct 1936:	Chief of Development Section, Naval Weapons Office, Naval High Command

14 Oct 1936 - 8 Oct 1937:	Commandant, Light Cruiser "*Leipzig*"
9 Oct 1937 - 21 May 1938:	Attached to Naval Weapons Office, Naval High Command
22 May 1938 - 6 Nov 1939:	Deputy Chief of Naval Weapons Office, Naval High Command
(1 Aug 1939:	Promoted to Konteradmiral)
7 Nov 1939 - 24 Dec 1939:	Chief of Artillery Section, Naval Weapons Office, Naval High Command

Admiralarzt (Konteradmiral) Dr. Hans-Releff **RIEGE**
(23 Apr 1892 - 27 May 1941)

1 Oct 1936 - 31 Mar 1939:	Section Chief, Naval Personnel Office, Naval High Command
1 Apr 1939 - 8 Dec 1939:	Chief of Military Section, Naval Medical Service, Naval High Command
9 Dec 1939 - 19 Dec 1940:	Chief Medical Officer, Kiel-Wik Naval Hospital
20 Dec 1940 - 27 May 1941:	Medical Officer, High Seas Fleet
(1 Nov 1941:	Promoted to Admiralarzt, posthumously)

Vizeadmiral Friedrich **RIEVE** (27 Jun 1896 - 16 Feb 1981)

9 Oct 1938 - 12 Nov 1939:	Staff Officer, High Seas Fleet Command
13 Nov 1939 - 10 Apr 1940:	Commandant, Cruiser "*Karlsruhe*"
April 1940:	Commander of Naval Group 4, Operation "Weserübung"
22 Apr 1940 - 3 May 1940:	Harbor Commandant of Oslo
4 May 1940 - 20 Aug 1940:	Commander of Sea Defenses, Oslo
21 Aug 1940 - 7 Apr 1943:	Chief of Staff, North Sea Naval Station
(1 Jan 1943:	Promoted to Konteradmiral)
11 May 1943 - 8 Sep 1944:	Admiral Commanding, Channel Coast
(1 Oct 1943:	Promoted to Vizeadmiral)
9 Sep 1944 - 10 Nov 1944:	Admiral attached to Army Group B
11 Nov 1944 - 10 Dec 1944:	Admiral attached to Army Group D
11 Dec 1944 - 3 Jan 1945:	Attached to the C-in-C, North Sea Naval Group
4 Jan 1945 - 31 Jan 1945:	Inspector, Naval Gas & Air Defense Inspectorate
1 Feb 1954 - 28 Feb 1945:	Attached to Naval High Command
1 Mar 1945 - 22 Jul 1945:	Chief of Administration, Naval High Command

Awards: *German Cross in Gold*

Konteradmiral Arthur **ROCHLITZ** (17 May 1882 - 7 Aug 1958)
1 Oct 1923 - 4 Oct 1925:	Commandant of Wilhelmshaven
5 Oct 1925 - 27 Mar 1929:	Commander, Baltic Naval Division
28 Mar 1929 - 31 May 1929:	Attached to the Commander, Baltic Naval Station
(31 May 1929:	Promoted to brevet Konteradmiral)
31 May 1929:	Retired

Vizeadmiral Bernhard **ROGGE** (4 Nov 1899 - 29 Jun 1982)
12 Feb 1938 - 5 Sep 1939:	Commandant, Training Sail Ship *"Albert Leo Schlageter"*
6 Sep 1939 - 18 Dec 1939:	Attached to Bremen Naval Office
19 Dec 1939 - 22 Nov 1941:	Commandant, Auxiliary Cruiser *"Atlantis"*
23 Nov 1941 - 14 Apr 1942:	Attached to the Commander, Baltic Naval Station
15 Apr 1942 - 28 Feb 1943:	Chief of Staff, Naval Training Inspectorate
(1 Mar 1943:	Promoted to Konteradmiral)
1 Mar 1943 - 19 Sep 1944:	Inspector of Naval Training
20 Sep 1944 - 4 Aug 1945:	Commander of Fleet Training Units
(1 Mar 1945:	Promoted to Vizeadmiral)

Awards: *Knight's Cross with Oakleaves; Knight's Cross*

Vizeadmiral Maximilian **ROGGE** (14 Mar 1866 - 6 Sep 1940)
22 Aug 1914 - Sep 1917:	Chief of Artillery and Hand Weapons Section, Armaments Department, Naval Office
(18 Sep 1915:	Promoted to Konteradmiral)
3 Oct 1917 - 28 Dec 1918:	Director of Armaments Department, Naval Office
(18 Sep 1918:	Promoted to Vizeadmiral)
28 Dec 1918 - 16 Feb 1919:	Acting State Secretary, Naval Office
17 Feb 1919 - 25 Mar 1919:	Commander-in-Chief of the Navy
26 Mar 1919 - 5 Sep 1919:	Attached to the Commander-in-Chief of the Navy
5 Sep 1919:	Retired

Konteradmiral Heinrich **ROHARDT** (13 Jul 1871 - 21 Dec 1945)
1 Apr 1913 - 16 Nov 1914:	Commandant, Heavy Cruiser *"Hertha"*
17 Nov 1914 - 31 Jul 1915:	Commander, 4. Sailor Regiment, Flanders Marine Corps
27 Aug 1915 - 21 Dec 1916:	Commandant, Battleship *"Rheinland"*
24 Dec 1916 - 10 Aug 1918:	Commandant, Battleship *"Bayern"*
1 Sep 1918 - 14 Jul 1919:	Chief of Section for Ships Construction & Weapons, Naval Office

8 Nov 1918 - 25 Nov 1918:	Acting Commander, IV. Reconaissance Group
5 Mar 1919 - 11 Apr 1919:	Acting Inspector of U-Boats
(14 Jul 1919:	Promoted to brevet Konteradmiral)
14 Jul 1919:	Retired

Marinedekan (Konteradmiral) Friedrich August **RONNEBERGER**
(21 Sep 1886 - 16 Jun 1968)

31 Aug 1936 - 8 May 1945:	Naval Chaplain, North Sea Naval Station & Naval Group North Sea
(2 Oct 1938:	Promoted to Marinedekan)

Vizeadmiral Hugo von **ROSENBERG** (3 Jun 1875 - 19 Oct 1944)

2 Aug 1914 - 30 Sep 1915:	Recalled from retirement; Commander, Baltic Blockade Ship Division
1 Oct 1915 - 24 Jan 1918:	Commander, Baltic Anti-Submarine Flotilla
25 Jan 1918 - 9 Dec 1918:	Commander, Baltic Anti-Submarine Forces
10 Dec 1918 - 28 Mar 1919:	Section Commander, II. Sailor Division
29 Mar 1919 - 28 Feb 1920:	Commander, Baltic Minesweeping Forces
1 Mar 1920 - 23 Mar 1920:	Deputy Commander, Baltic Naval Forces
24 Mar 1920 - 16 Jul 1920:	Placed on inactive status
17 Jul 1920 - 22 Sep 1923:	Commodore & Commander, Baltic Naval Forces
(31 May 1923:	Promoted to Konteradmiral)
30 Sep 1923:	Retired
(19 Aug 1939:	Promoted to brevet Vizeadmiral)

Awards: *Pour le Mérite*

Ministerialdirektor (Vizeadmiral) Dr. Ernst Heinrich **ROSENBERGER**
(19 Jun 1873 - 5 Sep 1956)

1 Mar 1929 - 2 Nov 1936:	Advisor for public law and patent questions, Ministry of Defense
(3 Nov 1936:	Promoted to Ministerialdirigent [Konteradmiral])
3 Nov 1936 - ?:	Section Chief, Armed Forces Legal Service, War Ministry
(?:	Promoted to Ministerialdirektor)
?:	Retired

Vizeadmiral Bernhard **RÖSING** (29 Oct 1869 - 10 Jan 1947)

5 Mar 1914 - 31 Oct 1916:	Director of Sea Transport Bureau, Naval Office
1 Nov 1916 - 24 Nov 1916:	Transferred to the Battleship *"Kronprinz"*

25 Nov 1916 - 27 Aug 1918:   Commandant, Battleship "*Kronprinz*"
28 Aug 1918 - 8 Mar 1920:   Director of Danzig Shipyards
(9 Oct 1918:   Promoted to Konteradmiral)
(21 Jan 1920:   Promoted to brevet Vizeadmiral)
8 Mar 1920:   Retired

Vizeadmiral Curt Freiherr von **RÖSSING** (13 Jul 1868 - 21 Dec 1942)
1 Mar 1914 - 14 Aug 1914:   Commander, 1. Sailor Division
15 Aug 1914 - 4 Oct 1914:   Commander, Sailor Brigade, Flanders Marine Division
5 Oct 1914 - 15 Nov 1914:   Commander, Sailor Artillery Brigade, I. Flanders Marine Corps
15 Nov 1914 - 26 Jan 1916:   Commander, I. Marine Brigade, Flanders Marine Corps
(27 Jan 1916:   Promoted to Konteradmiral)
27 Jan 1916 - 31 May 1917:   Commander, III. Marine Brigade, Flanders Marine Corps
1 Jun 1917 - 10 Nov 1917:   Commander, II. Marine Brigade, Flanders Marine Corps
11 Nov 1917 - 13 Dec 1917:   Attached to the Commander, Baltic Naval Station
(13 Dec 1917:   Promoted to brevet Vizeadmiral)
13 Dec 1917:   Retired
15 Aug 1918 - 17 Dec 1918:   Recalled from retirement; Chairman of Personnel Selection Committee, Flanders Marine Corps
17 Dec 1918:   Retired

Konteradmiral Richard **ROTHE-ROTH** (24 Mar 1898 - 9 Nov 1972)
17 Sep 1937 - 19 Dec 1940:   Staff Officer, High Seas Fleet
20 Dec 1940 - 12 Jun 1941:   Staff Officer to Deputy C-in-C, High Seas Fleet
13 Jun 1941 - 31 Aug 1941:   Attached to the C-in-C, High Seas Fleet
1 Sep 1941 - 6 Nov 1941:   Attached to Naval High Command
7 Nov 1941 - 31 Jan 1943:   Chief of Staff to Admiral Commanding, Aegean
1 Feb 1943 - 3 Apr 1944:   Commadant, Pocket Battleship "*Admiral Scheer*"
(1 Apr 1944:   Promoted to Konteradmiral)
5 Apr 1944 - 23 May 1945:   Chief of Staff, High Seas Fleet
5 Apr 1944 - 30 Jul 1944:   Chief of Staff, Naval Group North

Vizeadmiral Witold **ROTHER** (24 May 1888 - 27 Oct 1962)
28 Sep 1931 - 20 May 1937:	Commander of Mines Command
(1 Jan 1937:	Promoted to Konteradmiral)
1935 - 1937:	At various times, simultaneously Acting Commandant of Kiel
21 May 1937 - 31 Aug 1942:	Inspector of Mines
(1 Nov 1939:	Promoted to Vizeadmiral)
5 Aug 1937 - 22 Aug 1937:	Acting Deputy Commander, Baltic Naval Station
31 Aug 1942:	Retired
1 Sep 1942:	Recalled to reserve status
19 Oct 1942 - 10 May 1945:	Director of St. Nazaire Shipyards

Awards: *German Cross in Silver*

Admiralstabsrichter (Vizeadmiral) Dr. Joachim **RUDOLPHI** (26 Aug 1898 - 1 Feb 1990)
1 Jan 1934 - 30 Nov 1936:	Attached to the Court, Baltic Naval Station
(1 Oct 1936:	Promoted to Marineoberkriegsgerichtsrat [Konteradmiral])
1 Dec 1936 - 31 Oct 1937:	Attached to Naval High Command
1 Nov 1937 - 8 May 1945:	Chief of Naval Legal Service, Naval High Command
(20 Apr 1943:	Promoted to Ministerialdirektor [Vizeadmiral])
(1 May 1944:	Rank redesignated as Admiralstabsrichter)

Vizeadmiral Friedrich **RUGE** (24 Dec 1894 - 3 Jul 1985)
1 Jun 1937 - 31 Aug 1939:	Commander of Minesweepers
1 Sep 1939 - 14 Oct 1939:	Commander of Minesweepers, East
15 Oct 1939 - 16 Feb 1941:	Commander of Minesweepers, West
(1 Feb 1940:	Promoted to Kommodore)
Apr 1940:	Commander of Naval Group 10, Operation "Weserübung"
17 Feb 1941 - 21 May 1943:	Commander of Naval Security Forces, West
(1 Apr 1942:	Promoted to Konteradmiral)
(1 Feb 1943:	Promoted to Vizeadmiral)
12 Mar 1943 - 21 May 1943:	Chief of Special Staff, Tunisia
22 May 1943 - 12 Aug 1943:	Commander, German Naval Command, Italy
13 Aug 1943 - 9 Nov 1943:	Transferred to the Führer Reserve
10 Nov 1943 - 5 Aug 1944:	Special Purposes Admiral, Army Group B

6 Aug 1944 - 31 Oct 1944:	Attached to the Commander-in-Chief of the Navy
1 Nov 1944 - 9 May 1945:	Chief of Shipbuilding Directorate, Naval High Command

Awards: *Knight's Cross*

Marinegeneralstabsarzt (Vizeadmiral) Prof. Dr. Reinhold **RUGE**
(19 Apr 1862 - 15 Aug 1936)

(4 Mar 1914:	Promoted to Marinegeneralarzt with Konteradmiral rank)
4 Mar 1914:	Retired
29 Jan 1915 - 28 Jul 1915:	Recalled from retirement; Medical Officer, South Army
29 Jul 1915 - 30 Jul 1917:	Chief Medical Officer, South Army
(20 Feb 1917:	Promoted to brevet Marinegeneralstabsarzt with Vizeadmiral rank)
30 Jul 1917:	Retired

Konteradmiral Heinrich **RUHFUS** (14 Apr 1895 - 26 May 1955)

5 Oct 1937 - 15 Sep 1939:	Staff Officer, Mürwik Naval School
16 Sep 1939 - 10 Apr 1940:	Commandant, Light Cruiser "*Königsberg*"
11 Apr 1940 - 20 Aug 1940:	Sea Commandant, Bergen
21 Aug 1940 - 17 Sep 1942:	Commander of Sea Defenses, Oslo
(1 Sep 1942:	Promoted to Konteradmiral)
1 Oct 1942 - 16 Apr 1944:	Commandant, Mürwik Naval School
4 May 1944 - 28 Aug 1944:	Commandant of Sea Defenses, French Riviera, Toulon
28 Aug 1944:	Captured; POW

Konteradmiral Wilhelm **RÜMANN** (9 Nov 1881 - 31 Mar 1946)

1 Oct 1923 - 9 Sep 1925:	Commander, North Sea Naval Division
10 Sep 1925 - 23 Sep 1926:	Chief of Naval Training Office, Naval High Command
30 Sep 1926 - 28 Sep 1928:	Commandant, Battleship "*Schleswig-Holstein*"
30 Sep 1928 - 30 Sep 1930:	Chairman, Ships' Testing Commission
(30 Sep 1930:	Promoted to brevet Konteradmiral)
30 Sep 1930:	Retired
22 Mar 1939:	Recalled to reserve status
4 Sep 1939 - 9 Feb 1941:	Sector Commandant, Helgoland
(1 Sep 1940:	Confirmed as Konteradmiral from brevet rank)

10 Feb 1941 - 1 May 1941:	Sector Commandant, Cuxhaven
2 May 1941 - 8 Jun 1942:	Sick leave
9 Jun 1942 - 31 Aug 1942:	Sector Commandant, Cuxhaven
31 Aug 1942:	Retired

Marinegeneralstabsarzt (Vizeadmiral) Dr. Johannes **RUNKWITZ** (30 Apr 1859 - 16 Jul 1916)

(5 Sep 1909:	Promoted to Marinegeneralarzt with Konteradmiral rank)
28 Nov 1914 - 24 Apr 1916:	Recalled from retirement; Deputy Chief Medical Officer, Baltic Naval Station
(24 Apr 1916:	Promoted to brevet Marineobergeneralarzt with Vizeadmiral rank)
25 Apr 1916 - 31 May 1916:	Placed on inactive status
31 May 1916:	Retired

Generaladmiral Alfred **SAALWÄCHTER** (10 Jan 1883 - 6 Dec 1945)

24 Sep 1926 - 27 Sep 1927:	Commandant, Cruiser *"Amazone"*
28 Sep 1927 - 30 Sep 1928:	Commandant, Battleship *"Schlesien"*
15 Oct 1928 - 28 Sep 1930:	Chief of Staff, High Seas Fleet
29 Sep 1930 - 26 Sep 1933:	Chief of Naval Defense Office, Naval High Command
(1 Oct 1932:	Promoted to Konteradmiral)
2 Oct 1933 - 27 Oct 1938:	Inspector of Naval Training
(1 Apr 1935:	Promoted to Vizeadmiral)
(1 Jun 1937:	Promoted to Admiral)
2 Dec 1933 - 18 Jul 1936:	At various times, simultaneously Acting Inspector of Torpedoes & Mines
28 Oct 1938 - 22 Aug 1939:	Commander, North Sea Naval Station
23 Aug 1939 - 20 Sep 1942:	C-in-C, Naval Group West
(1 Jan 1940:	Promoted to Generaladmiral)
21 Sep 1942 - 30 Nov 1942:	Attached to the Commander-in-Chief of the Navy
30 Nov 1942:	Retired
1 Dec 1942:	Recalled to reserve status; no appointment conferred

Awards: *Knight's Cross; German Cross in Gold*

Konteradmiral Fritz **SACHSSE** (10 Jun 1875 - 12 Mar 1954)

16 Jul 1920 - 10 Aug 1920:	Acting Inspector of Naval Training

21 Aug 1920 - 20 Sep 1920: Acting Commandant of Kiel
21 Sep 1920 - 30 Sep 1922: Commander, Baltic Land Forces
10 Oct 1920 - 23 Mar 1921: Commander, Baltic Naval Division
1 Apr 1921 - 30 Sep 1922: Garrison Commander, Stralsund
1 Oct 1922 - 31 Dec 1922: Attached to the Commander, Baltic Naval Station
(31 Dec 1922: Promoted to brevet Konteradmiral)
31 Dec 1922: Retired

Konteradmiral Hermann, Baron von **SALZA** (16 Apr 1885 - 23 Jan 1946)
After a career in the Estonian Navy, including a period as Commander-in-Chief, Rear-Admiral Baron von Salza retired and moved to Germany in October 1939. He joined the Kriegsmarine on 17 February 1940 (with a seniority date of 1 December 1939) as a Konteradmiral.
17 Feb 1940 - 20 Feb 1940: Attached to Baltic Naval Station
20 Feb 1940: Retired

Vizeadmiral Heinrich **SASS** (21 Aug 1859 - 2 May 1941)
(26 Dec 1909: Promoted to Konteradmiral)
(14 Dec 1912: Promoted to brevet Vizeadmiral; retired)
1 Jun 1918 - 31 Mar 1919: Recalled from retirement; President, Pricing Commission, Naval Office
31 Mar 1919: Retired

Konteradmiral Ludwig **SAXER** (26 Nov 1869 - 3 May 1957)
19 Feb 1913 - 7 Nov 1914: Chief of Staff, Kiautschou Government
8 Nov 1914 - Jan 1919: Prisoner of War
Jan 1919 - 15 Jul 1920: Demobilization duties
(30 Jan 1920: Promoted to brevet Konteradmiral)
15 Jul 1920: Retired

Vizeadmiral Robin **SCHALL-EMDEN** (22 Mar 1893 - 29 Jan 1946)
4 Oct 1935 - 15 Feb 1937: Chief of Stettin Naval Office
16 Feb 1937 - 2 Nov 1938: Commandant, Light Cruiser "*Königsberg*"
5 Nov 1938 - 12 Sep 1939: Commandant of Stralsund & Commander, 1. Ships' Crew Regiment
13 Sep 1939 - 17 Mar 1940: Fortress Commandant of Gotenhafen
13 Jan 1940 - 17 Mar 1940: Commander of Coastal Defense, Eastern Baltic
10 Apr 1940 - 8 May 1940: Harbor Captain, Narvik
10 May 1940 - 20 Jun 1940: Commander of Coastal Defense, Eastern Baltic & Fortress Commandant of Gotenhafen

21 Jun 1940 - 3 Dec 1940:	Naval Commander, West France
(1 Dec 1940:	Promoted to Konteradmiral)
4 Dec 1940 - 18 Feb 1941:	Attached to the Commander-in-Chief of the Navy
19 Feb 1941 - 7 Mar 1941:	Chief of Calais Naval Office
8 Mar 1941 - 14 Nov 1944:	Admiral-in-Charge of Naval Offices
(1 Feb 1943:	Promoted to Vizeadmiral)
2 Jan 1945 - 15 May 1945:	Inspector of Recruiting, SchleswigHolstein

Awards: *German Cross in Silver*

Ministerialdirigent (Konteradmiral) Friedrich **SCHALLER**
(22 Oct 1876 - 25 Nov 1942)

11 Jan 1936 - 14 Nov 1939:	Advisor for Accommodations Questions, Naval Administration Office, Naval High Command
(20 Apr 1938:	Promoted to Ministerialdirigent)
15 Nov 1939 - 31 Mar 1940:	Chief of Accommodations Section, Naval Administration Office, Naval High Command
31 Mar 1940:	Retired

Vizeadmiral Carl **SCHAUMANN** (9 Oct 1865 - 23 Jun 1938)

(14 Dec 1912:	Promoted to Konteradmiral)
7 Dec 1913 - 1 Aug 1914:	Acting Director, Naval Academy
2 Aug 1914 - 11 Aug 1915:	Deputy Commander, III. Squadron
12 Aug 1915 - 4 Jan 1916:	Attached to the Commander, Baltic Naval Station
5 Jan 1916 - 29 Jan 1917:	Inspector of Artillery, Flanders Naval Corps
(22 Mar 1916:	Promoted to Vizeadmiral)
23 Jun 1916 - 7 Jul 1916:	Deputy Commander, 1. Marine Division, Flanders Marine Corps
30 Jan 1917 - 9 Jul 1917:	Inspector of Coastal Artillery and Mines
10 Jul 1917 - 17 Mar 1918:	Inspector of Coastal Artillery
31 Jan 1918 - 17 Mar 1918:	Commander of Cuxhaven Defenses
17 Mar 1918:	Retired

Konteradmiral Georg **SCHEDER** (19 Apr 1853 - 10 Jun 1938)

(27 Jan 1904:	Promoted to Konteradmiral)
2 Aug 19143 - 31 Jul 1918:	Recalled from retirement; Member, Kiel Prize Court
1 Aug 1918 - 9 Nov 1918:	Commissioner, Kiel Prize Court
9 Nov 1918:	Retired

Admiral Reinhard **SCHEER** (30 Sep 1863 - 26 Nov 1928)
(27 Jan 1910:   Promoted to Konteradmiral)
(9 Dec 1913:   Promoted to Vizeadmiral)
9 Dec 1913 - 26 Dec 1914:   Commander, II. Squadron
27 Dec 1914 - 15 Jan 1916:   Commander, III. Squadron
9 Jan 1916 - 6 Aug 1918:   C-in-C, High Seas Fleet
(5 Jun 1916:   Promoted to Admiral)
11 Aug 1918 - 14 Nov 1918:   Chief of Naval General Staff
15 Nov 1918 - 17 Dec 1918:   Attached to the Secretary of State, Naval Office
17 Dec 1918:   Retired
Awards: *Pour le Mérite, Oakleaves to the Pour le Mérite*

Konteradmiral Werner **SCHEER** (6 Jun 1893 - 27 Aug 1976)
14 Apr 1938 - 18 Sep 1939:   Commandant, U-Boat School
13 Oct 1939 - 3 Feb 1941:   Chief of Budget Office, Naval High Command
4 Feb 1941 - 21 Sep 1941:   Staff Officer, Wilhelmshaven Shipyards
(1 Sep 1941:   Promoted to Konteradmiral)
22 Sep 1941 - 12 Dec 1942:   Chief of Staff, Wilhelmshaven Shipyards
20 Dec 1942 - 7 Sep 1943:   Commandant, Toulon Naval Arsenal & Chief of German Naval Command, Toulon
15 Sep 1943 - 22 Nov 1943:   Chief of Special Staff for Billeting, Naval High Command
23 Nov 1943 - 27 Nov 1944:   Chief of Military Group, Shipbuilding Directorate, Naval High Command
28 Nov 1944 - 17 Apr 1945:   Commander, Recruiting Command Essen I

Konteradmiral (Ingeneur) Heinz **SCHEFFER** (8 Nov 1896 - 25 Jun 1977)
11 Apr 1938 - 18 Feb 1940:   Commander, 1. Naval NCO Training Detachment
26 Feb 1940 - 29 Jan 1941:   Section Chief, Kiel-Wik Naval School
30 Jan 1941 - 21 Jun 1942:   Engineer, Inspectorate of Naval Training
22 Jun 1942 - 28 Feb 1944:   Engineer, Naval Group West
13 Mar 1944 - 4 Apr 1945:   Commandant, Heiligenhafen Naval School
(1 Aug 1944:   Promoted to Konteradmiral Ingeneur)
5 Apr 1945 - 8 May 1945:   Senior Commander of Ships Construction Training Detachments

Vizeadmiral Georg **SCHEIDT** (6 Jul 1865 - 14 Jul 1943)
11 Apr 1911 - 1 Sep 1914:   Inspector of Naval Depot Inspectorate
3 Sep 1914 - 12 Dec 1914:   Commandant, Battleship *"Zähringen"*

13 Dec 1914 - 25 Jan 1915:	Attached to the C-in-C, High Seas Fleet
26 Jan 1915 - 3 Sep 1915:	Commander, IV. Reconnaissance Group
(23 Feb 1915:	Promoted to Konteradmiral)
16 Sep 1915 - 30 May 1917:	Inspector of Naval Depot Inspectorate
31 May 1917 - 16 Jul 1917:	Attached to the Commander, North Sea Naval Station
(16 Jul 1917:	Promoted to brevet Vizeadmiral)
16 Jul 1917:	Retired

Konteradmiral (Ingeneur) Max **SCHENITZKI** (21 Mar 1894 - 16 Feb 1977)

5 Nov 1938 - 7 Nov 1939:	Unit Engineer to Flag Officer, Battleships
10 Nov 1939 - 29 Feb 1940:	Engineer, Naval Group West
6 Mar 1940 - 29 Jul 1940:	Unit Engineer to Flag Officer, Battleships
30 Jul 1940 - 19 Dec 1940:	Attached to the High Seas Fleet
20 Dec 1940 - 27 Jan 1941:	Engineer to Deputy C-in-C, High Seas Fleet
1 Feb 1941 - 22 Jan 1944:	Section Chief, Shipbuilding Directorate, Naval High Command
(1 Apr 1943:	Promoted to Konteradmiral Ingeneur)
23 Jan 1944 - 23 Mar 1944:	Attached to Shipbuilding Staff, Naval Group West
24 Mar 1944 - 4 Oct 1944:	Chief of Shipbuilding Staff, Naval Group West
5 Oct 1944 - 31 Mar 1945:	Chief of Shipbuilding Staff, Naval Group Norway
1 Apr 1945 - 9 May 1945:	Attached to the C-in-C, Baltic Naval Group

Vizeadmiral Otto **SCHENK** (17 Feb 1891 - 19 Dec 1972)

30 Sep 1935 - 30 Sep 1937:	Commandant, Cruiser "*Leipzig*"
4 Oct 1937 - 25 Nov 1939:	Chief of Central Office, Wilhelmshaven Shipyards
26 Nov 1939 - 9 Jan 1940:	Attached to the Commander, Baltic Naval Station
(1 Jan 1940:	Promoted to Konteradmiral)
10 Jan 1940 - 18 Mar 1940:	Commander of Coastal Defense, Pomerania
9 Apr 1940 - 30 Aug 1940:	Admiral Commanding, Norwegian South Coast
31 Aug 1940 - 13 Aug 1942:	Admiral Commanding, Norwegian Polar Coast
(1 Mar 1942:	Promoted to Vizeadmiral)
14 Aug 1942 - 30 Sep 1942:	Attached to the Commander, Baltic Naval Station
1 Oct 1942 - 31 Jan 1945:	Chief of Testing Commission for New Ships
31 Jan 1945:	Retired
1 Feb 1945:	Recalled to reserve status

1 Mar 1945 - 2 May 1945: Commissioner-Designate, Hamburg Prize Court

Awards: *German Cross in Gold*

Marinegeneralstabsarzt (Konteradmiral) Dr. Friedrich **SCHEPERS** (9 Nov 1873 - 29 May 1944)
15 Sep 1920 - 30 Apr 1922: Attached to the Medical Department, Naval High Command
1 May 1922 - 15 Jul 1925: Medical Officer, Baltic Naval Station
15 Jul 1925 - 31 Mar 1926: Chief Medical Officer, Baltic Naval Station
(31 Mar 1926: Promoted to brevet Marinegeneralstabsarzt)
31 Mar 1926: Retired

Vizeadmiral Ernst **SCHEURLEN** (5 Dec 1894 - 8 Apr 1945)
30 Oct 1935 - 2 Nov 1938: Commander, III. Naval Artillery Detachment
31 Jul 1936 - 2 Mar 1938: At various times, simultaneously Acting Commander of Coastal Defense, Pomerania
3 Nov 1938 - 26 Jun 1939: Commandant, Light Cruiser "*Königsberg*"
27 Jun 1939 - 28 Feb 1943: Commandant, Coastal Artillery & Flak School
(1 Apr 1942: Promoted to Konteradmiral)
29 Aug 1940 - 27 Oct 1940: Simultaneously, Commander-Designate, Transport Fleet E
1 Mar 1943 - 15 May 1943: Chief of Naval Control Staff, Kerch
16 May 1943 - 22 Jun 1943: Attached to the C-in-C, Baltic Naval Group
23 Jun 1943 - 12 Aug 1944: Commander of Coastal Defense, Heligoland Bight
(1 Aug 1944: Promoted to Vizeadmiral)
13 Aug 1944 - 6 Sep 1944: Admiral Commanding, French South Coast
7 Sep 1944 - 10 Feb 1945: Admiral Commanding, Heligoland Bight
11 Feb 1945 - 8 Apr 1945: Commander, 2. Marine Division

Awards: *German Cross in Gold*

Konteradmiral Heinrich **SCHICKHARDT** (2 May 1885 - 25 Jun 1944)
12 Oct 1928 - 25 Sep 1933: Inspector, Naval Depot Inspectorate
(30 Sep 1933: Promoted to brevet Konteradmiral)
30 Sep 1933: Retired
1 Oct 1933 - 30 Sep 1935: Attached to the Commander, North Sea Naval Station (as retired officer)
15 Feb 1939: Recalled to reserve status; no appointment conferred
30 Nov 1940: Retired

Vizeadmiral Malte Freiherr von **SCHIMMELMANN** (1 Apr 1859 - 8 Jul 1916)
(27 Jan 1908:	Promoted to Konteradmiral)
(19 Nov 1910:	Promoted to brevet Vizeadmiral; retired)
1 Jan 1916 - 8 Jul 1916:	Recalled from retirement; Commissioner, Kiel Prize Court

Vizeadmiral Ernst **SCHIRLITZ** (7 Sep 1893 - 27 Nov 1978)
23 Sep 1936 - 16 May 1938:	Chief of Staff to Deputy Commander, North Sea Naval Station
8 Jun 1938 - 23 Sep 1939:	Chief of Staff, Naval Training Inspectorate
1 Aug 1938 - 20 Aug 1938:	Acting Inspector of Naval Training
24 Sep 1939 - 27 Oct 1939:	Chief of Staff, Commander of Naval Security Forces, Baltic
28 Oct 1939 - 14 Apr 1942:	Chief of Staff, Naval Training Inspectorate
1 Apr 1940 - 25 Aug 1940:	Acting Inspector of Naval Training
15 Apr 1942 - 13 May 1942:	Attached to the Commander, Baltic Naval Station
(1 Mar 1942:	Promoted to Konteradmiral)
14 May 1942 - 15 Jun 1942:	Attached to the Naval Commander, West France
16 Jun 1942 - 28 Feb 1943:	Commander of Sea Defenses, Brittany
1 Mar 1943 - 9 May 1945:	Admiral Commanding, Atlantic Coast
(1 Apr 1943:	Promoted to Vizeadmiral)
20 Aug 1944 - 9 May 1945:	Fortress Commandant, La Rochelle

Awards: *Knight's Cross; German Cross in Gold*

Vizeadmiral (Ingeneur) Alfred **SCHIRMER** (8 Sep 1892 - 31 Oct 1975)
1 Oct 1934 - 9 Sep 1935:	Engineer, Naval Training Inspectorate
10 Sep 1935 - 2 Oct 1936:	Station Engineer, Baltic Naval Station
7 Oct 1936 - 24 Nov 1939:	Commandant, Wesermünde Naval School
(1 Nov 1939:	Promoted to Konteradmiral Ingeneur)
28 Nov 1939 - 2 Apr 1943:	Deputy Commander, North Sea Naval Station
(1 Apr 1942:	Promoted to Vizeadmiral Ingeneur)
3 Apr 1943 - 19 May 1943:	Attached to the Commander, North Sea Naval Station
20 May 1943 - 20 Sep 1944:	Commandant, Brest Naval Arsenal
20 Sep 1944:	Captured; POW

Awards: *German Cross in Gold*

Feldbischof (Konteradmiral) Dr. Erich **SCHLEGEL** (24 Feb 1866 - 28 Apr 1938)
16 Aug 1918 - 1 Apr 1929:	Field Provost of the Army
1 Apr 1929 - 1 Dec 1933:	Field Provost of the Army & Navy
1 Dec 1933 - 31 Jan 1934:	Evangelical Field Bishop of the Armed Forces
31 Jan 1934:	Retired

Konteradmiral Max **SCHLICHT** (19 Sep 1870 - 12 May 1945)
4 Aug 1914 - 27 Aug 1914:	Commandant, Heavy Cruiser "*Freya*"
28 Aug 1914 - 1 Oct 1914:	Commandant, Heavy Cruiser "*Friedrich Carl*"
2 Oct 1914 - 14 Nov 1914:	Attached to the Commander, Baltic Naval Station
15 Nov 1914 - 29 Mar 1915:	Commander, I. Shipyard Division
30 Mar 1915 - 19 Nov 1915:	Commandant, Battleship "*Kaiser Barbarossa*"
20 Nov 1915 - 16 Jun 1918:	Commandant, Battleship "*Zähringen*"
17 Jun 1918 - 6 Feb 1919:	Director of Central Office, Danzig Shipyards
7 Feb 1919 - 7 Apr 1919:	Attached to the Commander, Baltic Naval Station
7 Apr 1919:	Retired
(18 Nov 1919:	Promoted to brevet Konteradmiral)

Konteradmiral Paul **SCHLIEPER** (29 Jun 1864 - 2 Oct 1950)
(19 Nov 1910:	Promoted to brevet Konteradmiral; retired)
2 Aug 1914 - 31 Dec 1918:	In charge of Prisoners of War, Berlin Prize Court
31 Dec 1918 - 23 Aug 1919:	Placed on inactive status
23 Aug 1919:	Retired

Konteradmiral Arno **SCHMIDT** (29 Jun 1890 - 4 May 1945)
29 Sep 1934 - 30 Sep 1936:	Director of Weapons & Navigation Section, Kiel Naval Arsenal
1 Oct 1936 - 31 Mar 1939:	Director of Central Office, Kiel Naval Arsenal
30 Sep 1937 - 29 Nov 1937:	Acting Commandant of Kiel Naval Arsenal
1 Apr 1939 - 14 Jan 1940:	Chief of Central Office, Kiel Shipyards
26 Feb 1940 - 5 Apr 1943:	Commandant of Gotenhafen Naval Arsenal
(1 Sep 1940:	Promoted to brevet Konteradmiral)
(1 Jan 1941:	Confirmed as Konteradmiral from brevet rank)
1 May 1943 - 31 Dec 1944:	Chief of Shipbuilding Staff, Naval Group Norway
31 Dec 1944:	Retired

Admiral Ehrhard **SCHMIDT** (18 May 1863 - 18 Jul 1946)
(19 Nov 1910:	Promoted to Konteradmiral)
(22 Mar 1914:	Promoted to Vizeadmiral)
31 Jul 1914 - 26 Aug 1915:	Commander, IV. Squadron
7 Jul 1915 - 25 Aug 1915:	Naval Commander, Baltic
27 Aug 1915 - 18 Jan 1918:	Commander, I. Squadron
19 Jan 1918 - 25 Apr 1918:	Placed on inactive status
(27 Jan 1918:	Promoted to Admiral)
25 Apr 1918:	Retired
11 Aug 1918:	Admiral à la Suite

Awards: *Pour le Mérite*

Konteradmiral Friedrich Traugott **SCHMIDT** (19 Apr 1899 - 21 Feb 1944)
9 Nov 1938 - 20 Jul 1940:	General Advisor, Naval Defense Office, Naval High Command
21 Jul 1940 - 25 Nov 1940:	Naval Liaison Officer to Army Group A
26 Nov 1940 - 11 May 1941:	General Advisor, Naval Defense Office, Naval High Command
12 May 1941 - 19 Jul 1942:	Chief of Supply Section, Naval Defense Office, Naval High Command
20 Jul 1942 - 9 Sep 1943:	Commandant, Light Cruiser "*Emden*"
30 Aug 1942 - 25 Sep 1942:	Acting Commandant, Light Cruiser "*Leipzig*"
10 Sep 1943 - 20 Feb 1944:	Commander of Sea Defenses, Istria/Northern Adriatic
21 Feb 1944:	CommanderDesignate of Sea Defenses, Attika
(1 Mar 1944:	Promoted to Konteradmiral, posthumously)

Ministerialrat (Konteradmiral) Heinrich **SCHMIDT** (6 Mar 1873 - 23 Jan 1955)
11 Aug 1925 - 28 Feb 1934:	Advisor, Naval High Command
1 Mar 1934 - 31 Aug 1937:	Chief of Ships & Vessels Group, Naval General Office, Naval High Command
(31 Aug 1937:	Granted Konteradmiral rank as Ministerialrat)
31 Aug 1937:	Retired

Marinegeneraloberstabsarzt m.d.R.e. Admirals Dr. Paul **SCHMIDT**
(29 Apr 1856 - 21 Oct 1921)
(5 Apr 1904:	Promoted to Marinegeneralstabsarzt with Konteradmiral rank)
5 Apr 1904 - 24 May 1916:	Chief Medical Officer of the Navy
(21 Jun 1907:	Promoted to Marinegeneralstabsarzt with Vizeadmiral rank)

(24 May 1916: Promoted to Marinegeneraloberstabsarzt with Admiral rank)
24 May 1916: Retired

Vizeadmiral Herwarth **SCHMIDT von Schwind** (2 Sep 1866 - 24 Jun 1941)
1 Aug 1914 - 2 Sep 1914: Commandant, Battleship "*Zähringen*"
3 Sep 1914 - 31 Aug 1915: Commander, VI. Squadron
(19 Sep 1914: Promoted to Konteradmiral)
1 Sep 1915 - 26 Jan 1916: Attached to the Commander, Baltic Naval Station
27 Jan 1916 - 31 Dec 1916: Commander, I. Marine Brigade, Flanders Marine Corps
3 Jan 1917 - 15 Aug 1917: Commander, Baltic Coastal Defense Division
16 Aug 1917 - 24 Jan 1918: Commander of Security Forces, Central Baltic
(14 Oct 1917: Promoted to Vizeadmiral)
25 Jan 1918 - 17 Mar 1918: Attached to the Commander, Baltic Naval Station
17 Mar 1918: Retired

Admiral Hubert **SCHMUNDT** (19 Sep 1888 - 17 Oct 1984)
25 Sep 1934 - 26 Sep 1935: Commandant, Cruiser "*Königsberg*"
27 Sep 1935 - 31 Oct 1935: Attached to the Cruiser "*Nürnberg*"
1 Nov 1935 - 13 Oct 1936: Commandant, Cruiser "*Nürnberg*"
14 Oct 1936 - 21 Aug 1939: Commandant, Mürwik Naval School
(1 Apr 1938: Promoted to Konteradmiral)
22 Aug 1939 - 18 Sep 1939: Chief of Staff, Naval Group East
19 Sep 1939 - 12 Oct 1939: Commander of Naval Units, Bay of Danzig
13 Oct 1939 - 5 Nov 1939: Chief of Staff, Naval Group East
6 Nov 1939 - 31 Mar 1940: Inspector of Naval Training
1 Apr 1940 - 31 Jul 1940: Deputy Flag Officer, Reconnaissance Forces
1 Aug 1940 - 14 Oct 1941: Flag Officer, Cruisers
(1 Sep 1940: Promoted to Vizeadmiral)
15 Oct 1941 - 27 Aug 1942: Admiral Commanding, Northern Waters
(1 Apr 1942: Promoted to Admiral)
31 Aug 1942 - 8 Mar 1943: Chief of Naval Weapons Directorate, Naval High Command
9 Mar 1943 - 21 Jun 1943: Admiral Commanding, Baltic Naval Station
22 Jun 1943 - 29 Feb 1944: C-in-C, Naval Group Baltic
1 Mar 1944 - 31 May 1944: Attached to the Commander-in-Chief of the Navy

31 May 1944:	Retired
1 Jun 1944:	Recalled to reserve status; no appointment conferred

Awards: *Knight's Cross*

Generaladmiral Otto **SCHNIEWIND** (14 Dec 1887 - 26 Mar 1964)
28 Sep 1932 - 21 Mar 1934:	Commandant, Cruiser "*Köln*"
22 Mar 1934 - 27 Apr 1934:	Attached to the Naval Training Inspectorate
28 Apr 1934 - 26 Sep 1934:	Attached to the Commander, Baltic Naval Station
27 Sep 1934 - 19 Oct 1937:	Chief of Staff, High Seas Fleet
(1 Oct 1937:	Promoted to Konteradmiral)
20 Oct 1937 - 30 Oct 1938:	Chief of Naval Defense Office, Naval High Command
31 Oct 1938 - 12 Jun 1941:	Chief of Naval General Staff
(1 Jan 1940:	Promoted to Vizeadmiral)
(1 Sep 1940:	Promoted to Admiral)
12 Jun 1941 - 30 Jul 1944:	C-in-C, High Seas Fleet
(1 Mar 1944:	Promoted to Generaladmiral)
2 Mar 1943 - 30 Jul 1944:	C-in-C, Naval Group North
31 Jul 1944 - 30 Apr 1945:	Attached to the Commander-in-Chief of the Navy

Awards: *Knight's Cross*

Marinegeneralstabsarzt (Konteradmiral) Dr. Rudolf **SCHOLTZ** (7 Nov 1868 - ?)
7 Mar 1914 - 31 Aug 1916:	Chief Medical Officer, Kiel Naval Hospital
1 Sep 1916 - 5 Jan 1919:	Chief Medical Officer, High Seas Fleet
6 Jan 1919 - 8 Jun 1919:	Attached to the Secretary of State, Naval Office
8 Jun 1919:	Retired
(7 Oct 1921:	Promoted to brevet Marinegeneralstabsarzt)

Konteradmiral Werner **SCHÖNERMARK** (24 Mar 1897 - 31 Dec 1945)
21 May 1938 - 2 Jul 1940:	First Officer, Battleship "*Gneisenau*"
25 Jul 1940 - 31 Aug 1942:	Chief of Naval Defense Department, Naval Defense Office, Naval High Command
1 Sep 1942 - 30 Apr 1944:	Chief of Naval Defense Office, Naval High Command
(1 Apr 1943:	Promoted to Konteradmiral)
1 May 1944 - 22 Jul 1945:	Chief of Naval Troops Office, Naval High Command

Vizeadmiral Friedrich **SCHRADER** (9 Feb 1865 - 24 Apr 1937)
(27 Jan 1913:	Promoted to Konteradmiral)
13 Nov 1913 - 15 Sep 1918:	Director of Construction Department, Naval Office
(24 Apr 1916:	Promoted to Vizeadmiral)
5 Dec 1917 - 27 Aug 1918:	Acting Director of Shipyards Department, Naval Office
16 Sep 1918 - 6 Nov 1918:	Attached to the Secretary of State, Naval Office
6 Nov 1918:	Retired

Admiral Otto von **SCHRADER** (18 Mar 1888 - 19 Jul 1945)
26 Sep 1932 - 24 Sep 1934:	Commandant, Cruiser "*Königsberg*"
27 Sep 1924 - 30 Sep 1937:	Fortress Commandant of Wilhelmshaven
(1 Apr 1937:	Promoted to Konteradmiral)
1 Oct 1937 - 31 Mar 1938:	Deputy Commander, North Sea Naval Station
1 Apr 1938 - 5 Apr 1940:	Commander, North Sea Naval Security Forces
(1 Nov 1939:	Promoted to Vizeadmiral)
9 Apr 1940 - 19 Jul 1945:	Admiral Commanding, Norwegian West Coast
(1 Mar 1942:	Promoted to Admiral)

Awards: *Knight's Cross; German Cross in Gold*

Ministerialdirektor (Vizeadmiral) Dr. Georg **SCHRAMM** (20 Aug 1871 - 13 May 1936)
4 Sep 1914 - 12 Mar 1916:	Chief of Accommodations Section, Naval Administration Department, Naval Office
(12 Mar 1916:	Appointed Geheime Admiralitätsrat [Konteradmiral])
12 Mar 1916 - 3 Jun 1919:	Director of Naval Administration, Naval Office
3 Jun 1919:	Retired
(23 Aug 1919:	Promoted to Ministerialdirektor)

Ministerialdirektor (Admiral) Theodor **SCHREIBER** (25 Oct 1874 - 10 Jul 1947)
1 Oct 1919 - 8 Apr 1923:	Chief of Dockyards Administration Section, Naval General Office, Naval High Command
(8 Nov 1919:	Promoted to Geheime Admiralitätsrat [Konteradmiral])
(20 Apr 1920:	Rank redesignated as Ministerialrat)
8 Apr 1923 - 15 Oct 1923:	On leave
16 Oct 1923 - 16 Apr 1934:	Chief of Dockyards Administration Section,

Naval General Office, Naval High Command	
17 Apr 1934 - 14 Dec 1939:	Chief of Naval Administration, Naval High Command
(24 Aug 1934:	Promoted to Ministerialdirektor [Vizeadmiral])
15 Dec 1939 - 31 Jan 1940:	Placed on reserve status
(29 Dec 1939:	Promoted to Ministerialdirektor with Admiral rank)
31 Jan 1940:	Retired
8 May 1940 - 26 Jun 1941:	Recalled; attached to Military District (Wehrkreis) III
27 Jun 1941 - 27 Aug 1943:	Chief Intendant to the Armed Forces Commander Norway
28 Aug 1943 - Apr 1945:	Chief Intendant to the Armed Forces Commander-in-Chief Southeast

Konteradmiral Hermann **SCHRÖDER** (6 May 1868 - 5 Jan 1946)

1 Apr 1913 - 10 Oct 1917:	Director of Central Bureau, Kiel Shipyards
11 Oct 1917 - 10 Nov 1917:	Attached to Flanders Marine Corps
11 Nov 1917 - 28 May 1918:	Commander, I. Marine Brigade, Flanders Marine Corps
(29 May 1918:	Promoted to brevet Konteradmiral)
29 May 1918 - Nov 1918:	Commander of Schelde Estuary Defenses & Harbor Commandant of Antwerp
Nov 1918 - 7 Nov 1919:	Attached to the Commander, Baltic Naval Station
7 Nov 1919:	Retired

Vizeadmiral Johannes **SCHRÖDER** (22 May 1858 - 11 Nov 1933)

(12 Sep 1908:	Promoted to Konteradmiral)
(22 Mar 1911:	Promoted to brevet Vizeadmiral)
30 Aug 1914 - 2 Feb 1919:	Recalled from retirement; Commander of Wesermünde Defenses
2 Feb 1919:	Retired

Admiral Ludwig von **SCHRÖDER** (17 Jul 1854 - 23 Jul 1933)

(14 Mar 1905:	Promoted to Konteradmiral)
(9 Nov 1907:	Promoted to Vizeadmiral)
(27 Jan 1911:	Promoted to Admiral)
23 Aug 1914 - 14 Nov 1914:	Recalled from retirement; Commander, Flanders Marine Division

11 Oct 1914 - 13 Oct 1914:   Acting Governor, Antwerp
15 Nov 1914 - 12 Dec 1918:   Commanding Admiral, Flanders Marine Corps
12 Dec 1918:   Retired
Awards: *Pour le Mérite, Oakleaves to the Pour le Mérite*

Vizeadmiral/General der Flakartillerie Ludwig von **SCHRÖDER**
(12 Sep 1884 - 28 Jul 1941)
12 Oct 1929 - 15 Jan 1930:   Commandant, Cruiser "*Amazone*"
16 Jan 1930 - 27 Sep 1932:   Commandant, Cruiser "*Köln*"
29 Sep 1932 - 31 Dec 1934:   Commandant & Harbor Captain of Kiel
(1 Oct 1934:   Promoted to Konteradmiral)
29 Sep 1932 - 30 Sep 1934:   Commissioner, Kaiser-Wilhelm Canal
1 Feb 1934 - 1 Oct 1934:   Acting Deputy Commander,
                               Baltic Naval Station
2 Jan 1935 - 31 Mar 1935:   Fortress Commandant of Swinemünde
1 Apr 1935 - 30 Sep 1937:   Commander of Defenses, Pomeranian Coast
(30 Sep 1937:   Promoted to brevet Vizeadmiral)
30 Sep 1937:   Retired
1 Dec 1937:   Joined the Luftwaffe as Generalleutnant
23 Dec 1937 - 29 May 1939:   Vice-President, Air Protection League
(1 Apr 1939:   Promoted to General der Flakartillerie)
30 May 1939 - 30 May 1941:   President, Air Protection League
31 May 1941 - 28 Jul 1941:   Military Commander, Serbia

Konteradmiral Franz **SCHRÖTER** (1 Feb 1883 - 28 May 1934)
31 Aug 1920 - 30 Apr 1930:   Commandant, Coastal Artillery School
17 Feb 1930 - 30 Mar 1930:   Acting Inspector of Naval Artillery
(30 Apr 1930:   Promoted to brevet Konteradmiral)
30 Apr 1930:   Retired

Konteradmiral Günther **SCHUBERT** (29 Dec 1898 - 29 Oct 1974)
7 Jan 1939 - 11 Sep 1941:   First Officer, Battleship "*Scharnhorst*"
12 Sep 1941 - 30 Mar 1945:   Chief of Organization Section, Quartermaster's Office, Naval High Command
(1 Mar 1943:   Promoted to Konteradmiral)
31 Mar 1945 - 22 Jul 1945:   Admiral Commanding, Western Baltic

Reichskriegsanwalt (Konteradmiral) Fritz **SCHUCK** (11 Jan 1881 - 26 Aug 1945)
(2 Oct 1936:   Promoted to Reichskriegsanwalt)
2 Oct 1936 - 3 Feb 1941:   Judge Advocate, Reich Military Court

4 Feb 1941 - 28 Feb 1941: Placed on reserve status
28 Feb 1941: Retired

Konteradmiral Rudolf **SCHULTE** (11 Apr 1885 - 23 Nov 1969)
6 Oct 1936 - 2 Jan 1939: Naval Liaison Officer to Military District (Wehrkreis) VI
3 Jan 1939 - 28 Feb 1940: Commander, Recruiting Command Essen I
1 Mar 1940 - 11 Jun 1941: Commander, Recruiting Command Wesermünde
12 Jun 1941 - 30 Sep 1942: Commander, Recruiting Command Hamburg IV
3 Oct 1942 - 1 Jan 1945: Inspector, Recruiting Inspectorate Schleswig-Holstein
(1 Dec 1942: Promoted to Konteradmiral)
2 Jan 1945 - 28 Feb 1945: Attached to the C-in-C, North Sea Naval Group
28 Feb 1945: Retired

Vizeadmiral Erich **SCHULTE-MÖNTING** (28 Aug 1897 - 17 Jan 1976)
5 Jan 1939 - 19 Feb 1944: Chief of Staff to the Commander-in-Chief of the Navy
(1 Mar 1943: Promoted to Konteradmiral)
15 Mar 1944 - 6 Sep 1944: Commander of Sea Defenses, Languedoc
8 Nov 1944 - 17 Aug 1945: Admiral Commanding, Norwegian North Coast
(1 Apr 1945: Promoted to Vizeadmiral)
Awards: *German Cross in Silver*

Admiralarzt (Konteradmiral) Dr. Egon **SCHULTE-OSTROP**
(23 Mar 1886 - 29 Mar 1968)
30 Sep 1935 - 24 Oct 1938: Chief Medical Officer, Wilhelmshaven Naval Hospital
29 Oct 1938 - 1 Nov 1939: Medical Officer, High Seas Fleet
(1 Nov 1939: Promoted to Admiralarzt)
2 Nov 1939 - 31 Aug 1942: Station Medical Officer, North Sea Naval Station
31 Aug 1942: Retired
1 Sep 1942: Recalled to reserve status
5 Jan 1943 - 29 Feb 1944: Chief Medical Officer, Reval Naval Hospital
31 Dec 1944: Retired

Admiral Friedrich **SCHULTZ** (14 Jan 1865 - 24 Mar 1945)
(27 Jan 1912:	Promoted to Konteradmiral)
1 Nov 1911 - 26 Oct 1914:	Fortress Commandant, Wilhelmshaven
7 Nov 1914 - 16 Aug 1915:	Commander, 2. Marine Division, Flanders Marine Corps
(17 Jun 1915:	Promoted to Vizeadmiral)
26 Aug 1915 - 18 Dec 1915:	Commander, IV. Squadron
26 Aug 1915 - 11 Jan 1916:	Naval Commander, Eastern Baltic
11 Jan 1916 - 3 Jun 1916:	Commander of Reconnaissance Forces, Eastern Baltic
4 Jun 1916 - 2 Oct 1917:	Fortress Commandant, Wilhelmshaven
20 Feb 1917 - 12 Apr 1917:	Acting Commander, 1. Marine Division, Flanders Marine Corps
3 Oct 1917 - 9 Jan 1918:	Attached to Flanders Marine Corps
10 Jan 1918 - 12 Dec 1918:	Commander, 1. Marine Division, Flanders Marine Corps
13 Dec 1918 - 31 Jan 1919:	In charge of demobilization of Flanders Marine Corps
1 Feb 1919 - 12 Feb 1919:	Attached to the Secretary of State, Naval Office
12 Feb 1919:	Retired
(4 Sep 1919:	Promoted to brevet Admiral)

Generaladmiral Otto **SCHULTZE** (11 May 1884 - 22 Jan 1966)
29 Sep 1924 - 30 Sep 1926:	Commander, Coastal Defense Detachment III
1 Oct 1926 - 29 Sep 1927:	Commander, I. Naval Artillery Detachment
30 Sep 1927 - 27 Sep 1929:	Commandant, Battleship "*Elsaß*"
28 Sep 1929 - 26 Feb 1930:	Commandant of Kiel, Commissioner, Kaiser Wilhelm Canal
3 Oct 1929 - 15 Oct 1929:	Acting Commander, Baltic Naval Division
3 Feb 1930 - 15 Mar 1930:	Acting Commander, Baltic Naval Division
27 Feb 1930 - 1 Oct 1933:	Inspector of Naval Training & intermittently Acting Inspector of Torpedoes & Mines
(1 Apr 1931:	Promoted to Konteradmiral)
2 Oct 1933 - 3 Oct 1937:	Commander, North Sea Naval Station
(1 Oct 1934:	Promoted to Vizeadmiral)
(1 Oct 1936:	Promoted to Admiral)
4 Oct 1937 - 31 Oct 1937:	Attached to the Commander-in-Chief of the Navy
31 Oct 1937:	Retired
1 Jan 1939:	Recalled to reserve status

23 Aug 1939 - 28 Nov 1939:	Commander, North Sea Naval Station
29 Nov 1939 - 1 Mar 1941:	Transferred to the Führer Reserve
2 Mar 1941 - 16 Aug 1942:	Commanding Admiral, France
17 Aug 1942 - 30 Sep 1942:	Attached to the Commander-in-Chief of the Navy
(31 Aug 1942:	Promoted to Generaladmiral)
30 Sep 1942:	Retired

Awards: *Pour le Mérite; German Cross in Silver*

Ministerialdirigent (Konteradmiral) Christian **SCHULZ**
(29 Apr 1874 - 18 Feb 1957)

20 Jan 1934 - 2 Apr 1939:	Chief of Construction Office, Naval High Command
(19 May 1934:	Promoted to Ministerialdirigent)
3 Apr 1939 - 30 Apr 1939:	Placed on reserve status
30 Apr 1939:	Retired

Konteradmiral Edmund **SCHULZ** (6 Apr 1877 - 15 Oct 1961)

10 May 1919 - 16 Dec 1919:	Chief of Personnel, Baltic Naval Station
17 Dec 1919 - 30 May 1920:	Advisor, Naval General Office, Naval High Command
31 May 1920 - 16 Jul 1920:	Commandant of Kiel
29 Jul 1920 - 20 Dec 1920:	Section Chief, Naval High Command
21 Dec 1920 - 16 Jan 1921:	Attached to the Commander, Baltic Naval Station
17 Jan 1921 - 26 Sep 1922:	Commandant, Battleship "*Hannover*"
19 Jul 1921 - 29 Jul 1921:	Acting Commander, Baltic Naval Forces
27 Sep 1922 - 30 Jun 1923:	Attached to the Naval Archives
(30 Jun 1923:	Promoted to brevet Konteradmiral)
30 Jun 1923:	Retired
1 Oct 1940 - 6 May 1941:	Recalled; Industrial Commissioner for Shipyards
7 May 1941 - 3 Dec 1941:	Commissioner of Shipyards, Southeast
(1 Aug 1941:	Confirmed as Konteradmiral from brevet rank)
4 Dec 1941 - 31 Jan 1942:	Attached to the Commander, Baltic Naval Station
31 Jan 1942:	Retired

Konteradmiral Otto **SCHULZ** (12 Mar 1900 - 28 Mar 1974)

30 Sep 1937 - 16 Mar 1943:	Staff Officer, North Sea Naval Station

1 Apr 1943 - 12 May 1944: Commander of Sea Defenses, Crimea
(1 Mar 1944: Promoted to Konteradmiral)
13 May 1944 - 27 Jun 1944: Attached to the Admiral Commanding, Black Sea
28 Jun 1944 - 14 Jul 1945: Chief of Foreign Navies Office, Naval High Command

Awards: *Knight's Cross*

Konteradmiral (Ingeneur) Alfred **SCHULZE** (17 Aug 1892 - 12 Dec 1972)
1 Jan 1938 - 30 Oct 1938: Commander, 14. Ships' Crew Detachment
2 Nov 1938 - 6 Dec 1939: Staff Officer, Kiel Naval School
7 Dec 1939 - 15 Oct 1941: Chief of Staff, Ships Equipment Inspectorate
16 Oct 1941 - 13 Nov 1942: Director of Naval Armaments & Repair Works, Salamis
(1 Nov 1942: Promoted to Konteradmiral Ingeneur)
4 Dec 1942 - 3 Mar 1943: Director of Suppy Office, Kiel Shipyards
4 Mar 1943 - 30 Jun 1943: Director of Bergen Shipyards
1 Jul 1943 - 8 May 1945: Commandant of Bergen Naval Arsenal

Konteradmiral Ernst **SCHUMACHER** (12 Nov 1881 - 1 Sep 1952)
28 May 1924 - 27 Sep 1927: Commander, Ems Estuary Defenses
4 Oct 1927 - 27 Sep 1929: Commandant of Kiel
4 Oct 1927 - 27 Sep 1929: Harbor Captain of Kiel & Naval Commissioner, KaiserWilhelm Canal
(30 Sep 1929: Promoted to brevet Konteradmiral)
30 Sep 1929: Retired
4 Sep 1939 - 22 Jun 1941: Recalled; Commandant of Sylt Sector
(1 Sep 1940: Confirmed as Konteradmiral from brevet rank)
23 Jun 1941 - 30 Sep 1941: Commander of Sea Defenses, Ukraine
1 Oct 1941 - 28 Feb 1942: Attached to the Commander, North Sea Naval Station
28 Feb 1942: Retired

Marinegeneralstabsarzt (Konteradmiral) Maximilian **SCHUMANN**
(7 May 1856 - 30 Oct 1942)
12 Mar 1912 - 24 May 1916: Medical Officer, North Sea Naval Station
24 May 1916: Retired
(9 Mar 1920: Promoted to brevet Marinegeneralstabsarzt)

Ministerialdirektor (Vizeadmiral) Dr. Friedrich **SCHÜRER**
(19 Jun 1881 - 27 Oct 1948)

15 Oct 1939 - 10 Jan 1944:	Chief of U-Boat Design Section, Naval Construction Department, Naval High Command
(1 Sep 1941:	Promoted to Ministerialdirigent [Konteradmiral])
11 Jan 1944 - 31 Oct 1944:	Chief of Ships Construction Group, Naval Construction Department, Naval High Command
(14 Feb 1944:	Promoted to Ministerialdirektor)
1 Nov 1944 - 14 Dec 1944:	Placed on reserve status
14 Feb 1944:	Retired

Awards: *Knight's Cross of the War Merit Cross with Swords*

Vizeadmiral Adelbert **SCHÜSSLER** (28 Oct 1887 - 1 Oct 1970)

27 Sep 1932 - 24 Sep 1934:	Chief of Budget Office, Naval High Command
28 Sep 1934 - 14 Aug 1938:	Commandant of Pillau
(1 Oct 1937:	Promoted to brevet Konteradmiral)
15 Aug 1938 - 6 Nov 1939:	Inspector of Recruiting, Elbing
(1 Apr 1939:	Confirmed as Konteradmiral from brevet rank)
7 Nov 1939 - 31 Aug 1942:	Inspector of Recruiting, SchleswigHolstein
(1 Apr 1942:	Promoted to Vizeadmiral)
31 Aug 1942:	Retired
1 Sep 1942:	Recalled to reserve status
3 Oct 1942 - 31 Mar 1943:	Judge, Berlin Prize Court
31 Mar 1945:	Retired

Admiral Karlgeorg **SCHUSTER** (19 Aug 1886 - 16 Jun 1973)

27 Sep 1933 - 28 Feb 1935:	Commandant, Battleship *"Schleswig-Holstein"*
1 Mar 1935 - 27 Jun 1935:	Attached to the Commander, North Sea Naval Station
(1 May 1935:	Promoted to Konteradmiral)
28 Jun 1935 - 24 Sep 1935:	Deputy Commander, North Sea Naval Station
25 Sep 1935 - 31 Mar 1938:	Deputy Commander, Baltic Naval Station
(1 Apr 1938:	Promoted to Vizeadmiral)
1 Oct 1937 - 31 Mar 1938:	Acting Commander, Baltic Naval Security Forces
19 Mar 1938 - 20 Apr 1938:	Acting Commander of Western Baltic Defenses
1 Apr 1938 - 27 Oct 1938:	Deputy Commander of Baltic Naval Forces & Deputy Commander, Baltic Naval Station
28 Oct 1938 - 1 Nov 1939:	Inspector of Naval Training
2 Nov 1939 - 26 May 1940:	Chief of Economic Warfare Staff, Armed Forces High Command (OKW)

(1 Jan 1940:	Promoted to Admiral)
27 May 1940 - 21 Jun 1940:	Admiral Commanding, West
22 Jun 1940 - 1 Mar 1941:	Admiral Commanding, France
1 Mar 1941 - 3 Apr 1941:	Admiral "Z"
4 Apr 1941 - 29 Jun 1941:	Admiral, Southeast
30 Jun 1941 - 20 Mar 1943:	C-in-C, Naval Group South
21 Mar 1943 - 30 Jun 1943:	Attached to the Commander-in-Chief of the Navy
30 Jun 1943:	Retired
1 Jul 1943 - 8 Apr 1945:	Recalled; Chief of Military Science Office, Naval High Command

Awards: *German Cross in Gold*

Vizeadmiral Christian **SCHÜTZ** (17 Apr 1861 - 9 Jul 1915)
(22 Mar 1911:	Promoted to Konteradmiral)
1 Nov 1913 - 28 Feb 1914:	Acting Commander, III. Squadron
1 Mar 1914 - 27 Aug 1914:	Sick leave
28 Aug 1914 - 16 Sep 1914:	Commandant of Kiel
17 Sep 1914 - 16 Apr 1915:	Sick leave
(27 Jan 1915:	Promoted to brevet Vizeadmiral)
16 Apr 1915:	Retired

Konteradmiral (Ingeneur) Adolf **SCHÜTZLER** (3 Aug 1860 - 13 Jan 1932)
30 Mar 1914 - 2 Apr 1918:	Chief Engineer, High Seas Fleet
3 Apr 1918 - 23 May 1918:	Placed on inactive status
23 May 1918:	Retired
(23 Aug 1919:	Promoted to Konteradmiral Ingeneur)

Konteradmiral Hans-Hermann Graf von **SCHWEINITZ und Krain**, Freiherr von Kauder (21 Jul 1883 - 4 Mar 1959)
29 Sep 1926 - 30 Sep 1931:	Commander, Elbe & Weser Estuary Defenses & Commandant of Cuxhaven
(30 Sep 1931:	Promoted to brevet Konteradmiral)
30 Sep 1931:	Retired
1 Jan 1934 - 28 Sep 1941:	Reactivated; Chief of Naval Printing Office
(1 Jan 1941:	Confirmed as Konteradmiral from brevet rank)
11 Oct 1941 - 2 Nov 1941:	Commander of Sea Defenses, Ukraine
3 Nov 1941 - 31 Mar 1943:	Commander of Sea Defenses, Crimea
1 Apr 1943 - 30 Jun 1943:	Attached to the Commanding Admiral, Baltic Naval Group

30 Jun 1943:   Retired
1 Jul 1943:   Placed on reserve status;
                                no appointment conferred

Vizeadmiral Albert Freiherr von **SECKENDORFF**
(11 Mar 1849 - 28 Jun 1921)
(27 Jan 1895:   Promoted to brevet Konteradmiral)
(27 Jan 1900:   Promoted to brevet Vizeadmiral)
13 Nov 1888 - 5 Nov 1918:   Marshal of the Court to
                                Großadmiral Prinz Heinrich von Preussen
5 Nov 1918:   Retired

Vizeadmiral Thilo von **SEEBACH** (30 Jun 1890 - 21 Oct 1966)
4 Sep 1930 - 24 Sep 1936:   Commandant, Coastal Artillery School
25 Sep 1936 - 29 Sep 1937:   Commandant, Battleship "*Schlesien*"
30 Sep 1937 - 29 Mar 1939:   Commander of Defenses, Pomeranian Coast
(1 Oct 1938:   Promoted to Konteradmiral)
23 Jan 1939 - 2 Apr 1939:   Acting Inspector of Naval Artillery
3 Apr 1939 - 3 Jun 1941:   Inspector of Naval Artillery
(1 Jan 1941:   Promoted to Vizeadmiral)
7 Apr 1940 - 3 Jun 1941:   Commander of Western Baltic Coast
4 Jun 1941 - 7 Sep 1941:   Sick leave
8 Sep 1941 - 31 Mar 1943:   Inspector of Naval Artillery
1 Apr 1943 - 31 May 1943:   Attached to the Commander-in-Chief
                                of the Navy
31 May 1943:   Retired
1 Jun 1943 - 30 Jun 1943:   Recalled; attached to the
                                Commander-in-Chief of the Navy
1 Jul 1943 - 8 May 1945:   Special Purposes Admiral,
                                Naval Group Norway

Awards: *German Cross in Silver*

Wirkliche Geheime Rat (Konteradmiral) Hermann **SEEBER**
(5 Jul 1857 - 19 Jun 1920)
10 Jun 1892 - 12 Mar 1916:   Chief of Section XII, Construction
                                Department, Imperial Naval Office
(18 Dec 1909:   Appointed Wirkliche Geheime Rat)
12 Mar 1916 - 3 Mar 1917:   Chief of Administration Section, Naval Office
3 Mar 1917 - 27 Jul 1917:   Attached to the Secretary of State, Naval Office
27 Jul 1917:   Retired

Konteradmiral Hans **SEEBOHM** (21 Nov 1871 - 25 Dec 1945)
9 May 1912 - 27 Mar 1914:	Commandant, Light Cruiser "*Bremen*"
28 Mar 1914 - 1 Aug 1914:	Attached to the Commander, North Sea Naval Station
2 Aug 1914 - 28 Aug 1914:	Commandant, Light Cruiser "*Ariadne*" & Commander, Jade & Weser Harbor Flotilla
2 Sep 1914 - 25 Jan 1916:	Chief of Operations, High Seas Fleet
31 Jan 1916 - 26 Nov 1918:	Chief of Central Section, Naval Office
27 Nov 1918 - 12 Feb 1919:	Attached to the Secretary of State, Naval Office
13 Feb 1919 - 10 Mar 1919:	Attached to the Commander, Baltic Naval Station
11 Mar 1919 - 24 Nov 1919:	Chief of Staff, Baltic Naval Station
24 Nov 1919:	Retired
(26 Jan 1920:	Promoted to brevet Konteradmiral)
1 Sep 1941 - 31 Mar 1943:	Recalled; attached to the Commander-in-Chief of the Navy
31 Mar 1943:	Retired

Vizeadmiral Karl **SEIFERLING** (21 Oct 1867 - 7 Feb 1936)
1 Oct 1914 - 30 Nov 1914:	Inspector of Naval Aviation
12 Dec 1914 - 25 Aug 1915:	Commandant, Battleship "*Zähringen*"
29 Aug 1915 - 1 Oct 1916:	Commandant, Battleship "*Markgraf*"
22 Dec 1915 - 31 Jan 1916:	Acting Deputy Commander, III. Squadron
11 Oct 1916 - 11 Dec 1916:	Commander, IV. Reconnaissance Group
(25 Nov 1916:	Promoted to Konteradmiral)
12 Dec 1916 - 31 Oct 1917:	Deputy Commander, III. Squadron
1 Nov 1917 - 1 Nov 1918:	Inspector of U-Boats
2 Nov 1918 - 13 Nov 1918:	Placed on inactive status
14 Nov 1918 - 14 Dec 1918:	Inspector of U-Boats
15 Dec 1918 - 7 Apr 1919:	Attached to the Commander, Baltic Naval Station
7 Apr 1919- 26 Nov 1919:	Placed on inactive status
(4 Sep 1919:	Promoted to brevet Vizeadmiral)
26 Nov 1919:	Retired

Senatspräsident (Konteradmiral) Dr. Wilhelm **SELLMER** (15 Jul 1877 - 13 Jun 1954)
1 May 1934 - 30 Sep 1936:	Attached to Armed Forces Criminal Senate
(1 Oct 1936:	Promoted to Senatspräsident)
1 Oct 1936 - 30 Sep 1943:	Senate President, Reich Military Court
1 Oct 1943 - 31 Aug 1944:	Senate President,

| | Armed Forces Criminal Court |
| 31 Aug 1944: | Retired |

Vizeadmiral Leopold **SIEMENS** (17 May 1889 - 7 Dec 1979)
21 Sep 1935 - 1 Sep 1937:	Commandant, Cruiser "*Karlsruhe*"
2 Sep 1937 - 28 Sep 1937:	Attached to Naval High Command
29 Sep 1937 - 1 Sep 1939:	Naval Attaché, London & The Hague
5 Sep 1939 - 18 Dec 1940:	Chief of U-Boat Directorate, Naval High Command
(1 Jan 1940:	Promoted to Konteradmiral)
20 Dec 1940 - 12 Jun 1941:	Deputy C-in-C, High Seas Fleet
27 May 1941 - 12 Jun 1941:	Acting C-in-C, High Seas Fleet
21 Jun 1941 - 6 Nov 1944:	Admiral Commanding, Norwegian North Coast
(1 Apr 1942:	Promoted to Vizeadmiral)
7 Nov 1944 - 31 Jan 1945:	Attached to the C-in-C, Baltic Naval Group
31 Jan 1945:	Retired
1 Feb 1945:	Recalled to reserve status; no appointment conferred

Awards: *German Cross in Gold*

Konteradmiral Werner **SIEMENS** (7 Mar 1873 - 21 Jul 1964)
9 Sep 1914 - 31 Oct 1917:	Acting Inspector of U-Boats
28 Nov 1917 - 3 Dec 1918:	Commandant, Battleship "*Großer Kurfürst*"
4 Dec 1918 - 22 Jun 1919:	Attached to the Commander, Baltic Naval Station
22 Jun 1919:	Retired
(22 Feb 1920:	Promoted to brevet Konteradmiral)

Konteradmiral Karl **SIEVERS** (22 Feb 1868 - 2 Mar 1940)
14 May 1913 - 25 Jul 1917:	Commandant, Battleship "*Kaiserin*"
26 Jul 1917 - 30 Sep 1917:	Attached to the Commander, Baltic Naval Station
1 Oct 1917 - 15 Jan 1919:	Inspector, I. Naval Inspectorate
(27 Jan 1918:	Promoted to Konteradmiral)
16 Jan 1919 - 28 Jan 1919:	Attached to the Commander, Baltic Naval Station
28 Jan 1919:	Retired

Vizeadmiral Kurt **SLEVOGT** (21 Mar 1892 - 23 Jul 1957)
21 May 1935 - 17 Sep 1937:	Commandant, U-Boat School
18 Sep 1937 - 3 Dec 1939:	Chief of Staff, Deputy Commander of Baltic Naval Station
4 Dec 1939 - 31 Mar 1943:	Deputy Naval Commander, Baltic
(1 Jul 1940:	Promoted to Konteradmiral)
(1 Sep 1942:	Promoted to Vizeadmiral)
1 Apr 1943 - 9 May 1943:	Attached to the C-in-C, Baltic Naval Group
10 May 1943 - 3 May 1945:	Judge, Hamburg Prize Court

Admiralarzt (Konteradmiral) Dr. Johannes **SONTAG**
(3 Aug 1884 - 24 Mar 1941)
29 Mar 1933 - 20 Dec 1940:	Chief Medical Officer, Baltic Naval Station
(1 Apr 1938:	Promoted to Admiralarzt)
21 Dec 1940 - 31 Jan 1941:	Attached to the Commander, Baltic Naval Station
31 Jan 1941:	Retired

Konteradmiral Siegfried **SORGE** (10 Jul 1898 - 13 Sep 1989)
21 May 1938 - 6 Dec 1939:	Navigation Officer, Battleship "*Gneisenau*"
7 Dec 1939 - 31 Mar 1943:	Chief of Staff to Deputy Naval Commander, Baltic
(1 Apr 1943:	Promoted to Konteradmiral)
1 Apr 1943 - 5 Jan 1945:	Deputy Naval Commander, Baltic
16 Jan 1945 - 9 May 1945:	Commander of Sea Defenses, West Prussia & Fortress Commandant of Gotenhafen/Hela

Admiral (Turkish Admiral) Wilhelm **SOUCHON** (2 Jun 1864 - 31 Jan 1946)
(10 Apr 1911:	Promoted to Konteradmiral)
23 Oct 1913 - 3 Sep 1917:	Commander, Mediterranean Division
(27 Jan 1915:	Promoted to Vizeadmiral)
16 Aug 1914 - 3 Sep 1917:	C-in-C, Turkish and Bulgarian Fleets
4 Sep 1917 - 12 Aug 1918:	Commander, IV Squadron
(11 Aug 1918:	Promoted to Admiral)
13 Aug 1918 - 27 Oct 1918:	At the disposal of the Kaiser
28 Oct 1918 - 8 Nov 1918:	Commander, Baltic Naval Station
9 Nov 1918 - 17 Mar 1919:	Attached to the Secretary of State, Naval Office
17 Mar 1919:	Retired

Awards: *Pour le Mérite*

Vizeadmiral Maximilian Graf von **SPEE** (22 Jun 1861 - 8 Dec 1914)
(27 Jan 1910:   Promoted to Konteradmiral)
(15 Nov 1913:   Promoted to Vizeadmiral)
15 Nov 1913 - 8 Dec 1914:   Commander, Cruiser Squadron

Marinegeneralstabsarzt (Konteradmiral) Dr. Richard **SPIERING** (23 Sep 1861 - ?)
Aug 1914 - Mar 1915:   Recalled from retirement; Chef Medical Officer, Stadthalle Heidelberg Reserve Hospital
Mar 1915 - Sep 1915:   Director of Military Hospital, Guards Corps
Sep 1915 - May 1916:   Chief Garrison Medical Officer, Graudenz
May 1916 - Dec 1918:   Medical Officer, XVIII. Army Corps
Dec 1918:   Retired
(17 Oct 1919:   Promoted to brevet Marinegeneralstabsarzt)

Konteradmiral/Generalleutnant Dr. Fritz **SPIESS** (28 Oct 1881 - 19 Feb 1959)
1 Oct 1919 - 15 Feb 1924:   Advisor for Naval Maps and Exploration, Naval High Command
1 Mar 1923 - 5 Jun 1923:   Acting Chief of Nautical Office, Naval High Command
15 Feb 1924 - 1 Nov 1924:   Acting Chief of Nautical Office, Naval High Command
15 Nov 1924 - 28 Sep 1927: Commandant, Survey Ship "*Meteor*"
1 Oct 1927 - 30 Sep 1928:   Attached to the Commander-in-Chief of the Navy
30 Sep 1928:   Retired
(1 Oct 1929:   Promoted to brevet Konteradmiral)
(14 Aug 1934:   Promoted to Ministerialdirektor with Generalmajor rank)
(14 Aug 1939:   Promoted to Ministerialdirektor with Generalleutnant rank)
14 Aug 1934 - 22 Jul 1945: President, Hamburg Naval Observatory

Konteradmiral Arno **SPINDLER** (10 May 1880 - 18 May 1967)
5 Sep 1919 - 26 May 1921:   Chief of Central Office, Wilhelmshaven Shipyards
27 May 1921 - 31 May 1923: Chief of Staff, Naval General Office, Naval High Command
1 Jun 1923 - 23 Jun 1923:   Attached to Fleet Office, Naval High Command
24 Jun 1923 - 30 Sep 1925: Chief of Fleet Office, Naval High Command (Chief of Naval Operations)

1 Oct 1925 - 31 Oct 1925:	Attached to the Commander-in-Chief of the Navy
(31 Oct 1925:	Promoted to brevet Konteradmiral)
31 Oct 1925:	Retired
1 Nov 1925 - 23 Apr 1943:	Expert attached to the Naval Archives
20 Aug 1940:	Recalled to reserve status
(1 Jun 1941:	Confirmed as Konteradmiral from brevet rank)
24 Apr 1943 - 31 May 1943:	Attached to the Commander, Baltic Naval Station
31 May 1943:	Retired
1 Jun 1943 - 8 May 1945:	Expert attached to the Navy Military Science Section

Vizeadmiral Rudolf **STANGE** (13 Nov 1899 - 25 Apr 1992)
22 Oct 1937 - 3 Jan 1942:	Group Chief, Naval Operations Office, Naval High Command
4 Jan 1942 - 10 Nov 1943:	Commandant, Pocket Battleship "*Lützow*"
(1 Oct 1943:	Promoted to Konteradmiral)
22 Nov 1943 - 11 Dec 1944:	Chief of Staff, Naval Group South
14 Dec 1944 - 31 Dec 1944:	Commander of Sea Defenses, West & East Prussia & Fortress Commandant of Gotenhafen
1 Jan 1945 - 9 Jun 1945:	Admiral Commanding, Netherlands
(1 Apr 1945:	Promoted to Vizeadmiral)

Awards: *German Cross in Gold*

Vizeadmiral Wilhelm **STARKE** (22 Mar 1866 - 21 May 1934)
(11 Jan 1913:	Promoted to brevet Konteradmiral; retired)
1 Aug 1914 - 11 Oct 1914:	Recalled from retirement; attached to the Naval Office
12 Oct 1914 - 13 Feb 1919:	Director of Aviation Bureau, Naval Office
(16 Sep 1916:	Confirmed as Konteradmiral from brevet rank)
14 Feb 1919 - 19 Feb 1919:	Attached to the Naval Office
19 Feb 1919:	Retired
(4 Sep 1919:	Promoted to brevet Vizeadmiral)

Konteradmiral Wilhelm Friedrich **STARKE** (28 Feb 1885 - 24 Oct 1941)
22 Sep 1926 - 30 Sep 1933:	Attached to the League of Nations Navy Group, Naval High Command
(30 Sep 1933:	Promoted to brevet Konteradmiral)
30 Sep 1933:	Retired

11 Sep 1939:	Recalled to reserve status
Aug 1941 - 24 Oct 1941:	Deputy Commissioner, Berlin-Southeast Prize Court

Konteradmiral Berthold **STECHOW** (3 May 1865 - 6 Jul 1941)
10 Apr 1909 - 29 Jul 1919:	Director of Printing Office, Naval High Command
29 Jul 1919:	Retired
(25 Sep 1920:	Promoted to brevet Konteradmiral)

Konteradmiral (Ingeneur) Johannes **STEENBOCK** (8 Dec 1894 - 19 Sep 1974)
30 Sep 1938 - 31 Jan 1944:	Commander, Armaments Command Essen
1 Feb 1944 - 28 Feb 1944:	Attached to Armaments Inspectorate XI
1 Mar 1944 - 18 Apr 1945:	Inspector, Armaments Inspectorate XI
(1 Aug 1944:	Promoted to Konteradmiral Ingeneur)

Konteradmiral Werner **STEFFAN** (26 Dec 1890 - 8 Aug 1973)
26 Sep 1932 - 26 Sep 1933:	Chief of Central Office, Kiel Naval Arsenal
19 Jul 1933 - 19 Aug 1933:	Acting Commandant of Kiel Naval Arsenal
27 Sep 1933 - 5 May 1940:	Naval Attaché, Scandinavian countries
(1 Apr 1939:	Promoted to brevet Konteradmiral)
(1 Nov 1939:	Confirmed as Konteradmiral from brevet rank)
6 May 1940 - 30 Jul 1940:	Attached to the Commander-in-Chief of the Navy
31 Jul 1940 - 31 Jul 1944:	Admiral-in-Charge, Danzig Naval Office
31 Jul 1944:	Retired

Ministerialdirigent (Konteradmiral) Johann Albrecht von **STEIN** (8 Aug 1874 - 5 Nov 1948)
1 Sep 1939 - 30 Jun 1943:	Advisor, Naval Administration Office, Naval High Command
1 Jul 1943 - 30 Jun 1944:	Chief of Personnel & Pay Section, Naval General Office, Naval High Command
(30 Oct 1943:	Promoted to Ministerialdirigent)
30 Jun 1944:	Retired

Konteradmiral (Ingeneur) Walter **STEINER** (14 Jul 1891 - 26 Mar 1975)
30 May 1938 - 17 Dec 1943:	Chief Engineer, Inspectorate of Torpedoes & Inspectorate of Mines
(1 Dec 1942:	Promoted to Konteradmiral Ingeneur)

30 May 1938 - 10 Nov 1938: Chief Engineer, Naval Communications Inspectorate
18 Aug 1939 - 16 Oct 1939: Chief Engineer, Naval Training Inspectorate
2 Aug 1940 - 29 Jan 1941: Chief Engineer, Naval Training Inspectorate
18 Dec 1943 - 31 Jan 1944: Attached to the C-in-C, Baltic Naval Group
1 Feb 1944 - 5 Oct 1944: Chief of Shipyards Staff to Admiral Commanding Aegean
6 Oct 1944 - 27 Nov 1944: Attached to the C-in-C, Baltic Naval Group
28 Nov 1944 - 25 Apr 1945: Commandant, Kiel Naval Arsenal

Konteradmiral (Ingeneur) Otto **STEINKOPF** (21 Jun 1874 - 2 Apr 1941)
1 Apr 1922 - 30 Sep 1924: Engineer Officer, Baltic Naval Station
1 Oct 1924 - 31 Oct 1924: Attached to the Commander, Baltic Naval Station
(31 Oct 1924: Promoted to brevet Konteradmiral Ingeneur)
31 Oct 1924: Retired

Vizeadmiral Wilhelm **STHAMER** (26 Apr 1864 - 18 Aug 1934)
(5 Sep 1911: Promoted to Konteradmiral)
2 Aug 1914 - 30 Sep 1917: Recalled from retirement; Inspector of I. Naval Inspectorate
15 Mar 1916 - 4 Apr 1916: Acting Commander, II. Marine Brigade, Flanders Marine Corps
(10 Jun 1916: Promoted to brevet Vizeadmiral)
1 Oct 1917 - 31 Jul 1918: Commissioner, Kiel Prize Court
1 Aug 1918 - 25 Nov 1918: Chairman, Personnel Selection Commission
25 Nov 1918: Retired

Konteradmiral Werner **STICHLING** (26 Nov 1895 - 29 Jan 1982)
7 Nov 1938 - 25 Aug 1939: Commander, 6. Naval Artillery Detachment
26 Aug 1939 - 19 May 1940: Commandant of Borkum District
20 May 1940 - 20 Jun 1940: Commander of Sea Defenses, Belgium & Commander, 22. Naval Artillery Regiment
22 Jun 1940 - 25 Jul 1940: Commander of Sea Defenses, Normandy
27 Jul 1940 - 30 Nov 1940: Chief of Staff to Naval Commander, North France
1 Dec 1940 - 29 Aug 1942: Commandant, Cruiser "*Leipzig*"
1 Nov 1941 - 10 Apr 1942: Acting Commander of Training Units, High Seas Fleet
18 Sep 1942 - 5 Nov 1943: Commander of Sea Defenses, Arctic Ocean

(1 Jan 1943: Promoted to Konteradmiral)
15 Nov 1943 - 24 Nov 1944: Coastal Commander, Western Baltic
25 Nov 1944 - 1 May 1945: Commander of Sea Defenses,
 SchleswigHolstein & Mecklenburg
15 Nov 1943 - 18 Apr 1945: Commander, I. Naval Flak Brigade
2 May 1945 - 8 May 1945: Attached to the C-in-C, Baltic Naval Group

Konteradmiral Oscar **STIEGE** (8 Sep 1852 - 25 Jan 1932)
(6 Dec 1902: Promoted to brevet Konteradmiral; retired)
30 Jun 1910 - 31 Dec 1914: Deputy Permanent Observer,
 Higher Naval Office
1 Jan 1915 - 31 Dec 1925: Permanent Observer, Higher Naval Office

Vizeadmiral (Ingeneur) Heinrich **STIEGEL** (7 Feb 1891 - 10 Apr 1964)
6 Oct 1934 - 27 Apr 1936: Chief of Naval Welfare Office, Swinemünde
28 Apr 1936 - 2 Oct 1936: Advisor, Naval General Office,
 Naval High Command
3 Oct 1936 - 8 Feb 1937: Station Engineer, Baltic Naval Station
10 Feb 1937 - 10 Dec 1939: Chief Engineer, High Seas Fleet
(1 Jan 1940: Promoted to Konteradmiral Ingeneur)
3 Jan 1940 - 31 Oct 1944: Chief of Ships Engine Works Directorate,
 Naval High Command
(1 Apr 1942: Promoted to Vizeadmiral Ingeneur)
1 Nov 1944 - 4 Jan 1945: Chief of Finished Ships & Shipyards
 Directorate, Naval High Command
5 Jan 1945 - 31 Mar 1945: Attached to the Commander-in-Chief
 of the Navy
1 Apr 1945 - 30 Apr 1945: Attached to Military Science Office,
 Naval High Command
30 Apr 1945: Retired
Awards: *German Cross in Silver*

Vizeadmiral (Ingeneur) Ernst **STIERINGER** (23 Jun 1891 - 23 Jul 1975)
25 Sep 1934 - 17 Sep 1936: Director of Armaments,
 Wilhelmshaven Shipyards
18 Sep 1936 - 27 Oct 1938: Chief Engineer, North Sea Naval Station
28 Oct 1938 - 28 Feb 1944: Inspector, Armaments Inspectorate XI
(1 Jan 1940: Promoted to Konteradmiral Ingeneur)
(1 Apr 1942: Promoted to Vizeadmiral Ingeneur)
1 Mar 1944 - 31 Dec 1944: Attached to the C-in-C,
 North Sea Naval Group

1 Jan 1945 - 30 Apr 1945:	Plenipotentiary for Motor Vehicle Assignment & Requisitioning, Armed Forces High Command (OKW)
30 Apr 1945:	Retired

Awards: *German Cross in Silver*

Vizeadmiral Hans-Herbert **STOBWASSER** (8 Mar 1885 - 10 Feb 1946)

8 Oct 1931 - 24 Sep 1933:	Commandant, Cruiser "*Leipzig*"
25 Sep 1933 - 24 Sep 1935:	Chief of Staff, North Sea Naval Station
(1 Apr 1935:	Promoted to Konteradmiral)
25 Sep 1935 - 30 Sep 1937:	Deputy Commander, North Sea Naval Station
(1 Oct 1937:	Promoted to Vizeadmiral)
4 Oct 1937 - 31 Dec 1939:	Chief of Testing Commission for New Ships
31 Dec 1939:	Retired
1 Jan 1940:	Recalled to reserve status
20 Jan 1940 - 13 Aug 1940:	Chief of West Shipyard, Wilhelmshaven Shipyards
14 Aug 1940 - 5 Oct 1940:	Director of Lorient Shipyards
21 Oct 1940 - 30 Nov 1940:	Chief of West Shipyard, Wilhelmshaven Shipyards
1 Dec 1940 - 19 May 1943:	Director of Brest Shipyards
20 May 1943 - 31 Oct 1943:	Attached to the C-in-C, North Sea Naval Group
31 Oct 1943:	Retired

Konteradmiral Albert **STOELZEL** (10 Jan 1872 - 16 Sep 1928)

1 Oct 1911 - 6 Oct 1916:	Attached to the Naval General Staff
7 Oct 1916 - 30 Nov 1917:	Section Chief, Operations Group, Naval General Staff
5 Jan 1918 - 2 Nov 1918:	Commandant, Heavy Cruiser "*Goeben*"
3 Nov 1918 - 24 Nov 1918:	Attached to the Secretary of State, Naval Office
25 Nov 1918 - 11 Feb 1919:	Attached to the Commander, Baltic Naval Station
12 Feb 1919 - 5 Nov 1919:	Chief of Staff, German Control Commission for the Disarming of the Aaland Islands
6 Nov 1919 - 24 Nov 1919:	Attached to the Commander-in-Chief of the Navy
24 Nov 1919:	Retired
(28 Dec 1919:	Promoted to brevet Konteradmiral)

Vizeadmiral Hans **STOHWASSER** (4 May 1884 - 30 May 1967)
6 Oct 1924 - 30 Sep 1926:	Chief of Staff, Naval Training Inspectorate
1 Oct 1926 - 27 Sep 1931:	Commander, Blockade Experimental Command
3 Jul 1927 - 31 Jul 1927:	Acting Inspector of Torpedoes & Mines
10 Aug 1928 - 10 Sep 1928:	Acting Inspector of Torpedoes & Mines
(30 Sep 1931:	Promoted to brevet Konteradmiral)
30 Sep 1931:	Retired
1 Sep 1933 - 31 Jan 1934:	Recalled; Blocade Weapons Instructor, Baltic Naval Station
1 Feb 1934 - 31 Mar 1935:	Blockade Weapons Instructor attached to the Deputy Commander, Baltic Naval Forces
1 Apr 1935 - 30 Sep 1936:	Instructor, Inspectorate of Torpedoes & Mines
1 Oct 1936 - 1 Nov 1936:	Instructor, Blockade Weapons Inspectorate
2 Nov 1936 - 31 Mar 1938:	Instructor, Signals Inspectorate
1 Apr 1938 - 21 Aug 1939:	Instructor, Baltic Naval Station
22 Aug 1939 - 15 Oct 1939:	Commander of Minesweepers, West
16 Oct 1939 - 9 Aug 1940:	Commander of Minesweepers, East
(1 Feb 1940:	Confirmed as Konteradmiral from brevet rank)
18 Jul 1940 - 5 Aug 1940:	Acting Chief of Security, Baltic
10 Aug 1940 - 13 Oct 1940:	Commander of Minesweepers, North
14 Oct 1940 - 7 Jun 1944:	Commander of Security Forces, Baltic
(1 Apr 1942:	Promoted to Vizeadmiral)
8 Jun 1944 - 30 Jun 1944:	Attached to the Commanding Admiral, Naval Group Baltic
30 Jun 1944:	Retired

Awards: *Knight's Cross*

Vizeadmiral Hans-Hubertus von **STOSCH** (3 Nov 1889 - 28 Apr 1945)
20 Feb 1933 - 22 Sep 1935:	Chief of Staff, Inspectorate of Naval Artillery
24 Sep 1935 - 3 Oct 1937:	Director of Artillery Workshops, Wilhelmshaven Shipyards
4 Oct 1937 - 13 Feb 1941:	Fortress Commandant of North Friesland
(1 Oct 1939:	Promoted to Konteradmiral)
14 Feb 1941 - 20 Apr 1941:	Naval Commander "A"
21 Apr 1941 - 30 Jun 1941:	Naval Commander, Greece
1 Jul 1941 - 26 Sep 1941:	Admiral Commanding, Aegean
(1 Sep 1941:	Promoted to Vizeadmiral)
27 Sep 1941 - 31 Jan 1942:	Attached to the Commander, North Sea Naval Station

1 Feb 1942 - 12 Jan 1943:	Chief of Artillery Office, Naval Weapons Directorate, Naval High Command
13 Jan 1943 - 22 Jun 1943:	Coastal Commander, Heligoland Bight
23 Jun 1943 - 31 Aug 1943:	Attached to the Commander, North Sea Naval Station
31 Aug 1943:	Retired
1 Sep 1943 - 30 Sep 1944:	Recalled to reserve status; Plenipotentiary for Naval Construction, Naval Group West
30 Sep 1944:	Retired

Vizeadmiral Herbert **STRAEHLER** (6 Jan 1887 - 16 May 1979)

29 Sep 1931 - 2 Oct 1933:	Commandant, Friedrichsort Naval School
3 Oct 1933 - 27 Sep 1934:	Chief of Central Office, Kiel Naval Arsenal
28 Sep 1934 - 26 Sep 1936:	Commandant, Kiel Naval Arsenal
27 Sep 1936 - 7 Nov 1939:	Chief of Shipyards Directorate, Naval High Command
(1 Apr 1939:	Promoted to brevet Konteradmiral)
(1 Nov 1939:	Confirmed as Konteradmiral from brevet rank)
8 Nov 1939 - 15 May 1943:	Inspector, Armaments Inspectorate XX
(1 Apr 1942:	Promoted to Vizeadmiral)
16 May 1943 - 31 May 1943:	Attached to the Commander-in-Chief of the Navy
31 May 1943:	Retired
1 Jun 1943:	Recalled to reserve status; no appointment conferred

Konteradmiral (Ingeneur) Johannes **STRAUCH** (29 Sep 1884 - 29 Dec 1957)

29 Sep 1929 - 29 Sep 1932:	Engineer, Inspectorate of Naval Training
30 Sep 1932 - 30 Sep 1934:	Station Engineer, Baltic Naval Station
(30 Sep 1934:	Promoted to brevet Konteradmiral Ingeneur)
30 Sep 1934:	Retired
1 Apr 1941:	Recalled to reserve status
22 Mar 1941 - 7 Nov 1944:	Armed Forces Commissioner for Industry, Warsaw
(1 Apr 1942:	Confirmed as Konteradmiral Ingeneur from brevet rank)
8 Nov 1944 - 31 Jan 1945:	Attached to Armaments & Defense Economics Office, Naval High Command
31 Jan 1945:	Retired

Konteradmiral Heinrich **STROMEYER** (8 Dec 1862 - 29 Jun 1922)
(19 Nov 1910:	Promoted to Konteradmiral)
13 Aug 1914 - 15 Jan 1915:	Recalled from retirement; Chief of Central Information Bureau, Naval Office
16 Jan 1915 - 31 Dec 1915:	Attached to the Military Section, Naval Office
31 Dec 1915:	Retired

Konteradmiral Ernst von **STUDNITZ** (5 May 1898 - 2 Dec 1943)
8 Apr 1938 - 18 Feb 1940:	Commander, 2. Naval NCO Training Detachment
19 Feb 1940 - 26 Mar 1941:	Commander, 1. Naval NCO Training Detachment
28 Mar 1941 - 6 Jun 1943:	Commandant, Light Cruiser "*Nürnberg*"
15 Jan 1942 - 30 Jun 1942:	Commandant, Battleship "*Schlesien*"
16 Jun 1943 - 25 Jul 1943:	Commander of Sea Defenses, Salonika
26 Jul 1943 - 2 Dec 1943:	Commander of Sea Defenses, Attika
(1 Sep 1943:	Promoted to Konteradmiral)

Konteradmiral Ludwig **STUMMEL** (5 Aug 1898 - 30 Nov 1983)
25 Sep 1935 - 27 Dec 1939:	Staff Officer, High Seas Fleet
28 Dec 1939 - 15 Jun 1941:	Chief of Naval Intelligence Office, Naval High Command
16 Jun 1941 - 30 Apr 1943:	Chief of Central Office, Naval Intelligence Directorate, Naval High Command
(1 May 1943:	Promoted to Konteradmiral)
1 May 1943 - 16 Aug 1944:	Chief of Naval Intelligence Directorate, Naval High Command
17 Aug 1944 - 13 Nov 1944:	Attached to the Commander-in-Chief of the Navy
14 Nov 1944 - 15 Mar 1945:	Senior Commander of Navy Communications Schools
16 Mar 1945 - 8 May 1945:	Attached to the Commander-in-Chief of the Navy

Konteradmiral (Ingeneur) Wilhelm **TACKENBERG**
(29 Dec 1893 - 24 Mar 1963)
28 Sep 1936 - 31 Oct 1938:	Chief Engineer, Inspectorate of Naval Training
1 Nov 1938 - 19 Nov 1939:	Station Engineer, North Sea Naval Station
20 Nov 1939 - 6 Sep 1942:	Section Chief, Naval Personnel Office, Naval High Command

(1 Jul 1942:	Promoted to Konteradmiral Ingeneur)
7 Sep 1942 - 30 Nov 1943:	Commandant of Wesermünde Naval School
6 Dec 1943 - 16 Apr 1945:	Chief of Shipyards Staff, Belgium-Netherlands

Konteradmiral Carl **TÄGERT** (29 Oct 1869 - 9 Jan 1946)

1 Oct 1913 - 14 Sep 1914:	Commander, II. Shipyard Division
15 Sep 1914 - 14 Nov 1914:	Chief of Supply Lines, Flanders Marine Division
15 Nov 1914 - Feb 1915:	Commander, 1. Sailor Regiment, Flanders Marine Corps
Feb 1915 - 19 Aug 1915:	Commander, 2. Marine Artillery Regiment, Flanders Marine Corps
20 Aug 1915 - 31 May 1917:	Commander, II. Marine Brigade, Flanders Marine Corps
1 Jun 1917 - 9 Nov 1918:	Naval Liaison Officer to 4. Army
10 Nov 1918 - 30 Jan 1919:	Attached to the Commander, North Sea Naval Station
30 Jan 1919:	Retired
(30 Aug 1919:	Promoted to brevet Konteradmiral)

Vizeadmiral (Turkish Rear-Admiral) Wilhelm **TÄGERT**
(24 Jul 1871 - 10 Sep 1950)

5 Aug 1914 - 23 Sep 1915:	Commandant, Battleship "*Mecklenburg*"
7 Nov 1915 - 27 Sep 1917:	Chief of Staff, Mediterranean Division & Chief of Staff, Turkish Fleet
1 Oct 1917 - 31 Oct 1917:	Acting Commandant, Heavy Cruiser "*Seydlitz*"
30 Nov 1917 - 4 Dec 1918:	Commandant, Heavy Cruiser "*Seydlitz*"
19 Jun 1918 - 19 Jul 1918:	Acting Deputy Commander, I. Reconnaissance Group
17 Nov 1918 - 4 Dec 1918:	Acting Flag Officer, Reconnaissance Ships & Acting Commander, I. Reconnaissance Group
5 Dec 1918 - 27 Dec 1918:	Attached to the Secretary of State, Naval Office
28 Dec 1918 - 21 Mar 1919:	Attached to the Commander, Baltic Naval Station
22 Mar 1918 - 5 Aug 1919:	Attached to the Naval High Command
6 Aug 1919 - 21 Aug 1919:	Attached to the Ship Oversight Commission
22 Aug 1919 - 10 Jan 1920:	President, Ship Oversight Commission
7 Nov 1919 - 10 Jan 1920:	Inspector, Coastal Defense Inspectorate IV
11 Jan 1920 - 29 Mar 1921:	Chief of Hamburg Naval Office
(21 Jan 1920:	Promoted to Konteradmiral)
(29 Mar 1921:	Promoted to brevet Vizeadmiral)
29 Mar 1921:	Retired

Vizeadmiral Arthur **TAPKEN** (9 Feb 1864 - 27 Jan 1945)
1 Mar 1914 - 25 Dec 1914:	Deputy Commander of Reconnaissance Ships
(22 Mar 1914:	Promoted to Konteradmiral)
26 Dec 1914 - 20 Oct 1915:	Chief of Staff, Baltic Naval Station
21 Oct 1915 - 16 Nov 1915:	Attached to the Commander, Baltic Naval Station
16 Nov 1915:	Retired
2 Mar 1916 - 28 May 1917:	Recalled from retirement; Commandant of Kiel
29 May 1917 - 25 Sep 1917:	Attached to the Commander, Baltic Naval Station & the Chief of Naval General Staff
(25 Sep 1917:	Promoted to brevet Vizeadmiral)
25 Sep 1917:	Retired

Admiralarzt (Konteradmiral) Dr. Otto Siegfried **TARNOW** (9 Sep 1893 - 19 Apr 1963)
5 Feb 1934 - 31 Aug 1939:	Senior Medical Officer, Kiel-Wik Naval Hospital
1 Sep 1939 - 31 Dec 1939:	Chief Medical Officer, Hospital Ship *Robert Ley*
5 Jan 1940 - Feb 1943:	Chief Medical Officer, Sanderbusch Naval Hospital
Feb 1943 - 25 Sep 1943:	Chief Medical Officer, Simferopol Naval Hospital
26 Sep 1943 - 30 Mar 1944:	Senior Medical Officer to Admiral Commanding, Black Sea
(1 Mar 1944:	Promoted to Admiralarzt)
31 Mar 1944 - 31 Dec 1944:	Senior Medical Officer, Naval Group West
1 Jan 1945 - 20 Jul 1945:	Chief Medical Officer, Naval Group North Sea

Wirkliche Geheime Baurat (Konteradmiral) Karl **THÄMER** (16 Jun 1851 - 8 Apr 1926)
26 Oct 1907 - 1 Mar 1918:	On inactive status
(14 Feb 1918:	Promoted to brevet Wirkliche Geheime Baurat)
1 Mar 1918:	Retired

Vizeadmiral (Ingeneur) Karl **THÄTER** (13 Sep 1886 - 14 Oct 1962)
29 Sep 1932 - 27 Sep 1935:	Instructor, Kiel Naval School
28 Sep 1935 - 20 Sep 1936:	Station Engineer, North Sea Naval Station
21 Sep 1936 - 9 Feb 1937:	Chief Engineer, High Seas Fleet

10 Feb 1937 - 22 Nov 1939:	Chief of Staff, Testing Command for New Ships
(1 Nov 1938:	Promoted to Konteradmiral Ingeneur)
23 Dec 1937 - 3 Jan 1938:	Acting Chief of Testing Command
25 Feb 1939 - 4 Mar 1939:	Acting Chief of Testing Command
27 Nov 1939 - 31 Aug 1942:	Commandant, Kiel Naval School
(1 Feb 1942:	Promoted to Vizeadmiral Ingeneur)
31 Aug 1942:	Retired
1 Sep 1942:	Recalled to reserve status; no appointment conferred

Konteradmiral (Ingeneur) Otto **THEDSEN** (1 Jan 1886 - 11 Feb 1949)

1 Jan 1936 - 11 Sep 1941:	Unit Engineer to Flag Officer, Submarines
12 Sep 1941 - 31 Jan 1943:	Chief Engineer to Deputy Flag Officer, Submarines
1 Feb 1943 - 8 May 1945:	Chief Engineer to Flag Officer, Submarines
(1 Mar 1943:	Promoted to Konteradmiral Ingeneur)

Awards: *German Cross in Silver*

Vizeadmiral August **THIELE** (26 Aug 1893 - 31 Mar 1981)

17 Sep 1936 - 27 Jan 1939:	Commandant, Training Sail Ship "*Horst Wessel*"
28 Jan 1939 - 20 Feb 1939:	Attached to the Inspectorate of Naval Training
21 Feb 1939 - 29 Mar 1939:	Attached to the Commander, Baltic Naval Station
30 Mar 1939 - 5 Oct 1939:	Fortress Commandant, Pomeranian Coast
6 Oct 1939 - 29 Nov 1939:	Attached to the Commander, Hamburg Naval Office
30 Nov 1939 - 18 Apr 1940:	Commandant, Pocket Battleship "*Lützow*"
19 Apr 1940 - 26 Apr 1940:	Commander of Sea Defenses, Drontheim
27 Apr 1940 - 19 Jun 1941:	Admiral Commanding, Norwegian North Coast
(1 Apr 1941:	Promoted to Konteradmiral)
30 Jun 1941 - 15 Feb 1943:	Chief of Staff, High Seas Fleet
28 Aug 1942 - Sep 1942:	Acting Admiral Commanding, Northern Waters
3 Mar 1943 - 19 Sep 1944:	Commander of Training Units, High Seas Fleet & Commander, II. Battle Group
(1 Apr 1943:	Promoted to Vizeadmiral)
20 Sep 1944 - 22 Mar 1945:	Commander, II. Battle Group
23 Mar 1945 - 27 Apr 1945:	Commander, Battle Group Thiele

28 Apr 1945 - 12 May 1945: Admiral Commanding, Eastern Baltic
Awards: *Knight's Cross with Oakleaves; Knight's Cross; German Cross in Gold*

Konteradmiral Ferdinand **THYEN** (28 Jun 1866 - 15 Apr 1939)
16 Oct 1909 - 17 Nov 1916:	Harbor Captain of Wilhelmshaven
(17 Nov 1916:	Promoted to brevet Konteradmiral)
17 Nov 1916:	Retired

Hafenbaudirektor (Konteradmiral) Karl **TIBURTIUS**
(23 Apr 1874 - 24 Feb 1953)
1 Oct 1937 - 31 Mar 1941:	Director of New Harbor Construction, Wilhelmshaven
(20 Jul 1938:	Accorded Konteradmiral rank as Hafenbaudirektor)
31 Mar 1941:	Retired

Admiral Werner **TILLESSEN** (22 Aug 1880 - 23 Aug 1944)
3 Jun 1920 - 16 Jul 1920:	Chief of Staff, Inspectorate of Naval Training
6 Jun 1920 - 15 Jul 1920:	Acting Inspector of Naval Training
17 Jul 1920 - 15 Sep 1920:	Director, Naval School "A"
16 Sep 1920 - 23 Sep 1925:	Commandant, Mürwik Naval School
24 Sep 1925 - 1 Mar 1927:	Commandant, Battleship "*Hannover*"
2 Mar 1927 - 27 Sep 1927:	Commandant, Battleship "*Schlesien*"
4 Oct 1927 - 4 Oct 1928:	Inspector of Torpedoes & Mines
(1 Oct 1928:	Promoted to Konteradmiral)
9 Jan 1928 - 29 Feb 1928:	Acting Inspector of Naval Training
5 Oct 1928 - 27 Sep 1932:	Commander, North Sea Naval Station
(1 Dec 1930:	Promoted to Vizeadmiral)
(30 Sep 1932:	Promoted to brevet Admiral)
30 Sep 1932:	Retired
24 May 1939:	Recalled to reserve status
8 May 1942 - 17 Dec 1942:	Chief of Naval Training Staff, Romania
17 Oct 1942 - 17 Dec 1942:	Chief of Naval Liaison Staff, Romania
18 Dec 1942 - 23 Aug 1944:	Chief of Naval Liaison Staff, Romania
(1 Feb 1943:	Confirmed as Admiral from brevet rank)

Großadmiral Alfred von **TIRPITZ** (19 Mar 1849 - 6 Mar 1930)
(13 May 1895:	Promoted to Konteradmiral)
15 Jun 1897 - 15 Mar 1916:	Secretary of State, Naval Office
(5 Dec 1899:	Promoted to Vizeadmiral)

(14 Nov 1903: Promoted to Admiral)
(27 Jan 1911: Promoted to Großadmiral)
15 Mar 1916: Retired; for services rendered, retained on Naval List.

Awards: *Order of the Black Eagle, Diamonds to the Order of the Black Eagle, Pour le Mérite*

Marinegeneralstabsarzt/Admiralarzt (Konteradmiral) Dr. Friedrich **TITSCHAK** (28 Aug 1876 - 22 Aug 1952)
10 May 1922 - 31 May 1926: Advisor, Naval Medical Service, Naval High Command
1 Jun 1926 - 31 Dec 1927: Medical Officer, North Sea Naval Station
(31 Dec 1927: Promoted to brevet Marinegeneralstabsarzt)
31 Dec 1927: Retired
15 Sep 1939: Recalled to reserve status as brevet Admiralarzt; no appointment conferred

Konteradmiral Erhard **TOBYE** (18 Apr 1894 - 16 Dec 1971)
13 Sep 1935 - 6 Nov 1939: Chief of General Artillery Section, Naval Weapon Office, Naval High Command
7 Nov 1939 - 31 Jan 1942: Chief of Artillery Weapon Directorate, Naval Weapons Office, Naval High Command
(1 Apr 1941: Promoted to Konteradmiral)
1 Feb 1942 - 1 May 1943: Chief of Staff, Kiel Shipyards
2 May 1943 - 30 Apr 1944: Naval Representative, Army Weapons Office
10 May 1944 - 15 Oct 1945: Chief of Naval Printing Office, Naval High Command

Vizeadmiral Karl **TOPP** (29 Sep 1895 - 24 Apr 1981)
1 Apr 1939 - 30 Dec 1940: Chief of Military Office, Shipbuilding Directorate, Naval High Command
15 Jan 1941 - 24 Feb 1943: Commandant, Battleship "*Tirpitz*"
(1 Feb 1943: Promoted to Konteradmiral)
1 Mar 1943 - 31 Mar 1943: Chief of Technical Office, Shipbuilding Directorate, Naval High Command
1 Apr 1943 - 12 Jul 1943: Chief of Military Office, Shipbuilding Directorate, Naval High Command
13 Jul 1943 - 30 Apr 1945: Chairman, Shipbuilding Commission of Ministry of Armaments
(1 Jan 1945: Promoted to Vizeadmiral)

1 May 1945 - 15 Oct 1945: Chief of Shipbuilding Directorate, Naval High Command

Konteradmiral Heinrich **TRENDTEL** (1 Jan 1864 - 29 Oct 1943)
8 Mar 1913 - 2 Sep 1914: Recalled from retirement; Inspector, Coastal Inspectorate V
3 Sep 1914 - 11 Jan 1919: Advisor for Mines & Explosives, Naval High Command
11 Jan 1919: Retired
(30 Aug 1919: Promoted to brevet Konteradmiral)

Konteradmiral Hans-Udo von **TRESCKOW** (25 Jun 1893 - 5 Jan 1955)
29 Sep 1936 - 30 Sep 1937: Commandant of Fortifications, Ems Estuary
4 Oct 1937 - 3 Aug 1942: Director of Artillery Office, Wilhelmshaven Shipyards
13 Aug 1942 - 12 Sep 1944: Commander of Sea Defenses, Seine-Somme
(1 Nov 1942: Promoted to Konteradmiral)
12 Sep 1944: Captured; POW

Ministerialdirigent (Konteradmiral) Guido **TRITTLER**
(13 Feb 1903 - 27 Sep 1981)
15 Apr 1936 - 31 Mar 1943: Advisor for Harbor Construction, Naval General Office, Naval High Command
1 Apr 1943 - 24 Jul 1944: Chief of Harbor Construction, Naval General Office, Naval High Command
25 Jul 1944 - 27 Mar 1946: Chief of Naval Construction Office, Naval High Command & Inspector of Naval Construction
(14 Aug 1944: Promoted to Ministerialdirigent)

Admiral Adolf von **TROTHA** (1 Mar 1868 - 11 Nov 1940)
20 Sep 1913 - 28 Jan 1916: Commandant, Battleship "*Kaiser*"
29 Jan 1916 - 10 Nov 1918: Chief of Staff, High Seas Fleet
(17 Dec 1916: Promoted to Konteradmiral)
11 Nov 1918 - 27 Nov 1918: Attached to the Secretary of State, Naval Office
28 Nov 1918 - 12 Dec 1918: Chief of Naval Cabinet, Naval Office
13 Dec 1918 - 25 Mar 1919: Chief of Naval Personnel, Naval Office
26 Mar 1919 - 22 Mar 1920: Commander-in-Chief of the Navy
(31 Oct 1919: Promoted to Vizeadmiral)
23 Mar 1920 - 5 Oct 1920: Attached to Naval High Command

5 Oct 1920:   Retired
(19 Aug 1939:   Promoted to brevet Admiral)
Awards: *Pour le Mérite*

Konteradmiral Clamor von **TROTHA** (6 Oct 1894 - 4 Nov 1988)
28 Sep 1935 - 10 Apr 1938:   Commander, 1. Naval NCO
                               Training Detachment
11 Apr 1938 - 15 Jul 1942:   Director of Torpedo Office, Wilhelmshaven
                               Shipyards
16 Jul 1942 - 28 Feb 1943:   Commandant of Torpedo Arsenal, West
(1 Nov 1942:   Promoted to Konteradmiral)
1 Mar 1943 - 5 Sep 1943:   Commandant of Torpedo Arsenal, East
6 Nov 1943 - 29 Aug 1944:   Commander of Sea Defenses,
                               Arctic Ocean Coast
9 Sep 1944 - 28 Jan 1945:   Commander of Sea Defenses, Bergen
29 Jan 1945 - 1 May 1945:   Attached to the Commander-in-Chief
                               of the Navy

Vizeadmiral Wolf von **TROTHA** (1 Oct 1884 - 31 Jan 1946)
21 Sep 1926 - 29 Sep 1928:   Commander, Torpedo & Signals School
3 Oct 1928 - 16 Apr 1929:   Commandant, Cruiser "*Nymphe*"
17 Apr 1929 - 2 Sep 1929:   Commandant, Cruiser "*Königsberg*"
3 Sep 1929 - 26 Feb 1930:   Attached to the Commander, Baltic
                               Naval Station
27 Feb 1930 - 25 Sep 1930:   Commandant & Harbor Captain of Kiel &
                               Commissioner, Kaiser Wilhelm Canal
29 Sep 1930 - 25 Sep 1932:   Chief of Naval Officer Personnel Section,
                               Naval High Command
30 Sep 1932 - 23 Sep 1936:   Commandant, Mürwik Naval School
(1 Oct 1933:   Promoted to brevet Konteradmiral)
(1 Apr 1934:   Confirmed as Konteradmiral from brevet rank)
16 Jul 1934 - 31 Jul 1934:   Simultaneoulsy, Acting Inspector
                               of Naval Training
(30 Sep 1936:   Promoted to brevet Vizeadmiral)
30 Sep 1936:   Retired
15 Feb 1939:   Recalled to reserve status
5 Sep 1939 - 3 Dec 1939:   Deputy Naval Commander, Baltic
4 Dec 1939 - 20 Jan 1941:   Transferred to the Führer Reserve
21 Jan 1941 - 8 Oct 1942:   Director of St. Nazaire Shipyards
(1 Sep 1941:   Confirmed as Vizeadmiral from brevet rank)

9 Oct 1942 - 30 Nov 1942: Placed on inactive status
30 Nov 1942: Retired

Vizeadmiral Konrad **TRUMMLER** (16 Jan 1864 - 27 Dec 1936)
(5 Sep 1911: Promoted to Konteradmiral)
10 Dec 1913 - 16 Dec 1916: Inspector of Coastal Artillery and Mines & Commandant of Cuxhaven Defenses
(17 Jun 1915: Promoted to Vizeadmiral)
16 Dec 1916: Retired

Konteradmiral Titus **TÜRK** (25 May 1868 - 7 Jun 1952)
7 Apr 1911 - 2 Sep 1914: Advisor for Mines & Blockade Weapons, Naval Office
3 Sep 1914 - 14 Nov 1914: Commander of Mines & Blockade Weapons, Flanders Marine Division
15 Nov 1914 - 21 Nov 1918: Commander of Mines & Blockade Weapons, Flanders Marine Corps
22 Nov 1918 - 12 Feb 1919: Attached to the Commander, North Sea Naval Station
12 Feb 1919: Retired
(30 Aug 1919: Promoted to brevet Konteradmiral)

Admiral (*Marshal of Turkey [Mushir]*) Guido von **USEDOM**
(2 Oct 1854 - 24 Feb 1925)
(14 Mar 1905: Promoted to Konteradmiral)
(27 Jan 1908: Promoted to Vizeadmiral)
(27 Jan 1911: Promoted to brevet Admiral)
19 Aug 1914 - 2 Nov 1918: Recalled from retirement; C-in-C, Dardanelles
(27 Jan 1916: Confirmed as Admiral from brevet rank)
26 Nov 1918: Retired
Awards: *Pour le Mérite, Oakleaves to the Pour le Mérite*

Vizeadmiral Ludolf von **USSLAR** (3 Jan 1867 - 28 Jul 1939)
1 Oct 1912 - 25 Aug 1915: Commandant, Battleship "*Nassau*"
26 Aug 1915 - 6 Dec 1917: Chief of Staff to C-in-C Baltic Fleet
(27 Jan 1916: Promoted to Konteradmiral)
7 Dec 1917 - 24 Jan 1918: Commander of Reconnaissance Forces, Eastern Baltic
17 Feb 1918 - 31 May 1918: Naval Commander, Courland
30 Apr 1918 - 31 May 1918: Commander of Baltic Special Forces

1 Jun 1918 - 19 Nov 1918:	Commander, Baltic Waters
20 Nov 1918 - 7 Apr 1919:	Attached to the Commander, Baltic Naval Station
7 Apr 1919:	Retired
(4 Sep 1919:	Promoted to brevet Vizeadmiral)
(21 Jun 1920:	Confirmed as Vizeadmiral from brevet rank)

Wirkliche Geheime Marinebaurat (Konteradmiral) Friedrich **UTHEMANN**
(18 Oct 1851 - 23 Jan 1921)

1 Oct 1906 - 18 May 1917:	Chief of Technical Bureau, Inspectorate of Torpedoes
(18 May 1917:	Promoted to brevet Wirkliche Geheime Marinebaurat)
18 May 1917:	Retired

Vizeadmiral Hans **UTHEMANN** (6 Nov 1866 - 25 Feb 1931)

1 Oct 1913 - 1 Jan 1916:	Commandant, Battleship "*Schleswig-Holstein*"
3 Jun 1915 - 30 Jun 1915:	Acting Deputy Commander, II. Squadron
12 Aug 1915 - 19 Aug 1915:	Acting Deputy Commander, II. Squadron
25 Jan 1916 - 18 Dec 1916:	Commander, 1. Torpedo Division
(17 Dec 1916:	Promoted to Konteradmiral)
19 Dec 1916 - 15 Nov 1917:	Commandant, Kiel Defenses
16 Nov 1917 - 10 Dec 1917:	Commandant, Wilhelmshaven Defenses
11 Dec 1917 - 17 Jan 1919:	Inspector of Torpedoes
18 Jan 1919 - 15 Jul 1919:	Attached to the Secretary of State, Naval Office
15 Jul 1919:	Retired
(4 Sep 1919:	Promoted to brevet Vizeadmiral)

Marinegeneraloberstabarzt (Admiral) Dr. Walter **UTHEMANN**
(28 Sep 1863 - 11 Mar 1944)

13 Apr 1914 - 27 Nov 1914:	Chief Medical Officer, Baltic Naval Station
28 Nov 1914 - 17 Apr 1916:	Chief Medical Officer, Flanders Marine Corps
(24 May 1916:	Promoted to Marinegeneralstabsarzt with Konteradmiral rank)
24 May 1916 - 30 Apr 1922:	Chief of the Naval Medical Service
(10 Nov 1919:	Promoted to Marinegeneralstabsarzt with Vizeadmiral rank)
(21 Aug 1920:	Rank changed to Marinegeneraloberstabsarzt)
(28 Apr 1922:	Promoted to Marinegeneraloberstabsarzt with Admiral rank)
30 Apr 1922:	Retired

Vizeadmiral Kurt **UTKE** (2 Dec 1893 - 30 Sep 1970)
27 sep 1934 - 3 Oct 1937:	Commander, IV. Naval Artillery Detachment
4 Oct 1937 - 17 Apr 1939:	Commandant, Torpedo School
20 Apr 1939 - 16 Nov 1939:	Commandant, Battleship "*Schlesien*"
18 Nov 1939 - 17 Feb 1943:	Commandant, Torpedo Testing Center, Eckernförde
(1 Mar 1942:	Promoted to Konteradmiral)
22 Feb 1943 - 3 Dec 1944:	Inspector of Torpedoes
(1 Feb 1944:	Promoted to Vizeadmiral)
6 Dec 1944 - 26 Apr 1945:	Inspector of Recruiting, Bremen

Awards: *German Cross in Silver*

Generalmajor der Marinefestungspionere Felix **VARA** (9 Jan 1881 - 3 Nov 1941)
1 Jan 1934 - 6 Nov 1939:	Recalled from retirement; Advisor for Fortress Construction, Naval Weapons Office, Naval High Command
7 Nov 1939 - 3 Nov 1941:	Inspector of Naval Pioneers, Naval High Command
(1 Oct 1939:	Promoted to Generalmajor der Marinefestungspionere)

Konteradmiral Eduard **VARRENTRAPP** (6 Mar 1869 - 23 Dec 1928)
6 Jul 1914 - 1 Jan 1916:	Commandant, Battleship "*Wettin*"
2 Jan 1916 - 2 May 1917:	Commandant, Battleship "*Schleswig-Holstein*"
12 Feb 1917 - 23 Feb 1917:	Senior Naval Commander, Sund
3 May 1917 - 25 Sep 1917:	Attached to the C-in-C, High Seas Fleet
26 Sep 1917 - 30 Nov 1917:	Commandant, Battleship "*König Albert*"
5 Nov 1917 - 27 Nov 1917:	Acting Deputy Commander, IV. Squadron
1 Dec 1917 - 19 Dec 1917:	Attached to the Commander, Baltic Naval Station
20 Dec 1917 - 30 Jan 1919:	Commandant, Wilhelmshaven Defenses
(28 Apr 1918:	Promoted to Konteradmiral)
30 Jan 1919:	Retired

Wirkliche Geheime Oberbaurat (Konteradmiral) Dr. Rudolph **VEITH**
(1 Jun 1846 - 13 Mar 1917)
27 Oct 1906 - 13 Mar 1917:	Director of Engine Construction Section, Naval Office
(13 May 1909:	Promoted to Wirkliche Geheime Oberbaurat)
13 Mar 1917:	Retired

Generalmajor der Marinefestungspionere Heinrich **VIERKORN**
(2 Sep 1884 - 18 Apr 1944)

21 Apr 1933 - 30 Sep 1935:	Recalled from retirement; Pioneer Officer to Commandant of Cuxhaven
1 Oct 1935 - 19 Nov 1941:	Pioneer Officer to North Sea Naval Station
20 Nov 1941 - 18 Apr 1944:	Inspector of Naval Pioneers, Naval High Command
(1 Jun 1943:	Promoted to Generalmajor der Marinefestungspionere)

Konteradmiral Waldemar **VOLLERTHUN** (14 Apr 1869 - 2 Nov 1929)

1 Apr 1912 - 7 Nov 1914:	Head of Central Administration Section for the Kiautschou Government, Naval Office
8 Nov 1914 - 9 Mar 1920:	Prisoner of War; inactive status
(30 Jan 1920:	Promoted to brevet Konteradmiral)
9 Mar 1920:	Retired
22 Jun 1920 - 20 Aug 1920:	Reactivated; Chief of Imperial Navy Decommissioning Office, Naval High Command
21 Aug 1920 - 31 Mar 1921:	Chief of Decommissioning Office, Ministry of Finance
31 Mar 1921:	Retired

Konteradmiral (Ingeneur) Hans **VOß** (28 Apr 1894 - 29 May 1973)

26 Oct 1938 - 25 Jul 1943:	Advisor, Operations Office, Naval High Command
1 Aug 1943 - 10 Oct 1944:	Chief of Shipyards Staff, Baltic
(1 Jan 1944:	Promoted to Konteradmiral Ingeneur)
11 Oct 1944 - 31 Mar 1945:	Senior Commander of Ships Construction Training Detachments
1 Apr 1945 - 10 May 1945:	Chief of Shipyards Staff, Naval Group Norway

Vizeadmiral Hans-Erich **VOß** (30 Oct 1897 - 18 Nov 1969)

23 Aug 1939 - 1 Nov 1939:	Staff Officer, Naval Group East
2 Nov 1939 - 3 Oct 1942:	Chief of Command Section, Naval Command Office, Naval High Command
5 Oct 1942 - 28 Feb 1943:	Commandant, Heavy Cruiser *"Prinz Eugen"*
(1 Mar 1943:	Promoted to Konteradmiral)
1 Mar 1943 - 30 Apr 1945:	Permanent Naval Representative to Führer Headquarters
(1 Aug 1944:	Promoted to Vizeadmiral)

Konteradmiral Gerhard **WAGNER** (23 Nov 1898 - 26 Jun 1987)
5 Oct 1937 - 4 Apr 1939:	Commandant, Destroyer "*Leberecht Maaß*"
5 Apr 1939 - 12 Jun 1941:	Group Chief, Operations Office, Naval High Command
13 Jun 1941 - 28 Jun 1944:	Chief of Naval Operations
(1 Mar 1943:	Promoted to Konteradmiral)
29 Jun 1944 - 30 Apr 1945:	Special Purposes Admiral to C-in-C of the Navy
1 May 1945 - 23 May 1945:	Director of the Military Cabinet to the Head of State, Großadmiral Dönitz

Awards: *German Cross in Gold*

Konteradmiral Heinrich **WAGNER** (10 Dec 1886 - 6 Jul 1950)
29 Mar 1930 - 4 Dec 1939:	Chief of Remote-Control Units
1 Oct 1933 - 30 Sep 1936:	Director of Armaments Works, Wilhelmshaven Shipyards
5 Dec 1939 - 22 Nov 1942:	Section Chief for Military Questions (Shipyards), Naval High Command
23 Nov 1942 - 3 Jan 1944:	Commandant, Bordeaux Naval Arsenal
(1 Dec 1942:	Promoted to Konteradmiral)
4 Jan 1944 - 31 Jan 1944:	Attached to the C-in-C, Naval Group West
1 Feb 1944 - 8 May 1945:	Chief of Staff Questions Group, Naval Defense Office, Naval High Command

Admiral **WALDEMAR**, Prince of Denmark (27 Oct 1858 - 14 Jan 1939)
Admiral à la Suite (Honorary title)
Awards: *Order of the Black Eagle*

Konteradmiral Johannes **WALLMANN** (30 Sep 1852 - 3 Mar 1935)
(27 Apr 1907:	Promoted to brevet Konteradmiral)
3 Aug 1914 - Jun 1916:	Recalled from retirement; Prize Commissioner for the Baltic
Jun 1916:	Retired

Konteradmiral Hans **WALTHER** (25 Dec 1883 - 4 Jan 1950)
1 Oct 1936 - 31 Dec 1940:	Recalled from retirement; Chief of Naval Group, Recruiting Inspectorate, Koblenz
(19 Aug 1939:	Promoted to brevet Konteradmiral)
(1 Jan 1941:	Confirmed as Konteradmiral from brevet rank)
1 Jan 1941 - 31 Aug 1942:	Commander, Recruiting Command Essen I
31 Aug 1942:	Retired

1 Sep 1942: Recalled to reserve status; no appointment conferred

Awards: *Pour le Mérite*

Generaladmiral Walter **WARZECHA** (23 May 1891 - 30 Aug 1956)
24 Sep 1934 - 28 Sep 1937: Chief of Staff, Baltic Naval Station
2 Oct 1937 - 31 Oct 1938: Commandant, Pocket Battleship *"Admiral Graf Spee"*
(1 Nov 1938: Promoted to Konteradmiral)
1 Nov 1938 - 31 Aug 1942: Chief of Naval Defense Office, Naval High Command
(1 Jan 1941: Promoted to Vizeadmiral)
(1 Apr 1942: Promoted to Admiral)
15 Nov 1939 - 30 Apr 1944: Chief of Naval General Office, Naval High Command
(1 Mar 1944: Promoted to Generaladmiral)
1 May 1944 - 22 Jul 1945: Chief of Naval Defense
26 May 1945 - 22 Jul 1945: Acting Commander-in-Chief of the Navy

Awards: *German Cross in Silver; Knight's Cross of the War Merit Cross with Swords*

Konteradmiral Erwin **WAßNER** (1 Mar 1887 - 24 Aug 1937)
26 Sep 1931 - 8 Dec 1932: Commandant, Cruiser *"Karlsruhe"*
23 Jan 1933 - 31 Mar 1933: Attached to Naval High Command
1 Apr 1933 - 24 Aug 1937: Naval Attaché, London & The Hague
(1 Oct 1936: Promoted to Konteradmiral)

Awards: *Pour le Mérite*

Konteradmiral Georg **WAUE** (1 Feb 1901 - 8 May 1945)
5 May 1938 - 3 Apr 1939: Commander, 4. Torpedo Boat Flotilla
4 Apr 1939 - 4 Mar 1940: Commander, 6. Torpedo Boat Flotilla
5 Mar 1940 - 9 Mar 1942: Staff Officer, Naval Group West
10 Mar 1942 - 23 Oct 1943: Staff Officer, High Seas Fleet
4 Nov 1943 - 23 Nov 1944: Chief of Staff to Admiral Commanding, Aegean
25 Nov 1944 - 8 May 1945: Fortress Commandant of Pola
(1 Mar 1945: Promoted to Konteradmiral)

Awards: *German Cross in Gold*

Konteradmiral (Ingenieur) Carl **WEBER** (23 Apr 1896 - 5 Nov 1975)
31 Oct 1938 - 15 Nov 1939: Commander, 14. Ships Crew Detachment
19 Nov 1939 - 20 Aug 1940: Station Engineer, North Sea Naval Station

21 Aug 1940 - 13 Oct 1941:	Chief of Transport Section to Admiral Commanding, France
15 Oct 1941 - 14 Nov 1943:	Chief of Staff, Ships Equipment Inspectorate
(1 Apr 1943:	Promoted to Konteradmiral Ingeneur)
15 Nov 1943 - 3 Jan 1944:	Attached to the C-in-C, North Sea Naval Group
4 Jan 1944 - 22 Aug 1944:	Commandant of Bordeaux Naval Arsenal
23 Aug 1944 - 19 Sep 1944:	Commander, Marine Brigade Weber
19 Sep 1944:	Captured; POW

Vizeadmiral Carl **WEDDING** (30 Sep 1867 - 13 Jul 1952)

7 Aug 1914 - 14 Nov 1914:	Commander, 1. Shipyard Division
15 Nov 1914 - 31 May 1917:	Commander, IV. Marine Brigade, Flanders Marine Corps
(25 Nov 1916:	Promoted to Konteradmiral)
1 Jun 1917 - 11 Nov 1918:	Commander, III. Marine Brigade, Flanders Marine Corps
12 Nov 1918 - 18 Dec 1918:	Commander, 2. Marine Division, Flanders Marine Corps
19 Dec 1918 - 8 Jun 1919:	Placed on inactive status
8 Jun 1919:	Retired
(4 Sep 1919:	Promoted to brevet Vizeadmiral)

Vizeadmiral Wolfgang **WEGENER** (16 Sep 1875 - 29 Sep 1956)

14 Feb 1919 - 30 Sep 1919:	Director of Artillery Depot, Wilhelmshaven
1 Oct 1919 - 8 Nov 1919:	Chief of Staff, Ships Artillery Inspectorate
9 Nov 1919 - 17 Oct 1922:	Chief of Staff, Naval Artillery Inspectorate
24 May 1920 - 17 Oct 1922:	Acting Inspector of Naval Artillery
18 Oct 1922 - 30 Sep 1926:	Inspector of Naval Artillery
(1 Mar 1923:	Promoted to Konteradmiral)
(30 Sep 1926:	Promoted to brevet Vizeadmiral)
30 Sep 1926:	Retired

Konteradmiral Oskar **WEHR** (20 Jan 1886 - 1 Jun 1968)

25 Sep 1928 - 20 Mar 1932:	Chief of Staff, Inspectorate of Mines & Torpedoes
29 Mar 1932 - 27 Sep 1934:	Commandant of Kiel Naval Arsenal
30 Sep 1934:	Retired
1 Oct 1934 - 8 Sep 1935:	Recalled; Naval Commissioner, Kaiser-Wilhelm Canal

9 Sep 1935 - 17 Nov 1939:	Chief of Torpedo Testing Center, Eckernförde
(16 Apr 1938:	Promoted to brevet Konteradmiral)
(1 Apr 1939:	Confirmed as Konteradmiral from brevet rank)
18 Nov 1939 - 14 Mar 1940:	Attached to the Inspectorate of Torpedoes
15 Mar 1940 - 25 Aug 1940:	Admiral-in-Charge, Danzig Naval Office
26 Aug 1940 - 31 Oct 1942:	Attached to the Commander-in-Chief of the Navy
31 Oct 1942:	Retired

Vizeadmiral Eberhard **WEICHOLD** (23 Aug 1891 - 19 Dec 1960)

28 Apr 1934 - 31 Dec 1936:	Commandant of the Naval Academy
1 Jan 1937 - 26 Feb 1937:	Attendance at Destroyer training course
27 Feb 1937 - 26 Oct 1938:	Commander, 1. Destroyer Flotilla
27 Oct 1938 - 20 Oct 1939:	Staff Officer, High Seas Fleet
2 Nov 1939 - 20 Jun 1940:	Chief of Staff, Special Staff for Economic Warfare, Armed Forces High Command (OKW)
28 Jun 1940 - 15 Aug 1941:	Chief of Naval Liaison Staff to Royal Italian Navy (Regia Marina)
(1 Jul 1940:	Promoted to Konteradmiral)
16 Aug 1941 - 4 Mar 1943:	Admiral-in-Charge, Naval Staff attached to Royal Italian Navy
(1 Apr 1942:	Promoted to Vizeadmiral)
22 Nov 1941 - 4 Mar 1943:	Commander of German Naval Command, Italy
12 Apr 1943 - 31 Mar 1944:	Special Advisor to the Naval High Command
1 Apr 1944 - 8 May 1945:	Chief of Naval Training Staff

Awards: *German Cross in Gold*

Ministerialdirigent (Konteradmiral) Dr. Andreas **WEISSMÜLLER**
(2 Feb 1882 - 11 Oct 1950)

11 Nov 1939 - 18 Aug 1943:	General Advisor on Construction Matters, Naval High Command
18 Aug 1943 - 8 May 1945:	General Advisor on Legal & Tax Questions, Naval Construction Office, Naval High Command
(20 May 1944:	Promoted to brevet Ministerialdirigent)

Konteradmiral Carl Wilhelm **WENIGER** (4 Aug 1874 - 9 Sep 1945)

5 Aug 1914 - 28 Jul 1915:	Staff Officer, IV. Squadron
29 Jul 1915 - 3 Jun 1916:	Commandant, Light Cruiser "*Stralsund*"
22 Jun 1916 - 9 Jul 1916:	Commandant, Light Cruiser "*Graudenz*"

10 Jul 1916 - 11 Aug 1916:	Attached to the Light Cruiser "*Königsberg*"
12 Aug 1916 - 21 May 1917:	Commandant, Light Cruiser "*Königsberg*"
24 May 1917 - 5 Nov 1918:	Commandant, Battleship "*König*"
6 Nov 1918 - 22 Jun 1919:	Attached to the Commander, Baltic Naval Station
22 Jun 1919:	Retired
(19 Aug 1939:	Promoted to brevet Konteradmiral)

Admiral Paul **WENNEKER** (27 Feb 1890 - 17 Oct 1979)

28 Dec 1933 - 23 Aug 1937:	Naval Attaché, Tokyo
24 Aug 1937 - 2 Sep 1937:	Attached to the Commander-in-Chief of the Navy
3 Sep 1937 - 15 Nov 1939:	Commandant, Pocket Battleship "*Deutschland*"
(1 Oct 1939:	Promoted to Konteradmiral)
24 Jul 1938 - 15 Aug 1938:	Acting Commander of German Naval Forces, Spain
15 Nov 1939 - 29 Nov 1939:	Commandant, Pocket Battleship "*Lützow*"
30 Nov 1939 - 6 Feb 1940:	Attached to Naval High Command
21 Mar 1940 - 8 May 1945:	Naval Attaché, Tokyo & Admiral Commanding, East Asia
(1 Sep 1941:	Promoted to Vizeadmiral)
(1 Aug 1944:	Promoted to Admiral)

Awards: *German Cross in Silver; Knight's Cross of the War Merit Cross with Swords*

Vizeadmiral Alexander **WERTH** (2 May 1879 - 20 Apr 1942)

17 Jul 1920 - 29 Sep 1922:	Commandant, Cruiser "*Medusa*"
30 Sep 1922 - 5 Oct 1924:	Chief of Staff, Baltic Naval Station
6 Oct 1924 - 10 Sep 1927:	Chief of Naval Defense Office, Naval High Command
(1 Apr 1927:	Promoted to Konteradmiral)
11 Sep 1927 - 11 Oct 1928:	Commander, North Sea Naval Forces & Deputy Commander, Battleship Division
12 Oct 1928 - 31 Dec 1928:	Attached to the Commander-in-Chief of the Navy
(31 Dec 1928:	Promoted to brevet Vizeadmiral)
31 Dec 1928:	Retired
24 May 1939:	Recalled to reserve status
3 Sep 1939 - 20 Apr 1942:	Commissioner, Hamburg Prize Court
(1 Feb 1941:	Confirmed as Vizeadmiral from brevet rank)
20 Apr 1942:	Retired

Vizeadmiral Hugo **WESTPHAL** (25 Mar 1855 - 18 Sep 1924)
(9 Jan 1904: Promoted to brevet Konteradmiral; retired)
2 Oct 1914 - 28 Jan 1917: Recalled; President, Technical Research Commission
(22 Mar 1916: Confirmed as Konteradmiral from brevet rank)
28 Jan 1917: Retired
(4 Feb 1920: Promoted to brevet Vizeadmiral)

Vizeadmiral Paul **WEVER** (28 Jan 1893 - 11 Aug 1944)
31 May 1937 - 5 Jun 1938: Chief of Staff, Inspectorate of Naval Training
19 Jul 1937 - 17 Aug 1937: Acting Inspector of Naval Training
15 Jun 1938 - 5 May 1939: Commandant, Cruiser "*Emden*"
6 May 1939 - 22 Aug 1939: Attached to the Commander, North Sea Naval Station
23 Aug 1939 - 4 Dec 1939: Chief of Staff, Naval Group West
1 Jan 1940 - 21 Jun 1940: Chief of Naval Intelligence Evaluation Office, Naval High Command
22 Jun 1940 - 15 Jan 1943: Chief of Naval Group, Armistice Commission, France
(1 Sep 1941: Promoted to Konteradmiral)
16 Jan 1943 - 1 Sep 1943: Attached to the C-in-C, Naval Group West
2 Sep 1943 - 11 Aug 1944: Admiral Commanding, French South Coast
(1 Oct 1943: Promoted to Vizeadmiral)

Konteradmiral Kurt **WEYHER** (30 Aug 1901 - 17 Dec 1991)
28 Jan 1939 - 5 Sep 1939: Commandant, Sail Training Ship "*Horst Wessel*"
6 Sep 1939 - 8 Dec 1939: Attached to Hamburg Naval Office
9 Dec 1939 - 24 Aug 1941: Commandant, Auxiliary Cruiser "*Orion*"
25 Aug 1941 - 20 Nov 1941: Attached to the Commander, Baltic Naval Station
21 Nov 1941 - 11 Apr 1942: Staff Officer to Admiral Commanding, Aegean
12 Apr 1942 - 11 Jan 1944: Staff Officer, Naval Group South
12 Jan 1944 - 21 Jun 1944: Chief of German Naval Command, Constanta & Commander, 10. Security Division & Chief of Escorts, Black Sea
22 Jun 1944 - 10 Oct 1944: Commander of Sea Defenses, Crete
2 Nov 1944 - 22 Jul 1945: Commander of Sea Defenses, East Friesland
(1 Jan 1945: Promoted to Konteradmiral)
Awards: *Knight's Cross; German Cross in Gold*

Vizeadmiral Franz **WIETING** (27 Oct 1876 - 20 Feb 1966)
4 Oct 1919 - 10 Jan 1920:	Inspector, Coastal Inspectorate II
11 Jan 1920 - 6 Oct 1923:	Chief of Stettin Naval Office
15 Oct 1923 - 8 Jan 1925:	Commandant, Battleship "*Braunschweig*"
10 Jan 1925 - 31 Mar 1925:	Commander, Light Naval Forces, Baltic
1 Apr 1925 - 23 Sep 1925:	Commander, North Sea Naval Forces & Deputy Commander, Battleship Division
(1 May 1925:	Promoted to Konteradmiral)
24 Sep 1925 - 15 Mar 1927:	Commander, Baltic Naval Forces & Flag Officer, Reconnaissance Forces
16 Mar 1927 - 31 Mar 1927:	Attached to the Commander, Baltic Naval Station
(31 Mar 1927:	Promoted to brevet Vizeadmiral)
31 Mar 1927:	Retired
24 May 1939:	Recalled to reserve status
12 May 1941 - 30 Nov 1941:	Director of La Pallice Naval Shipyards
1 Dec 1941 - 28 Feb 1942:	Attached to the Commander, Baltic Naval Station
(1 Feb 1928:	Confirmed as Vizeadmiral from brevet rank)
28 Feb 1942:	Retired

Vizeadmiral Karl **WILBRANDT** (12 Dec 1864 - 6 May 1928)
(18 Nov 1912:	Promoted to brevet Konteradmiral; retired)
15 Nov 1914 - 26 Jan 1916:	Recalled from retirement; Commander, III. Marine Brigade, Flanders Marine Corps
(27 Jan 1916:	Confirmed as Konteradmiral from brevet rank)
6 Mar 1916 - 31 Dec 1918:	Commander of Volunteer Motor Boat Corps
31 Dec 1918:	Retired
(23 Sep 1919:	Promoted to brevet Vizeadmiral)

Konteradmiral Wilhelm **WILKE** (6 May 1878 - 5 Jan 1963)
24 Mar 1921 - 15 Aug 1921:	Chief of Personnel Office, North Sea Naval Station
16 Aug 1921 - 30 Sep 1921:	Acting Chief of Nautical Office, Naval High Command
1 Oct 1921 - 31 Mar 1922:	Inspector, Naval Depot Inspectorate
1 Apr 1922 - 30 Sep 1923:	Commandant of Wilhelmshaven
1 Oct 1923 - 31 Dec 1923:	Attached to the Commander, North Sea Naval Station
(31 Dec 1923:	Promoted to brevet Konteradmiral)
31 Dec 1923:	Retired

25 Jul 1939: Recalled to reserve status; no appointment conferred

Vizeadmiral Raimund **WINKLER** (15 Dec 1855 - 16 Jul 1941)
(27 Jan 1907: Promoted to Konteradmiral)
(18 Dec 1912: Promoted to Vizeadmiral)
Aug 1914 - 31 Dec 1918: Chief of Care Parcels Section, Naval Office
3 Feb 1915 - 13 May 1915: Acting Director of Nautical Department, Naval Office
31 Dec 1918: Retired

Konteradmiral Waldemar **WINTHER** (12 Jun 1897 - 6 Apr 1983)
27 Oct 1937 - 25 Sep 1942: Chief of Officer Personnel Office, North Sea Naval Station
26 Sep 1942 - 24 Feb 1943: Commandant, Light Cruiser "*Leipzig*"
25 Feb 1943 - 16 Apr 1944: Commander, 1. Security Division
(1 Apr 1943: Promoted to Konteradmiral)
17 Apr 1944 - 24 Sep 1944: Commandant of Mürwik Naval School
25 Sep 1944 - 22 Jul 1945: Inspector of Naval Training

Konteradmiral Max **WITSCHEL** (30 Nov 1863 - 22 Aug 1916)
(8 Feb 1913: Promoted to brevet Konteradmiral; retired)
2 Aug 1914 - 29 Aug 1914: Recalled from retirement; Commander of Wesermündung & Geestemünde Defenses
30 Aug 1914 - 15 Oct 1914: Attached to the Flanders Marine Division
16 Oct 1914 - 14 Nov 1914: Artillery Inspector, Flanders Marine Division
15 Nov 1914 - 15 Jan 1916: Artillery Inspector, Flanders Marine Corps
16 Oct 1914 - 15 Jan 1916: Naval Artillery Advisor, III. Reserve Corps
16 Jan 1916 - 22 Aug 1916: Commander, Liepaja (Libau) Special Command
(27 Jan 1916: Confirmed as Konteradmiral from brevet rank)

Vizeadmiral Robert **WITTHOEFT-EMDEN** (29 Aug 1886 - 4 Dec 1960)
1 Nov 1926 - 23 Jun 1929: Commander, Friedrichsort Naval School
24 Jun 1929 - 26 Sep 1930: Commandant, Cruiser "*Königsberg*"
11 Oct 1930 - 21 Mar 1932: Commandant, Cruiser "*Emden*"
22 Mar 1932 - 23 Sep 1932: Attached to the Commander, North Sea Naval Station
24 Sep 1932 - 24 Sep 1933: Chief of Staff, North Sea Naval Station
25 Sep 1933 - 8 Nov 1933: Attached to the Commander-in-Chief of the Navy

9 Nov 1933 - 11 Dec 1941:	Naval Attaché, Washington D.C.
(1 Apr 1935:	Promoted to Konteradmiral)
(1 Nov 1937:	Promoted to Vizeadmiral)
12 Dec 1941 - 5 May 1942:	Interned
17 May 1942 - 9 Nov 1942:	Attached to the Commander-in-Chief of the Navy
10 Nov 1942 - 28 Feb 1943:	Admiral Commanding, Black Sea
1 Mar 1943 - 31 May 1943:	Attached to the Commander-in-Chief of the Navy
31 May 1943:	Retired
1 Jun 1943:	Recalled to reserve status; no appointment conferred

Generaladmiral Karl **WITZELL** (18 Oct 1884 - 31 May 1976)

1 Oct 1928 - 31 Aug 1942:	Chief of Naval Armaments Office, Naval High Command
(1 Sep 1933:	Promoted to Konteradmiral)
(1 Dec 1935:	Promoted to Vizeadmiral)
(1 Nov 1937:	Promoted to Admiral)
(1 Apr 1941:	Promoted to Generaladmiral)
1 Sep 1942 - 30 Sep 1942:	Attached to the Commander-in-Chief of the Navy
30 Sep 1942:	Retired
1 Oct 1942:	Recalled to reserve status; no appointment conferred

Awards: *Knight's Cross of the War Merit Cross with Swords*

Vizeadmiral Ernst **WOLF** (21 Jul 1886 - 29 Jul 1964)

6 Oct 1929 - 20 Mar 1932:	Commander, Torpedo & Signals School
21 Mar 1932 - 27 Sep 1936:	Chief of Bremen Naval Office
(1 Jun 1936:	Promoted to Konteradmiral)
5 Oct 1936 - 30 Sep 1942:	Admiral-in-Charge, Hamburg Naval Office
(1 Jan 1939:	Promoted to brevet Vizeadmiral)
(1 Jan 1941:	Confirmed as Vizeadmiral from brevet rank)
1 Oct 1942 - 28 Feb 1945:	Commissioner, Hamburg Prize Court
31 Mar 1945:	Retired

Feldpropst (Konteradmiral) Dr. Max **WÖLFING** (8 Sep 1847 - 1 Dec 1928)

6 May 1905 - 1 Oct 1918:	Evangelical Provost of the Army and Navy
1 Oct 1918:	Retired

Vizeadmiral Eberhard **WOLFRAM** (24 Jul 1882 - 6 Jan 1947)
13 Oct 1924 - 9 Feb 1928:	Chief of Central Office, Wilhelmshaven Shipyards
10 Feb 1928 - 15 Oct 1930:	Chief of Staff, Naval General Office, Naval High Command & Chief of Shipyards Office, Naval High Command
16 Oct 1930 - 31 Jan 1931:	Attached to the Commander-in-Chief of the Navy
(31 Jan 1931:	Promoted to brevet Konteradmiral)
31 Jan 1931:	Retired
1 Jan 1939:	Recalled to reserve status
28 Sep 1939 - 5 Apr 1940:	Commander of Patrol Boats, West
(1 Feb 1940:	Confirmed as Konteradmiral from brevet rank)
6 Apr 1940 - 3 Apr 1943:	Commander of Naval Security Forces, North Sea
(1 Apr 1942:	Promoted to Vizeadmiral)
4 Apr 1943 - 30 Jun 1943:	Attached to the Commander-in-Chief of the Navy
30 Jun 1943:	Retired
1 Jul 1943:	Recalled to reserve status; no appointment conferred

Awards: *Knight's Cross*

Konteradmiral Paul **WOLFRAM** (30 Sep 1871 - 28 Jan 1946)
27 Sep 1913 - 13 Sep 1914:	Commandant, Light Cruiser "*Hela*"
14 Sep 1914 - 14 Apr 1915:	Staff Officer, Kiel Commandant's Office
15 Apr 1915 - 3 Jun 1915:	Director of Engineer & Deck Officer School, Kiel
4 Jun 1915 - 13 May 1916:	Commander, IV. Torpedo Boat Flotilla
14 May 1916 - 24 Jan 1918:	Commander, Trade Protection Flotilla
25 Jan 1918 - 19 Feb 1918:	Attached to the Commander, Baltic Naval Station
20 Feb 1918 - 31 May 1918:	Commander, Reval Naval Command
1 Jun 1918 - 11 Dec 1918:	Commander of Naval Installations, Estonia
12 Dec 1918 - 7 Jul 1919:	Attached to the Commander, Baltic Naval Station
8 Jul 1919 - 8 Mar 1920:	Appointed to dismantle Baltic Waters Command
8 Mar 1920:	Retired
(10 Sep 1920:	Promoted to brevet Konteradmiral)

Konteradmiral Karl-Friedrich **WOLLANKE** (10 Oct 1884 - 7 Mar 1968)
1 Oct 1926 - 15 Apr 1928:	Commander, II. Naval Artillery Detachment
16 Apr 1928 - 10 Nov 1929:	Attached to Ministry of Defense
11 Nov 1929 - 27 Sep 1932:	Commander, Ems Estuary Defenses
(30 Sep 1932:	Promoted to brevet Konteradmiral)
30 Sep 1932:	Retired
1 Oct 1932 - 30 Sep 1933:	Recalled; Staff Officer, Stettin Recruiting Office
1 Oct 1933 - 31 Mar 1935:	Military Economics Officer, II. Military District
1 Apr 1935 - 6 May 1937:	Inspector, II. Military Economics Inspectorate
31 May 1937:	Retired
3 Sep 1939 - 11 Dec 1939:	Recalled; Commandant, Mecklenburg Coastal Sector
12 Dec 1939 - 15 Apr 1941:	Transferred to the Führer Reserve
16 Apr 1941 - 30 Jun 1943:	Chief of Technical Office for Auxiliary Cruisers, Hamburg Naval Office
(1 Sep 1941:	Confirmed as Konteradmiral from brevet rank)
30 Jun 1943:	Retired

Konteradmiral Fritz **WOSSIDLO** (4 Aug 1877 - 9 Sep 1942)
6 Oct 1918 - 3 Dec 1918:	Commander of Naval Airships
4 Dec 1918 - 31 May 1920:	Fortress Commandant of Cuxhaven
4 Dec 1918 - 30 Sep 1919:	Acting Inspector of Coastal Artillery
1 Jun 1920 - 31 Mar 1921:	Attached to Military District (Wehrkreis) II
1 Apr 1921 - 30 Sep 1923:	Commandant of Swinemünde
1 Oct 1923 - 31 Dec 1923:	Attached to the Commander, Baltic Naval Station
(31 Dec 1923:	Promoted to brevet Konteradmiral)
31 Dec 1923:	Retired
19 Jul 1939:	Recalled to reserve status; no appointment conferred

Vizeadmiral Paul **WÜLFING von Ditten** (13 Sep 1880 - 1 Nov 1953)
7 Aug 1920 - 9 Feb 1921:	Chief of Central Office, Naval High Command
10 Feb 1921 - 25 Sep 1923:	Chief of Staff, Naval High Command
1 Oct 1923 - 18 Jul 1925:	Commandant, Cruiser *"Berlin"*
19 Jul 1925 - 27 Sep 1925:	Commandant, Cruiser *"Hamburg"*
28 Sep 1925 - 11 Oct 1927:	Commandant, Mürwik Naval School

15 Jul 1927 - 31 Jul 1927:	Acting Inspector of Naval Training
12 Oct 1927 - 30 Sep 1928:	Inspector of Naval Training
(1 Jan 1928:	Promoted to Konteradmiral)
22 Dec 1927 - 4 Jan 1928:	Acting Inspector of Torpedoes & Mines
9 Jul 1928 - 14 Jul 1928:	Acting Inspector of Torpedoes & Mines
11 Sep 1928 - 16 Sep 1928:	Acting Inspector of Torpedoes & Mines
1 Oct 1928 - 28 Feb 1929:	Attached to the Commander-in-Chief of the Navy
28 Feb 1928:	Retired
(25 Jan 1937:	Promoted to brevet Vizeadmiral)
3 Sep 1939 - 28 Nov 1939:	Recalled; Deputy Commander, North Sea Naval Station
6 Jun 1940 - 29 May 1942:	Under-Secretary of State, Ministry of Transport
(1 Feb 1941:	Confirmed as Vizeadmiral from brevet rank)
30 May 1942 - 28 Feb 1943:	Attached to the Commander-in-Chief of the Navy
28 Feb 1943:	Retired
1 Mar 1943:	Recalled to reserve status; no appointment conferred

Admiral Hans-Heinrich **WURMBACH** (12 May 1891 - 16 Dec 1965)

5 Oct 1934 - 21 Sep 1936:	Naval Attaché, Rome
1 Oct 1936 - 28 Oct 1938:	Chief of Naval Defense Office, Naval High Command
31 Oct 1938 - 24 Oct 1939:	Commandant, Battle Cruiser *Admiral Scheer*
25 Oct 1939 - 14 May 1942:	Chief of Staff, Baltic Naval Station
(1 Sep 1940:	Promoted to Konteradmiral)
6 Nov 1939 - 20 May 1940:	Chief of Staff, Naval Group East
15 May 1942 - 9 Nov 1942:	Admiral Commanding, Black Sea
(1 Sep 1942:	Promoted to Vizeadmiral)
10 Nov 1942 - 18 Mar 1943:	Sick leave
19 Mar 1943 - 15 Apr 1944:	Admiral Commanding, Denmark
16 Apr 1944 - 8 May 1945:	Admiral Commanding, Skagerrak
(1 Oct 1944:	Promoted to Admiral)
9 May 1945 - 4 Aug 1945:	Chief of German Naval Command, Denmark

Awards: *German Cross in Gold*

Vizeadmiral Otto **WURMBACH** (8 Jun 1864 - 25 Apr 1940)

1 Oct 1912 - 21 Dec 1916:	Chief of Staff, North Sea Naval Station

(8 Mar 1913: Promoted to Konteradmiral)
(25 Nov 1916: Promoted to Vizeadmiral)
22 Dec 1916 - 6 Feb 1919: Inspector of Naval Training
7 Feb 1919 - 17 Mar 1919: Attached to the Commander, Baltic Naval Station
17 Mar 1919: Retired

Konteradmiral Georg **WUTHMANN** (25 May 1863 - 9 Jun 1940)
18 Aug 1914 - 15 Jan 1916: Recalled from retirement; Commander, 2. Sailor Division
(15 Jan 1916: Promoted to brevet Konteradmiral)
15 Jan 1916: Retired

Konteradmiral/General der Flieger Konrad **ZANDER** (9 Mar 1883 - 3 Feb 1947)
27 Sep 1926 - 24 Sep 1928: Chief of Staff, Inspectorate of Torpedoes & Mines
28 Sep 1928 - 19 Sep 1929: Chief of Staff, Baltic Naval Station
20 Sep 1929 - 30 Sep 1932: Chief of Aviation Office, Naval High Command
(1 Oct 1932: Promoted to Konteradmiral)
1 Oct 1932 - 31 Mar 1934: Inspector of Torpedoes & Mines
23 Jan 1933 - 31 Feb 1933: Acting Inspector of Naval Training
1 Aug 1933 - 27 Aug 1933: Acting Inspector of Naval Training
9 Mar 1934 - 19 Mar 1934: Acting Inspector of Naval Training
31 Mar 1934: Retired
1 Apr 1934 - 31 Mar 1935: Transferred to the Luftwaffe; President, Kiel Air Office
(1 Mar 1935: Accorded Generalmajor rank)
(1 Apr 1935: Promoted to Generalleutnant)
1 Apr 1935 - 31 Jan 1938: Commanding General, Luftkreis (Air District) VI
(1 Oct 1936: Promoted to General der Flieger)
1 Feb 1938 - 28 Feb 1939: Commanding General of Naval Aviation
28 Feb 1939: Retired
1 Mar 1939: Recalled to reserve status
28 Mar 1941 - 14 Oct 1942: Attached to Luftflotte (Air Fleet) 4
15 Oct 1942 - 15 Mar 1943: Air Commander, Crimea
16 Mar 1943 - 31 Mar 1943: Placed on inactive status
31 Mar 1943: Retired

Admiral Hans **ZENKER** (10 Aug 1870 - 18 Aug 1932)
2 Aug 1914 - 31 Jan 1916:	Chief of Staff, Supreme General Headquarters
5 Feb 1916 - 27 Apr 1917:	Commandant, Heavy Cruiser "*Von der Tann*"
28 Apr 1917 - 10 Aug 1918:	Section Chief, Operations Group, Naval General Staff
22 Dec 1917 - 18 Feb 1918:	Acting Chief of Naval Operations
8 Oct 1918 - 7 Nov 1918:	Commander of Security Forces, North Sea
10 Nov 1918 - 12 Nov 1918:	Chief of Staff, High Seas Fleet
13 Nov 1918 - 29 Nov 1918:	Commander of Security Forces, North Sea
3 Jan 1919 - 1 Aug 1919:	Acting Chief of Naval General Staff
2 Aug 1919 - 9 Nov 1919:	Attached to the Commander-in-Chief of the Navy
10 Nov 1919 - 23 May 1920:	Inspector of Naval Artillery
(21 Jan 1920:	Promoted to Konteradmiral)
24 May 1920 - 30 Sep 1923:	Commander, North Sea Naval Station
(1 Jan 1921:	Promoted to Vizeadmiral)
15 Oct 1923 - 17 Sep 1924:	C-in-C, High Seas Fleet
18 Sep 1924 - 30 Sep 1928:	Commander-in-Chief of the Navy
(1 Oct 1924:	Promoted to Admiral)
30 Sep 1928:	Retired

Konteradmiral Erich Graf von **ZEPPELIN** (10 May 1873 - 26 May 1927)
4 Aug 1914 - 17 Jan 1915:	Commandant, Light Cruiser "*Medusa*"
18 Jan 1915 - 31 Aug 1915:	Commandant, Light Cruiser "*Nymphe*"
1 Sep 1915 - 9 Jan 1916:	Commandant, Coastal Battleship "*Hildebrand*"
26 Dec 1914 - 9 Aug 1916:	Commander, Elbe Harbor Flotilla
10 Aug 1916 - 29 Jun 1920:	Member, Military Tribunal
(29 Jun 1920:	Promoted to brevet Konteradmiral)
29 Jun 1920:	Retired

Konteradmiral (Ingeneur) Paul-Willy **ZIEB** (3 Jun 1892 - 9 Aug 1972)
1 Apr 1935 - 6 Oct 1936:	Commander, Wesermünde Naval School
7 Oct 1936 - 28 Oct 1938:	Unit Engineer to Flag Officer, Reconnaissance Forces
31 Oct 1938 - 17 Aug 1939:	Chief Engineer, Inspectorate of Naval Training
18 Aug 1939 - 1 Nov 1939:	Engineer, Naval Group East
2 Nov 1939 - 18 Nov 1939:	Attached to Wilhelmshaven Shipyards
19 Nov 1939 - 28 Aug 1940:	Director of Armaments Office, Wilhelmshaven Shipyards

1 Apr 1940 - 19 Jan 1943:	Director of Supply Office, Wilhelmshaven Shipyards
(1 Apr 1942:	Promoted to Konteradmiral Ingeneur)
3 Feb 1943 - 25 Aug 1944:	Chief of Shipyards Staff, Black Sea
26 Aug 1944 - 7 Sep 1944:	Commander of Naval Units, Lower Danube
23 Oct 1944 - 8 May 1945:	Director of Wilhelmshaven Shipyards

Awards: *German Cross in Gold; German Cross in Silver*

Admiral (Ingeneur) Erich **ZIEGER** (12 Jul 1889 - 21 Mar 1945)

26 Sep 1933 - 30 Sep 1935:	Station Engineer, North Sea Naval Station
1 Oct 1935 - 20 Sep 1936:	Chief Engineer, High Seas Fleet
25 Sep 1936 - 10 Dec 1939:	Chief of Ships Equipment Office, Naval High Command
(1 Oct 1937:	Promoted to Konteradmiral Ingeneur)
11 Dec 1939 - 28 Mar 1943:	Inspector of Ships Equipment
(1 Jan 1940:	Promoted to Vizeadmiral Ingeneur)
(1 Sep 1942:	Promoted to Admiral Ingeneur)
29 Mar 1943 - 30 Jun 1943:	Attached to the Commander-in-Chief of the Navy
30 Jun 1943:	Retired
1 Jul 1943:	Recalled to reserve status; no appointment conferred

Awards: *German Cross in Silver*

Marineoberbaudirektor (Vizeadmiral) Karl **ZIMMERMANN** (5 Apr 1889 - 20 Jul 1965)

1 Jun 1938 - 31 Mar 1939:	Attached to Kiel Naval Arsenal
(12 Aug 1938:	Promoted to Schiffbaudirektor [Konteradmiral])
1 Apr 1939 - 30 Jun 1943:	Director of Construction Yards, Kiel Naval Dockyards
(26 Jun 1943:	Promoted to Marineoberbaudirektor)
1 Jul 1943 - 31 Aug 1943:	In charge of reorganizing Kiel Naval Dockyards
31 Aug 1943:	Retired

Konteradmiral Karl **ZIMMERMANN** (18 Jan 1863 - 23 Feb 1916)

(27 Jan 1911:	Promoted to Konteradmiral)
6 Aug 1914 - 23 Feb 1916:	Recalled from retirement; Inspector, II. Naval Inspectorate

Konteradmiral Adalbert **ZUCKSCHWERDT** (1 Jan 1874 - 1 Jul 1945)

29 Aug 1940 - Nov 1940:	Recalled from retirement; Harbor Commandant of Nieuport
Nov 1940 - 22 Feb 1941:	Harbor Commandant of Calais
23 Feb 1941 - 21 Nov 1942:	Commander of Sea Defenses, Loire Estuary
22 Nov 1942 - 25 Jun 1943:	Commander of Sea Defenses, Languedoc
(1 Mar 1943:	Promoted to Konteradmiral)
26 Jun 1943 - 31 Aug 1943:	Admiral Commanding, French South Coast
1 Sep 1943 - 4 Apr 1944:	Commander of Sea Defenses, Languedoc
5 Apr 1944 - 31 May 1944:	Placed on inactive status
31 May 1944:	Retired

APPENDIX:

ALPHABETICAL INDEX OF SHIPS (1914 - 1945)

Admiral Graf Spee (Pocket Battleship, 1934)
Admiral Hipper (Heavy Cruiser, 1937)
Admiral Scheer (Pocket Battleship, 1933)
Amazone (Light Cruiser, 1900)
Anton Schmitt (Z 22) (Destroyer, 1938)
Arcona (Light Cruiser, 1902)
Ariadne (Light Cruiser, 1900)
Atlantis (Auxiliary Cruiser, 1939)
Augsburg (Light Cruiser, 1909)
Baden (Battleship, 1915)
Bayern (Battleship, 1915)
Beowulf (Coastal Battleship, 1890)
Berlin (Light Cruiser, 1903)
Bernd von Arnim (Z 11) (Destroyer, 1936)
Bismarck (Battleship, 1939)
Blücher (Heavy Cruiser, 1908)
Blücher (II) (Heavy Cruiser, 1937)
Brandenburg (Battleship, 1891)
Braunschweig (Battleship, 1902)
Bremen (Light Cruiser, 1903)
Bremse (Cruiser Minelayer, 1916)
Breslau (Light Cruiser, 1911)
Brummer (Cruiser Minelayer, 1915)
Bruno Heinemann (Z 8) (Destroyer, 1936)
Cöln (Light Cruiser, 1909)
Cöln (II) (Light Cruiser, 1916)
Coronel (Auxiliary Cruiser, 1942)
Danzig (Light Cruiser, 1905)
Derfflinger (Heavy Cruiser, 1913)
Deutschland (Battleship, 1904)
Deutschland (II) (Battleship, 1931)
Deutschland (III) (Battleship, 1937)
Diether von Roeder (Z 17) (Destroyer, 1937)
Dresden (Light Cruiser, 1907)
Dresden (II) (Light Cruiser, 1917)
Elbing (Light Cruiser, 1914)
Elsaß (Battleship, 1903)

Emden (Light Cruiser, 1908)
Emden (II) (Light Cruiser, 1916)
Emden (III) (Cruiser, 1925)
Erich Giese (Z 12) (Destroyer, 1936)
Erich Koellner (Z 13) (Destroyer, 1937)
Erich Steinbrinck (Z 15) (Destroyer, 1936)
Frankfurt (Light Cruiser, 1915)
Frauenlob (Light Cruiser, 1902)
Frauenlob (II) (Light Cruiser, 1918)
Freya (Heavy Cruiser, 1897)
Friedrich Carl (Heavy Cruiser, 1902)
Friedrich Eckoldt (Z 16) (Destroyer, 1937)
Friedrich der Grosse (Battleship, 1911)
Friedrich Ihn (Z 14) (Destroyer, 1935)
Frithjof (Coastal Battleship, 1891)
Fürst Bismarck (Heavy Cruiser, 1897)
Gazelle (Light Cruiser, 1898)
Gefion (Light Cruiser, 1893)
Georg Thiele (Z 2) (Destroyer, 1935)
Gneisenau (Heavy Cruiser, 1906)
Gneisenau (II) (Battleship, 1936)
Goeben (Heavy Cruiser, 1911)
Graf Spee (Heavy Cruiser, 1917)
Graf Zeppelin (Aircraft Carrier, 1938)
Graudenz (Light Cruiser, 1913)
Grosser Kurfürst (Battleship, 1913)
Hagen (Coastal Battleship, 1893)
Hamburg (Light Cruiser, 1903)
Hannover (Battleship, 1905)
Hans Lody (Z 10) (Destroyer, 1936)
Hans Lüdemann (Z 18) (Destroyer, 1937)
Hansa (Heavy Cruiser, 1898)
Hansa (II) (Auxiliary Cruiser, 1943)
Heimdall (Coastal Battleship, 1892)
Hela (Light Cruiser, 1895)
Helgoland (Battleship, 1909)
Hermann Künne (Z 19) (Destroyer, 1937)
Hermann Schoemann (Z 7) (Destroyer, 1936)
Hertha (Heavy Cruiser, 1897)
Hessen (Battleship, 1903)
Hildebrand (Coastal Battleship, 1892)
Hindenburg (Heavy Cruiser, 1915)
Hindenburg (II) (Battleship, 1938)

I (Aircraft Carrier, 1918)
Imperator (ex-Volga) (Battleship, 1914)
Kaiser (Battleship, 1911)
Kaiser Friedrich III (Battleship, 1896)
Kaiser Karl Barbarossa (Battleship, 1900)
Kaiser Karl der Grosse (Battleship, 1899)
Kaiser Wilhelm II (Battleship, 1897)
Kaiser Wilhelm der Grosse (Battleship, 1899)
Kaiserin (Battleship, 1911)
Kaiserin Augusta (Heavy Cruiser, 1892)
Karl Galster (Z 20) (Destroyer, 1938)
Karlsruhe (Light Cruiser, 1912)
Karlsruhe (II) (Light Cruiser, 1916)
Karlsruhe (III) (Cruiser, 1927)
Kolberg (Light Cruiser, 1908)
Köln (Cruiser, 1928)
Komet (Auxiliary Cruiser, 1939)
König (Battleship, 1913)
König Albert (Battleship, 1912)
Königsberg (Light Cruiser, 1905)
Königsberg (II) (Light Cruiser, 1915)
Königsberg (III) (Cruiser, 1927)
Kormoran (Auxiliary Cruiser, 1940)
Kronprinz (Since 1918, *Kronprinz Wilhelm*) (Battleship, 1914)
Leberecht Maaß (Z 1) (Destroyer, 1935)
Leipzig (Light Cruiser, 1905)
Leipzig (II) (Light Cruiser, 1918)
Leipzig (III) (Cruiser, 1929)
Lothringen (Battleship, 1904)
Lützow (Heavy Cruiser, 1913)
Lützow (II) (Pocket Battleship, 1931)
Lützow (III) (Pocket Battleship, 1939)
Mackensen (Heavy Cruiser, 1917)
Magdeburg (Light Cruiser, 1911)
Magdeburg (II) (Light Cruiser, 1917)
Mainz (Light Cruiser, 1909)
Markgraf (Battleship, 1913)
Max Schultz (Z 3) (Destroyer, 1935)
Mecklenburg (Battleship, 1901)
Medusa (Light Cruiser, 1900)
Michel (Auxiliary Cruiser, 1940)
Moltke (Heavy Cruiser, 1910)
München (Light Cruiser, 1904)

Nassau (Battleship, 1908)
Niobe (Light Cruiser, 1899)
Noske (Cruiser, 1920)
Nürnberg (Light Cruiser, 1906)
Nürnberg (II) (Light Cruiser, 1916)
Nürnberg (III) (Light Cruiser, 1934)
Nymphe (Light Cruiser, 1899)
Odin (Coastal Battleship, 1894)
Oldenburg (Battleship, 1910)
Orion (Auxiliary Cruiser, 1939)
Ostfriesland (Battleship, 1909)
Paul Jacobi (Z 5) (Destroyer, 1936)
Peter Strasser (Aircraft Carrier, 1940)
Pillau (Light Cruiser, 1914)
Pinguin (Auxiliary Cruiser, 1940)
Pommern (Battleship, 1905)
Posen (Battleship, 1908)
Preussen (Battleship, 1903)
Prinz Adalbert (Heavy Cruiser, 1901)
Prinz Eitel Friedrich (Cruiser, 1920)
Prinz Eugen (Heavy Cruiser, 1938)
Prinz Heinrich (Heavy Cruiser, 1900)
Prinzregent Luitpold (Battleship, 1912)
Regensburg (Light Cruiser, 1914)
Rheinland (Battleship, 1908)
Richard Beitzen (Z 4) (Destroyer, 1935)
Roon (Heavy Cruiser, 1903)
Rostock (Light Cruiser, 1912)
Rostock (II) (Light Cruiser, 1918)
Sachsen (Battleship, 1916)
Scharnhorst (Heavy Cruiser, 1906)
Scharnhorst (II) (Battleship, 1936)
Schlesien (Battleship, 1906)
Schleswig-Holstein (Battleship, 1906)
Schwaben (Battleship, 1901)
Schwalbe (Light Cruiser, 1887)
Seydlitz (Heavy Cruiser, 1912)
Seydlitz (II) (Heavy Cruiser/Aircraft Carrier, 1939)
Siegfried (Coastal Battleship, 1889)
Stettin (Light Cruiser, 1907)
Stier (Auxiliary Cruiser, 1941)
Stralsund (Light Cruiser, 1911)
Straßburg (Light Cruiser, 1911)

Stuttgart (Light Cruiser, 1906)
Theodor Riedel (Z 6) (Destroyer, 1936)
Thetis (Light Cruiser, 1900)
Thor (Auxiliary Cruiser, 1939)
Thüringen (Battleship, 1909)
Tirpitz (Battleship, 1939)
Undine (Light Cruiser, 1902)
Victoria Louise (Heavy Cruiser, 1897)
Vineta (Heavy Cruiser, 1897)
Von der Tann (Heavy Cruiser, 1909)
Weser (Aircraft Carrier, 1942)
Westfalen (Battleship, 1908)
Wettin (Battleship, 1901)
Widder (Auxiliary Cruiser, 1939)
Wiesbaden (Light Cruiser, 1915)
Wiesbaden (II) (Light Cruiser, 1917)
Wilhelm Heidkamp (Z 21) (Destroyer, 1938))
Wittelsbach (Battleship, 1900)
Wolfgang Zenker (Z 9) (Destroyer, 1936)
Wörth (Battleship, 1892)
Württemberg (Battleship, 1917)
Yorck (Heavy Cruiser, 1904)
Zähringen (Battleship, 1901)

Z 23 (Destroyer, 1939)
Z 24 (Destroyer, 1940)
Z 25 (Destroyer, 1940)
Z 26 (Destroyer, 1940)
Z 27 (Destroyer, 1940)
Z 28 (Destroyer, 1940)
Z 29 (Destroyer, 1940)
Z 30 (Destroyer, 1940)
Z 31 (Destroyer, 1941)
Z 32 (Destroyer, 1941)
Z 33 (Destroyer, 1941)
Z 34 (Destroyer, 1942)
Z 35 (Destroyer, 1942)
Z 36 (Destroyer, 1943)
Z 37 (Destroyer, 1941)
Z 38 (Destroyer, 1941)
Z 39 (Destroyer, 1941)
Z 43 (Destroyer, 1943)
Z 44 (Destroyer, 1944)

Z 45 (Destroyer, 1944)
Z 46 (Destroyer)
Z 47 (Destroyer)
ZG 3 (Hermes) (Destroyer, 1938)
ZH 1 (Destroyer, 1940)

LIST OF PRINCIPAL SOURCES

Title	Author
The Breaking Wave (WWII in 1940)	Telford Taylor
Chronik des Seekrieges 1939 - 1945	J. Rowehr/G. Hümmelchen
Deutschlands Admirale 1849 - 1945, Band I - IV	H. Hildebrand/E. Henriot
Encyclopedia of the Third Reich	Louis L. Snyder
German Warships 1815 - 1945, Vol. I: Surface Vessels	Erich Gröner
Hitler's Elite Guards: Waffen SS, Parachutists, U Boats	W. Victor Madej
The Last Year of the Kriegsmarine	V.E. Tarrant
Men Around the Kaiser	Frederic William Wile
My Life	Erich Raeder
Operationsgebiet Ostliche Ostsee, 1944	Mil.Geschichtl. Forschungsamt
Preussisch-Deutsche Generalfeldmarschälle und Grossadmirale	Jürgen Hahn-Butry
Ten Years and Twenty Days	Karl Dönitz
23 Days: The Final Collapse of Nazi Germany	Marlis G. Steinert
Die Wehrmacht Elite	Reinhard Stumpf
Warships of the World	Roger Kafka/Roy Pepperburg
World War II Almanac, 1931 - 1945	Robert Goralski